D1564946

The Practice of Sociotherapy

Books by Marshall Edelson

Termination of Intensive Psychotherapy (1963)
*Ego Psychology, Group Dynamics, and the Therapeutic
    Community* (1964)
Sociotherapy and Psychotherapy (1970)

The Practice of
Sociotherapy:

A Case Study

by Marshall Edelson, M.D., Ph.D.

New Haven and London, Yale University Press 1970

Library of Congress catalog card number: 73-118728
International standard book number: 0-300-01351-5
Designed by Marvin Howard Simmons,
set in Caledonia type,
and printed in the United States of America by
the Vail-Ballou Press, Binghamton, N.Y.
Distributed in Great Britain, Europe, and Africa by
Yale University Press, Ltd., London; in Canada by
McGill-Queen's University Press, Montreal; in Mexico
by Centro Interamericano de Libros Academicos,
Mexico City; in Australasia by Australia and New
Zealand Book Co., Pty., Ltd., Artarmon, New South
Wales; in India by UBS Publishers' Distributors Pvt.,
Ltd., Delhi; in Japan by John Weatherhill, Inc.,
Tokyo.

For Zelda

Contents

Introduction

The following chapters constitute a case study in sociotherapy. In a previous volume (*Sociotherapy and Psychotherapy,* University of Chicago Press, 1970), I have set forth, in some detail, a theoretical foundation for sociotherapy. Here, that general conceptual formulation is applied in detail to the ordering of a specific empirical realm: namely, a psychiatric hospital considered as a social system. In addition, the body of knowledge and skills required of the sociotherapist and sociotherapy staff, the immense variety of their interventions, and the consequences of such interventions, are illustrated in a presentation of the day-by-day vicissitudes of an attempt to build a therapeutic community.

This book depicts the intergroup relations of staff, made up of adults with professional roles, and patients, who are predominantly alienated youth; it is written for, and I hope will interest and be of use to, the members of both groups. It may, however, find other readers as well, because the value-dilemmas of such a community, its intragroup and intergroup conflicts, and its debates and struggles concerning sex, noise, the control of space and facilities, and the use of drugs and alcohol, are not only representative of communities within psychiatric treatment centers but ubiquitous throughout our society.

Most of all, however, this book is written for the practicing sociotherapist—who may be psychiatrist, psychologist, nurse, social worker, nursing aide, administrator, group worker, activities therapist. He is a new kind of clinician, who faces a new task and requires the conceptual tools and skills appropriate to it. He brings an orientation to the situation or social system rather than the personality system as the object of analysis and intervention. He has discovered that he cannot understand the impact of the therapeutic community upon its individual members or the impact of individual members upon the capacity of the therapeutic community to solve its primary functional problems without understanding the therapeutic community as social system. His interventions—including (but not only) interpretations—are informed by his awareness of group processes, including intergroup relations, and by his knowledge of the covert or unconscious, and often shared, meanings groups and organizations or their parts have for the individuals participating in them, and of the covert aims group members share, which determine to some extent their relation to one another, to their leaders, to other groups, and to the tasks that presumably they have joined together to achieve. The ultimate goal of the sociotherapist's interventions is skillful contribution to the attainment of community ends—particularly perhaps skillful contribution to the resolution of intragroup and intergroup strains interfering with the attainment of various group ends generated by the requirements of community life in the hospital or militating against the institutionalization of the treatment values constituting that community insofar as it is "therapeutic."

I have used the clinical data in this book—the selections from a sociotherapist's journal—in my teaching. Typically, a chapter involves a description of a series of community meetings, often for many pages without comment, and then a discussion or analysis of these data from the point of view of the theoretical framework sketched in the first chapter of this book and reported in detail in the previous volume, *Sociotherapy and Psychotherapy.* I have presented the material of the community meetings to seminar groups, challenging the members of the group at various points: "What would you, as the sociotherapist, have done then, if anything? Why? How do you think about what was going on? What do you think the consequences of your intervention (including the decision to say or do nothing) would be? Can you predict possible dysfunctional as well as functional consequences?" I have found no better way to prepare a sociotherapist in training for the chaos, the multiplicity, the complexity of such community meetings and, indeed, group life in general, and no better way to encourage the attempt to master such experiences rather than the inclination merely to succumb to, or retreat in disorder from, them.

How is one to organize an enormous quantity of data—innumerable meetings, events, chains of events, reports, impressions—so that the possibility of meaningful order can be communicated to others? Careful analysis of a single meeting might be helpful to most workers in the field, but missing would be the sequence of events constituting a total process the awareness of which can give meaning to an isolated comment or interaction in a single meeting. In the following chapters both are included: detailed analysis of single meetings, and an overview of a series of such meetings.

The selections are limited to a study of community meetings (the purpose of which in any event is to serve as a window to the entire therapeutic community), since attempting to describe all that happened at any one time, even in the various committees of the therapeutic community, much less in the whole hospital, would result in a bog of material not easily encompassed within two book covers. Necessarily, this means that the end of certain sequences of action, occurring outside the community meeting, might be lost to the reader; but that repeats well the experience of the sociotherapist in the meeting. He cannot know everything that is happening in the therapeutic community as he participates in the community meeting. He must deal with what is presented. He may not know in many cases what was the fate of his efforts in the community meeting; if one is to respect the limits within which one must operate, that must be tolerated.

The question an investigator must answer: what is a meaningful unit for observation? is answered by the axiomatic concepts of his conceptual frame of reference. Here, any act defines a meaningful unit for observation that includes the following analytically distinguishable elements: (1) an intentional orientation to an *end*, a future state of affairs, a cathected goal; (2) a *situation* in which the act occurs, including conditions and means; (3) normative elements, *norms*, which govern choices between alternatives; and (4) motivational commitments to *values*, that is, internalized or institutionalized obligations to expend effort or energy to actualize such values. The actor may be individual or collective. (I have acknowledged previously and acknowledge now and later in this book the debt to Talcott Parsons and his colleagues for their formulations of the theory of action.)

In looking at any particular meeting, then, the following questions are suggested by the frame of reference. (I have not asked every question about every meeting; I hope the reader is stimulated to do so.)

One, which subsystems (functions, aims) of the community—*adaptation* (having to do with the situation), *consummation* (having to do with the attainment of ends), *integration* (having to do with selection among alternatives according to shared norms), *motivation* (having to do with the mobilization and maintenance of commitment to values)—are manifest, which latent? What goals are being pursued—and instead of what other goals? In what phase is the pursuit of a particular goal; what component of a subsystem is involved?

Two, what is the relation among these aims, these subsystems of the community? Do they conflict? Do they compete? Is their input-output exchange with each other as well as with aspects of the situation (personality systems, behavioral organisms, cultural systems) such as to facilitate or inhibit the attainment of various goals? Relations between subsystems may be manifested by value questions or conflicts, involving value-orientations of more than one subsystem, combinations of the six pairs of alternatives facing an acting system: external-internal orientation (autonomy-heteronomy); time orientation (potentiality-actuality); way of classifying objects (being-doing, personal-impersonal); type of object relation (inhibition-discharge, restriction-expansion). (These alternatives have been described in *Sociotherapy and Psychotherapy*.) Is there evidence of such value conflicts?

Three, how are conflicts between subsystems (or the values associated with them) resolved? What is the current balance among them, and what is the equilibrium to which processes tend to return the entire system?

Four, what criteria are being employed by participants or investigator to evaluate a particular outcome? Do these specify a desired relation between subsystems, for example, a desired prepotency of any one subsystem or a relative insulation of a particular subsystem from influence by processes in others? Do these criteria specify a desired prepotency of a particular value? Do they specify a particular outcome of a process within a particular subsystem: a change in the *utility value* of an object, or a change in the ratio of *confidence* or knowledge and *uncertainty* or confusion, as a result of a process of action in an adaptation group; a change in the *cathectic value* of an object, or a change in the ratio of *gratification* and *deprivation*, as a result of a process of action in a consummation group; a change in the extent to which an object is *identified* with, or a change in the ratio of *solidarity* and *anomie*, as a result of a process of action in an integration group; a change in the extent to which an object is *esteemed* and *respected*, or a change in the ratio of *commitment* and *alienation*, as a result of a process of action in a motivation group? Or is output to personality systems of primary concern?

Five, on a technical level, what was or would have been a useful intervention on the part of various staff members, from the point of view of the sociotherapeutic function? When should one enter in? What are those moments of relaxed stability when new information from an individual might influence a group? How are these to be recognized? What perspective should be encompassed by a particular intervention? Is it possible to roll with the endless change in a group, not tormented by the need to control events, but rather fascinated by them?

Finally, I hope that the following chapters will give the reader a sense of the great issues and themes in group life: for example, the continual tension between values such as autonomy and heteronomy, between imperatives such as integration and adaptation; the continual tension between the need to act synchronously with data about the outside, to recognize the situation, and the need not to lose the pulsebeat within; the continual tension between group and individual. The individual depends upon social life for a framework of meanings and for the attainment of ends requiring collective effort. Yet he comes to social life with fear; he dreads losing his moorings in the complex group process; he dreads ridicule, shame, being hunted down by the group. Even as he knows that he is inevitably a part of the group, in some aspect of himself also he must be not of it. The individual must maintain his own vision and judgment, lest he join others to say, "How beautiful are the Emperor's clothes!" For that effort, he depends upon both knowledge and skill. This book is intended to contribute, in some small way at least, to both.

1. The Individual and Society

If you ask a professional in the mental health field what ails the individual he treats, he is likely to answer in one of two ways.

If he is an advocate of the therapeutic community movement, he may tell you that his individual patient suffers from too little connection with his fellows. What the professional means by this is that his patient is alienated from the values, shared with others, that legitimize action and give wants finite compass, thus making satisfaction possible. He has lost a sense of continuity with other generations. He has no guide to what is legitimate or preferable to seek and achieve; nothing is worthwhile, because nothing is valued more than anything else. The patient is apathetic and undisciplined; he feels no obligation; he is unable to mobilize effort to attain ends. Aimless, he is prey to a chaos of random impulses, none valued more than any other, and all engaged in endless strife within him. The appropriate treatment milieu is, then, a therapeutic community which makes possible personal relatedness, belongingness, and involvement, and, therefore, the creation, renewal, and strengthening of motivational commitments and meaningful identity. If the professional is a psychotherapist, and this is his point of view about his patient, he is likely to attribute what is curative in psychotherapy primarily to the involvement of the patient in a relationship with a psychotherapist.

On the other hand, the professional may have it that his individual patient suffers from inhibition, constriction, or irrationality, caused by

Parts of this chapter and of the concluding chapter of this book were presented at a seminar at Austen Riggs Center, Stockbridge, Massachusetts, in spring, 1968; at a meeting of the Illinois Psychological Association in Peoria, Illinois, on March 15, 1968; at a program sponsored by the Allan Memorial Institute, Department of Psychiatry, McGill University, Montreal, Canada, on April 8, 1968; and at a Research Seminar of Yale University's Department of Psychiatry on December 3, 1968.

the repressive dominance of traditional social values, authority, and obligations distorting his essential nature and interfering with his self-expression and self-realization. From these he needs to be released. If the patient is in a hospital, the best thing to do is to let him do what he wants as much as possible without interference. In the last analysis, he will know what is best for himself, or at least, in making his own decisions, pursuing what he believes is his own interest, seeking his own opportunities for self-expression, and examining the consequences of his own actions, he will learn to behave rationally. Similarly, what is curative in psychotherapy for such a patient is primarily the insight or the conscious awareness of what was once unconscious, which frees him to be rational.

These two no doubt oversimplified ways of looking at what primarily ails the individual patient have many bases, but are, I think, interestingly related to two traditions of thought about the relation of the individual and the social. I shall describe these two traditions, because we should be clear about them to study individuals in society or, more particularly, to evaluate the consequences of our interpretive interventions in a treatment milieu. Although I do not expect to alter personal preferences for one or the other of these traditions, I hope to show, as a preliminary to considering the consequences and difficulties of interpretation in a social-theoretical rather than psychological-theoretical frame of reference, that we are not compelled, certainly at least in studying the individual and social system, to choose between these two traditions as mutually exclusive, dichotomous alternatives.

With respect to the relation between the individual and society, two views predominate.[1] One, articulated by such sociologists as Durkheim and Weber, holds that an individual finds fulfillment only within the context of the social. The social is prior to the individual; insofar as an individual discovers himself in actualizing the values of his community, community determines the nature of his individuality. An individual's identity, when it has enduring, coherent meaning to himself, is constituted by his membership in a community of individuals who share sentiments, values, and beliefs. Memberships in such associations

1. For discussions of the sociological tradition represented by the work of such men as Durkheim and Weber, and the sociological tradition to which it is a reaction, see Robert Nisbet, *The Sociological Tradition* (New York: Basic Books, 1966); Talcott Parsons, *The Structure of Social Action* (New York: The Free Press of Glencoe, 1937). For another excellent explication of the work of Durkheim and Weber, see Raymond Aron, *Main Currents in Sociological Thought II* (New York: Basic Books, 1967).

as class, kin, guild, and local community, and participation in networks of personal relationships, protect individuality from the gray sameness of, and dominance by, a universal, all-powerful state, and guarantee the individual a place in society in which to express and realize himself.

Individual wants, if they are to be organized and satisfied, must be disciplined. They must be governed by community values, or sources of traditional authority representing these values, which specify desirable ends and their hierarchy, and are associated with an internal sense of obligation to realize them in action. In the absence of such discipline, there arises a chaos of wants, which never find cessation, but only a perpetual motion of discontent, exemplified, for example, by insatiable hunger for statuses or possessions.

Since the desirable ends signified by community values are ultimate, that is, are preferred without regard to their utility as means to any other ends, and since such shared values are the emergent characteristic of community, community is ineluctably nonrational. Ultimate values are embodied in sacred objects, which derive their sacredness from their symbolic connection with community and the values constituting it. The sacred is a necessary ground for the meaningfulness of action. Relation to the sacred is the source of renewal of commitment, strengthening of purpose, and mobilization of effort to achieve ends, which rationality itself is powerless to effect, since rationality—which is concerned with means-ends relations—is irrelevant to the cathexis of ultimate ends. Respect for the sacred is the basis for moral consensus and social solidarity, and, therefore, a prerequisite for order and stability. Secularization, which undermines shared values and beliefs, rather than indicating progress, issues in alienation and a cacophony of egoisms, isolation and placelessness, and the loss of meaningful, coherent identity—the condition of individuality in a rationalized, technological society.

The second view—perhaps, as ideology, both root and bloom of the Industrial Revolution and the French Revolution—holds that the individual is prior to society. Individualism, not community, is the theme; individuals do not emerge from community, but rather society is a combination of the sum of individual atom-parts. Social institutions are essentially contracts between individuals actuated by rational considerations of self-interest; each individual sees it to his own benefit to adhere to a social contract.[2]

2. Proponents of the opposing view state that expediency is not adequate to account for adherence to contract. They point out that conformity often occurs

Rationality is the sine qua non of individuality. Reason determines action, except when it is superseded by irrationality, due to ignorance or error, to lack of knowledge or incorrect knowledge. (A variant of this position is that instinctual, innate, hereditarily given forces determine individual action; social phenomena are the "blind" outcome of the clash between or combination of such individual forces. Both rationalistic individualism and anti-intellectualistic individualism [3] tend to conceive history in terms of evolution, progress or lack of progress from a state of irrationality to a state of rationality, or survival of the fittest, rather than as a succession or co-existence of different value systems.[4]) Individual rationality is compromised when the individual is dominated by the sacred—irrational (in this view) values and beliefs—or by traditional authority. The secularization of society releases the individual from the obligations exacted by the sacred and traditional, frees him from the hold of superstition.

The rationalization of society, aimed at making rational action maximally possible throughout the social body, involves undercutting membership in local personal communities and associations, so that nothing interferes with the individual's loyalty to the large state, which is centralized and organized to achieve ends by effective means, and therefore provides the conditions in which an individual has freedom to act rationally.[5] To be free is to be free from ignorance, error, the

---

when it is not in the self-interest of the conformer, when in fact it is much more in his interest to deviate from the contract, and even when deviance is unlikely to incur negative sanctions. Such phenomena, they argue, require the recognition that prior internalized value-commitments underlie fidelity to contractual arrangements. See Aron, *Main Currents;* Nisbet, *Sociological Tradition;* and Parsons, *Structure.*

3. See Parsons, *Structure.*

4. Pareto argued the distinction between logical (rational) and nonlogical (nonrational, *not* irrational) action. The former is action in which means are effective in achieving ends, according to practical, empirical, verifiable knowledge. The latter is action in which, in accord with a tendency to make action seem rational whether it is or not, reason, making use of ideological systems, rationalizes or justifies, with more or less sophistry, action having its origins in enduring dispositions, which are often unrecognized or unacknowledged by the actor, are linked to sentiments, and have the status of ultimate preferences. See Aron, *Main Currents,* and Parsons, *Structure.* Freud described rationalization as a defense against the recognition of the role of unacceptable instinctual impulses in determining action; in some of his work at least, he seems to suggest that action so determined is irrational rather than nonrational—that is, that accurate knowledge of what is unconscious might and probably would result in more rational action.

5. Proponents of the opposing view would say that a rationalized society is one dominated by the values giving prepotency to instrumental action and the stand-

weight of tradition; freedom implies rational action. The dissolution of traditional bonds results above all in progress, not alienation but knowledge and the freedom knowledge confers, not isolation but the possibility of rational contractual agreements with others based upon recognition by each party of what effectively serves his self-interest.

All men are equal, in the sense that all are elements of the same rational society, having no commitments that have priority over participation in such a society; all are subject to the same rules or laws; all are impersonally rather than personally regarded in terms of universal categories rather than local or particular relationships. No difference between individuals depending on membership in traditional communities or associations matters; only each one's actual or potential performance with respect to the rational achievement of the ends of the total society matters.

Each individual is, then, free to make his unique contribution to the attainment of desired ends. Such contributions are rationally organized by society to bring about desired ends efficiently and effectively. The complementariness of differentiated, interdependent roles, each different from, but requiring and at the same time regulating, the other, each recognized and valued as a necessary ingredient in the effort to achieve a given end, constitutes, to use Durkheim's terminology, the "organic solidarity" of such a society, as distinct from the "mechanical solidarity" of a community whose members are alike, sharing common sentiments, values, and beliefs—what I shall refer to, also, as homogeneous solidarity. Bureaucracy, the hierarchization of individual role-contributions in terms of their logical, instrumental relation to each other and to the end to be achieved, is the basis for social integration and order in the secular, technological society.

The therapeutic community as a social movement in the mental health field seems, on the whole, to adopt the first view about the relation of individual and society; it is in reaction to the rationalization of society. Its equalitarianism is not the equalitarianism of the rationalized mass society, but is rather anti-hierarchical and anti-bureaucratic. The objection is to inequality based on roles and the different degrees of authority, status, and prestige which come to be attached to such roles and the individuals who occupy them. What is valued rather are networks of personal—interpersonal, as they are called—relationships,

---

ards of efficiency and effectiveness in guiding such action; the rationalistic individualist conceives no other legitimate positive value orientation but only values representing debasements or corruptions of this one.

the bonds between people being based not on complementary, differentiated roles, but rather on the similarity of their values, sentiments, and beliefs. Individuals are equal in their adherence to common values and beliefs or in the feelings and sentiments they share; other characteristics have less importance. In other words, the solidarity of such a community is of the homogeneous rather than organic variety.

Enthusiasm is for shared effective expression, shared activities and facilities, informality, free communication, and group rituals (for example, meetings of various kinds, which like all group rituals serve primarily to renew commitment to the values of the community and to strengthen purpose to actualize these values in the treatment endeavor). Such enthusiasm tends to be accompanied by anti-intellectual attitudes and suspicion of performance "in role" as nonhuman, insincere, reserved, or, at the least, constricted.

The aspect of therapeutic community ideology often termed "reality confrontation," [6] does not in my experience involve cognitive-adaptation values primarily—that is, the acquisition of instrumental knowledge about oneself and the world one lives in—but rather serves to make the individual more a part of the community, to involve him more intensely with the values, beliefs, and sentiments of his fellows, by exposing him to what others *feel* about his behavior. (It is not unusual for a staff member to exhort patients and sometimes other staff as well to let a deviant patient know how others *feel* about the way he has been acting.) This kind of interaction tends to result in an increase in the bonds of union and likeness among community members, or in the exclusion of the offender—in either event, in strengthening the homogeneous solidarity of the community.

To the extent that permissiveness is also a part of the ideology of the therapeutic community, it usually denotes not permission to challenge or evade the sentiments, values, or beliefs held in common—not the legitimacy of such a challenge or evasion—but rather the desirability of community members orienting to each other in terms of personal ties, group belongingness, and particularistic criteria—"he's one of us," "he's my friend," "he should be understood not punished"—rather than in terms of impersonal universal categories or actual performance in relation to given tasks or norms.

Now, I think, there are at least four reasons why, as we study individuals and groups, we should not choose one and reject the other of

6. See, for example, Robert Rapoport, *Community as Doctor* (Springfield, Ill.: Charles C. Thomas, 1960).

these two views of the relation between the individual and society, nor seek always and exclusively in our milieu—or, for that matter, individual—therapy to actualize only the values of either the traditional community or rationalized society.

First, the meaning of individuality, if enhancing individuality be the end to determine our choice, changes from one view to the other. In the first view, individuality is thought to be achieved insofar as an individual most completely represents in himself and his actions that which is valued by the members of his community. Such values are not mere external social facts, to which he must adapt, but constituents of his own personality, which he wants to actualize.[7] He is not compelled, but wills himself to do that which he is by virtue of the group to which he belongs. In other words, he realizes himself to the extent that his action is disciplined by the internalized sense of obligation to actualize the values he shares with others. At the moment he is most of others, he is most himself. Then he knows who he is, where he is going, and what his life means. In the second view, individuality is thought to be achieved insofar as an individual most completely separates himself from the claims of tradition and differentiates himself from others; only then is he free to follow rationally the dictates of self-interest. The individual finds himself in standing apart from the world and mastering, understanding, or making use of it; and in differentiating himself from others and priding himself on doing his job, on the unique contribution he brings to relationship, and on the fidelity of his commitment to skill and discipline in his interdependent, complementary interaction with others whose difference from himself he recognizes and respects as they recognize and respect his own from them.[8]

Second, if the welfare of the individual be the concern to determine our choice, the concrete individual does not appear to be unequivocally benefited in either kind of social situation. In the homogeneous, traditional community the individual knows who he is and where he is going—so long as he is of the group. Paring away the parts of himself that do not fit, suppressing idiosyncratic inclinations and judgments, he may slide imperceptibly, caught up in community, into acts of altruistic suicide. If he be different from others with respect to the important

7. Therefore, the importance of a concept like the superego; see Sigmund Freud. *The Ego and the Id*, The Standard Edition of the Complete Psychological Works of Sigmund Freud, vol. 19 (London: Hogarth Press, 1961); and Parsons. *Social Structure and Personality* (New York: The Free Press of Glencoe, 1964).

8. Proponents of the other view might well claim that this is, in fact, the value system shared and actualized by the members of the rationalized society.

sentiments, values, and beliefs that constitute the community, if he thereby violates what is regarded as sacred, he is expelled or repressively punished—such punishment itself becoming not a means of rehabilitation but the ritual by which commitment to the community and the values it represents are renewed in all its members. The homogeneous group is exclusive: aggressive toward individuals and groups outside holding different values and beliefs, and cruel to its own deviants. This kind of group inevitably creates the category outcast. Since innovation, the product of the solitary thinking mind, threatens group tradition and solidarity, it is discouraged. Because the community does not encourage change, its relation to its situation may be less than optimally adaptive; and as the community suffers from this disadvantage, so of course do its individual members.

In the rationalized society, on the other hand, where all individuals are equal as objects of utility, to be used expediently and efficiently, there is an inexorable drift toward subordination of the individual to the tyranny of collective purpose, to the organization which is the means of achieving that purpose rationally, and to the centralized concentration of power required to effect and maintain that organization. There is a tendency increasingly to subordinate the minority to the will of the majority, the sum of whose self-interests supposedly creates the collective purpose. The individual is valued and values himself according to his use; before the majority and the effective organization that carries out its will, he is powerless to assert himself in terms of other values, which have no meaning in such a society. Individuality in this society, optimally manifested in acts of mastery and skillful, disciplined role-performance, may slide imperceptibly into robotization, when the role calls upon an increasingly narrow segment of the individual's resources and an increasingly limited range of experience and value is relevant to its validation. Or individuality may become a chaotic egoism, to which nothing matters but the inclination of the moment whose satisfaction is justified in the name of the rational pursuit of self-interest.

Third, in our attempts to study the relation between the individual and society, we must remember that the "individual" and "social" are analytical cenceptions, not concrete entities. The individual and the social are inextricably interrelated aspects of phenomena; the individual is not observable apart from what is social, nor is the social observable apart from individuals. Therefore, "individual" and "social" should not be reified and opposed, as if there were two entities whose concrete existence might be incompatible. An individual personality system may be theoretically distinguished from a social system as a focus of scientific interest, but these two systems do not exist apart from one another in reality.

A single phenomenon may be studied from the point of view either of personality system or social system. A personality system may be viewed, for example, as a distinctive organization of need-dispositions, a social system as a distinctive organization of roles, roles and need-dispositions each being necessary for meeting the requirements of a particular kind of system. Roles and need-dispositions are integrated by a value-system, which is internalized as a constituent of an individual personality system, or—the emergent characteristic of the "social"—shared by the members of, or institutionalized in, a social system. In the integration of role-expectations with need-dispositions, and at the point of articulation where values internalized in individual personality systems are at the same time shared by persons to form the basis of solidarity in the social system, personality and social system intersect in the phenomenal world.

The physiological behavioral organism and the cultural system are also theoretically distinguishable from social system and personality system. Each system is an organization of distinctive components, and for its description and the discovery of lawful relations in it, different concepts are relevant. Attempts to deal with questions apparently concerning the relation between individual and social may necessarily involve consideration of the inputs and outputs to and from these different systems in relation to one another.[9]

The individual and social are, then, inextricably interrelated in, and observable aspects of, both the homogeneous, traditional community and the rationalized society. In neither can one say that what is individual has some concrete existence apart from, and is in perpetual opposition or expedient adaptation to, what is social, nor that what is individual is lost in, secondary to, or indistinguishable from, what is social. The question of which is prior, causally or ontogenetically—the individual or social—will someday soon, if it has not already, join such questions as which is prior, heredity or environment, in the graveyard of social science theory.

9. Inputs from the physiological organism to the personality system cannot be considered the ultimate foundation of the individual as opposed to the social, since such inputs are essential to the personality system's orientation to and dependence upon social objects, and also since such inputs do not activate the personality system until they are transformed into symbolic meaning, a process dependent upon social experience.

Fourth, the homogeneous, traditional community and the rational-ized society may be considered forms of the social giving different priorities to the various functional requirements of any social system. To the extent that a social system is differentiated to meet such func-tional requirements, one may expect to find within it collectivities hav-ing the characteristics of the homogeneous, traditional community and other collectivities having the characteristics of the rationalized so-ciety. Some collectivities, primarily concerned with establishing and maintaining *motivational commitments* to values and mobilizing in-centives for the *attainment of cathected ends,* emphasize shared values, beliefs, and sentiments and a shared perception of the way things are in relation to the way things ought to be, to the ultimately desirable. Some collectivities, primarily concerned with *adaptation* to, or mastery of, the situation, or with the *integration* of the differentiated roles of the members of the social system (crucially related to the survival of the social system in its situation), are characterized by the organic solidarity of interdependently interacting persons.

A so-called therapeutic community and the other collectivities of a rationalized hospital organization within which such a community may exist offer examples of such contrasting collectivities. Within a patient-staff therapeutic community, which has differentiated groups carrying out different functions, family-like *small groups* may give highest pri-ority to homogeneous solidarity; a *work program* or *governing com-munity council* may give highest priority to organic solidarity. A patient-staff community meeting itself may move through phases. Some phases are devoted to the establishment of motivational commitments or the arousal of interest in desired ends; in these phases a value con-sensus and a shared cathexis of ends provide the foundation for group cohesion. Other phases are devoted to a cognitive examination of means-ends relations which may be used to master a particular situa-tion, or to a moral evaluation of the ways in which people are or are not doing their parts and consequences of these for the group; in these phases, the integration of differentiated specific contributions with each other and with the situation provides the foundation for the group's organic solidarity.[10]

10. See Marshall Edelson, "The Sociotherapeutic Function in a Psychiatric Hos-pital," *Journal of the Fort Logan Mental Health Center,* 4, no. 1, 1–45; Marshall Edelson, "Sociotherapy and Psychotherapy in the Psychiatric Hospital," in vol. 47 of the Association for Research in Nervous and Mental Disease series, *Social Psy-chiatry* (Baltimore: Williams and Wilkins Company, 1969), pp. 196–211; Marshall Edelson, *Sociotherapy and Psychotherapy* (Chicago: University of Chicago Press,

A crucial relation between the individual and the social system may be stated as follows. Any social system, if all its functional problems are to be solved, requires of its members capacities for both *involvement* with others—joining with others, being like others, feeling with others, seeing and valuing as others see and value—and *individuation*—the separation or distinguishing of self from others and the detachment of self from the situation to be understood or mastered.[11] A particular group within a social system may give priority either to involvement or individuation. Such priority depends upon the nature of the group's contribution to the social system of which it is a part—that is, the particular functional problem that is prepotent for it—or upon what phase the group is in with respect to meeting its own functional requirements. A social system as a whole, or a particular group, may give a more or less enduring priority to one or another kind of values or ends, and therefore to special requirements for involvement or individuation, but no group or social system can long survive by sacrificing beyond certain limits the solution of other kinds of functional problems, which require a different emphasis on involvement or individuation.

Requirements for involvement or individuation may or may not fit the capacities or dispositions of particular personality systems. As is evident from subsequent chapters in this book, in a therapeutic community one has an unusual opportunity to study the impact of the social system's requirements for involvement and individuation upon its individual patients and staff members—for example, the anxieties aroused by such requirements. One may also study the impact upon functional problem-solving processes in such a community (as in any group) of characteristic limitations in its individual members' capacities for, their characteristic value-attitudes toward, and their collusive defenses against, involvement or individuation.

1970); Talcott Parsons, Edward Shils, and Robert Bales, *Working Papers in the Theory of Action* (New York: The Free Press of Glencoe, 1953); Talcott Parsons, "Pattern Variables Revisited," *American Sociological Review*, 25 (August 1960); Talcott Parsons, "An Outline of the Social System," in Parsons et al., *Theories of Society*, vol. I (New York: The Free Press of Glencoe, 1961), pp. 30–79.

11. For a discussion of individuation and involvement in human life, see Susanne Langer, "Man and Animal: The City and the Hive," in *Philosophical Sketches* (New York: Mentor Books, 1964), pp. 95–106. For an assertion of the inevitability of both self-regard and social impulse in human life, see Reinhold Niebuhr's critical survey of idealist and realist political theories in *Man's Nature and His Communities* (New York: Charles Scribner's Sons, 1965).

In recent works,[12] I have suggested that the fundamental distinction between *person* and *situation*, both of which are essential aspects of any process of action, is reflected by the differentiation of the treatment enterprise in a psychiatric hospital into *psychotherapy* and *sociotherapy*.

The most general formulation is the distinction between any acting system—whether the actor be a person or a collective such as a group, organization, or society—and its situation. All actors—personal or collective—may be distinguished, or are separated by definable boundaries, from the situation to which they relate; all actors are oriented to the anticipated attainment of future ends. This definition provides the fundamental framework of the theory of action.[13]

The boundary between action system and situation, and the process of attainment of ends or actualization of values through time, provide two dimensions according to which the primary functional problems of the system may be classified. An acting system may choose in any particular process of action to focus upon the future (potentiality) or the present (actuality), and to focus upon what is within the system (autonomy) or upon its relation with its external situation (heteronomy). Potentiality-heteronomy means a focus upon *adaptation* or a concern with the means, resources, or constraints to be mastered or accommodated to in the service of the attainment of future ends. Actuality-heteronomy means a focus upon *consummation* or the actual attainment of ultimate ends, valued in and of themselves, and not as the means to other ends.

Potentiality-autonomy means a focus upon *motivation,* or the condition of the units of the system with respect to motivational dispositions or commitments required for the attainment of future ends. Actuality-autonomy means a focus upon the *integration* of the units of the system.[14]

In a previous volume, *Sociotherapy and Psychotherapy,* I have described adaptation, consummation, motivation, and integration group

12. See Marshall Edelson, "Review of *Social Psychology in Treating Mental Illness: An Experimental Approach*, edited by George Fairweather," *Psychiatry,* 29, no. 4, 428–32; and the first three references cited in footnote 10.

13. See Talcott Parsons, et al., *Toward a General Theory of Action* (New York: Harper and Row, Torchbook edition, 1951). A. K. Rice has independently analyzed organizations in this conceptual framework, that is, as systems related across boundaries to situations and seeking to achieve tasks and subtasks; see *The Enterprise and Its Environment* (London: Tavistock Publications, 1963).

14. See Parsons, "Pattern Variables Revisited," and Edelson, "Theory of Groups," in *Sociotherapy and Psychotherapy,* chap. 2.

functions, each one of which gives primacy to one of these alternatives, to the solution of one of these system problems. In other words, I have described the characteristics and aims of the adaptation group, consummation group, motivation group, and integration group in relation to and interacting with each other in a social system. Outputs of the adaptation, consummation, and integration groups are, respectively, instrumental action, expressive action, and responsible action. Processes in the motivation group are directed to the internalization and institutionalization of values.

Sociotherapy and psychotherapy are complementary, inextricably interrelated enterprises in any attempt to understand and influence persons, but enterprises differentiated by having different systems as foci of intervention and analysis: psychotherapy the personality system, sociotherapy the social system in which the person participates. Psychotherapy is concerned with intrapersonal states, conflicts, and determinants of motivation. Sociotherapy is concerned with the object-situation, the locus of means, constraints, and goal-objects, and the source of norms and values adapted to or internalized. The aims of psychotherapy are the identification and mitigation of strains within, or the integration of, the personality system. The aims of sociotherapy are the identification and mitigation of strains within, or the integration of, the relevant social system, which in a hospital organization is the hospital community or "therapeutic community," as it may be called. Any clinical phenomenon may be—and for effective treatment in a hospital should be—considered both from the point of view of psychotherapy, focusing upon the patient's personality system, and from the point of view of sociotherapy, focusing upon the social system of which the patient is a member, most saliently, the hospital community itself. The differentiation of responsibility for the psychotherapeutic and sociotherapeutic enterprises in the hospital organization facilitates the articulation of both points of view and tends to ensure that both will be brought to bear in any attempt to understand or cope with clinical phenomena.

A sociotherapy staff, broadly speaking, is constituted by all those who are primarily concerned with the structure of the object-situation with its inducements and opportunities for expressive, instrumental, and responsible action, and its value patterns and orientations, which may be internalized and actualized in such processes of action. Various staff members may operate primarily along the axis of the primary functional problems motivation and consummation, that is, the creation and maintenance of shared value commitments and the attainment of cathected ends.[15] Therapy staff members, for example, often participate in the therapeutic community as numinous leaders,[16] representing and inspiring respect for the values of the treatment enterprise. A medical or clinical director may lead the community toward some end by mobilizing a shared cathexis of it as a more desirable state of affairs than a present state of affairs. Activities staff members may lead by stimulating desires to attain gratifying, expressive ends.

Other staff members may operate primarily along the axis of the primary functional problems adaptation and integration. Leaders in a work program are sources of knowledge and skill; they know what will work, and how to get and use the necessary means to achieve a given end. Nurses frequently specialize in defending the norms of the community against the deviance of individual members; such staff leaders stand for the requirement that each individual and each group do his or its part in a way that contributes to the harmony and stability—or organic solidarity—of the whole.

Leaders operating along the first axis require involvement from others; leaders along the second axis require individuation. Members of the group have characteristic value-attitudes toward and may collusively defend in a variety of ways against these leaders and their demands. Such processes are illustrated in the subsequent chapters of this book.

In *Sociotherapy and Psychotherapy*, I formulated a theory of groups, and a system theory of organization, leading to a particular model of psychiatric hospital organization and view of the therapeutic community. In that work, I concluded that the therapeutic community comprises the interdependent patient, staff, and patient-staff collectivities, whose primary focus is the social system of the hospital community, rather than the individual personality system or the relation between the individual patient and groups in the extended society. As a reflection of the institutionalization of the values of psychotherapy, a therapeutic commuity may involve a collective effort by patients and staff to learn to understand the situation in which treatment proceeds, and in particular the nature of a social system integrated around treatment values; the often conflicting values, aims, and interests struggling within such a social system; the complex equilibria represented by its

15. For the theoretical formulation that makes sense of the word "axis" in this context, see Parsons, "Pattern Variables Revisited."

16. To use Erik Erikson's felicitous adjective; see his relevant discussion of the numinous in the "Ontogeny of Ritualization," in *Psychoanalysis—A General Psychology* (New York: International Universities Press, 1966).

institutions; and the complicated reciprocal influence of personality systems and the social system. Patients and staff, informed by skills and knowledge pertinent to sociotherapy, collaborate in participating in, and investigating, a social system, in a way that is analogous to the participant-investigation of the personality system that goes on in intensive psychotherapy.

Such investigation of the hospital community as social system is facilitated by its organization into collectivities—the community meeting; governing community council; work program, committee, or crew; expressive activity, program, or committee; and small groups. Each such collectivity is differentiated to contribute to the solution of different primary functional problems of the community, for example, adaptation, consummation, integration, and motivation. In the process of solving such problems, these collectivities require involvement and individuation from the members of the therapeutic community. For example, a work program may be considered to give primacy to adaptation group functions or to exemplify the adaptation group; an activities program may be considered to give primacy to consummation group functions or to exemplify the consummation group; a community council may be considered to give primacy to integration group functions or to exemplify the integration group; and small groups may be considered to give primacy to motivation group functions or to exemplify the motivation group. Another way of putting this is that the work program is part of the adaptation subsystem of the therapeutic community as social system; the activities program is part of the consummation subsystem; the community council is part of the integration subsystem; and the small group program is part of the motivation subsystem. Each of these subsystems in turn may be viewed as having to meet problems of adaptation, consummation, integration, and motivation, and, therefore, as having adaptation, consummation, integration, and motivation components. Similarly, a process of action in each such subsystem will have adaptation, consummation, integration, and motivation phases.

With respect to output to individual personality systems, such organization provides clear models of adaptation, consummation, integration, and motivation groups. In participating in such groups, patients may not only learn to experience and understand the relation among these different kinds of social processes, but may also internalize patterns or orientations relevant to instrumental action, expressive action, responsible action, and processes involving commitment to, and respect for, systems of values and the social objects representing them.

To summarize, in this first chapter, preliminary to the consideration throughout this book and explicitly in the final chapter of the consequences and difficulties of interpretation in a social-theoretical rather than psychological-theoretical frame of reference in clinical situations, two views of mental illness and its treatment have been related to two traditions of thought about the relation of the individual and the social. One view emphasizes the internalization by the individual of values shared with others in the traditional community, as explicated by such sociologists as Durkheim and Weber. The other view emphasizes the individual's rational pursuit of self-interest in a secularized society.

The therapeutic community as a social movement in the mental health field seems, on the whole, to adopt the first view about the relation of individual and society; it is in reaction to the rationalization of society. However, there are four reasons why, as we study individuals and groups, we should not choose one and reject the other of these two views, nor seek always and exclusively in our milieu—or, for that matter, individual—therapy to actualize only the values of either the traditional community or rationalized society.

First, we cannot choose between the values of the traditional community and the rationalized society on the basis of a preference for enhancing individuality, since the meaning of "individuality" changes from one tradition of social thought to the other.

Second, we cannot choose between them on the basis of concern for the welfare of the individual, since the concrete individual does not appear to be unequivocally benefited in either the traditional community or the rationalized society.

Third, we cannot choose between them on the assumption that we are choosing between the social and the individual, since "individual" and "social" are analytical conceptions, not concrete entities, and should not be reified and opposed, as if they were entities whose concrete existence might be incompatible. An individual personality system may be theoretically distinguished from a social system as a focus of scientific interest, but these two systems represent different, inextricably interrelated, abstracted aspects of phenomenal reality.

Fourth, the traditional community and rationalized society are forms of the social. The values of both are to be found in any social system since the values of each are relevant to the solution of some of the primary functional problems of any social system. The values of the traditional community are relevant to groups or group processes giving priority to the solution of the social system's primary functional problems *motivation* and *consummation,* requiring *homogeneous solidarity* of the group and *involvement* from individual group members. The values of the rationalized society are relevant to groups or group processes giving priority to the solution of the social system's primary functional problems *adaptation* and *integration,* requiring *organic solidarity* of the group and *individuation* of individual group members.

Finally, I have described how sociotherapy may be distinguished from psychotherapy, and how the aims of a sociotherapy staff may be delineated in terms of the primary functional problems of the hospital community as a social system.

2. Group Life in a Psychiatric Hospital

This chapter is a study of the group life of a psychiatric hospital, and especially of the relations between groups—between patients and staff, between staff groups—as these are effected by the overall organization of the hospital. The striking characteristic of the organization of this particular hospital is that the organization appears to be, in large part, a function neither of the hospital's task nor of situational exigencies or available resources, but rather of commitment to a value system, for example, the values of autonomy and equalitarianism. Commitment to autonomy is expressed in permissiveness of staff members toward patients and toward other staff members, and of patients toward each other, in a completely open hospital or residential treatment center. The consequences of the primacy of these and other values for adaptation to situational exigencies and for task achievement have been discussed in a previous volume, *Sociotherapy and Psychotherapy,* and are suggested in this chapter and illustrated in other chapters of this book as well.

In this study of a psychiatric hospital I have emphasized characteristics of organization in accounting for various phenomena. This does not mean that I do not appreciate that strains within, or optimal motivational states of, personality systems, and the inadequacies or unusual skills of behavioral organisms, make an important contribution to such phenomena. I did not feel it was appropriate, nor had I any inclination, in this chapter to write about personalities or individual capacities, which tend, in any event, to be overemphasized by most "human relations" experts to the exclusion of an appreciation of the determining role of organization itself. Often what is regarded as the peculiar expression of a personality is an "average" expectable manifestation of role characteristics or reaction to the pressures and strains associated with the occupancy of that role in a particular organization.

In general, special motivations leading a particular individual to occupy a given role-position or the singular personal satisfactions he experiences in it, as well as his unique gifts of leadership, receive more interest than is justified by the effect of these upon the achievement of organizational ends. Neglected are the degree of fit between particular gifts and the current needs of the organization, and the role-occupant's actual performance, especially as this is determined by the characteristics of the role itself—the nature of the expectations, value orientations, associated available resources, opportunities, and prescribed relations to other roles defining it within a particular organization. (This is true of patients as well as staff.) The no doubt colorful variety of motivations leading to participation in an office or enterprise seems to matter less in determining the behavior of participants, and therefore their effect upon the achievement of organizational tasks, than what in a particular organization is expected of and permitted to these participants, and how and to what degree adherence in conduct to such expectations and (enabling as well as constraining) regulations is maintained.

The particular hospital examined offers an exceptional opportunity to its staff to study intensively both individual lives during periods of developmental crisis and a small, in many ways unique, hospital social system. The treatment program and staff are generally recognized as of unusually high quality compared to average psychiatric facilities.

The observations were made over an approximately two-and-a-half year period, which was marked by upheaval and portentous change. The medical director during many months of this period suffered what was ultimately a fatal illness; the staff tried not only to maintain but to improve the treatment program, even while its members experienced the anguish of personal loss and, inevitably, some anxiety about the future. Many observations are now no longer applicable; many situations described too statically as existent were already in a process of change. Problems focused upon here have been "solved"; as is always true, the solutions have given rise to new, unpredicted problems.

Even in a situation in which the very nature of the tasks to be performed implies intrinsic dilemmas, one may be tempted to suppose that a change in someone's qualities or an improvement in interpersonal relations will lead to a "resolution" of difficulties. However, in dealing with most problems in a psychiatric hospital, one finds oneself ultimately choosing between alternatives each one of which has associated dysfunctional and functional effects, and accommodating as best one can to the pain of one's position; one rarely indeed finds anything even resembling a completely satisfactory final "resolution." It is hoped, therefore, that nothing in the following descriptions suggests the impatient, shortsighted, optimistic criticism: if this or that had been changed, if he or she had been different, how much better it would have been!

Finally, the view of the hospital and its organization is that of a relatively new member of the organization, seeing it inevitably in part from the particular perspective of his own experiences, values, and concerns.

PATIENT AUTONOMY AND PLEASING THE THERAPY STAFF

In a small psychiatric residential treatment center, approximately fifty patients live in an old inn; they come and go as they please. Next door there is an office building where the psychotherapy or therapy staff "lives." [1] Here each patient is seen for psychoanalytic individual psychotherapy, usually in fifty-minute sessions, usually four times a week.

The therapy staff rarely meets together as a group in itself. There are no "management" conferences; the therapy staff rejects the concept that therapists are engaged in "managing" patients. There is no person other than the medical director charged with overall responsibility for the psychotherapeutic enterprise. Each psychotherapist presumably has maximum autonomy in areas concerning the conduct of individual psychotherapy sessions and the direction of his work or his way of working with any patient; day-to-day medical (if he is a physician) and most administrative decisions (there are relatively few) concerning his patients are largely in his hands.

Recommendations about a patient's remaining for treatment and about approaches to treatment are made at a staff conference.[2] Usually,

1. The therapy staff consists of approximately twelve permanent staff and about twelve fellows in training. Of the permanent staff, somewhat over half are psychiatrists and somewhat less than half are psychologists; about one half are psychoanalysts (half of these are training analysts) and a small number are in psychoanalytic training. Of the fellows, about four are psychologists receiving postdoctoral training and about eight are psychiatrists who have had at least two years of residency in psychiatry before coming to the hospital. Two of the therapy staff do not see patients in psychotherapy because of their administrative positions; one of the therapy staff who is engaged in research also does not see patients in psychotherapy. Other members of the therapy staff see from two to five inpatients for four fifty-minute psychoanalytically oriented psychotherapy sessions a week. Each fellow receives one hour a week of individual supervision with a senior member of the permanent staff for each patient with whom he works.

2. Each patient is presented to the staff conference (including all therapy staff, members of the nursing staff, and the director of the activities staff) after a month's intense study and evaluation, which result in a report from the psychotherapist

although not without exception, the presenting psychotherapist's attitudes and conclusions are quite influential, if not decisive, in determining whether the patient will remain. If the patient needs financial aid to remain in the hospital, other staff opinion is likely to have more weight; the psychotherapist's opinion is still given much consideration, although to some extent its effect is dependent upon his experience.

Discharge arrangements are often made between a patient and therapist without consultation with the rest of the staff, although usually after some discussion with a supervisor or medical administrator. Strains most often develop over such decisions when they concern arrangements with a patient for him to move out of the hospital and live in town but continue to be seen by his psychotherapist as an outpatient; different therapists and different staff groups hold different attitudes toward, and different criteria for, such a status.

The therapy staff has difficulties in making decisions about such matters as acceptance for treatment and discharge, as well as difficulties in making judgments about patients' social behavior. Members of the therapy staff frequently express uncertainty about the extent to which the values and norms to which staff members appeal are intrinsic to the treatment enterprise and the extent to which these, in fact, arise from therapists' own backgrounds and personal preferences. It is hard to assess how much such difficulties are related to the facts that the patients, for the most part, come from a socio-economic class different from that of most staff members (the patients are and have been wealthier than the therapists and are used to luxuries and services most staff members cannot afford); and how much such difficulties are

---

detailing a life history and clinical-diagnostic impression, a report from a psychologist of inferences concerning personality psychodynamics and ego-functioning derived from psychodiagnostic testing, a report from an internist concerning physical status, and reports from a nurse and from the director of the activities staff about participation in the hospital community.

The patient most likely to be accepted for treatment is a young adult (average age twenty-two), who has had some college (about two-thirds of the patients are college "drop outs"), has above-average intelligence, needs treatment for schizophrenia, a schizophrenic or severe neurotic character disorder, or a borderline condition, and whose family can afford—and is willing—to pay the relatively high fees. (The hospital is a private, nonprofit institution; since it lacks endowment, it depends on fees to support its expensive treatment program.)

A patient is usually re-presented once a year to the staff conference with focus upon the course of therapy; recommendations concerning such matters as possible change of therapist, continuation in inpatient status, and plans for the future are often discussed.

related to staff members' witting and unwitting ambivalence about that fact.

An official policy is that after a period of treatment a patient's inability to continue paying the fees will not result in his discharge, if he has gained, or shows promise of gaining, from the treatment program. In many cases, decisions are made according to this policy, the patient's additional hospitalization being supported by a Patient-Aid Fund. In other cases, some rationalization and sophistry inevitably creep into discussions at staff conference to cover difficult dilemmas for the hospital as an organization, arising for example from excessive drains on its resources or the refusal of families, who can afford to do so, to support further hospitalization for a patient in whose treatment the patient and staff have invested.

The hospital exists, officially, for patients with severe character disturbances, severe neuroses, borderline states and psychoses. Nevertheless, patients with alcoholism (except what appears to be reactive alcoholism in a previously hard-working, successful person) or drug addiction, or with acute psychosis (if the patient does not seem to be able to take care of himself adequately in an open setting), are ordinarily not accepted for treatment. Patients who require much physical care, especially if physical disability confines them to their rooms or threatens their lives, are ordinarily not accepted for continued treatment. Similarly, patients with a record of serious antisocial behavior, especially if they are narcissistic, defiant, or give the impression of "conning" the staff, are ordinarily not accepted for treatment.

Patients who are destructive of property, or who frighten others through intimidating or assaultive behavior or gross disorganization of thought processes (including patients who develop catatonic states even in the absence of any overt assault) are likely to be sent from the hospital to a hospital with closed facilities. Such disruption of a treatment process and relationship between patient and psychotherapist is at considerable variance with the avowed commitment to relationship and continued, prolonged treatment and causes much strain among and between patient and staff groups. Interestingly enough, although immense anxiety and anger are typical reactions to patients who commit self-destructive acts (cutting their wrists or taking pills), these patients are much less likely to be sent from the hospital than the previously mentioned group who attack others or the values of others; it is rare indeed for a patient to be refused continued treatment following evaluation on the basis that the patient is a suicidal risk.

Many members of the therapy staff prefer to have some older de-

pressed patients, who have been previously hard-working and successful, in the hospital community;[3] as one therapy staff member put it,
"such patients are more mature and help to present good social values
to the younger patients." As one might guess, some older patients slip
into the role of representing values and positions important to the
therapy staff to the rest of the patient group,[4] often identifying primarily with the therapy staff and holding themselves somewhat aloof
from the younger patients; sometimes scolding the latter self-right-
eously, giving them advice, often being helpful, but never quite feeling or being felt to be one of the group. Such older patients tend to
regard the younger patients as wild, impulsive, undependable, and not
objective; on the other hand, they extoll the experience, wisdom,
thoughtfulness, and objectivity of therapy staff. This is an example of
how relations between patients and staff affect relations among patients.

The ability and willingness of a patient to participate in hospital
community activities, particularly in the work program,[5] are said to be
preconditions for acceptance for treatment and for remaining at the
hospital. However, if a patient is passive, apparently compliant, states
that he believes in the values—and wishes to behave according to the
norms—of the community but that (for some reason he does not understand but hopes to be able to understand through psychotherapy) he
cannot; if he makes some show of an effort—even if for the most part
unsuccessful—to meet the expectations of the program; then, the
therapy staff will tolerate—with fairly vociferous objections from a
minority—a great deal of evasion of responsibilities, non-participation,

3. "Community" and "hospital community" are used interchangeably in the
text; "community" does not mean the extended community outside the hospital
unless so specified. Similarly, "community program" refers to the therapeutic community program within the hospital.

4. It is not, of course, difficult for patients to determine what members of the
therapy staff want, like, or value. The town in which the hospital is located is
very small. Patients and staff see each other on a variety of occasions, share many
of the same facilities, and exchange views at all sorts of programs. The children of
many staff members are cared for by patients acting as assistant teachers in the
nursery school sponsored by the activities program. Some patients work on research
projects of therapy staff members (other than their own therapists).

5. The patients work about an hour a day on chores on the grounds, in the inn,
the greenhouse, the shop, the patient office; such work is organized by a patient-
staff work committee, consisting of one or two members of the therapy staff (one
of whom has the position of staff representative to the work committee), the director of the activities staff, intermittently a nurse, two patient schedulers, and patient
foremen from each work area.

and withdrawal. The prepotent attitude seems to be that the patient should have every chance and should be allowed a rather wide leeway as far as social mal-integration is concerned, if he indicates that he knows that he is ill, that he needs help, and that he wants to enter into a relationship with a competent therapist, telling his therapist "everything," presumably to receive such help. This attitude, of course, is not different from the general social distinction between illness and malingering or criminality.

The patient who is not likely to be accepted for treatment or to remain long, if once accepted, is the patient who aggressively and provocatively flouts community norms, justifies and rationalizes his doing so as evidence of some superior desirable qualities in himself, repetitiously and verbally flaunts his disbelief in, mockery of, and lack of commitment to, community values, and tries to recruit others to join him in such behavior. (Another patient who is likely to be considered for an early discharge is the patient who for one reason or another makes the nurses feel helpless, anxious, or incompetent. Sometimes these characteristics overlap in the same patient, but not always.)

Of course, aggressive challenge is the kind of deviance that is enormously difficult for any social system to cope with. When the question whether or not to discharge such a patient is being discussed, that part of the staff which was previously a minority, insisting that social standards be maintained and conformity to norms be upheld as a precondition for membership in the community, now becomes the leadership of the therapy staff. Such statements as "We can't go along with this!" are now heeded. The doubts of those who remind the therapy staff of the treatment mission of the hospital are quieted with an assertion of humility: "We have to accept that we can't treat every kind of patient, and protect the kind of place we are so that the patients we can help will be helped here."

Selection of and relating to patients depend upon being able to make and maintain in the face of ambiguities the distinction between *illness*—deviance which is acceptable so long as the patient is making an effort to get better, no matter what the effect of such deviance is upon the community—and *criminality* or *malingering*—deviance which is unacceptable, though its behavioral manifestations may at times be quite similar, and its effects upon the community as little or as greatly contributing to dysfunction in the social system as illness. Moral judgments are held to interfere with the acceptance and permissiveness required for treatment. On the other hand, how are such acceptance and permissiveness to be given in a way that does not positively sanction the patient's pathological formations? The therapy staff is ingenious in its accommodation to such strains.

With respect to patients who passively withdraw and evade, without overtly challenging values and norms, the therapy staff is able to reassure itself that it is treating, not judging, ill people and giving them the patience, acceptance, and time they need to work out their problems. With respect to patients who aggressively flout norms and values, the therapy staff is able to reassure itself that it is maintaining consistent firm social expectations and standards and thereby combatting the regressive tendencies that would be exacerbated in a setting where no responsibilities are required.

Difficulties, however, inevitably arise in the treatment of patients whose previous social mal-integration has in fact involved ritualistic compliance, overconformity, dependence, submission, evasion, and withdrawal. The socially dysfunctional consequences of this kind of deviance tend to be overlooked or, when observed, hard to overcome in the hospital community itself—because such behavior is characteristic of the kind of patients with whom the therapy staff wants to work. The therapy staff believes that such patients are the only ones who can be treated in an open setting with its absence of external restraints or controls.

Here is a paradox indeed! The therapy staff, for a variety of reasons, values above all autonomy and independence. Many of the staff came to the hospital as pioneers, partly in rebellion against the formal structures and authoritarian hierarchies of other hospitals, to set up a psychoanalytic center, where a small staff and a small group of patients could meet face-to-face and work democratically together.

Psychologists and psychiatrists at the hospital pride themselves on the absence of pernicious status and prestige distinctions between their professional groups. (The absence of such distinctions, interestingly enough, does not extend to professional groups outside the therapy staff.) The opinions and judgments of psychologists are highly respected. They have tended to be seen as the creative thinkers and theorists of the therapy staff, drawing heavily upon and contributing to "ego psychology" in the psychoanalytic body of knowledge. Over and over, statements are made at the staff conference concerning the superiority of psychodiagnostic test reports to psychiatric clinical impressions in evaluating patients, the greater diagnostic accuracy of the test reports, and the deeper understanding of the healthy as against the pathological aspects of the patient's personality psychologists have in comparison to psychiatrists. (The hospital is rarely referred to as a "hospital"; strictly medical attitudes toward patients tend to be deprecated as inhuman, depersonalizing, pathology-oriented, or authoritarian.) Contributing, then, to the maintenance of an apparently equalitarian relationship between these two professional groups—and highly valued, therefore—are the emphases on democratic processes, on the importance of autonomy and independence rather than dependence upon and submission to authority, and on the patient's ego-assets, as evidenced in life in the hospital community outside the individual psychotherapy session, and in his roles as citizen, worker, student, rather than his pathology or his role as patient.

That the staff prides itself on ignoring or blurring distinctions between psychologists and psychiatrist, analyst and non-analyst, results, unfortunately for task performance, in displacement of concerns about, and strains involving, such distinctions and people's feelings about them into intense ideological quarrels about the hospital community itself and whether or not patients are being treated as equals by staff or constrained in a dependent patient role by staff.

The paradox is that encouraging independence and autonomy in the patient group is often at odds with the need to have relatively dependent, conforming, compliant patients, who are highly sensitive to staff wishes and values, as the chief mechanism of social control in a social system that eschews authoritarianism, overt interference with patients by staff, and external controls.

DYSFUNCTIONAL AND FUNCTIONAL EFFECTS OF THE INSULATION OF THERAPY STAFF

The official policy about the relation between the psychotherapists and the therapeutic community program is that the responsibility of the psychotherapist qua psychotherapist is the individual psychotherapy of the patient, and the responsibility of the hospital (therapeutic) community is its own social life: work, play, policies, regulations, and social problems. The psychotherapist is not to intervene in the social processes of the community to explain the behavior of, or intercede for, his patient; nor is he to claim for his patient on "therapeutic" grounds exemptions from the responsibilities or expectations of the community; nor is he—if the policy is to be consistent—to manipulate covertly those participating in the structure of that community to apply sanctions to, or limit or control the behavior of, his patient. As a logical corollary, the staff and patients working together in the patient-staff groups of the community program, on the other hand, should not expect the psychotherapist to solve the social problems of the community by "disciplining," "analyzing," or "setting limits for," his patient.

Needless to say, this policy is as much honored in the breach as in the observance. Patients and nurses continually ask a difficult patient, "What does your psychotherapist say? Have you talked to him about this?" The patient, in turn, often stops discussion dead by saying, "My therapist says . . ." (there is no way of checking this, of course) or "This is none of the community's business—I'll discuss it with my therapist" or "I cannot change my behavior until I have time to work this out in my therapy."

Nurses send a twenty-four hour bulletin to the therapy staff, supposedly describing life in the community, but actually often detailing their distress about various situations and the degree to which they are increasingly finding their contacts with a particular patient intolerable. In addition, nurses regularly meet with small groups of psychotherapists to discuss their individual patients: how the nurses are to understand each patient and how the nurses may deal with and be helpful to them. This nurses' conference is an interview of each psychotherapist about each of his patients and is only incidentally concerned with the group life of the hospital.

On the whole, though, the psychotherapist is relatively insulated from pressures arising from his patient's behavior and effect on others. This does tend to mean that dramatic and "impossible" crises must be developed and nourished, so to speak, with many demonstrations of incompetency in dealing with them, if others are to force the psychotherapist to intervene. But that usually takes time. Meanwhile, many situations do get worked out in one way or another or at least subside. Stormy periods may be weathered without pressure from others' distress or insistence on the patient's discharge so impinging upon the psychotherapist that he feels he must *do* something, something that may disrupt the psychotherapeutic work—as sometimes happens in settings where communication is felt to be important and there is much daily continuous discussion between the psychotherapist and a host of others having to do with his patient.

THE ELDER STATESMEN

Most psychotherapists feel two ways about the community program. They would like to have the feeling they are doing more than "private practice" in a hospital setting, that they are in addition having some effect on the milieu in which they work, that they have a say in the running of the hospital. Since the administration of the hospital is organized, on the whole, so that most members of the staff have little say in the day-to-day decision-making concerning most of its aspects, these longings tend to focus in the direction of the patient-staff community program. This is especially so since members of the therapy staff often lack confidence in the competency of other staff groups functioning in the community program. On the other hand, most members of the therapy staff are uninterested in actually participating day-to-day in groups, meetings, activities—often rationalizing their disinclination as a fear that such participation would interfere with the orderly unfolding and understanding of the "transference" in psychotherapy.[6]

The accommodation to this ambivalence is the structuring of an "elder statesman" role for many members of the therapy staff, who in the name of defending and maintaining the "values" of the hospital—which often means defending its existing structures—criticize, advise, and veto the proposals and actions of those staff members "on the front line," without themselves having any extensive knowledge of, or direct involvement in, current social processes, and without their having to cope with the immediate consequences of such intervention.

In addition, the difficulty of unambiguously deriving specific prescriptions for action from general principles and values being what it is, members of the therapy staff hold a variety of points of view about what to do in any specific situation—although in comparison to other hospital organizations the staff is relatively homogeneous as far as basic values are concerned. Those staff members directly involved in the community program are able to choose among these views whatever one is least anxiety-arousing, although not necessarily most useful at a particular time, or they may become paralyzed, since some members of the therapy staff will always be "displeased" or feel that something "wrong" is happening.

The function of this "elder statesman" role is, therefore, to oppose or delay change; it contributes, thereby, to the stability and maintenance of the internal arrangements of the hospital—to an emphasis on endur-

6. As a matter of fact, many although not all therapists who do participate in the community program have become quite disciplined about acting in their role as community member (committee member, administrator)—not in the role of individual psychotherapist. They rather consistently focus on the content of "reality" issues, on the nature of the task to be accomplished or goal to be achieved in the community. They avoid interpretations about the "unconscious" dynamics of group processes. They avoid seeking information about or making interpretations in group settings of individual psychodynamics or psychopathology.

ing structures, traditions, systems of rules, "the way it has always been done," rather than on rapidly and flexibly meeting current exigencies, developing processes for solving problems as they occur, innovating and changing.

No One Is Happy with the Nursing Staff

A working-in-shifts arrangement makes regular participation in any aspect of the community program impossible for any nurse other than the head nurse, who usually, although not invariably, works the 7 AM to 3 PM shift.[7] The suggestion that one or more nurses be assigned for a prolonged period to particular aspects—programs or committees—of the community program (and to one shift to make this possible) was rejected. The reason given was that special assignments for some members of such a small nursing group would make for prestige and status differences and exacerbate envy and competitiveness.

Inferences about the prepotent functions of the nursing staff may be made from their activities and listed as follows in order of relative importance.

1. It is necessary, above all, to be in the inn to cover this building at all times. This despite the fact that patients come to and go from this building as they please, and are assumed to be able to care for themselves, not requiring the continual presence of nursing personnel appropriate on a medical or surgical ward or closed psychiatric unit. Nurses maintain a sense of the importance of the job, perhaps, by insisting that patients will become very upset if all the nurses go next door to the medical office building at the same time for a meeting or seminar, or that it is impossible to have just one nurse on from 11 PM– 7 AM who might simply go to bed. Patients complain of the nurses' hovering over them, and complain also if the nurses are not immediately available when wanted.

2. An important job is handing out medication, because no one but a nurse may do this. Since the principal modalities of treatment are individual psychotherapy and the community program—and "chemical" solutions to problems in living are regarded by most of the therapy staff as a poor, and perhaps competing, alternative to these preferred treatment modalities—this job is regarded ambivalently by patients,

7. There are approximately ten registered nurses; usually, two nurses work each eight-hour shift: 7 AM to 3 PM; 3 PM to 11 PM; 11 PM to 7 AM. The nurses rotate frequently among these shifts, so that with the exception of the head nurse no nurse works for any length of time on a single shift.

therapy staff, and the nursing staff itself. Furthermore, as far as the indispensability of this function is concerned, patients have free access to many other sources of supply of medicines, drugs, tranquilizers, intoxicants, and stimulants—including parents' and friends' medicine cabinets, drugstores, physicians in the locality or in other areas, and the local tavern. Both patients and nurses appear comfortable to have one of their main interactions occur around demand for pills (which are usually ordered by therapists "as the patient requests") and the response to these demands; in this situation, the role of the nurse is conventional and patients may gratify needs for personal contact on a relatively undemanding level without mobilizing anxiety in themselves or in the nurses.

3. Nurses help individual patients in distress usually by talking to them. Again, an ambivalently valued and practiced function. It is true that this resembles the highly valued individual psychotherapy session, and often is a way for the patient to send a message to or have extra contact with a therapist. However, the practice of psychotherapy or variants thereof by others outside the psychotherapy session is not encouraged by the therapy staff; the role of other staff members is usually conceived by the therapy staff to involve doing things with patients in the setting of everyday life including the community program which is activity-, project-, or task-oriented.

One might suppose that the community program would be the ideal arena for a psychiatric nursing function to be exercised—if that function involved a focus on interpersonal relations in the hospital community, an understanding of group phenomena, and an ability to care for the "group life" of the patients. Then patients might in turn be able to care, and provide a hospitable matrix, for each other.

However, most nurses are ill-at-ease in groups and do not participate in them; even in groups where an obvious nursing function is involved, such as the sponsors' committee, which is concerned with integrating new patients into the community, or the small groups, which are often concerned with interpersonal processes in the hospital community and particularly at the inn, participation by nurses is infrequent, irregular, and often non-existent; instead regular staff participation is provided by members of the therapy staff.[8] Besides the head nurse, a few nurses

8. Small groups of six to eight patients, one or two members of the therapy staff, and occasionally a nurse, meet once a week. Originally, these groups were political in nature, having a formal agenda, voting on issues referred to them by the community council, and electing representatives to that council. The groups, while still electing representatives to the community council, do not now formally

do participate somewhat irregularly and on a volunteer basis in small groups. Nurses attend the community meeting who are on duty the day and shift during which it meets.

Recently, nurses have begun serving tea in the afternoon or evening in the nurses' office—a large comfortable room—and appear to be increasingly comfortable about informal patient groups gathering for discussions there. Fewer comments are heard to the effect that nurses cannot get their work done because patients keep interrupting them by coming into the office. Occasionally, some nurses have called patient groups together to help cope with some crisis or social disturbance.

The suggestion that there be a regularly scheduled nursing report with the patients present was rejected by the nursing staff on the grounds that nurses would write different reports if they knew patients were to hear them. Although this was discussed as though confidentiality were the main issue—such an issue does not seem relevant to other than the individual psychotherapy enterprise—it was clear that nurses felt insecure about their ability to write reports that would be skillful, objective, and useful, and not be heard as personal reactions to which patients in turn would react with anger.

Nurses rarely attend the work or activities committees, and rarely join patients as companions in work or activities.[9] The nurses have rejected suggestions that they share with the patients chores in the work program.

At the community meeting, some nurses inevitably become upset by patients' criticisms, feeling that the nursing staff is being attacked or that patients are telling nurses how to do their jobs. Understandably,

---

instruct or bind their representatives; small group meetings consist of free-wheeling discussions of whatever is on members' minds, often involving a sharing of views by patients and staff about current issues in the hospital community, a consideration of relations between group members, or an attempt to help a group member who is in some kind of difficulty in the community. Many therapy staff members who participate in a small group do not belong to any of the patient-staff committees, do not attend the patient-staff community meeting, and have little or no discussion about the community with the staff who do belong or attend.

9. Patients plan parties, cook occasionally in a patient kitchen, show movies, act as assistant teachers in a nursery school, play volleyball, baseball, and ping pong, put out a community journal, sponsor patient-staff evening programs, attend a variety of classes, participate in a drama group, sculpt, paint, learn crafts, sell their products through the shop. Activities are planned by a patient-staff activities committee, consisting of the director of the activities staff, occasionally a nurse, and patient chairmen of what are often non-existent subcommittees: party, shop, kitchen, journal, movies, recreation, program. A member of the therapy staff works with the evening program committee but does not participate on the activities committee.

open discussions at the community meeting about relations between patients and nurses and involving specific examples are rare. "Who is in charge?" is always a question for staff members relating to patients in the community program; for example, an activities staff member also is likely to feel his expertise questioned or position depreciated if his wishes are challenged—"It's a question whether I'm an expert in my own field and able to make the decisions there, or just a pal."

At staff conferences, nurses are always sensitive to criticism, and some frequently feel they have been treated disrespectfully if their opinions or experiences have been disregarded. The interpretation "we are scapegoating the nurses again" is, of course, often at least partly true, but it is also used by some members of the therapy staff to protect the nurses by cutting off discussion which might lead attention to a specific nurse—it is almost unheard of that one should mention a nurse by name in a staff discussion where nurses are present rather than speak about "the nursing staff"—or to the examination of specific doings in a definite time and place.

The following appear to be some of the factors accounting for these characteristics of the nursing staff.

The nurses are themselves split as a group; conventional nursing roles, duties, and prerogatives are upheld by an old guard; new nurses with less conservative ideas about nursing tend to become frustrated and leave. The head nurse functions skillfully and sensitively in the community program, but she has some difficulty teaching others—except by example; unfortunately the administrative arrangements of the nursing staff militate against anyone else having her opportunity for continuous, regular participation and therefore emulating her example. The head nurse has not been able to integrate the nursing staff, partly perhaps because of leadership deficiencies, but perhaps also because she has been left "high and dry" by the organization, which has left it largely up to the nurses to improvise their own role, subject less to the requirements of a task and more to their own wishes and anxieties. The organization as a whole has not defined clearly the nursing role and indicated unambiguously this staff's task-requirements and task-priorities, and therefore its particular part in the achievement of the entire organization's goal. The problem is, in a sense, one of this group's identity.

None of the nurses is trained as a psychiatric nurse. In the absence of a sense of specialized competence and a sense of having a definite, unique, and highly valued contribution to make toward the achievement of the hospital's goals, the nurse tends to fall back on conventional nursing behavior and becomes preoccupied with the trappings of autonomy, suspicious of any interference, and hypersensitive to possible slights or disrespect.

In-service training to increase the level of competence has been difficult to arrange. Being faced with the necessity of learning new skills and the possibility of failing to use these adequately mobilizes anxiety. What consultation the nurses have is often, apparently necessarily, a kind of counseling, devoted to reassurance and short-term efforts to mitigate feelings of humiliation, anger, offended pride, or failure and inadequacy—rather than to the transmission of new knowledge and skills. The nurses have insisted on inviting their own consultant from the therapy staff—someone who understands them and whom they like but not necessarily any person who is in an organizational position to provide them with the leadership or with the tools needed to perform their particular task. Some nurses especially are edgy that their own authority and prestige will be undercut if skills or definitions of nursing roles are introduced from outside the nursing staff. Furthermore, they fear that if they learn a role at this hospital which departs too far from traditional expectations of the nurse, they will lose by dis-use what skills they have and gain skills that, if anything, will unfit them for work as nurses in any other setting.

In relation to patients who are of superior intelligence and another socio-economic class, the nurses are easily intimidated—oscillating in responses to the patients between defensiveness and moralistic judging. An additional source of anxiety for nurses, located as they are most closely to the patient group, serving as a buffer between the patient group and the therapy staff, is that nurses will be drawn into participating in deviant behavior themselves, reciprocate pathological expectations, become too "involved," show their own emotional problems—become like patients. On the other hand, if too impersonal, the nurses run the risk of being regarded as inhuman.

The therapy staff gives a vote of lack of confidence in the nurses by performing a psychiatric nursing function in the community program, presenting themselves—and accepting others' definition of them—as the experts in interpersonal relations. Some members of the therapy staff thus gratify their wishes to participate with patients in the life of the community. The nurses, for reasons mentioned above, are happy to relinquish what might be their unique nursing function to the therapists. The patients' belief that therapists are—since they are the ones responsible for the main task, treatment—the most valued members of the community and that they should be omnipotent and omniscient, is, when asserted by the patients, thus reciprocated by the staff.

The anxiety then felt by the nurse is that there is no special need for her in this community, no valued job for which she is responsible; she retreats further into conventional nursing activities, baffled because these are obviously not appreciated as a prepotent contribution in this setting. On the other hand, she may attempt to fulfill the function assigned to her by the therapy staff in lieu of the psychiatric nursing function: to represent the administration by seeing that rules are upheld. Such an effort of course makes her position in a group largely made up of intelligent, rebellious adolescents and young adults an unenviable and negatively valued, if not intolerable, one, involving her in a series of interactions in which inevitably she is cast as the "bad mother."

In addition to these factors, the nurses interestingly enough—for example, in their preoccupation with autonomy, equalitarianism, and rebellion against the assignment of special jobs which might lead to prestige and status differentiations—often reflect the concerns and values of the therapy staff. One wonders if many times a nursing staff may resist change in the interest, and responsive to the wishes and values, of the very group or groups who seem most exasperated by this resistance.

THE INDEPENDENT ARTISANS

The director of activities is a woman with a background of civic service, who has many contacts in the area, where she has lived for many years, especially among people in art, theater, and music. The activities staff consists also of the two craftsmen who work as instructors in the shop, one of whom is the assistant director of activities and both of whom are practicing creative artists; a drama director; the director of the nursery school; and a greenhouse supervisor.

Teachers from the surrounding area are usually hired to teach classes in such subjects as sculpture, oil painting, languages, typing, current events, the novel, and poetry. For the activities staff to organize a class, which is scheduled to meet for ten sessions, an expression of patient interest and the likelihood of attendance by at least six patients are usually required. Although the patient-staff activities committee usually sponsors and plans programs, recreational events, movies, and parties, and takes care of such facilities as the kitchen and the library at the inn, the activities staff usually sponsors and plans classes. For some reason, in a program emphasizing collaboration between patients and staff, the activities staff continues to plan and make decisions about activities, whenever the participation of the skilled and independent artisan is involved.

Other interesting observations may be made about the activities committee. A patient-trustees committee is part of the activities committee. The formation of such a committee implies the disruption of many role and task boundaries in order for the patients to deal directly with trustees. "Going around" the medical director—by patients, by staff?—appears to be involved. The drama group, nursery school, and greenhouse are not represented formally by patients on the activities committee. This appears to represent a failure on the part of the activities staff to think through the nature of the formal organization, in which these are *patient-staff* enterprises, or to catch up in such thinking with developments in the community, emphasizing the importance of collaboration between these two groups. Some activities staff members no doubt share the wish to leave responsibility for these activities more completely in the hands of the independent artisan members of the activities staff. The decorating committee is part of the patient-staff policy-making community council rather than the activities committee. Here, the wish of the head nurse to remain in control of the inn decor may have influenced this disposition, when in fact a decorating committee should be primarily concerned with expressive action and appreciative standards, the province of the activities committee, rather than with norms, moral standards, and responsible action, the province of the community council. Over and over, in fact, the interests of staff groups vis-a-vis patients are reflected in non-rational (from the point of view of task achievement) organization.

A strange lack of collaboration between the independent artisans of the activities staff and the therapy staff is reflected in organizational anomalies. Although a therapy staff member works with the program committee, which as a subcommittee of the activities committee plans monthly evening programs for staff and patients but has no activities staff person on it, and therapy staff members occasionally teach classes in such subjects as group development, child development, or creative writing, there are no therapy staff members who meet with either the activities committee or the activities staff. The director of activities has long felt that a therapy staff person's participation on the activities committee would create problems by linking "activities" to "therapy." At the least, this attitude suggests that the activities staff—by contrast with the nursing staff—has a sense of its own identity and mission which it is able to maintain through a relative isolation from the therapy staff. This independence is no doubt related to the fact that at least three important members of the activities staff—the two shop instructors and the drama director—maintain separate careers in their fields and the director of activities is an appreciated member of her own community; thus they have a sense of their own competence independent of the vicissitudes of their work in the hospital and their relations with other staff groups there.

NO SOCIAL WORK

There are no social workers in this hospital. This fact may reflect a number of historical vicissitudes, including the predilections of the medical director, for example, but it also seems related to another fact, that the hospital mainly treats young patients, who leave their homes to live away in a residential treatment center as they might go away to college. Their developmental task is to leave their families of origin as well as their previous communities and to move toward creating new families or at least new primary groups and discovering—in some creative-participant sense—their relation to community. Therefore, the integration of the patient either with his family of origin or with his previous community is not viewed as a major part of the task of this organization; indeed, efforts in this direction might be viewed by some staff members as interfering with the particular imperatives of treatment with patients of this age group, who face these particular developmental tasks.

The idea that a "moratorium" on usual age-appropriate social demands is also necessary for this group, because of the developmental distortions or deficiencies of its members, also militates against emphasis on integration of patient with family of origin or outside community—as well as creating a curious tendency to view even the claims of the patient-staff "therapeutic" community as primarily hostile to, or interfering with, individual aims or treatment. (This tendency may be related to the classical psychoanalytic view that there is an irreconcilable conflict between the needs and claims of society and individual instinctual aims.)

EQUALITARIANISM AND DISTRUST OF AUTHORITY: CONSEQUENCES FOR ADMINISTRATION

Why in this particular organization is there no director of treatment, no director of training, no director of research? [10] One reason is that the medical director—a gifted clinician and teacher and a man of

10. In this organization, highest priority is assigned to treatment imperatives, and especially to individual psychotherapy. Opportunities to do research are eked out by those staff members who are already motivated in this direction; there has

great moral stature, of whom the staff tended to stand in awe—preferred to be his own director of psychotherapy and his own director of training, unofficially arrogating these functions to himself; various committees in these and other areas tended to exist in name only. Another reason is the widespread distrust and suspicion of authority, manifested by reluctance to delegate authority or responsibility to any one individual, fear of becoming depersonalized or constrained by an assigned role, and antipathy for anything resembling formal organization.

The positive valuation of "sharing responsibility equally," "democracy," and "equalitarianism" is related to the cultural background of the members of the organization, the history of the organization and the nature of its origins, and the dynamics of the relationship between psychiatrists and psychologists in the organization. It is also perhaps intensified to the extent that "democracy" is an illusion and staff members must cope, for example, by denial and rationalization, with various frustrations, or with regret over the nature of their own contribution to the situation, as they live in what closely resembles a benevolently paternal autocracy. It is this latter kind of factor especially that may make for difficulty, militating against the dispassionate view of organization as a means to desired ends and of a particular organization as merely potentially useful or not useful. Organization tends to be viewed as interfering with individual autonomy and "wholeness," rather than as, potentially at least, enhancing the autonomy of individuals and groups—for example, by establishing and protecting necessary, task-related boundaries—and therefore indispensable for the achievement of ends or the actualization of values shared by members of the organization.

In an organization that involves blurred boundaries and an equalitarian ethos, organizational committees often appear to be exercises in mutual paralysis and futility.

---

been little persistent, organized effort for some years to motivate staff members to devote more time to research or to raise money to support the exploratory and clinical research the hospital is especially equipped to do—for example, studies of psychotherapy, clinical studies of individual lives, naturalistic studies of a small society, biographical or metatheoretical studies—which are not likely to be supported by research foundations; there is no director of research. The heart of the training program is the opportunity to do intensive individual psychotherapy and to receive individual supervision in psychotherapy from senior members of the staff. Other areas of training—for example, social or group processes in the therapeutic community or community psychiatry—compete with varying degrees of success for time in the informally organized "curriculum."

An administrative conference [11] sought to make decisions concerning the community program; it was a large, unwieldy aggregate of many groups and individuals who worked with varying degrees of distance from that program. Apparently interminable arguments, ending in stalemate, indecision, and resentments, were frequently its products.

However, although all found the meetings frustrating as far as the decision-making process was concerned, the exchange of views was widely felt to be valuable. Above all, the administrative conference represented an apparent actualization, at least, of a "democratic" ideal—that all the staff should participate in making decisions that shape "the kind of hospital we want to work in." (It was generally assumed that this kind of hospital would do the best job treating patients; this assumption was not questioned or—the state of knowledge being what it is—was in particular cases justified by rationalizations rather than by validated scientific theory or empirical evidence.)

The fact was that most of the important decisions about the hospital at that time and subsequently were made by the medical director, sometimes in consultation with various selected staff groups, often not. Consultation when it did occur was often with those chosen on the basis of personal preferences and associations, not necessarily according to the specific responsibilities of the people consulted. The area in which the staff as a whole was actually permitted to make decisions was quite limited—all the more prized, therefore, and all the more likely to become the focus of many feelings, conflicts, and concerns displaced from elsewhere to find expression in the administrative conference in discussions about the patients and the community program. For various reasons impossible to go into here, administrative conferences ended ever more frequently in anger and paralysis; they were increasingly cancelled, or simply not scheduled, by the medical director, and finally ceased to meet.

---

11. The now defunct administrative conference consisted of the entire staff (therapy, nursing, activities, and administrative staffs) and met sometimes once a week, sometimes once a month, sometimes even less frequently. The administrative conference considered policies for the community program: for example, what form should the work program take; what principles underlie the small group program; what staff policy about drinking is. Although a smaller coordinating committee had the nominal responsibility for planning and calling administrative conferences, it rarely exercised its authority to do so; such meetings were usually called—or cancelled—at the discretion of the medical director, who was often openly exasperated by them.

An executive committee [12] made a wide variety of decisions, especially concerning personnel (both professional and nonprofessional) and money; also including, for example, questions about financial aid to patients that would enable them to remain in the hospital. Its deliberations and the decisions themselves were not communicated consistently or systematically to the rest of the staff. "Secrecy" is not to be unexpected, when authority is exercised in an organization espousing equalitarian ideals. This committee ceased to function after the death of the superintendent and a serious illness of the medical director. It was succeeded by a staff council, which had been occasionally convened in the past.[13] The five members of the therapy staff on the staff council were "elder statesmen." They were not chosen because each represented a specialized task, group, or delegated area of responsibilty; their longevity in the organization was felt to qualify them to represent the values, vested interests, and cathected arrangements of the hospital: to protect these against forces tending to change them. Such a group was vulnerable to challenge, of course, on the ground that values are most potently actualized in task-performance, not in protecting traditions which may or may not any longer be relevant to such task-performance. The staff council was considered, when reconvened, an advisory group to the acting medical director, rather than a decision-making one. It has so far not communicated its deliberations to other members of the staff.

The coordinating committee was also originally conceived to be advisory to the medical director, particularly with reference to the community program.[14] An original task of this group was to ensure the

12. The executive committee consisted of the medical director, clinical director, business manager, and the superintendent in charge of the dietary department, the maintenance of buildings and grounds, purchasing, and nonprofessional personnel.

13. The staff council consisted of the acting medical director, the clinical director, the five members of the therapy staff with most seniority, and the business manager now in charge of the dietary department, the maintenance of buildings and grounds, purchasing, and nonprofessional personnel.

14. The coordinating committee consists of the acting medical director, the clinical director, the superintendent (when he was alive), the business manager, the head nurse, the director of activities, and a representative of the therapy staff. More recently, it has also included the therapy staff member with chief responsibility for the work program, and—as a consultant—the community program coordinator. The coordinating committee deals with all requests by patient-staff groups for money, approves in detail the budget of the activities committee and decorating committee, makes decisions about the use and alterations of any facility, and often "holds the line" for certain policies and rules in which the administration has a strong interest—for example, those concerning the extent of drinking at the

integration of the administrative operations of the superintendent with the therapeutic aims of the community program—for example, to see that work was not assigned to the maintenance department that belonged to the patients in the work program. That is, its hidden agenda was to cope with the superintendent by group discussion rather than according to line organization.

COLLUSION BETWEEN PATIENTS AND STAFF

The coordinating committee is often uncertain about making, and rarely initiates, positive decisions or innovations; it acts to check, to apply cautions and warnings, to appeal to tradition, to test fittingness with the staff's values, and sometimes to veto, the proposals and requests of others—particularly patients, or those representing patient wishes. This committee tends to view the patients as impulsive, incessantly demanding, and wanting things to be easy for themselves— itself as thoughtful, sober, careful, and responsive to the values and traditions of the hospital. Its functioning is an exemplification of the process of splitting in the relation between groups, where one group, the staff, is assigned all wisdom, and the other group, the patients, is assigned all folly. This tends to be detrimental to the self-esteem of the latter group, but the former group is able to manage the latter "in its own best interests" without recourse to "authority."

The patients also share with the staff responsibility for formulating, and maintaining adherence to, the rules of hospital life, and for the social problems arising in the hospital community—usually represented by some unacceptable patient (not staff) behavior. Social problems are referred for discussion and action to the community council, which is responsible for policies and rules governing life at the inn and for the atmosphere or morale in that community.[15]

---

inn, the possession of firearms, and parking and fire regulations. The present coordinating committee has functions overlapping those of both the community program staff and staff council. It consists of a majority (but not all) of the members of the community program staff as well as members of the staff council. In the coordinating committee, members of the former group report to the latter essentially; the latter must respond to all such reports with the unknown reaction of the rest of the staff council at least in mind. More effective intergroup relations would probably result if the community program staff through a director of sociotherapy (or, if and when appointed, through a director of treatment) reported directly to the medical director and the staff council.

15. Members in the community council include: one or two therapy staff members (one of whom is the clinical director), the head nurse, and patient represen-

In making decisions about ends, the community council is hesitant; often, various staff groups have communicated a vote of no confidence by imposing delays, expressing doubts, or questioning the values of the patient group, when the community council has been involved in such decision-making. Since the community meeting portrayed in subsequent chapters does not have the executive decision-making role of an older patient-staff meeting, which during this period of change has apparently become defunct, there is throughout this time no adequate mechanism for making joint patient-staff decisions about ends.

In its establishment of norms, the community council is largely influenced by what the staff communicates is required for the maintenance of the hospital organization. Since frequently these norms are not felt to be those really chosen by the community council, sponsorship of them by the members of the council is halfhearted or hypocritical. Furthermore, the staff communicates a vote of no confidence by establishing an all-staff group, the social problems council, higher in the hierarchy, to perform the same function: supporting the norms of the community. (Some members belonging to this staff social problems council may have no other role in the community program.) The community council colludes with this vote of no confidence. It is willing to abrogate its responsibility to do anything more than talk with patients who are breaking rules or deviating from community norms, since any action that might interfere with the life of a patient more seriously is bitterly resented, and the repercussions of such action in the informal life of the patient group are intense and painful. In addition, patient members of the community council are themselves likely to be involved presently or in the future in similar deviant behavior, and are cautious about protecting their own positions.

SOCIAL PROBLEMS IN A PSYCHIATRIC HOSPITAL:
THE PRIMACY OF INTEGRATION IMPERATIVES

One might suppose the work program ideally would be designed to perform an adaptation group function, the activities program a consummation group function, the community council an integration group function, and the small group program a motivation group func-

---

tatives from the work committee, the activities committee, and from each small group. Subcommittees of the community council include a decorating committee and a committee to sponsor new patients. The head nurse is a member of the former; a therapy staff member, who is not on the community council, works with the latter.

tion.[16] However, in point of fact, in this treatment center the work program arose historically to deal with problems of deviant conduct, to perform an integration group function. For example, it was thought that scheduling an early morning period for work would mitigate the tendency of patients without responsibilities to stay up all night and sleep all day (so-called day-night reversal). Work was made a moral obligation, that is, a precondition for membership in the hospital community, an obligation to which a patient was to commit himself upon admission. Difficulties in patients' making and adhering to such a commitment, especially in a therapeutically oriented community which tended to be much more concerned with consequences to and difficulties of an individual than with consequences to and difficulties of the community, created many strains. Since all work had to be done immediately following breakfast—no matter what time would suit the needs of a particular job—patients caricatured by a persistent refusal to work more than one hour a day, even if a job to be done well required more time, the disregard in the program both for work-requirements and for the instrumental ends to which such work was intrinsically related. This refusal was exacerbated by the absence of some patients from work every day; since work-assignment was obligatory, regardless of the amount of work actually to be done, some patients simply had to be absent to ensure the others would have an hour of work to do. In the background were members of the administrative staff, who depreciated the work of patient workers (a depreciation with which patients colluded) partly in order to maintain jobs for non-patient workers.

It was thought that a dependent relationship between staff and patients in the area of being physically cared for and waited upon was undesirable, tending to stimulate regressive tendencies; patients caring for themselves and the physical setting in which they lived might mitigate such tendencies. This introduced a "therapeutic" or "moral" (the kind of community we would like to have) rationale for work, which competed with a purely instrumental orientation to it. ("Moral" means that consideration of the consequences to the integration of a personality, group, or social system precedes and governs action.)

In addition, at least some members of the staff have always given an especially high value to manual work, so that in fact "work" has come to mean "manual work." In part, this seems to be because the only

16. See chapter one of this book; also, the theory of groups, theoretical model of psychiatric hospital organization, and view of the therapeutic community in *Sociotherapy and Psychotherapy*.

kind of work for which the hospital will compensate the patients financially (by contributing money into a fund to aid patients who would not otherwise be able to remain in treatment) is work that would presumably otherwise have to be done by hired laborers. In part, the emphasis on manual work seems to be related to the traditional value placed on hard work in a Calvinist culture, the historical role of work in the psychiatric rehabilitation of those patients who expect to be doing such work after they leave the hospital—which most of the patients in this hospital do not, feelings in the staff (and the patients) about the wealth of the patients with perhaps some lack of understanding about what is the work of such a socio-economic group in our society and what constitutes adequate preparation for it, and a kind of Rousseauan nostalgia for the simple activities of a rural culture in the days of an increasingly mechanized, automatized, complex, urban one. In part, the emphasis on manual work is also a reaction to the introspective intellectualization flourishing in a treatment center in which psychotherapy is a primary treatment modality; there is no doubt that at times such introspective intellectualization serves trends of passivity, regression, and loss of interest in external reality. However, all kinds of cognitive activity and any kind of discussion, no matter how purposeful, have come to be regarded with suspicion and excluded from the positive value given to "work." So, for example, not the drama group learning how to act or building a set, nor the community council struggling to understand problems of community mal-integration, nor the activities committee preparing a party or program, are considered "work" groups or part of the work program.[17]

The activities program, similarly, is frequently preoccupied with issues of commitment and responsibility, rather than issues of expression and gratification. The activities program early developed in a direction away from traditional occupational therapy with its aura of "therapeutic" prescriptions from physicians for arts and crafts activities. The program is designed rather to provide opportunities for patients to develop and maintain interests as they are inclined to do so. The activities staff are teachers, usually well-trained and working currently and often creatively in their own fields. For the most part they are

---

17. The work program continues to be disrupted by the conflict between integration or moral values and adaptation or instrumental values. A recent attempt to cope with this consisted of splitting off a job unit—to do "real work" (still largely manual) on the model of labor or business—from the program involving chores on the model of a family. Another recent suggestion was the development of an independent patient "industry."

divorced from the clinical concerns of the therapy staff; they do not wish to know about patients' psychopathology, but rather to know patients as students, artists, and artisans. Since many of the teachers are seriously working in their own fields, they tend to emphasize commitment and responsible effort, looking somewhat askance at amateurism and dilettantism. They complain that patients' enthusiasm for classes arranged by the activities staff does not outlast the second or third class session. Since this staff eschews understanding individual or group behavior psychodynamically—lest it make for "therapist" attitudes—such knowledge is often not available to them in their teaching. Their response to difficulties then tends to be in the "moral" realm; patients do not act as they should: they are "lazy, irresponsible, uncommitted"; they should be "busy." The activities staff's proudest boasts concern patients who go on to make a career in the area introduced to them in the activities program. "Playing around at things," momentary fun, transient curiosities tend to be deprecated unless they lead to something, such as the acquisition of skills. It is not surprising that this activities program has difficulty at times competing with the "forbidden, nontherapeutic, unlawful" pleasures offered by informal patient groups acting as consummation groups.

Within the activities staff itself, there is competition for patients between, for example, the director of the drama group and the shop instructors. Such competition is exacerbated by sharing of the same physical space (the drama group's improvised theater is on the second floor of the shop). The drama group is also seen as drawing people away from commitment to the work program, late-night rehearsal revels and performance-nights and their aftermath apparently resulting in patients' not awakening to do their share of the chores.

In both cases, pleasure and sober responsibility, lighthearted irregularity and commitment, unprepared-for stardom and craftsmanship are pitted against each other, with a tendency on the part of all groups to play down the "fun" aspects of work or shop activities or to avoid realistic recognition of the hard work, even drudgery, of theater life, as though the manifestation of the controversy itself were essential.

Why this contest between the imperatives of integration and those of adaptation and consummation? Specific aspects of the hospital's history probably contribute. But the characteristics and primary task of any psychiatric hospital also imply such a contest. The psychiatric hospital, from the viewpoint of the social system of which it is a part, is an integration group. Its task from that viewpoint is to convert individuals, whose mal-integration with society or some part of it has necessitated their hospitalization, from mal-integrated into socially functioning entities. This task alone would tend to give rise to preoccupation with responsible action, and to assign primacy to the "moral" values of the integration group function throughout the groups of the hospital, regardless of their other group functions.

In addition, patients cannot merely be the passive objects of a treatment process. As human individuals with passions and values of their own, they are inevitably active participants in that process. Since the nature of that participation is of crucial importance to the outcome of the process, the hospital must be concerned that patients become integrated members of the hospital community, sharing commitment to its aims and values.

Patient-members of the hospital community constitute a selected group of individuals who have failed in some way to meet the integrative requirements of society. The process of their treatment inevitably results in a relatively high turnover (for a social system) of such membership: the continual loss of socialized contributing individuals and the acquisition of new individuals. These facts make the problem of integrating not only a continuous stream of new members, but new members having special problems in functioning within any social system, especially difficult for the hospital community. Problems of deviance from, and challenge to, the values and norms of the community are rather naturally regarded as prepotent.

In fact, the question that is raised by these conditions is whether the hospital community does not make its primary contribution to the treatment of the patient by struggling with the problems that arise as that patient becomes a more or less integrated member of it. Is the chief output of a "therapeutic community" to the personality system of a patient to his superego, that is, a change in his ability to internalize, and relate less self-defeatingly or more creatively to, the values and norms of a social system, to identify and participate interdependently with others to achieve common ends and actualize shared values?

How patient-members are integrated within a hospital community, how challenges to, and deviations from, the values and norms of that community are met, will determine the nature of the contribution of the "therapeutic community" to the treatment process. Does a patient simply learn expediently to conform to—or evade—specific norms for conduct existing in his situation in the hospital; or does he internalize shared general values, from which a wide variety of function- and situation-specific norms are derivable? What values, if any, are available to a patient as a result of experiences in the hospital community? What values are actually internalized, so that commitment to them is no longer dependent upon external sanctions? To what extent is the patient asked to acquiesce to values or norms in the society of which the hospital community is a part; to what extent is he encouraged by his experiences in the hospital community to examine, question, and choose among these?

Strains, of course, are inevitable, as professional personnel, for example, imbued with the values of science or of the adaptation group, among which is the attitude that values themselves should be regarded dispassionately merely as objects for study in the situation, perforce must wrestle with issues of responsibility and commitment. Additional strains arise from the fact that no social system can survive if the imperatives of adaptation and consummation group functions are continuously ignored in favor of attention to the imperatives of integration and motivation group functions. No human being will participate for long or constructively in a society in which the aims of the adaptive and libidinal ego are continuously sacrificed to those of the ego-ideal and the superego.

Despite the fact that prepotent concerns with integration will exist, given the primary task of the psychiatric hospital and the conditions with which it must cope, recognition of—and opportunity for the achievement of the aims of—all four group functions should exist in a "therapeutic community," manifested by well-differentiated programs to ensure this outcome. The safeguarded existence, however, of differentiated group-function, each represented by one or more groups promoting its own aims and values, creates inevitable competition, conflict, and perpetual dilemmas concerning which values and which aims in any specific situation are to have priority.[18]

SOCIAL PROBLEMS IN A PSYCHIATRIC HOSPITAL: WHO HAS RESPONSIBILITY?

Refusal to participate in some aspect of the community program (especially the work program), excessive drinking, use of proscribed drugs, flouting rules, behavior that is destructive or disturbing to others, behavior that brings discredit upon the organization, are all likely to be defined as social problems, and to result in referral to the community council. Any member of the staff or patient group, or any patient-staff

18. See Appendix A for a detailed note on the value dilemmas exemplified by the work program.

committee, has the right to refer a patient as a social problem directly to a social problems council,[19] bypassing the ordinary route through the community council. This may happen when a staff person such as the superintendent is outraged by some behavior (usually involving hospital property) and wants it dealt with immediately and "at the top"; or when someone feels the community council will not deal firmly with the offender: the work committee, for example, is apt to feel that the community council (some of whose members are themselves having difficulty with work obligations) is not tough enough with people who are scanting their work obligations and will not back up the work committee.

The community council ordinarily tries to see a patient having social problems over a period of time, hoping that talking things over will result in the patient's "coming around" without the necessity to apply sanctions. The community council has increasingly thought that people who come to its attention, for example, through discussions in the community meeting, as withdrawn, isolated, or upset, and likely to get (although not yet) in trouble, should be invited to come and talk with the community council, in an effort to relieve strains and avert further difficulty, even though such patients are not referred as social problems. There is some evidence that the community council has had to adopt this function because of the failure of the small groups to cope with the distress of individuals arising from, or likely to have an effect upon, their life in the hospital community. The community council has become, therefore, increasingly preoccupied with individuals, rather than with its business agenda—action having to do with the community as a whole. Such a priority, of course, also conforms to

19. The social problems council consists of the head nurse and two senior members of the therapy staff. A patient having difficulty meeting his commitments in the work program is referred to the work committee for discussion of his problems with the program. If such discussions do not result in the patient's meeting his obligations, he may be referred to the community council for further discussion. If he continues to have difficulty, or if others continue to feel that he creates a social problem by his behavior, he may be referred by the community council to the social problems council—a kind of "court of last appeal." The social problems council keeps the referring group informed in writing of its experiences with the patient and recommendations about him, such reports being transmitted to the entire hospital community by the referring group following its acceptance of the report. If the social problem continues even after discussion between the patient and the social problems council, the latter usually refers the matter to the medical director, either recommending that the patient be discharged or that a staff conference be held to review his course in therapy, his use of the treatment center, and whether or not he should remain in the hospital.

the prepotent value in the organization as a whole of treating and caring for the individual.

The community council's reluctance to apply sanctions is related to the fact that many of its members are often or have been engaged in the very behavior they are being asked to sanction, and also to the high value placed on individual autonomy, individual freedom from interference by a group, and the expectation that a person will control himself rather than submit to controls from outside.

Since many patients are ambivalent about external controls, often longing for help in their struggles with unruly impulses but quite unable to acknowledge this wish, there often develops a spiral of increasingly intense problem behavior in an effort to provoke someone to clamp down. This wish is often for long periods almost cruelly frustrated, as is inevitable in any hospital relying primarily on normative sanctions (the response of others) rather than coercive sanctions, and hoping thereby to achieve internalization of shared values and norms rather than mere expedient conformity to or evasion of values and norms. The therapy staff for the most part believes that the imposition of sanctions by authority figures will exacerbate ambivalence toward authority, intensify psychopathological formations, interfere with the development of individual autonomy (on the supposition, apparently, that patients would never be motivated to graduate from dependence upon external controls to the development of inner controls unless these external controls emanate from the peer group), and thereby militates against the aims and conduct of individual psychotherapy. (What difference it might make to these expected results if the authority figures were staff members collaborating with the patients in the community program, but were not also individual therapists, is an open question.) The therapy staff takes this position, therefore: "We do not wish to impose sanctions on you, the patients, but would prefer that you, through your community program structures, such as the community council, decide upon and impose such sanctions yourselves."

As a corollary of, if not part of the foundation for, such opinions, the therapy staff and other staffs in their participation with patients in the community program, proud of their own individuality and defensive of their own independence, tend to emphasize the individual differences between and the disagreements and variations in the points of view of staff members—rather than their commitment to a shared enterprise, their disciplined acceptance of the limits within which each member of the staff works and relates to others, or their abiding by rules they set for themselves. It is relatively easy for the patient group or part of it to get one or another staff member to join with it in some expression—often but not always covert—of rejection or defiance of some aspect of the organizational structure or its rules and regulations.

The patients, probably in part because of the factors described in previous paragraphs and in part because of the lack of a staff model for the firm, consistent, impersonal application of controls with which to identify (or, conversely, because of the presence of a staff model for the reluctant imposition of, and rebellion against, external controls), refuse through the community council to apply intermediate sanctions, such as taking away a driver's license from a reckless driver or barring the use of a room to someone who has been destructive with its equipment. Such sanctions are rare. The principal mechanism of social control in the community are offers of help (which varies in skill and tact, consistency of follow-through after a meeting is over, and persistence in the face of rebuff); grumblings of disapproval, often shot through with expressions of baffled frustration and angry rejection; and the ultimate threat—discharge from the hospital. The latter sanction the patients are reluctant to impose on one of themselves, turning instead to the staff—through the social problems council—for ultimate solution of a social problem by initiating such action.

These phenomena are related to widespread ambivalence among patients and staff members about the responsibility for social problems; such responsibility, one would think, is an inevitable corollary of the freedom apparently so valued in the hospital community. The patient members of the hospital community, of course, must face together rather than flee from the tormenting complexities and impossible dilemmas that are part of freedom, if they are to take and share responsibility for their own lives, including the inevitable social problems around noise, liquor, drugs, sex, and malingering that arise when people live, work and play together. These social problems are, of course, never simply solved, nor does any formula serve in every situation with every person; the community, while it is a community and especially one continually taking in new members and discharging old ones, cannot rid itself once and for all of social problems but can only struggle with them inventively and every day anew.

This freedom, this responsibility, are heavy burdens. The dilemmas of freedom and responsibility are everyone's dilemmas. Each community group looks for other groups to whom to pass such burdens; dependency of one group upon another group is a reaction to the difficulty of the continuous day-by-day effort to examine what is going on—in order to understand and make better the lives of community members, in order to make real the values (and to achieve the goals) they share.

Each group has its refuge from the difficulty of such a shared task. The patient: "I'm only a patient; I'm too sick to understand or attempt anything; I'm here to be taken care of"; the nurse: "I'm only a nurse; I'm likely to be blamed by everyone so it is best for me to do nothing"; the therapist: "It is not my job to tell patients what to do; I'm neutral"; the administrator: "Since this is a democracy, it is best to wait and see what the group wants to do; I shall refer the matter to a committee."

New patients enter the hospital. There is deviant behavior, individual upset, collective upset. The patient: "I can't follow this discussion, I forget, I get confused," or "I'm willing and hard-working but the apathy of other patients keeps me from doing or changing anything," or "If the therapists were here, more interested, things would be better; they're wise, objective, know about these problems." The nurse: "If the therapists would meet with us and tell us about their patients, whom they understand so well, then we would know what to do."

Therapists and patients meet together in a special patient-staff meeting to discuss the work program or join in evening programs to discuss drugs or alcohol. Everyone feels better. "Now the patients know what the therapists think and value." At the same time, administrators may acquiesce to requests for money or facilities from patients. This is seen as part of a collaborative relationship with patients, but such actions often seem to suggest that at times administrators find it easier to let patients be dependent upon them for problem-solutions than to insist to such a group that it is capable of innovating and carrying out its own solutions by its own efforts.

The social problems, of course, are solved by none of these moves; after a pause, they may even worsen. Patients abandon all pretense at problem-solving. "I don't care. I only care about myself, I can't do anything about these difficulties. I'm sick. It's too much for me." One crisis, one problem-patient, after another; soon, the nurses will be "driven crazy." The nurses complain about being on the spot, about having an impossible job, about wanting to quit. Their distress is intense. They do nothing, let the situation worsen. Soon, the patients are in a state of helpless rage. Both patients and nurses are "fed up," suffer, make gloomy predictions about the hospital. "We're being asked to do what we can't do." Finally, members of the therapy staff are aroused. Passing a colleague in the hall, someone exclaims: "Someone will have to do something or the hospital will go to pot!"

The social problems council sends out memos berating the community for its laxness and asserting sternly about a referred patient's behavior: "We can't go along with it!" Pressure to discharge a patient builds up, is resisted, is displaced from patient to patient; perhaps discharge may be considered for someone in trouble who in other circumstances would be allowed to stay, or for a new patient at evaluation who might otherwise have been recommended for further treatment. Promiscuity or suicidal tendencies are now considered too great a risk. The staff, lacking confidence in the community, considers that a particular patient will find it boring or that another patient will be corrupted by it. Following a discharge, especially of a patient who has been in trouble, everyone is relieved; patients begin to behave. Soon, the entire sequence of events begins again.

The social problems council is, to be sure, often effective in its contacts with socially deviant patients in bringing about greater conformity to hospital community norms. Its work may result in an expedient conformity to norms in public, because of fear of discharge, and an expedient evasion of norms when it is possible to get away with it— rather than an identification with other members of the therapeutic community and an internalization of values and norms shared with them; the maintenance of such values and norms no longer then depends upon external sanctions.

Two of the members of the social problems council are separated from the day-by-day workings of the community program. Because of this fact, the pervasiveness of the focus upon the individual in a treatment organization, and the nature of the function of the social problems council, this group tends to see problems that come to its attention as the fault of the individual it sees. It tends to present this view both to patients and to other staff members, supplementing it with a view of the community as essentially an external constraint upon the individual, which enforces regulations and rules, and should insist that expectations be met, requirements be fulfilled, and obligations be accepted. Not seeing the community as an internalized part of the individual or the individual as a constituent of the community, or regarding the community primarily as enabling the individual to actualize values he shares with others, the social problems council tends to judge the relation between community and individual solely in terms of the effectiveness with which the community acts as an adequate external constraint upon the individual's behavior.

The social problems council—in responding to pressures to save the community from the depredations of an individual; in seeming to join the community, hungering for simple answers to complex questions, in attributing blame to one individual; in ignoring, for the most part, the contributions made to an individual's deviance by community ways of life, structures, and values—may contribute to the illusion that the problem will be solved if that individual "reforms" or is discharged, only to be dismayed along with the community that as soon as the individual does reform or leaves the hospital, another individual takes his place. The impossible behavior of the new "delinquent" is in turn also used by the patients often in collaboration with nursing staff to force the therapy staff to be stricter, to lay down the law, to set limits—to save the community from the burdens of freedom and responsibility.

It is rare for the recommendations of the social problems council not to be accepted by the medical director; when he refuses to accept the recommendation, the members of the social problems council and those members of the staff agreeing with the recommendation feel that the structure of the entire community program is being undercut and attribute subsequent difficulties in the community to the fact that now patients are not able to depend upon expectations and obligations being upheld by the staff, and they now feel that "anything goes."

Theoretically, of course, the therapy staff eschews *sole* responsibility for the establishment and enforcement of norms; not—as the misinterpretation is made—that this staff is reluctant or opposed to these functions being carried out at all. What is deemed desirable is that responsibility for these integration functions be shared by patients and staff and that it be delegated to a patient-staff committee, the community council.

On the whole, identification with staff leaders or patients allied with them (so that values represented by these leaders are internalized, resulting in adherence to the norms derived from such values) is much preferred by patients and staff to the use of coercion or rewards and punishments as a means of enforcing norms. There is, therefore, a heavy reliance on the qualities and effectiveness, the charisma parhaps, of individual leaders.

However, the staff leader on the community council, for example, may lack the qualities leading to such identification; or he may, because of his position or lack of prestige or influence in the organization, be unable to represent staff values. Assignment of a fellow in training to such a position, or a non-therapist, may result in the patients' feeling that the staff is not actually sharing the responsibility with—but rather passing a dirty job to—the patient group. The patients' passing the responsibility back, through inaction, for example, to the staff via the social problems council creates additional strains, since the staff-constituted social problems council represents and at times explicitly wields a coercive threat: that a patient who does not adhere to norms may be discharged. Resort to such coercion violates values of both groups.

Difficulties in, and opposition to, the use of coercion and utilitarian rewards or punishments have their roots in the values and imperatives of the psychotherapeutic enterprise. Such an institution of psycho-therapy as confidentiality, for eaxample, may be used to legitimize secrecy, so that it is difficult for the community to discover whether norms are being evaded or flouted and by whom. The status of illness, and the declared effort to get well, are used to claim exemption from obligations. The importance to psychotherapy of personal autonomy, of the individual's need to experiment and grow, and of concern with self or the integration of the personality system continually gives rise to perplexing questions for the therapeutic community about what norms are appropriate for all its members, under what circumstances excep-tions are justifiable, and what regulation of—or interference with—the individual for the sake of the community can be tolerated.

As might be expected in such a community, there is a general, some-what utopian, assumption that most social problems can be solved through an improvement in interpersonal relations, especially of a private personal nature. There is little recognition that the specific de-tails of a social structure and the values and goals shared by its mem-bers determine to a great extent what kinds of interpersonal relations are possible within it.

As is true in much psychoanalytic writing, the community or society is generally regarded somewhat suspiciously by many therapists as limiting, restraining, or interfering with, individuals—rather than as a system for the actualization of the shared values of its members. De-parting from Freud in a direction rather common to many American psychoanalysts, therapists are inclined to hold that most difficulties in such a community are due to faults in society's dealings with individ-uals, rather than any inevitable instinctual characteristics of individ-uals, especially not any innate aggressive or destructive instincts. Com-munity difficulties are thought mitigable by changing the community—usually in the direction of the community's making fewer claims on an individual—or helping an individual to unlearn what he has been taught by previous "bad" social experience. There is much optimism about the possibility of such change, and enthusiasm about the devel-opment of a society characterized by rational problem-solving.

The therapeutic community movement, in general, seems often to be based upon such views: that everyone is basically good, except insofar as he is distorted by previous social experience, that a hospital community can be integrated around the value of people helping each other, and that in such a society group processes (if not interfered with by an optimal minimum of organization), unlimited communication, and good intentions, will inevitably lead to therapeutic outcomes for every individual.[20]

SOCIOTHERAPY OR PSYCHOTHERAPY: WHAT IS THE TASK?

The confusion about the task of the patient-staff small groups is reflected in ambiguities of staff participation. As has been previously discussed, participation by nurses in small groups is problematical; those who attend do so voluntarily and often irregularly. There is no clear organizationally assigned priority for nurses to work with groups; the nurse is not sure that this is part of her job, that skill in carrying it out is part of the expectation of her as professional staff, and that other more traditional nursing roles and duties do not in fact have priority (as far as others are concerned) over this part of her work—so that work in groups must be considered secondary, worked in voluntarily on her time off at cost to her personally, or in general left to her individual inclinations. The small group staff is, therefore, dominated by therapists, many of whom are not otherwise involved in the community program and who are primarily interested in psychotherapeutic processes (with focus upon intrapersonal phenomena) rather than in sociotherapeutic processes (with focus upon social phenomena). This creates a somewhat anomalous situation in those groups in which there is both a therapist and a nurse, since the male therapist tends to behave primarily like a mother, concerned with emotional and interactional matters within the group itself, and the female nurse, when she is confident enough to participate at all, tends to behave primarily like a father, concerned with what is going on in the world outside the group—with the claims, requirements, and tasks of the hospital community.

20. In many ways, the present social problems council does not make sense. (Possible reasons for this "nonrational" organizational arrangement are outlined in the previous discussion.) If decisions or recommendations have to be made concerning patients who are having difficulty conforming to community norms, this is clearly the function of the community council, which should be strengthened, not displaced. If decisions or recommendations have to be made concerning evaluation of a patient's participation in the entire treatment enterprise, this might be clearly the responsibility of a director of treatment, consulting with a group consisting at least of a director of psychotherapy and director of sociotherapy, were such positions occupied, as they are not.

The small group staff members [21] have had difficulty deciding upon the function of the small groups in which they work and, a related matter, integrating the small group program with other aspects of the community program. The small group staff tends to think of the small group program in terms of its output to individual patients rather than its output to a small society or community of both staff and patients. The small group is supposed to provide an individual patient with an opportunity to share his ideas and feelings with others, to test out his perception of reality, including of himself, and to discover the consequences of his behavior, through exposure to others' views and values. In the direction of thinking about output to the community, the small group is seen as a setting where adaptive social interaction is facilitated; mutual influence is made possible by sharing experiences and viewpoints, particularly in the area of current problems in community life.[22]

Small groups are often considered "family-like" groups. With or without the conscious intent of the participants, such groups, when going well, through discussion in a situation characterized by solidarity and mutual acceptance, probably make possible the reduction of individual tensions mobilized by decisions, task-requirements, social interactions, and other aspects of community life, as well as the tensions arising from strains within the personality. These tensions ordinarily have a disturbing influence upon the commitment of an individual patient to the values of the treatment enterprise and upon his motivation to participate in community programs devoted to carrying out aspects of that enterprise. Small groups, ideally, mitigate the disrupting effects of such tensions. Similarly, in the small group, there is an opportunity to interpret events in community life, the misunderstanding of which, for example, have made people angry, disaffected, or upset and thereby disrupted their commitments to community structures, goals, and values. To some extent, also, specific patterns of motivational commitment—usually at a general value-level rather than a specific skill-level—

21. The small group staff consists of members of the therapy and nursing staffs who participate in small groups. The small group staff's task is to examine each staff member's participation in the small group and to help him and other staff members understand the factors affecting such participation as well as its consequences; to study small group processes; to make week-by-week administrative decisions concerning the small groups; to formulate policy recommendations to other groups concerning the small group program.
Press Waiting Practice of Social Therapy 8|10|26 Cal mag* 47 8-17-70 1168
influence all segments of the community, should happen in the community meeting.

to join others in working, understanding, enjoying, or sharing responsibilities may be taught or reinforced by discussions in small groups of
community issues, problems, and events and people's responses to
these.

The small group, then, from the point of view of the community or
social system *is* focused upon the individual—specifically, upon the
condition of his motivational commitments, his relation to the community in which he currently lives. (This focus upon the relation between individual and the therapeutic community should include a consideration not only of the individual's use of and impact upon the
community, but also the community's exploitation of the individual's
psychopathology and predilections, as well as his skills, toward its own
ends. Therapists often learn to be sensitive to efforts by an individual
to recreate old life situations in the hospital community, in order to be
able to seek anew to solve old problems or achieve long wished-for
gratifications; but therapists tend to be less aware of the way in which
group processes involve projections of group affects or problems into
individuals, or the covert encouragement by the group of "suitable" individuals to represent certain wishes, fears, impulses, or affects—often
so that these may be disowned, along with the patient representing
them, by the rest of the group.)

For staff members, however, who are new to the hospital, whose only
model for participation in small groups has been a psychotherapeutic
rather than a sociotherapeutic one, or whose participation in other
aspects of the community program is minimal, the structure of the
small group seems to invite efforts at conducting psychotherapy. Such
efforts take the form of either psychotherapy of the individual in a
group setting—perhaps by conducting group interviews of individuals
aimed at abreaction or insight, by focusing upon fantasies and trans-
ferences shared by group members, or by confronting members with
the consequences of their interactions with each other in the group—
or "therapy of the group," with analysis of intragroup processes and
relations among members of the group.

The external reality of life together that group members share not
only with each other but with other members of the hospital community dims in interest next to such fascinating inward-looking preoccupations. Regressive immersion in introspection (to the relative exclusion of alloplastic concerns with understanding, adapting to, and
changing the reality in which one lives) may be enhanced. The desired
output to the social system itself is diminished; the distress, anger, or
disaffection of a particular patient may go ignored, be exacerbated, or

continue unrelated to the immediate community events and processes that have given rise to them—with a continuation or intensification of the effect of deviant dysfunctional behavior upon community activities. The group members act as if what goes on in the meeting is private and has nothing to do with everyday life; interactions in the group are isolated from group members' relations outside the group; it is an hour a week of "therapy" which is not evaluated in terms of, or expected to change, the life of the hospital community outside the group. Absurd artificialities abound; members of a group may know for six days that one of them is very upset, but they do not get together to discuss this or help each other to cope with it until the hour of the seventh day when the small group meets.

It is as if a family existed with predominant emphasis on emotional, interactional, and graitfying processes within the family (the mother and her functions are all-important), meanwhile neglecting all links to the society in which the family is embedded and which gives the lives of its members meaning and direction (the father and his functions are of secondary importance).

None of this, of course, is meant to imply that group psychotherapy as a psychotherapy rather than a sociotherapy modality cannot be part of an intramural program. However, in an organization where intensive individual psychotherapy is an important treatment modality, the effect of these two forms of psychotherapy upon each other, and the effect upon other aspects of the hospital community and upon individual patients of this degree of emphasis upon introspective, autoplastic processes, must be considered. Furthermore, not enough attention has been paid to the consequences for group psychotherapy, its purposes and methodology, of having members who are not only otherwise known to each other, but who are in fact interdependent in their life situations, who need each others' cooperation for the achievement of a multitude of tasks and gratifications, and whose behavior in relation to each other in reality outside the group could indeed give rise to serious deprivation and pain.[23]

23. As one might expect, there are strains associated with ambiguity about who among a group of staff members participating together in a small group is the leader of the team. It has not been clear whether or not direction for staff partici-pation should come primarily from the therapy staff member in the small group, the nurse, or, more recently, the representative of the community program staff. This unclarity is ultimately related to ambiguities about the function of the small group: are the small groups part of the psychotherapy or sociotherapy enterprise? Within the sociotherapy enterprise should such groups be primarily concerned

INNOVATION: THE COMMUNITY PROGRAM STAFF AND
THE COMMUNITY MEETING

When community meetings and the community program staff [24] were innovated, largely at the instigation of the community program coordinator, who was a relatively new member of the staff at that time, the community program staff had great difficulty functioning. It had little

with nursing problems, narrowly conceived, or with the entire range of phenomena having to do with relationships between individual and community?

24. The community program staff consists of those staff members who have immediate responsibility for day-to-day participation in the community program and who attend the community meeting regularly. This includes heads of staff groups the main function of which is in the community program, and those who have assignments in some group, committee, or program requiring or involving patient-staff collaboration: for example, the community program coordinator; the therapy staff representative on the community council (who also is a member of the coordinating committee); the therapy staff representative to the work committee; the director of the activities staff (who is a member of the activities and work committees); and the head nurse (who is a member of the community council, the social problems council, and the coordinating committee). In addition, a research associate is a member of the community program staff and attends the community meeting; with the community program coordinator he studies aspects of the community program, was for a long time an observer in the community meeting, on at least one occasion reported with the community program coordinator some findings to the patient and staff members of the community meeting, and is more recently a verbal participant in the community meeting with the task of enhancing cognitive aspects of problem-solving processes—promoting, for example, the use of memory of past events in the group, learning from previous experiences, and hypothesis-formation and evaluation in the carrying out of innovations. There are also fellows in training who are members of the community program staff, usually as associates to those permanent staff members having these previously mentioned roles.

The tasks of the community program staff include:

1. studying day-to-day the details of the community program's current functioning—what parts are in difficulty, what parts are doing well, and causes and (when indicated) remedies;

2. increasing the skill of its members, through mutual consultation, and through developing understanding of the group processes involved in the program;

3. developing, at a general theoretical level, a framework for considering the goal or goals of the community program, and the functions of its various parts—such a framework to help in evaluating the output of any aspect of the program, in anticipating the possible consequences of proposed changes in the program, and in suggesting desirable innovations;

4. integrating and coordinating various aspects of the community program

potency for its own members and was distrusted by other members of the staff. The following actions were all contrary to traditional procedures and some established interests: the delegation of operational responsibility for the community program to a specific subgroup of the total staff; the delegation of operational responsibility for the community program to a group in which a nurse and activities person had important roles and many senior therapy staff members no role at all; and the delegation of key responsibility for the performance of the sociotherapy function in the hospital and for the coordination of community programs, committees, groups, and staffs to one therapy staff member, and a new member at that. The result was much suspicion and dissension.

After many months of floundering, the community program staff was disbanded; it did not meet for about eight months, and was then reconvened by the coordinating committee. Following this reorganization, the community program staff functioned with increasing cohesiveness and confidence as an increasingly accepted staff group. During this time, however, it tended to be regarded essentially as being on the side of patient interests and representing these to other staff groups (for example, the coordinating committee), and as a potential source of as yet unknown but probably disruptive change (against which, for example, such staff groups as the staff council might have to find some way to uphold old and valued traditions). There was also question about how the community program staff was to be related to other staff members and staff groups, so that it did not carry out its functions isolated from others.

Also in a state of flux at that time was the relation of staff groups functioning in the community program, such as the nursing staff, the activities staff, and the small group staff, to the community program staff, on which each of these staffs was represented. Its task was to promote the coordination of the efforts of these staffs and cooperation among them.

Theoretically, activities, nursing, and small group staffs might refer problems to the community program staff, and consider issues, questions, ideas, and recommendations referred by the community program staff to them. However, representatives of these groups on the com-

---

and promoting collaboration and cooperation between staff groups and patient-staff committees participating in that program;

5. collaborating with the staff training committee (responsible for the training of fellows in psychiatry and psychology) in making possible the education of fellows in the area of the therapeutic community program—the study of social structures and processes, and the development of skills in sociotherapy.

munity program staff participate in relation to the community program staff primarily in terms of their roles in patient-staff committees and enterprises, and tend to neglect that aspect of their role which involves acting as liaison between the community program staff and their own staff group. This phenomenon is probably related in part to anxiety about the autonomy of these staff groups, and a desire to protect them from encroachment and interference by a new supraordinate body which encompasses them all as constituent elements.[25]

A precursor of the community meeting was a patient-staff meeting.[26] Patient-staff meetings were called to cope with crisis and usually held at the height of the emotional response to the crisis, when it was most difficult to think. It was often felt by various staff members that such meetings made matters worse, encouraging "witchhunts" or pseudo-psychotherapeutic analyses in the group of the behavior of this or that troublesome patient. Staff members felt relatively impotent to influence the course of such group processes.

As is so often the case, the staff had neither an adequate conceptual model to understand group phenomena nor a methodology for intervention in group processes. Often, then, in a position of helplessness or confusion, unable to see sense, pattern, or order in the complex, rapidly changing phenomena of a large group meeting, staff members would feel "bored" and were subsequently reluctant to call or attend such meetings, or, attending them, were relatively passive. Attempts to impose order through a highly organized business agenda and adherence to parliamentarian procedures resulted in somewhat obsessive, colorless meetings—again experienced as "boring."

When the community program coordinator joined the staff, he and

25. Also, as a remnant of past arrangements during a time of change, and consistent with a preoccupation with maintaining the autonomy of various staff members and enterprises, therapy staff members who are assigned to work with the sponsors' group (subcommittee of the community council responsible for the integration of new patients into the community), with the program committee (subcommittee of the activities committee responsible for evening programs to which both patients and staff are invited), and the patient-trustees committee (subcommittee of the activities committee concerned with communication between patients and trustees), have no relation to the community program staff and do not attend the community meeting.

26. The patient-staff meeting ordinarily included all patients and all members of the therapy staff, nursing staff, and activities staff. The patient-staff meeting was usually convened by the community council and staff administrative conference to respond to some crisis in the community or to take action on the model of a town meeting—for example, to consider and vote upon a proposal for change in some aspect of the community program. A majority vote of the patient group and a majority vote of the staff were required for approval.

the therapy staff representative to the work committee initiated a morning meeting, following breakfast and around the breakfast tables, of all patients and some staff to assign work for the day and air any current problems in work areas or in the work program. Patients felt that the often angry discussions early in the morning were intolerable and upset them for the rest of the day. The therapy staff representative to the work committee, along with the members of the work committee, came to feel that the meeting was substituting talk for work, and that the community program coordinator's attempts to foster discussions of current aspects of community life other than the work program (on the grounds that patients' feelings about these might be affecting their participation in the work program) would sabotage the business of the meeting, which was to assign people to work and to deal with administrative problems in the work program.

On an organizational level, this disagreement represented a conflict between two group functions, the adaptation group function with its emphasis on instrumental action, and the integration group function, as well as the technical difficulty of carrying out two such complex functions in one meeting with very limited time at its disposal.

On a personal level, the disagreement reflected strains brought about by the arrival of the community program coordinator and his introduction into an area in which among the staff the therapy staff representative to the work committee had been especially active, not only in his role in the work program, but as a person primarily interested in studying, thinking out a conceptual framework for, and initiating proposals for change in, the community program. The personal strain between these two men was maintained and exacerbated by the behavior of patients, who took sides, and by other members of the staff, who, for example, insisted on emphasizing the theoretical differences of the two men—although their theoretical differences from each other were not so great as their differences from the positions of some other members of the staff—and on keeping their organizational relation to each other and their organizational roles as ambiguous as possible, thereby fostering mutual suspicion and competitiveness. The maintenance of this strain, of course, had the effect of relatively immobilizing both men, so that neither of them could take effective action to disturb the status quo.

After four or five months, the community meeting was formed to meet separately from the morning meeting; some months after the community meeting had begun to meet, the morning meeting ceased to meet.

In proposing the community meeting, the community program co-ordinator emphasized the expected output to individual patients and their psychotherapy, rather than the output to the community program itself; this, instead of winning support from the therapy staff, aroused suspicion concerning possible interference by the community meeting with psychotherapy.

He proposed that he be a co-chairman of the community meeting, a patient to be the other co-chairman. He thought that only in this way could he lead the group, establish new values, and participate flexibly enough to demonstrate what could be done in the community meeting as he visualized it; at this time, for example, as a member of the group he would have had to raise his hand and wait his turn to speak, making prompt intervention, when necessary, impossible. This open bid for a position in which to wield influence also aroused suspicion.[27]

The community program coordinator also proposed that the community meeting be a consultation mechanism rather than a decision-making group, a place where people would influence each other by sharing views, opinions, experiences, information, and feelings, rather than by simply raising hands to vote "yes" or "no"—a variety of opinions and much information often being concealed from a group behind a series of apparently the same "yes" (or "no") votes.

The proposal was motivated by the desire to thwart a number of tendencies of the members of the group. They tended to turn to precipitate, easiest solutions when anxious. They tended to settle for simple solutions, even though such solutions meant maintaining a status quo involving splits, dissensus, and an obviously unreconciled minority. They tended to bully others through appeals to the power of a majority vote (rather than attempting to influence others through the thoughtful presentation of facts, memories of previous experiences, reason, or appeals to different values)—especially when faced with the tensions, delays, and difficulties involved in finding solutions based on negotiation, information, attempts to meet objections by formulating and test-

27. Later, as the community meeting developed, parliamentary procedures were considerably relaxed, and people chimed in when they had something to say without raising their hands; those who had difficulty getting into the discussion would raise a hand so that the chairman could help them do so. As the patient co-chairman picked up skills in chairing the meeting, as new values became institutionalized, as informal participation became possible, there seemed less need for the community program coordinator to continue as co-chairman. As time went on, his continuing in this office made sense primarily as a symbol of the fact that the community meeting was a shared venture of both patients and staff and as a representation of his leadership role in the community program.

ing alternative hypotheses, compromise, and accommodation. The proposal was also designed to prevent supersession of the decision-making groups in the community—the community council, the work committee, and the activities committee.[28]

A typical committee meeting (a pattern evolving over a two-year period) starts with the patient co-chairman announcing the time and asking that the doors of the room be closed. (A tradition was established early of starting and ending on time. Previous meetings had not recognized time boundaries, resulting therefore in interference with other enterprises. Similarly, the patients' view that they could not stay in a room the doors of which were closed because their anxiety made it necessary to get up and walk out as they felt like it was challenged early on the grounds that if work was to get done interruptions and noise from within and from without had to be defended against.)

The patient co-chairman typically protects the working conditions of the meeting—dealing with such matters as interruptions, noise, seating arrangements, people who have difficulty entering the discussion, un-identified people who are present, time boundaries. Optimally, he reminds the group, when appropriate, of the values of the meeting, its purposes, ground rules, and organization. Sometimes, he comments on the past history of a particular issue or makes a referral of an issue to a decision-making group for further action. The staff co-chairman also makes some of these latter contributions, as well as making interpretations about such things as intergroup relations, individual-group relations, and value conflicts bearing upon some current problem. Occasionally, he interprets events in the light of, or offers, information about the hospital situation available to him as a result of his participation in the organization.

Other staff personnel participate in terms of the tasks with which they are prepotently concerned because of the nature of their organizational assignment and relevant to which they have special skills and resources. For example, work program staff are most likely to be active in discussions involving not only work but problems of adaptation, means-ends hypotheses, information and knowledge about reality, and

28 This is not to say that a community meeting should never be a decision-making group, or that these difficulties cannot be met by some other way of planning the formal organization of a community program. However, meeting them in some other way in this situation would have required considerable change in the existing organizational structure; attempts to bring about these additional changes would probably have aroused such intense resistance that it might not then have been possible at that time to bring about the existence of any community meeting at all.

instrumental action in general; activities staff in discussions involving not only activities but problems of consummation, the satisfaction of wishes, and expressive action in general; nursing staff in discussions not only of interpersonal relations, norms, and deviant behavior, but problems of integration and responsible action in general; small group staff in discussions not only concerning the distress of individuals but problems of motivation, participation, incoherent or inconsistent value-systems, and alienation from or commitment to the values of the hospital community.

Announcements are made at the beginning of the meeting: the amount of chemotherapeutic agents and sedatives taken during the week; introduction of visitors or new patients; staff members' comings and goings; patients' departures; scheduled activities; requests for assistance or information; actions being considered or taken by the community council, activities committee, work committee, or small groups. (The results of a patient's staff conference are usually reported by him at the end of the next community meeting after a discussion between him and his therapist has taken place.)

After the announcements, discussion proceeds about any information now before the meeting or about any other topic anyone else wishes to raise. The co-chairmen have responsibility for deciding the direction to be taken if there is more than one claim for discussion at a time, for encouraging participation, and for bringing a discussion to some conclusion—for example, summarizing where the group is with respect to a particular problem or making referral to a decision-making group for action—before going on to another item. Priority is usually given to reports and discussion of events in the current life of the community—i. e., since the last community meeting.

The meeting often ends with a statement by the staff co-chairman about some theme in the meeting and with calling of time by the patient co-chairman.

Four types of community meetings can be described. One is concerned with problems of *adaptation:* efforts to plan how to bring about a desired end—for example, how to win the approval of the coordinating committee for a new budget item; or efforts to discover the nature of the situation in which the group is operating—for example, what is behind some mysterious occurrence, what actually did hpapen last night? Many work program issues are included here: how to get a desired job done—especially, how to organize the workers to do a job; who wants what work to be done, what work is needed; what needs to be known or obtained to get a job done.

The second is concerned with problems of *consummation:* a wish of some members or a number of members, and the fears (within him, them, or others) or competing wishes interfering with its consummation—for example, the wish to have pets in the hospital and the fears preventing its gratification, the wish to have a swimming pool and the other priorities opposing its gratification. Frequently, issues involving the activities committee are at stake in this type of meeting: what do we want and what other wants might have to be sacrificed to get it? Gradually, the activities committee has changed from a priori planning a year's program to attempting to respond to current needs emerging in the group for fun, recreation, and self-expression. (Often, discussion of some activity such as a party or game—about which there is little disagreement or difficulty—is used by the group to "warm up" for a discussion of some distressing problem which people recognize but are not quite ready to tackle.)

The third type of meeting is concerned with problems of *integration:* usually with the deviation by a member of the group from established social norms. Typical topics are episodes of stealing, drunkenness, excessive noise, use of illegal drugs, flouting of rules—and what to do about such behavior. The community council is the group that frequently raises such issues and takes action in relation to them.

The fourth is concerned with problems of *motivation.* An event has occurred, for example, which people are not able to reconcile with what they understand the values of the community to be or with some important values they bring to the community. Community members are, therefore, resentful, disaffected, and disinclined to participate in furthering the ends of an unjust or corrupt community. For example, a patient has been discharged or not permitted to remain; or doctors leave, go on vacation, go off to a conference. These events are perceived as betrayals of the hospital's obligation "to take care of." Discussion of the "facts"—and it is their interpretation, not what they are, that is at stake—often involves reinterpreting the relation of the event to the value in question or bringing to bear upon its interpretation other values, or the hierarchy of values of the community, in order to restore respect for and commitment to the hospital. Members of small groups may initiate or continue such discussions in their own meetings; these are community groups that, from the point of view of output to the social system rather than to particular individuals, function to cope with individual tensions—often arising in response to current community events—or with deficient patterns of motivational commitment for other reasons, for example, lack of adequate learning or socialization or skills. The commitment of members of the community to its goals are thereby reestablished or enhanced and their participation in achieving its goals maintained.

The goals of discussion—as far as output to the hospital community as a social system is concerned—in the first type of meeting have to do with orientation to the situation and the discovery and mobilization of means, opportunities, and facilities, and the use of media such as verbal communication, to achieve given ends; in the second type, with establishment of and investment in ends and acceptance of priorities; in the third type, with maintaining the power of norms to govern conduct or maintaining the integration between individuals, between individual and group, or among groups in the community; in the fourth type, with the maintenance of those intrapersonal conditions necessary to ensure the participation of individuals in the community, their expenditure of effort to actualize shared values through goal-achievement.[29]

We may now turn to the following chapters for illustrations of these types of processes and analyses of them in these terms.

29. For some documents related to the inauguration of the community meeting, and a later reconsideration of it, see Appendix B.

3. In the Beginning

WEEK ONE

1. *Wednesday.* The dining room was hot, humid, and crowded. An angry kitchen staff noisily cleared the lunch dishes. It was difficult to hear anyone speak. Members of the therapy staff arrived at different times, two arriving twenty-five minutes late and immediately joining in a vote although they had not heard the discussion leading up to it.

A work committee report was given; then it was suggested that that report belonged in the morning meeting.

A question was raised about my being elected chairman. The group was told by the clinical director that I would want to observe and report later, and that the other members of the staff would like to pop up and say whatever they wanted. Another staff member was also nominated; he declined, saying he could participate more actively if he were not chairman. A patient was elected.

A patient refused to discuss in front of forty-two people why she had not signed up for work; she would discuss it with the patient who was work scheduler.

A patient challenged the idea that this was a patient meeting. There was no response. Instead there was a discussion of meeting in the dining room, the noise, the possibility of meeting in the living room. Two patients thought that might not be a good idea because people would hide behind the furniture. A patient, supported by a member of the staff, said the real issue was not being discussed; there was no statement about what the real issue was.

A committee to arrange the seating so people could hear each other was suggested; two patients and a staff member volunteered.

A patient requested that the doors of the room be opened; when this was not done, he walked out.

2. *Thursday*. A group had met to plan the seating arrangement, which was posted on the dining room door "so people would not be angry and shocked." It had been difficult to get volunteers to set up the chairs according to the new arrangement, because many were opposed to it; the change in customary seating arrangements aroused an unbelievable amount of upset and anger.

There was some attempt to discuss what the purpose of the meeting was, much concern about my silence, and fear of a meeting with no agenda.

A new patient was present but not introduced.

WEEK TWO

3. *Tuesday*. There was no difficulty hearing.

A patient thanked two others for stopping her from drinking. Another patient reported that the group development seminar (a ten-meeting seminar sponsored by the activities staff) had had difficulty for four meetings but then did well after that; he encouraged the group to "plug along" with this meeting.

I made a statement that I wanted to help but was trying to figure out how to do this without disrupting important values of the hospital.

A lively discussion ensued concerning people's fears of being "confronted" in the meeting. Patients gave examples of how well such "confrontations" had turned out at the morning meeting. A patient proposed the meeting meet four times a week instead of two. Another questioned why proposals for the meeting had to be sent to a committee: "why can't we work it out here?"

4. *Thursday*. A visitor was present. I questioned the presence of an unidentified visitor; following my doing so, two patients questioned his presence on the grounds that the group wanted to be able to discuss personal things in the meeting. The visitor left.

There was some discussion of "tension" in the community. A staff person wanted to know how the group was to develop some callousness to Patient X's frequent upsets. A patient commented that he felt new patients like himself were being excluded from the community.

I commented about the visitor that perhaps visitors might prevent people from bringing up things they wanted to bring up, and that the community council might consider this problem and decide upon some policy for the group. I also commented about Patient X that people were finding it difficult to respond to her intensity and scolding, and found her repetition of things I said embarrassing. There was a statement from a patient indicating that it was easier for a member of the staff to make such statements than for patients to make them.

5. *Tuesday.* Attendance at the meeting had fallen off. There was a twenty-minute discussion about a patient who refused to participate in the work program and mocked it as senseless: "What shall we do about him?"

I interrupted to ask if the shop instructor had been informed that the shop would not be cleaned on a particular occasion. Upon being assured that he had been, and knowing that he had not been, I commented on the polite deception being practiced at the meeting, and wondered if the presence of staff was responsible; if so, would it be better to meet without staff? There were immediate denials, followed by attempts to attribute blame for what had happened. A staff member said he did not understand the issue, another staff member said that he had not been notified about a meeting about Synanon, a residential program for drug addicts, held that morning, and the first staff member said the second sounded as if he felt deceived by me. The patient who had denied practicing deception applauded. I was rescued by the patient co-chairman of the meeting who said that what I had been saying was that we cannot have a meeting unless we are honest, and that the discussion had been a good one because now at least we were talking about people at the meeting instead of outside the meeting.

6. *Thursday.* The activities staff objected to a proposal that the community meeting meet at 11.30 AM: this was an important period for work at the shop. A patient objected to the idea of having a patient and me as co-chairmen.

A nurse protested some breaking of windows by patients and wanted to know why the community did not register more objection to this.

A patient about to be discharged burst into tears as she said good-bye: "This is a wonderful place." A staff member asked her about her future plans.

I questioned someone's assertion that the value of my being co-chairman was that the meeting would then be more orderly and businesslike. I thought the achievements of the meeting would be of a different kind, such as a patient's facing the pain and pleasure of saying good-bye and the group's having the opportunity to hear from the activities staff and nursing staff about their concerns.

7. *Tuesday.* There were about twent-five patients present. Two patients left during the meeting.

Patients discussed their feelings about not knowing who their doctors would be when new fellows-in-training came and some left. The feeling was that selection was haphazard, careless, and random: "No one cares." A new fellow would not know much about the hospital: "Can he help me?" Some anger was expressed toward the medical director and some anxiety about who would be taking care of particular patients in the interim period.

A patient interrupted to scold the group for wasting time and not discussing the fact that another window had been broken. Another patient came in to say she felt she had a responsibility to the first patient to shut her up. Others berated the first patient, telling her that if her doctor were leaving she would not regard the discussion as a waste of time.

8. *Thursday.* New fellows were present. No staff participated in the discussion.

There was a discussion of a "synanon" group that had been formed in the hospital by a staff member (staff representative to the work committee) and a group of patients, on the pattern of group sessions in which drug addicts in the Synanon community talked to each other with great candor. Members of the synanon group said that in that group they were honest; in the community meeting, they were not able to be. Fears were expressed that candor was being and would be used as a weapon.

9. *Monday.* (Patients and staff had met last week and voted in the following proposal: community meetings would meet four times a week in the living room for the purpose of discussion. There would be no decision-making or pre-arranged agenda; items for discussion would come from the meeting. The co-chairmen would be a patient serving a two-month term and I.)

The meeting was well attended. The patient co-chairman shut the doors and two end windows leading into a hallway.

There was some question as to whether an outpatient should attend the meeting. The general feeling seemed to be that all outpatients should be able to attend the meeting. A patient said, in answer to questioning of this position, "Why do we have to be so tight?"

A patient told the group that he would not straighten up the living room after Sunday night movies; he expected help from the group in this.

There was a discussion of a patient who was receiving Thorazine. Questions were asked about the dosage, the reason for her appearing so sedated. The clinical director made the inpterpretation that the patients were angry at the staff: "We criticize you for using drugs, and now you criticize us for giving them." A patient said the group should be discussing negative feelings about the patient under discussion. This led to comments about her stereotyped or childish behavior, and her statements that she was a genius.

I remarked that many patients shared with this patient the fantasy of being special—that, for example, one of the patients was at this moment hiding behind one of the chairs, lifting his hand to speak, as though he expected that he could be seen through the chair. Another patient said angrily, "We know we have problems."

The patient co-chairman started and ended the meeting on time. The mood throughout was somewhat tense, quiet, subdued.

10. *Tuesday.* There was a discussion of a patient who was not participating in, but rather challenging, the work program. Another patient challenged the right of the work committee to interfere with his therapy by asking to see him (because of his failure to work) during his therapy hour (when the work committee regularly met).

I commented that the group saw the first patient as irresponsible and insisting upon being special, and that he saw the group as arbitrary and inconsiderate.

A patient accused the group of being very punishing. Others immediately, in a guilty way, said they were sorry; they were only trying to help. I asked why the group was being seen as punishing the patient (who did not work) by insisting upon seeing him. A therapist might, for example, hope that such a patient would take the responsibility for managing his life in such a way that he would be able to get to his therapy hours, rather than that committees should reorganize their work or abrogate their responsibilities to make his attendance at therapy sessions possible.

After further discussion I wondered why others were not speaking. One patient said, "We're bored." Toward the end of the meeting, the patient under discussion launched into an attack on the meeting, the organization, the hospital. I said to him, "You're not looking at the faces of the people around you; they look bored and sleepy."

11. *Thursday.* This meeting was characterized by very lively affect, much anger, laughing, and apparently fairly open talk.

A patient was angry that the staff representative to the work committee had insulted a patient at the morning meeting by saying she acted like a five-year old. Others pointed out how repetitive his attack had become. Reference was made to the synanon groups and fear of the verbal assaults upon patients that were going on there.

I wondered if such assults were indirectly attacks upon this meeting. The staff representative to the work committee wondered if there was not a split in the group, those in the synanon groups and those who felt left out of them. This led to more discussion of what was going on and people's fear of destructive "honesty." Another staff member made the interpretation that the great fear in the meeting seemed to be that to say what one thinks means being destructive.

12. *Friday.* There were twenty-eight patients present. I left a staff conference to be at the meeting on time. Other staff members came late.

A patient brought up the suggestion that the patients make their own breakfast; this suggestion came from the experience of visiting Synanon and seeing the population of drug addicts there take care of themselves completely. There were complaints about the night watchmen and the kitchen staff. I wondered if these complaints had to do with feelings about staff coming late to the meeting. A pateint said the group knew the staff members had been at a staff conference. There was further discussion about whether or not people wanted to make their own breakfast. One of the fellows interpreted the interest in new ventures as an interest in the new fellows. Another fellow raised questions about contact outside of therapy between therapists and patients. My experience of the meeting was that so many things were being brought up and so many interpretations made of them that it was difficult to follow the discussion.

13. *Saturday.* A new fellow, who had been on duty the night before, called a special community meeting to discuss a self-destructive act by a patient. The meeting started off with the patient telling in a rather vague, platitudinous way what had happened. Patients explained his behavior in terms of his relation to a girl at whom he was angry and his desire to demonstrate to his parents he needed to stay in the hospi-

tal. The tone of the discussion was rather sympathetic and interpretative.

A patient who had known about the self-destructive act did not call the doctor on duty or inform the nurses because she felt the patients could handle the matter, and she distrusted what the staff would do.

Interventions by the staff were of a varied nature. One discussed the confession and sympathetic discussion as an undoing which now made everything okay. Another agreed, suggesting that further discussion would contribute to this and recommending adjournment with the community council managing the matter from then on. The clinical director tried to get the patients to show that they were fed up with this kind of behavior. Still another staff member suggested that use of alcohol was to blame and that this patient should be told not to use alcohol.

I pointed out that there had been no discussion of how the community as a whole joins together to cover up this patient's way of life that leads to the self-destructive act. At this, a number of hands went up, but then the staff representative to the work work committee suggested the meeting be adjourned; the fellow who had called the meeting who was now chairing it did adjourn it.

WEEK SIX

14. *Monday.* A patient told the group that guests of his had brought drugs to a party two weeks before and that the patient who had been self-destructive had used the drugs. I questioned his withholding the names of the guests, stating that his doing so again raised the question of what would be shared at this meeting. A staff member challenged this, saying, "Why is this meeting so special?'"

Patient members of the group attacked the patient for withholding the information. He said, "You all think your way and I'll think mine. I don't believe using drugs is anti-therapeutic." A staff member said he didn't think the names should be given; it might just give people a source of such drugs.

I stated the ways in which I thought the use of drugs had implications for a therapeutic community. The act of using drugs had a specific meaning in the relationship between therapist and patient, for example, expressing anger at the therapist. It was a cynical expression of the lack of alliance between patient and staff, since the use of the drugs had gone on surreptitiously at a party to which staff were invited. It had resulted in a disruption of psychotherapeutic work, since secrets had to be kept from psychotherapists in order to cover the patients who had used the drugs. Further, the use of psychotherapy by others as a sanctuary in which such secrets could be confessed and kept, as though there were no consequences to the life of the community, was a perversion of the real purposes of psychotherapy.

15. *Tuesday.* The attack on the patient who withheld the names continued. Another visit to Synanon by a group was discussed.

I commented on the pattern of the meetings, a focus by those who do participate of attack upon some one other person, and a number of nonparticipants who like the attackers also prefer not to talk about themselves. Patients responded with protests. What secrets of our own are we supposed to tell? What are the agreements among us at this meeting? What will we do with secret information when it is told? How can we be a group here, when we immediately split up after the meeting?

A staff member wondered about the synanon groups, which were outside this meeting and secret. Another staff member made a play on the words "Sin Anon," commenting that all sin in the community is anonymous and goes on in someone else. Still another staff person thought that cohesiveness was being forced by focusing an attack upon one person.

16. *Thursday.* A patient who was sitting outside was called in by another patient. When she came in she discussed, weeping, her sense of aloneness in the community: her best friend had been discharged; her doctor was leaving. Many patients asked her questions. A patient interpreted slips of the tongue. The discussion was general, with one exception: a patient reported a fight between her and the patient under discussion.

I commented that this was a contribution to the meeting, a description of a specific incident happening between two people in the community. As to the rest of the discussion, I continued to wonder if it was useful to divide up the group into a patient who acted the role of patient and the rest of the group who responded to the "patient" with approval or disapproval. The patient co-chairman was angry: "We were working hard and you interrupt us with your evaluation of how the group is working."

I commented that somehow I was also either speaking or being heard as speaking in terms of right and wrong. Other patients defended my interruption, on the grounds that my job was to help the group to do its work better.

17. *Friday.* Seventeen patients were absent. There was a brief dis-

cussion of my presentation at a patient-staff program the evening before on the therapeutic community, and about my comment at the end of last meeting which had angered people. Two patients were sitting together outside talking, ostentatiously not attending the meeting; people were angry about this. There was a discussion of three or four patients whom other patients experienced as problems.

The general theme was discouragement. What can we do with this meeting? There was anger at the staff who criticize and say what should be; every staff person who talked about the goal of the meeting was ignored. What can we do with the people who come to the meeting late? What can we do about the patients at whom we become angry?

WEEK SEVEN

18. *Monday.* I reviewed comments about the weekend and wondered how it had gone.

There had been a meeting of the synanon group, a two-day party (during which drinking had gone on and the police had been called), and some patients had gone boating. A pateint reported some belongings stolen; another patient was reported to have intruded into someone else's room. The discussion focused on the intruder. A patient brought up the new patients. A staff member commented on the theme of intruders, new patients, and new doctors. I said the meeting seemed to have a choice, to "do good to someone" or to discuss the problems we all share in living together.

19. *Tuesday.* The meeting started with a patient's requesting concert tickets anyone might not be using and getting a positive response. A new patient asked how to get to the concerts. The patient co-chairman of the meeting remarked that this was an example of what this meeting was for. A patient commented that the staff commentators make patients feel that it is not their meeting. "They take us out of ourselves."

One of the patients said that one of the staff had suggested we get to know the new patients. Should we welcome new patients or not?

A patient who had been at the hospital some time wanted to know how people saw her. She was told people got angry at her and were afraid of her.

A new patient volunteered a lengthy story of his illness. A staff member questioned: "Is this what we need to know to help us live together?" Another staff person said, "Yes, understanding illness is important to the community." A patient said, "We each want to talk about ourselves."

I commented that the issue seemed to be not whether it was good to talk about "health" or "illness" but what did we need to know to help us to live togther.

At the end of the meeting, I said I was not sure but I wondered if the meeting might be less awkward if people did not have to raise their hands. A patient immediately raised his hand: there was a burst of laughter.

20. *Thursday.* The meeting started with a question about the synanon groups, leading to discussion about the purpose of the community meeting. Staff asked why people attend the community meeting. Patients asked why the staff members don't say why they're here. Why doesn't the staff participate? "Can it be the patients think there are disagreements among the staff?" Laughter.

There was mention of a patient's leaving shortly after arrival. Had the community failed? The patient had insisted on having breakfast in bed, after she was told she shouldn't because that isn't the way things are done here.

During the meeting, the patient co-chairman called on someone who looked as if he wanted to say something but hesitated to break in.

21. *Friday.* The community council reported that two patients had been kicked off that committee because of absences and having been referred to it several times as social problems; it was felt they should not, therefore, be representing the community on the community council. This action was supported by the clincial director as necessary for dealing with the two patients.

I tried to focus on the question what kind of community it is in which people, for example, sleep in the meeting or sit silently outside the meeting, rather than on such questions as what is going on in each of these individuals and what can we do about him or her. My comment was ignored; the group members began to criticize one of the patients.

Synanon groups were mentioned again. *P:* [1] Why does the staff representative to the work committee, who is working with those groups, not participate in the community meeting? That staff member spoke movingly of his effort to be honest in a group. This led to questions

---

1. P and S represent paraphrases of statements by patient or staff members, respectively. These paraphrases are not quotations and sometimes represent summaries or abstractions of the point of view of more than one person. If a statement is clearly part of a discussion, but not identified as patient or staff, it may be assumed to belong to the patient group.

about why he had left the small group in which he had been participating; the speculation was that it had to do with disagreements with me. One patient said that I was now the important staff person in the community; another asked, "Why can't they both be important?"

22. *Monday.* There was a fairly lively discussion of the two sides in the community, those who wanted the synanon groups and those who did not. There was some indication that the synanon groups were a protection against the individual's being swallowed up in the new "community." The value of being open with others was explained in terms of increased awareness of self. A wish was expressed to have me tell the group how to deal with this split, but also the wish to "decide for ourselves." The prevailing mood seemed to be: "We can't figure it out ourselves; the staff has to tell us what to do."

A patient's question about the weekend was ignored. A patient reported that he had kept track and noted eighteen to twenty people talking in the meeting. There were some complaints that it was hard to get into the discussion since raising hands had been abandoned. Another patient raised the question about what was relevant in the meeting: "Was a patient's feelings about her therapist, just expressed, really that crucial for a whole community to know?"

At the end of the meeting, a patient said he was shocked, that he didn't like a question addressed to him by another patient about what he thought, nor did he like the way people talked to their therapists in the meeting.

23. *Tuesday.* A patient reported trying to help another patient by getting her involved in an activity; but she had responded by threatening to bring his action up at the community meeting. She said she didn't believe he was trying to help, and found him obnoxious. The patient co-chairman said that we all have this kind of problem; let's discuss all of us rather than just these two. He was ignored. The interpretation was made by a staff member that the meeting was like the Christians and the lions with the rest of us the jury.

24. *Thursday.* Members of the activities staff showed up at this meeting. There was a heavy silence. The absence of therapy staff members was commented on: "Don't they value the meeting?" Other comments: "There are enough doctors here; why worry about the ones not here?" "Why do I have to come if others don't?"

I commented that there was a large group of patients absent too.

What is the purpose of the meeting? People don't want to discuss themselves.

I said that the meeting was to discuss life at the hospital and how to make it better.

A discussion of the work program ensued. People were not showing up for work in the morning. A patient complained about the finickiness of his foreman about the exact time he worked: "I'll do my assignment." Two patients commented that another patient was sleeping during the discussion and that no one paid attention. The clinical director said, "I envy him!" A patient said, "Why do we keep discussing the work program?" Another said, "The new patients need to. You older patients should help and have patience."

25. *Friday.* A patient asked for help in pinning up her skirt. She would pay seventy-five cents. No takers? The men laughed.

The patient co-chairman announced that a patient was going to have a staff conference, another was leaving, and a third was getting a job. The first patient of the three mentioned commented on the sense of helplessness in the meeting, the second said he was planning on doing nothing after he left, and the third said he thought a job was worth more than the community meeting.

In connection with vandalism, trespassers on hospital property were mentioned.

I commented that Friday meetings felt different, moody. Another staff member interpreted the feeling: "We'll kill anyone who trespasses our barriers."

There was much discussion of what was going on among the staff, staff disagreements, staff influence upon different groups of patients.

I interpreted a feeling of helplessness in the face of absenteeism and nonparticipation.

WEEK NINE

26. *Monday.* A patient announced that tickets were available through the activities committee for a play in the area. Another patient said that guests at dinner last night ate up all the food like pigs. There was considerable anger. A patient left the meeting to get the patient whose guests they were. When she came in, she and another patient carried on a lively discussion with the group, defending themselves and their friends. The patient co-chairman pointed out the concern with intruders might also have to do with feelings about new patients and new staff.

It came out during the discussion that the guests had been under the influence of drugs. People had hesitated to speak to them because it looked as though they were looking for a fight. Were the drugs responsible for their behavior? One staff member refused to believe that the patients defending the guests were as troubled by the guests' behavior as others were; another interpreted the two patients' comments as expressing contempt for the group.

I said what I heard was that everyone feels helpless in coping with many situations arising in life at the inn, things no one seems to be able to do anything about: nonparticipation, nonattendance, vandals, intruders, the guests. It seemed as if the group's solution was to be to make two patients completely responsible, although it was not clear to me why they were supposed to be less uncertain and helpless in this situation than anyone else. Another solution is to do nothing, saying, "We'll talk about it tomorrow in the community meeting."

At this, a patient expressed his fear of his own anger in the situation involving the guests, and other patients joined in to say that they also didn't know what to do. One patient said that it was a satisfactory solution to bring it up in the community meeting and let the two patients who had invited the guests know just how everyone felt about them.

The patient co-chairman said, referring to the fact that a number of patients had referred to the inn as "our home," "If we really felt this was our home, we'd work more, and not feel so helpless in these situations."

This was the first community meeting in which there had been a sustained discussion throughout the meeting about one subject.

27. *Tuesday.* This was a very difficult meeting, with long heavy silences, digressions, whispering. There were many absences.

The head nurse raised a question about two patients coming in during the early morning hours; she had asked one of them to come to the meeting to discuss this. Her concern was the way these two patients were living; they seemed to be using the inn merely as a hotel. The patient she had asked to come to the meeting justified his behavior, minimizing his drinking. A staff person commented on the group's apathy. I pointed to the sense of secrecy. A third staff member changed the subject, asking a third patient if she had used false names to register guests for dinner. These turned out to be the same guests who had introduced drugs at a patient-staff party some weeks back; the group rancorously attacked the two patients whose guests they were, telling them these people were not wanted at the hospital, at the same time recognizing that the two patients were becoming increasingly defensive.

I commented that the discussion had started out about two patients, that apparently no one wanted to ask questions about these two patients' secrets, and so the discussion had shifted to attack two other patients about their secrets.

A patient said, "You know the answer. If they tell their secrets, we have to tell ours." Another said, "We don't care: let them keep their secrets and we'll keep ours." The patient who had been asked by the nurse to attend the meeting said, "What makes you think there are any secrets?"

A number of patients said that they don't feel the inn is their home. One patient said angrily about another that she was saying screw the hospital; this made him angry because he had a stake in the hospital.

28. *Thursday.* There was a discussion of the recommendation to the medical director by the social problems council that a patient who had been referred to it for not participating in the work program and for undermining others' participation by his scorn and contempt should be discharged. There were two points of view. One: "We are not to blame. He did it to himself. Don't try to make me feel guilty." The other: "Aren't we somewhat responsible? Why do people not make it here?"

I said that the patient's failure had been discussed in the community council, the work committee, and the social problems council; that in this meeting perhaps we had the only opportunity to discuss the community's contribution to this failure. How do we fit in? How did we cooperate with the patient in bringing about this outcome?

One patient said, "It's every man for himself in this community; that's the philosophy here despite all the groups."

Toward the end of the meeting, two patients who had taken the position that the patient had brought this upon himself got up and left the meeting, without comment by anyone.

A member of the activities staff slept through most of the meeting.

29. *Friday.* It was announced that a new synanon group was starting if people wanted to sign up for it. There was discussion about what staff person might be interested in working with it.

Most staff were still at the staff conference and there were sixteen patients absent. There was a long silence.

I wondered what the hell we were here for. I felt dissatisfied but maybe everyone else was satisfied by the kind of community we have. A patient asks for help in sewing a skirt and has to offer to pay for the help. The only response she gets is from someone who says I'll show you how but I won't do it for you, as though the request for help were being interpreted as abnormal dependency. A patient does not participate in the work program; response to him is self-righteous indignation rather than questions about what there might be about what the work program itself that contributes to such non-participation. Newcomers to the community feel coldly greeted: every man for himself. Is this the kind of community people want?

There were various responses. One: "You are confused; aren't we supposed to confront people realistically about their behavior?" Two: "I was afraid to get too intimate with him [the patient who did not work]." Three: "How much responsibility can we take for each other?" Four: "We put in our time in the work program; why should he get away with it, and not us?"

One patient said that the patient under discussion really wanted people to like him, but was afraid they wouldn't; so he acted obnoxiously. Another patient said that that patient had a raw deal, referring to the fact he had had a frequent change in therapists. A patient suggested that there be a referendum asking the medical director not to follow the recommendation of the social problems council. One response to this from a patient: "The same thing would just keep on happening if he were allowed to stay."

I announced I would be absent the following Monday and Tuesday.

WEEK TEN

30. *Monday.* and 31. *Tuesday.* I did not attend these two meetings.

32. *Thursday.* There was a discussion about having a meeting without the doctors, and anger at me for not answering questions. A patient refused to discuss what happened at his small group meeting when asked to do so by another patient.

When I commented that there seemed to be divisions in the community, a patient said, "I don't see any."

A patient said, "Let's discuss whether we really do want a different community." Another patient said, "What can we do?"

A patient angrily accused the staff of being more interested in money than in patients—apparently in response to the recent discharge of a patient. That patient's therapist confessed he had misled the group concerning the circumstances of the patient's discharge.

During the meeting, when a patient tried to get the group to discuss the work program, there was no comment by the staff representative to the work committee. When the patient co-chairman said he thought people seemed to be making speeches rather than talking with each other, the director of activities took issue with him.

33. *Friday.* There were two professional visitors at this meeting. There was some discussion of staff behavior. The nurses objected to being criticized. When I commented about the criticalness in the group, a patient said that I kept dangling a utopia before the group. There was some discussion of the role of the head nurse in the meeting, and the nursing potential represented by patient skills in the area of mutual help.

WEEK ELEVEN

34. *Monday.* All staff were present on time. The staff representative to the work program was not present. There was a dog in the room. The patient co-chairman asked that the dog be taken out. There were general objections. The patient co-chairman appealed to me; I said I thought it would be a good idea to take the dog out. A patient took it out.

Some information about a new patient and announcements were followed by a patient's mentioning that one of the patients had been writing bad checks in town. The patient in question discussed his tangled relationship with his father. The problem was discussed matter-of-factly and without righteous indignation.

The pros and cons of not having doctors at the meeting, and the feeling that there were too many meetings, were considered. I commented that one reason the meeting was set up not to take action though voting was so that every time we got into a jam it couldn't be resolved by changing the meeting, but rather we would have to stick it out and work the difficulties through. *P:* What is the meeting for? *P:* The meeting is to help us deal with our common problems. *P:* We have the meetings so that it won't be like the weekend when there is nothing planned. Director of activities: We could plan things for the weekend.

A patient then asked what a good meeting would be like. Wouldn't it have some humor? She stated she was afraid to bring something up because the group might not take it seriously. She then referred to a memo from the medical director to the effect that pets were not allowed in the inn. She said her dog meant a great deal to her; it was given to her by her therapist before he left. She wanted to be able to keep the dog with her in the inn. There was a lively discussion of this. The patient chairman of the community council said he was planning to see the medical director to find out if there was any use in discussing this: could the rule be changed?

I wondered if there was a feeling that the patients had little power to change anything about the hospital.

A staff member supported the dog-owner: "You're not able to give the dog up." Then he asked the group to consider my comment.

Patients began to express their dislike of animals. The head nurse supported the need for such a rule. When the zoning laws were mentioned, a patient offered to find out what these actually were. The difficulties in caring for animals were pointed out. P: We shouldn't do anything until the medical director says it's okay.

I made the interpretation that the group wanted the medical director to decide the matter so that it would not have to deal will all the thorny problems involved. There was an angry "No!"

Another staff member said that if the group were serious, it would make a concrete proposal to the medical director. It would not send someone to ask him, "May we have pets?" That might mean one hundred animals. No medical director is going to give the group carte blanche. The group would have to come to an agreement about how many animals its members were prepared to stand. The owner could not be responsible twenty-four hours a day; there would need to be agreements about what responsibilities other members of the community were willing to take.

35. *Tuesday.* A new patient was introduced.

The chairman of the community council reported on his visit to the medical director. He had asked the medical director if the patients had any room to maneuver as far as the administration was concerned on the question whether inpatients could have pets. The administration's position on this issue was reported to be inflexible; the explanation of this position was the housekeeping problems involved; it was impossible to make an exception, since granting one patient the right to keep a pet would make it impossible to deny the right to others, and therefore the situation could quickly get out of hand.

Q:[2] What can a patient who wants to keep his dog do now? A: Board him at a kennel nearby and visit him. The feeling that this was an unsatisfactory arrangement was expressed; to some it sounded silly.

P: What are the implications of an inflexible administrative rule? P: The medical director has not given his real reason for his ruling; there is certainly no state law against having pets in hospitals. P: The medi-

2. Q and A stand for "question" and "answer."

cal director knows very well there are dogs around, since one had visited the small group of which he was a member; why has he chosen this time to lay down or reiterate the rule about pets? *P:* The medical director knows that people are bothered by dogs and that these people don't feel free to say so, since a rejection of a person's pet tends to be taken as a rejection of the person; he is, therefore, acting to get those people who object to pets and can't say so off the hook. The group was reminded in this connection that the patient who had raised this issue had said that if her dog were forced to go, she would go. One patient suggested that dogs were not the only annoying intruders at the inn since the presence of some outpatients' children had also been viewed with annoyance; she wondered if the presence of her children, when they visited, was annoying to others, and welcomed comments about this to her. The director of activities noted that the patient who felt so strongly about her own dog's staying had commented about a large dog around the inn that she could understand why anybody would be annoyed with that dog.

P: Is it possible to get the medical director to change his mind? *P:* I don't think he should be put on the spot by our pursuing the issue further; he had to lay down the law because there has been an increase in the number of dogs highly visible around the inn. *P:* Those people who now own dogs are not even at this meeting. *P:* We ought to discuss the meaning to a person of having a pet at the inn: it is a public declaration of loneliness. *P:* Having a pet is a rejection of human companionship; the people who have pets are rejecting the rest of the community.

I suggested that making therapy-like interpretations in the group might be a way of avoiding the question: how was it that whatever had been stirred up by the question of patients' having pets at the inn had been handled in a way that provoked a statement from the administration that the patients could take no action about this matter?

P: The chairman of the community council's going to see the medical director has really solved the problem for the group. It was recalled that a member of the staff had pointed out at the last meeting that any administrator faced with the kind of request that the community council chairman was going to make would have no choice but to say no.

I commented that, therefore, since the group knew that the medical director would probably say no and did nothing to prevent the community council chairman from proceeding, the group could now grumble rebelliously at the medical director's response while appearing to comply obediently, all the time feeling secretly relieved that the problem of having to face the difficulties of, or doing something about, this issue was solved.

The chairman of the community council became very angry. He said that he had a mandate from the community council to see the medical director. Nothing he had heard at the community meeting convinced him that he shouldn't act on that mandate. The community council was as important as this meeting! Besides, the medical director might have asked for a specific and reasonable proposal from the patient group, saying he would consider such a proposal.

P: What would a reasonable proposal be like? *P:* We might suggest building a kennel near the inn and taking care of the pets there. *P:* Since the patients are doing the housekeeping at the inn, staff concerns about the dogs' making messes in the inn are not as valid as they would be if the housekeeping staff were faced with the messes. *P:* We really can't do anything or make any decisions in this community.

I wondered if there was a sense of helplessness in the community meeting because this group didn't know what its relationship was to the action-taking committees in the community such as the community council, the activities committee, and the work committee. The group found it difficult to respond to this comment. Instead, there was some further discussion of dogs as child-substitutes, to which I responded with the observation that we were turning from doing something about the problems of community living to making therapy-like interpretations.

Another staff person made an attempt to define what the work of the community meeting might be. Although patient attitudes and opinions were supposedly represented by the patient leaders of the various decision-making committees, there was no other meeting than the community meeting where what the patient group as a whole really felt and thought about an issue could be expressed. No executive group could take action unless it knew such facts as how many dogs the group would put up with or how cleaning up would be arranged. This staff person ended by wondering what the group really felt about the question of patients having pets in or around the inn; until people began to say what they thought and felt, no work could be done on the matter.

P: I am against pets because they're noisy and messy, just as I'm against people, children, and motorcycles that are noisy and messy. *P:* You're hypocritical since you're noisy and messy yourself. *P:* I'm not willing to clean up other people's dogs' messes. *P:* I don't want dogs inside the inn, but I'm bothered that someone would say she will leave if her dog is not allowed to stay.

I commented that there seemed to be two sides to the problem: not only how to get pets in the inn, but also how to get rid of those which are not wanted. The group, if it considers this problem, may have to face the real differences of opinion among its members.

At the end of the meeting, I brought up the absence of the patient who had been recommended for discharge to the medical director by the social problems council. The medical director had placed him on probation. It turned out he was working outside the inn at a job fifty-six hours a week, but that he was off the day of this meeting and presumably could have attended it. I suggested that members of the group mention to him that his participation in the community was a condition of his probation, and that it would be helpful to keep people posted about his activities. *P:* And get my head snapped off! *P:* I didn't get my head snapped off when I talked to him about getting to work here on time.

36. *Thursday.* I noticed a patient was reading and commented on it. He put the book aside, complaining that nothing was happening. I wondered if he meant that nothing will be happening. He said, "No."

The director of activities noted that kitchen utensils were missing from the patient kitchen, according to community council minutes, and that the activities committee had discussed that books, records, and magazines were missing from the library.

Additional information emerged during the discussion. The absence of current issues of magazines irked some. A patient had been unable to bake a cake because of the absent equipment. An outpatient had been asked by an inpatient if he had taken the kitchen utensils; he had said, "No." (There was some anger expressed about his having been accused.) A patient reported he had fifteen records in his room, which he would return; he did not know records were not to be borrowed from the library. An inpatient reported that she knew an outpatient had a number of books from the library in his apartment, but had never mentioned this to him. It turned out an inpatient had that morning asked him if he had library books in his apartment and he had said no. Another patient confirmed that he had. Late in the meeting, a patient mentioned the fact that his bike was missing; he wondered how people felt about that. Details about the disappearance were obtained, as well as a description of the bike. A patient discussed guilt feelings about borrowing people's bicycles.

Suggestions for dealing with these problems made at various times during the meeting included the following. There should be a system for keeping track of books, records, and kitchen utensils, because people are forgetful and no library can operate on an honor system.

The head nurse, in this connection, commented she had assumed there was a system for signing out books and records; she asked who the library chairman (on the activities committee) was. That chairman described the state in which she had found the library on taking office, and her attempt to catalogue and keep records about the use of books and phonograph records. These comments provoked a defense from the previous library chairman, and a recounting of the experiences of another ex-chairman. There were suggestions about how the activities committee or library chairman should set up rules for keeping track of books and records; the director of activities suggested that magazines be chained in place. A patient, clearly to stimulate others to make suggestions, proposed that all the bookcases and the record cabinet be kept under lock and key, the key to be kept by the nurses; the proposal was loudly rejected. At the end of the meeting, a patient who was concerned about the missing magazines asked that others who were also bothered get together with him after the meeting.

Dilemmas and issues were stated during the course of the meeting. The library chairmanship should be included in the work program; because of the amount of work involved, a patient doing this job should be excused from other chores. It is no use trying to solve the problem; people don't give a damn; the inn is not looked on as a home. Things get better treatment here than in my home. If people cared, things wouldn't disappear; the newspaper never disappears because people would be furious if it were not at the receptionist's desk when they wanted it. People won't respond to others' requests. A patient said he was glad when someone asked him to stop playing his record player loudly one night and that he has tried to avoid doing so again. What is the relationship between these problems and the current proposal by the work committee that patients take more responsibility for their life in the inn, for example, doing more housekeeping, and working in the dining room?

Early in the meeting I commented that it was difficult to tell how much people cared about the inconveniences being reported, and what people were willing to do to change the situation.

Later, I summarized three solutions being sugegsted. One: "Let's trust each other." Two: "Let's delegate finding a solution to these difficulties to a committee." One involved an ideal, but no dependable degree of performance; two might merely be a way to get rid of the difficulty. Committees may propose rules and regulations, but these will be ineffective in the absence of knowledge about what the members of the group wanted and were willing to do. A third solution seemed to have something to do with increasing the responsibility the entire group was willing to take for life at the inn; that solution involved considerable work by the group to arrive at some understanding of what people cared about and what steps they were willing collectively to take with regard to problems in group living. I mentioned three names as examples of people about whose feelings and opinions we knew nothing.

When a patient called for a vote as an indication of how many people were concerned about the missing magazines, I pointed out that voting was outside the group rules of the meeting, since we were interested in hearing what might be behind any "yes" or "no" vote. This resulted in both challenge and compliance.

At the end of the meeting, a patient said she wanted to say goodbye and thank the community for the many things she had learned here. She was asked about her plans. The comment was made that it felt good to have someone think the community was worthwhile enough for someone to say good-bye like this rather than just disappear. A patient called for a round of applause for the patient who was leaving despite his feeling that such a display might be viewed as "indecent." The applause ended the meeting.

37. *Friday.* The meeting opened with silence; there were a lot of people absent.

The patient co-chairman noted that the community council had decided they would not or could not enforce the medical director's rule about pets. I commented on the convenient arrangement managed by the community, which had gotten the medical director to make the decision, and which could now disown this decision, leaving it to each person to accept it or not as he chose.

The discussion that followed included the following kinds of comments. The community council should be expected only to implement those rules it makes. Rules are foolish. This community, which can't make a rule about pets, is foolish. The medical director would find it inconvenient to hang around the inn trying to enforce his decision; perhaps the group needn't worry about it any more. Nurses are delegated responsibility for enforcing such rules; that's a difficult position to be in. What do nurses feel about this question? The head nurse commented that she personally would enjoy having a few dogs around. Anything that would make the place more like home would be welcome. *P:* I don't want hairs all over. *P:* I don't like other people's dogs. *P:* Animals are like humans; so-and-so's dog is being spoiled by being left to run wild. *P:* He's not ready to go to college yet. Laughter.

I commented that we can't live with the messy lovable little beasts and we can't live without them. Somewhat later, I said that the discussion had centered largely around questions of mess and discipline; no one had mentioned, however, that a person's love for her pet might be a part of the matter.

A patient discussed her love for her pet, how useful he was to her during periods of withdrawal and depression since he continued to make demands upon her according to his own needs, how comforting that was. There were some interpretations about her attachment to her dog, namely that it was serving to justify her neglect of the problem of relating to other people.

I wondered who else wanted to keep a pet. A patient said she wanted to keep her two dogs. A patient said she had once minded these two animals but no longer did. Another patient, who had very rarely participated, said she too would like a dog.

I commented that direct expressions of wishes were of great help to the group in indicating what needed to be considered in any solution of the problem.

There was a call from the opposite side. Concern about mess, scuffling, and noise was expressed. Again the possibility of a kennel was raised. No one had heard again from the patient who had once volunteered to find out about zoning laws.

I mentioned the problem of still not knowing what many members of the group thought and felt, and wondered if instead of voting we might poll some members of the group, asking them what they thought about the matter of pets. This was objected to because people might feel forced to participate, but a patient did ask another what he thought. He said he hadn't spoken because it made no difference to him either way, but that too many dogs around the inn would no doubt create a problem. Other patients were queried. One said that he wouldn't mind having a few animals, but he thought it would be impossible to keep the number to a few. Another said she feared animals jumping on her, but she didn't care because she was leaving. A patient said but others might feel as you do. The head nurse said she would like to see some pets but was concerned about the housekeeping and the matter of putting them out at night; she wondered if there was some way to keep the number down.

WEEK TWELVE

38. *Monday.* At the beginning of the meeting, a patient said he had heard that someone was going to bring up a fight that had taken place

over the weekend. A nurse said the nurses had heard nothing about any "casualty lists." There were a number of evasive comments: the inn had seemed upset; on the other hand, perhaps someone made up the rumor to liven up the inn, which was dull.

A patient complained that two nurses were chattering behind him. They said he hadn't said anything to them. He said that he was saying something now.

The group was variously described as apathetic and hostile.

I said I thought that perhaps the search for the meaning of the rumor might not be leading anywhere; I wondered if anyone in the room had a specific concern he wanted to bring to the attention of the group.

A nurse said she was concerned about a patient who had "done some injury to himself" during the previous night. The patient was asked how he had injured himself. Questions were asked further to find out if anyone knew he had been feeling desperate enough to injure himself and to find out if he expected to get help from anyone. He said he didn't expect that there was anyone who could help him. P: I know what you mean about the unavailability of help.

Patients reported experiences with him before the incident, indicating their awareness of his distress, also their inability to help him. P: I didn't know what I could do about it, so I left. P: I was too upset about my own problems to be of any use to him with his. P: I saw him put his fist through a pane of glass, but there was nothing I could do to reach him. P: I went for a short walk with him, knowing he was upset.

A young woman patient alluded vaguely to some time she had spent with him. (All the contacts mentioned had been with women patients.) There was some attempt to find out if anything had made him more upset. A male patient asked if going to a movie had bothered him. "No." The young woman asked if their exchange had upset him. "Probably."

A nurse who had been on duty the previous night reported that he had gone to sleep in the nurses' room on the couch. She had awakened him and told him to return to his room. She had accompanied him to his room. Five minutes later, he had returned, having injured himself. She now took this to mean that she shouldn't have sent him back to his room. She wished he had spoken to her and told her of his need to stay in the nurses' room.

He said there were other ways than words to communicate that kind of need: "you had to force me off the couch and push me out." She denied any scuffle and added that going to sleep on the nurses' couch was unusual and that she understood he had been sent back to his own room on previous occasions without incident. She also mentioned that it was the first time she had been on night duty.

There were some comments from patients to him that one has to know how to ask for help.

I commented that his signals of distress had been clear: he had been increasingly depressed at the community meetings; he had recently in a community meeting asked for a weekend meeting because he wanted something to do over the weekend; and he had gone to the nurses' office. Perhaps the problem was that people didn't know how to respond to such signals.

There were a number of comments explaining why people could not help someone in trouble: you have to devote yourself to the person needing help and forget your own concerns; people are too preoccupied with their own needs and anxieties to be selfless even briefly. A patient said he had to decide whether to join in at a party or stay with a woman patient he knew was in trouble; he finally took her back to the inn and returned to the party. Sometimes patients don't have the wherewithal to come to the aid of another patient.

I wondered if patients had any suggestions for the nurses.

One patient suggested that some patients be allowed to sit in on the closed meeting of the nurses, when the evening shift came on duty. Patients in distress might find it easier to turn to nurses if this meeting were open.

There was some argument between patients about whether or not patients couldn't help each other or just didn't want to; a lot of guilt was expressed.

I commented that there was a kind of luxuriating in feelings of being guilty that I didn't think would be helpful. One problem remaining was to figure out what would make sense as responses in the community to signals of distress. Second, it was clear that the patient in question continued to require nursing attention; the nurses could not supply all the help he needed by themselves; he needed some help only patients could contribute. Maybe the nurses and patients could meet together to discuss how to provide what was needed together.

39. *Tuesday.* A movie committee meeting was announced. A community council proposal for extending the hours during which guests would be allowed to visit private and common rooms in the inn was brought up for patient and staff approval. Why does the staff have to approve it? A staff member asked what needs had led to this proposal. Do these regulations apply to outpatients? Some seem to hang around

the inn at all hours. *Nurse:* Previously there has been no need to decide what to do about outpatients. *Nurse:* Whether or not an outpatient is given permission to visit seems to depend upon who is the receptionist on duty. A patient reported that two patients had been in another's room after midnight, contrary to rules against visiting in a private room then; was this with the nurses' permission? *Director of activities:* As a member of the coordinating committee, I do not get any sense that there is strong feeling for changing the regulations. Several patients spoke for the proposed changes: present regulations were inconvenient; if a few want them changed, they should be. *P:* I hope late visitors will be courteous, remembering that others want to sleep. *P:* I don't care either way.

I asked the community council chairman if he had the information he needed; he said "Yes."

A question was raised about having doubles in a tennis tournament.

A question was raised about an anonymous, cryptic message that had been put in people's mailboxes. There was a flurry of comments, including the rumor that there were to be seven such messages. A patient defended anonymity because of the tendencies to recrimination when someone tries to communicate. Asked if she sent the messages, she confessed. She then spoke of her distress about outpatients (the subject of the messages), and especially about a patient who had gone home for two weeks. *P:* Is she gone?! *P:* Why should a patient be expected to tell the community that? I'm sure she told her friends. A number of people told the sender of messages they couldn't understand what she was talking about. *P:* The issue of outpatients is still worth talking about. *P:* Thinking about becoming an outpatient has raised a lot of questions and doubts in my mind. There was some discussion of inpatients who behave like outpatients, that is, are never around; a particular patient was mentioned.

I asked if anyone wanted to comment on the way the meeting was going.

What do you mean? Why do we have to go on talking about [the patient whose self-destructive act had been discussed the previous day]?

Referring to that patient, I said he obviously had a good night; people had been helpful to him; everyone seemed comfortable about the incident and assumed it was over. I wondered if we had to wait for another such incident before becoming concerned about what events bring on such incidents.

The patient was asked how his evening had gone; he said it had been a "good scene." He didn't want to be talked about, because it was not right for the group to focus on one individual during the meetings. He had been asked to attend the rehearsal of the drama group's play; he hadn't thought he would enjoy it but he did. He had been asked to join someone for lunch on the porch, and by someone else about his plans for the evening, which he appreciated. He had a late evening talk session with two patients which had been helpful to him but perhaps not to one of them who had stayed in bed all day.

A patient pointed out that the patient being discussed had been elected to an important office in the community that morning; was this the way the community handles this kind of problem?

P: I don't understand! *P:* He was a favorite candidate before this happened! *P:* Explain the implications of your remark! *P:* I'm not sure what they were myself.

P: I would like to hear the suggestion to open up the nurses' night meeting discussed further. *Nurse:* I am interested in that idea and it is going to be discussed at the nurses' meeting. *Nurse:* I don't think waiting until 11:00 PM for nurses and patients to get together is a good idea; why not an earlier meeting, closer to dinner?

P: I want to return to the subject of outpatients; there are many ways of being an outpatient; although I am an inpatient I feel outside the life of the community; although I have chosen to be outside and have been thrust outside, I still want some attention paid to people like me.

I commented after some time about the work still remaining for us as a group. First, the problem of how to respond to signals by individuals; I noticed a patient at this meeting, who was silent, looked worried, and had chosen to sit where everyone could see him. Second, the community did not know what had taken place between [the patient who had been upset] and [the young woman] although the exchange at the meeting indicated that it was something of significance; perhaps because there seemed to be something about sex involved, it was assumed that to pursue this was taboo. Third, we cannot evaluate sleeping in the nurses' room as a solution to a problem unless we know what led to wanting to sleep there.

Only the first comment received a response. A patient asked the silent patient for me if he was upset. *P:* Not more than usual; I prefer not to be talked about. *P:* I still don't know how to respond to someone in distress; I saw [the patient being discussed] sitting off by himself, but though he looked upset I didn't go up to him, not knowing what to say or what was the right thing to do.

I commented that I knew people cared about the subjects being discussed but the silences and "damped down" quality of the discussion may result from their preferring to discuss these matters elsewhere, perhaps feeling loyal to other groups which expect that discussions should be held elsewhere "with more honesty."

Evidence for this was presented: who would be a good candidate had been discussed after nominations were closed and a meeting was over. An alternative explanation was that one had no thoughts at the meeting, only afterthoughts when it was over.

40. *Thursday.* A nurse noted that the group had been working on the matter of people in difficulty. She was, therefore, bringing to the group's attention that [a particular patient] felt people didn't like her, and was growing more and more distressed. This patient, who was relatively new, had written a note to another patient, who had turned the note over to the nurses because he was worried about this patient's threats to harm herself.

The patient in question discussed her attempts to make friends. Three male patients had offered friendship but no one else was friendly; others have been unkind; if that keeps up she will harm herself. She was afraid she would not be kept here and during the few weeks since she had come she had not unpacked. She felt the only people who were nice to her were the staff. Her doctor had advised her to relax a little and not try so hard to make friends; he was worried about her desperation. In answer to a nurse's question how she would know she was getting friendship, she replied that she liked her friends to show they liked her, to tell her they liked her. "With a real friend, I can say what I want, do what I want, visit at any time of the day or night." She also said her problem went back a long time; her parents had never showed her any affection.

Members of the group told her that she was aggressive; that she had shown she really didn't want anything to do with the women, her first question being how many boys were here; that she had made it clear that friendship with her must be expressed publicly and physically, for example, by holding people's hands; that she had gone into people's rooms uninvited and used their personal possessions without permission, violating the important principle of right to privacy in one's own room; that she had forced herself between people on a couch where there was no room. One patient said he didn't mind staying up with her until four in the morning; others said that she had done better than most new patients in establishing friendly relations. She was told, however, that friendships have to be worked for, that they involve giving as well as getting.

The director of activities suggested that people might approach her through the committees, that she had expressed interest in the nursery school and in helping with the parties. A patient said she ought to try to make it in the work program before getting involved in those activities.

Concern was expressed about her promiscuity, her desire to relate to all the men physically. A number of the women commented acerbically that they could not pass that kind of test for friendship. A male patient wondered about his sounding so priggish in discussing this; a woman said she was uncomfortable with physical contact; and another that she was perhaps jealous of this open sexuality. A male patient said he had gone out with her but had not liked it when she took his hand.

A patient commented that he thought the group was now too ready to respond to dramatic presentations of individual difficulty. Friendships should be based on something other than needfulness and problems. Another said he would refuse any friendship offered on the terms, "Accept me as I am unconditionally." There was a good deal of anger expressed about the patient's threats to harm herself; although others also admitted having done this, the general feeling was that such a threat was unfair.

A woman patient said she had offered to help [the new patient] unpack. The latter said she appreciated it, but thought it was done because after all they shared the same bathroom. That response made another woman patient angry: "That's how you slap people in the face when they make a friendly gesture!"

Toward the end of the meeting, I commented that it sounded as if there were a lot of good care to be had in the group. There seems to be some jumpiness that now that has been seen, a lot of people will want that care and be making requests. Maybe we will have more requests. General laughter.

41. *Friday.* I did not attend this meeting. A patient said she wanted to discuss with the group the fact that she has to reject the sexual advances of men here, leaving her feeling destructive and guilty and the men impotent. She wanted to hear from other women about this. Various patients made comments about the rules of society and how these conflict with sexual needs; how people use sex as a kind of "sounding board" in relations with others; how feeling rejected hurts even when you know the problem may be in the person doing the rejecting. People use sex in different ways and for different purposes: to exploit fantasies of being a movie star or Don Juan; to get close to others, even while fearing this; to avoid closeness with others; to validate one's own person. There was some argument about whether discussing this subject

in the community meeting was appropriate; did confession not belong in therapy? There was some attempt to define the values about sex currently held in the community: so long as it isn't public knowledge, it is okay behind closed doors; affectionate displays in public make people want to look the other way; sexual activity used to be flaunted and apparently approved by the administration, but is now handled in better taste and more circumspectly.

WEEK THIRTEEN

42. *Monday.* There was an announcement about the expected arrival of two new patients and the need for patient sponsors. There was some effort to elicit information from a staff member about a group relations conference he had attended; his disinclination to discuss this experience at this meeting led to the proposal for a patient-staff evening program on the conference.

A nurse reported that she was in a dilemma and wanted help from the group. What should she do, knowing that there was a patient in trouble, who was not at the meeting, who was closeted in her room with a "Do Not Disturb" sign on her door? The patient had asked the nurse not to discuss her at the community meeting, and yet she (the nurse) felt she ought to bring the patient's needs to the attention of the community, especially since the latter had been rejecting contacts with members of the community and had slept overnight at a motel over the weekend to get away from the inn.

The patient's name emerged. The nurse was told by patients that she should not make a promise not to discuss a patient at the community meeting, when it was part of her job as a nurse to do so, especially since the instruction, "Don't bring me up in the meeting," is often a patient's way of requesting to be brought up at the meeting. The formulation that appeared most acceptable to patients and the nurse was that the nurse should tell a patient she plans to bring her up at the meeting because she is worried about her.

Various patients reported efforts to be with this patient. The suggestion was made that her friends, not her acquaintances, should try to see her now. A nurse suggested about the sign that people knock and see what happens: "all she can do is not answer."

I pointed out that it was a nurse who had asked for the group's help, not the patient in question, and that we were not clear why the nurse felt that the sign on the door was a problem and not simply an indication that a patient wanted to be alone for a while.

The nurse said she was worried that the patient might do herself some harm and therefore about her being alone.

I wondered if the nurse was then asking the group how attention and companionship could be supplied to this patient around the clock.

The group's attention was drawn to someone weeping. She was upset because she had tried to talk to the patient being discussed and was told by the latter she didn't want help, that she only wanted attention from the nurses, because she didn't want to be in debt to other patients. In addition another patient was in trouble; he had been drunk at four in the morning and left the inn: "why had he been allowed to drive away in a drunken state?" According to the nurse, the patient had not been drunk, and had left with his wife, who apparently was going to drive.

Difficulties in "helping" were discussed: the person being helped doesn't want to be under obligation to others; the helper wants to see immediate visible results; the helped person then feels he has to repay attention by a change in attitude or expression, which is an additional burden for someone who is miserable.

I commented that "help" was apparently thought of with a capital "H," rather than in terms of simple practical things that might be done in a specific situation.

43. *Tuesday.* A new patient co-chairman took office at this meeting. He announced the meeting was open in a way that led me to say, "That sounds ominous, as if we're at the edge of a pit."

The next comments concerned the flowers in the room, and a call for appreciation for the work of the greenhouse crew.

A nurse commented on the sequence of patients who had attempted to harm themselves in the same way. What do we do about this?

The events of the previous evening were recounted with considerable feeling. A young woman had harmed herself. The doctor on duty had called a special meeting to tell people what had happened. This was described as getting people out of their beds and baths and rounding them up, arousing anxiety; then people found the act involved didn't seem very serious. Others resented this patient's "bouncing good spirits" both before and after the special meeting. Anger was expressed at the doctor who had called the meeting. Is hurting oneself becoming a model for asking for help? Patients reported that their attempts to control their own self-destructive impulses were being threatened by the acting out of these impulses by others.

I commented that I heard the anger in the room.

The next problem preoccupying the group was whether or not the act constituted a serious suicidal effort. No, because the hospital doesn't take suicidal patients. The patient being discussed said that she didn't intend to kill herself, but also that her smiling and bouncing behavior might be deceptive. The interpretation was made by another patient that the patient in question might be getting some satisfaction out of this situation.

I commented on the difficulty of distinguishing the degrees of seriousness of various signals of distress.

The events of the evening were reported further. A patient had seen her beginning to hurt herself; the behavior was made light of and she was asked not to mention it, but she did tell the nurses. Another patient reported inviting her to the movies; she refused.

Another patient also saw her hurting herself and was shocked to hear from her that the nurses knew about this behavior. She left not knowing what to do.

I commented that everyone seemed to have the psychotherapist in mind as the model for help: sitting and talking to someone, exploring with them what the trouble is. Simple, practical things are not mentioned.

P: What should I have done? *I:* Take [the implement used for self-injury] away. *P:* Yes.

I discussed the recent events in the community: how angry people were at the expectation that they could be helping and caring for people; how this seemed to be experienced as a burden, so that patients competed to be the person being helped rather than the person expected to give help. I thought that perhaps skills other than talking skills might have to be learned.

A patient said that if he didn't try to think about these people as a psychotherapist would, he'd just think they were silly.

I suggested that each situation might have to be examined as a different one, especially the social context in which someone is asking for help, and that each situation might require different action. I asked the patient who had harmed himself after being sent from the nurses' room why he had gone there. He said, "because I was afraid to go to my own room." I commented that the specific problem then in that situation was what do we do when someone is afraid to go to his room. *P:* A lot of people feel that way at times. *Nurse:* How about some arrangement whereby someone could have a temporary roommate? *P:* How about sleeping in the living room, library, nurses' room? *P:* I'm not in favor of a lot of bodies lying around the common rooms of the inn at night.

I said I thought the suggestion about roommates was interesting. *P* (exposing secrets): That's what goes on now! *P:* That's a nutty idea. It will upset the whole place. *P:* What are you afraid of? You make it sound as if everybody is going to need a roommate all the time. We're talking about emergencies.

44. *Thursday. P:* A long weekend is coming up; it looks like a bad scene for me and maybe for some others.

Various activities available over the holiday weekend were mentioned: a party Friday night; concerts in the area on Saturday and Sunday. Organizing a baseball game was suggested and rejected. A volleyball game was a possibility. How about an outing to the ocean? The ocean's far away. How about making up skits making fun of this place; has that ever been done? Not in an organized way.

A member of the activities staff reminded the group that the activities committee had a budget and a variety of subcommittees; "why is the machinery being ignored?"

There were further listings of the activities available in the area. One patient accused another of saying that the activities committee meetings were boring: "Why don't you change your attitude toward the meetings and the weekends?" Another patient said she would not be in the inn over the weekend; in this community, there is no one to talk to and no quiet companionship. There was a discussion of the contradiction involved in her complaint about lack of companionship and her plan to go away to be alone.

I commented that the effort to plan for the weekend seemed to be undercut by the statements that everything is hopeless, so why try to do anything.

There were a few more suggestions; a member of the activities staff wondered about the program committee. The response was that the program committee does not plan programs for weekends because of the lack of audience then for speakers or performers.

A patient asked if the staff were invited to the Friday night party. A stammering and somewhat embarrassed-sounding explanation was given by a patient concerning the traditions and nature of these parties; that staff do not come was a fact of community life.

A discussion of the legality of bingo—as a possible party activity—followed, as well as complaints about the TV room and TV set.

A staff person discussed the intolerable burden that a day off often seems to be for people, and how in hospitals frequently some patient chooses and is "chosen" by the group to be the sickest one so that the other patients can busy themselves with taking care of somebody rather than be burdened with the pleasure of a holiday.

P: The competition for the sick role around here would be fierce. *P:* Why don't we have a treasure hunt and discharge the winner? Laughter. There were reminiscences of a weekend hunt for archeological relics at the farm of a staff member.

I commented on the usefulness of planning for such happenings, and wondered why the apparatus for initiating activities was ignored. Why does no action seem possible?

There were pleas for spontaneous activities and arguments against planning. *P:* I think that if you have a good idea you ought to keep it to yourself and then let it pop out at the right moment as if you, also, were surprised that you had just thought of it. It was pointed out that traditionally the group either does something over such a weekend as a matter of duty or abandons itself to a bacchanal. *P:* If people are doing nothing, it is because that is what they want to do, and no one should bother them. *P:* But people who look unhappy keep others from having fun; when someone looks like that, I feel it's wrong to go on enjoying myself.

I commented that the party sounded as if it was going to be a dreary affair. *P:* It is interesting how we plan to have parties knowing that these always turn out to be disastrous for some people. *P:* Yes, the worst things around here happen during and after parties.

45. *Friday.* A patient member of the synanon groups requested that these groups be discussed in the community meeting, because of the increasing awareness of members of these groups of opposition from patients (on the whole, silent) and especially from staff (increasingly apparent).

Information emerged during the discussion. Two patients and one staff person had left the groups, the former on the recommendations of their doctors, the latter because he felt it conflicted with his job in the community. Other patients were mentioning their doctors' warnings that these groups might be detrimental to them. A review of the origin of the groups was given by a patient. Some patients had been impressed after a visit to a Synanon House; the ex-addicts there had sneered at how much money the patients here spent for therapy; the members of the Synanon House eschewed the help of professionals. At a patient-staff meeting on drugs, a staff member had described his visit to a Synanon House; what struck one patient was that ex-addicts could tell one another not to be babies, to grow up and start acting like mature adults. The work committee decided to go and visit Synanon; on the way back, in the car of the staff representative to the work committee, the group found themselves speaking differently to one another. The staff representative to the work committee had been so impressed by the honesty and directness of this encounter that he had suggested, and others had agreed, to go on meeting and trying to relate to one another in this way.

Dilemmas and issues were stated during the course of the meeting. Patients believe they are having honest, open discussions on their own, but are actually dependent upon the participation of such staff members as the staff representative to the work committee. Patients have been heard to say that they are getting more out of their synanon group than psychotherapy. The Synanon theory is that insight is not essential, that it is helpful to "go through the motions." Are the synanon groups opposed to psychotherapy and what the hospital stands for? Patients join the synanon groups for companionship, which is not available elsewhere in the community. Does leaving such a group mean you can't get back in or that the group will be so far ahead of you that you'll feel out of place should you return? Q: Why are the groups closed? Why can't people attend to see what they're like? A: Commitment is required. The frankness sought depends upon not discussing elsewhere what is discussed in the group. Q: Do members of synanon groups tend not to speak up at community meetings? Are these groups opposed to the community program? A: No, some participate and some do not; some are among the most responsible members of the community. P: Members of synanon groups try to talk to one another, not make speeches at one another or hide from one another as this meeting and room encourage.

My interventions were along the following lines. Let us approach these groups as social scientists. What are the satisfactions these groups offer their members? Are these satisfactions unavailable within the formal structure of the community program as it now exists? For example, a "couch group" used to meet in the front hall; it seemed to be the only place where patients could poke fun at the goings-on at the hospital. Perhaps now that some of these feelings can be expressed in the community meetings, such a group may be no longer necessary and in fact seems to have disappeared. If the synanon groups are viewed partly as involving a criticism of the hospital, understanding what that criticism is might be turned into something useful for the community.

Another staff member interpreted the participation in the synanon groups as the experience of freedom from some kind of oppression. However, frankness of communication—for example, in public toilets— is not necessarily responsible communication. Rebellion against oppression can take two forms: flight (for example, emigration) or fight (stand one's ground and try to change things). Why don't the members of the synanon groups return from their emigration and try to work within the community?

The response to his comments largely consisted of denial that any rebellion motivated the members of these groups.

Toward the end of the meeting I was challenged by one patient to give my reasons for being against these groups. When I said that it was up to the synanon groups to decide whether they wanted to continue meeting or not, that it was my job to point out that the existence of these groups is a comment on the hospital and its program, which I felt we should try to understand, I was heatedly accused by another patient of using my power to get rid of the groups.

At the end of the meeting, a patient said good-bye to the group.

WEEK FOURTEEN

Monday. Holiday.

46. *Tuesday.* A new patient was introduced. A movie committee meeting was announced. *P:* It was a pretty good weekend.

A series of angry statements and challenges by patients directed at staff followed. *P:* Where is the sheet telling where patients' money goes that used to be on the bulletin board? *P:* It's outdated since the fees have been raised. *P:* Can I see a copy of it? *P:* It's available at the business office.

P: Why are there so many nurses here; are we expecting a crisis or is this just the usual inefficiency? *Nurse:* Three nurses are on duty and have to be at the meeting, and I'm here because I'm interested. *P:* Why are there two nurses on duty in the evening, when all they do is sit around and knit? *Nurse:* The nursing station must be covered to take care of all eventualities; nurses knit to stay awake. *P:* Why has nothing been done to establish open patient-nurse meetings in the evening? *Nurse:* The idea is both good and bad; I, personally, would like to see a meeting earlier in the day; isn't the community meeting a type of patient-nurse meeting? *P:* Patients want a late evening meeting with the nurses to discuss potential trouble spots. *Nurse:* Nurses need to discuss things which cannot be shared with patients, for example, purely staff matters or confidences of patients; I wouldn't want to have a closed part of the meeting, when I would have to say: "Go home now, kiddies." *P:* That's what you're saying now! *P:* Why are you so defensive?

I commented: "Perhaps because she is being attacked." I used as an example the statement about "inefficiency."

P: Perhaps the hospital is set up to be inefficient; a cost accounting or time study of the hospital would show this. *P:* Patients pay too much. *P:* Now that patients are about to take on new work responsibilities, maybe we could do away with some staff and save ourselves some money. *P:* People become outpatients because they can't afford to stay in the hospital. *P:* Why can't outpatients attend community meetings? *P:* Maybe they don't attend because they're not interested. *P:* Because of not having money, outpatients are denied important aspects of the program.

I commented that one function of the synanon groups might be to meet the need of outpatients (who were active in these groups) for continued contact with the hospital.

P: The Friday night party's only purpose was to get people drunk: the room is dark; the music is loud; people don't communicate; it is impossible for anyone to have a good time. *P:* I communicated; I had a good time; I like it dark; I like loud music. *P:* That's why people don't speak up at these meetings; when they do, they immediately get attacked.

I commented that perhaps the patients feel themselves to be rich, spoiled kids, who have everything but don't work, so cannot allow themselves to have fun. For this reason, perhaps, the help of others has to be rejected; the poor people of Synanon or at [an English hospital recently discussed at a patient-staff program] are envied.

P (angrily): I see red; you call us rich, spoiled kids! *P:* Only rich people are supposed to be able to afford to get sick. *P:* I'm supposed to be sick, but I don't feel sick; I can enjoy myself.

A member of the activities staff, going back to the discussion of the party, wondered who says what kind of party it shall be. It sounds as if the rules were imposed from outside, he added, but actually the party subcommittee of the activities committee could make arrangements that would be more satisfactory.

I wondered if the group did not have a stake in the activities committee's not making satisfactory arrangements for real fun.

P: I think you go too far; perhaps that's what it looks like to you as a member of the staff. We are not guilty because we are rich but because each of us has done things he regrets and because of that guilt we can't enjoy ourselves.

I wondered if perhaps the fact that the patients tend to be wealthy, and members of the staff not, colored relations between these two groups. How much do patients feel they have to suffer and make up for that?

P: I have feelings about that. *P:* The patients are getting poorer and the staff is getting richer. Laughter. *P:* The staff here makes much less than they could in private practice. *P:* The staff should be paid more. *P:* Or we should pay less.

The patient co-chairman wondered if a rearrangement of the chairs in the room might make for a better discussion.

47. *Thursday.*. The seats were arranged in a single row semi-circle facing the couch on which the chairmen sit; people were encouraged to sit within the semi-circle after chairs were filled rather than behind it. *P:* I'm glad; now I'll be able to hear everyone. It was suggested jokingly that a patient lie on the table in front of the couch "to be dissected."

P: I've noticed the new doctors [fellows] are no longer speaking in the meeting; have they been told not to?

I said they had been asked to participate as observers. All the staff participating do so as part of some job they have in the comunity. I explained the structure of the community program staff.

P: Do you realize the dampening effect of having so many observers?

I said that the community program staff had discussed this and did not know how many observers the meeting could tolerate; another possibility would be to have fellows rotate in the role of observers, perhaps one at a time.

There were many angry comments about this arrangement largely directed at me. Issues of importance to the group included the following. Does staff presence here as part of their jobs mean their attendance is involuntary and unwilling? Are other therapy staff members being kept out of the meeting? What does this do to our efforts to improve patient-staff relations? Is the community becoming a series of compartments? Why was this information not given to us before?

I said that the staff had discussed the question about communication of its thinking about staff participation, and the decision had been to wait until there was some concern about this matter.

A patient commented to me that I was being seen as pulling all the strings and that the way out for someone in my position was to share responsibility with the rest of the staff so that I would not have to bear the brunt of the patient's attacks.

Another concern expressed was that the perception of the new doctors as "in training" depreciates their worth.

I commented that the fact that some of the doctors come to the hospital for training is one of the things everyone knows but doesn't want to mention openly.

A member of the activities staff was asked if he was supposed to keep quiet. He said, "certainly not." P (sotto voce): He just doesn't dare to speak.

P: Now I feel I'm being observed. P: Patients don't participate at these meetings; are we calling for more staff participation to cover up that fact? P: If more staff participated, more patients would. P: I am disgusted by this arrangement; I'm being told that I'm different, that I'm sick; I don't want to come to these meetings anymore. P: We don't have any real say in how the meetings are conducted, even though we were told we do. A patient asked me if I was going to be staff chairman for life. P: Why should we be asked to have open discussions, when the staff has secret discussions?

I commented that the patients had been making many decisions in fact about what to bring up at the meetings (for example, the synanon groups) and what not to bring up (the new work program proposals).

P: I think we're going back to our earlier preoccupations with what the staff thinks and does; the group has made progress since we left those preoccupations behind; now maybe everything the meeting is on the way to achieving will be lost. P: I can't accept an arrangement which stops some doctors from speaking and keeps others from coming to the meeting altogether.

I interpreted the anger at the failure of some therapy staff members to attend as based on a conception of the meeting as extra therapy. But it was actually a meeting to work on the problems of living together in a community like this.

This comment was greeted by threats that patients would become silent observers too, by many expressions of being "sunk in depression," and by tentative decisions not to come anymore. P: Haven't you all been looking for an excuse to justify feelings you already had? Surely the information shared at this meeting couldn't have caused these feelings.

I wondered if the anger that had been present in the meetings for some time might have to do with the fact that people are being asked to be, and have made steady progress in becoming, the competent people they are.

P: Now I know why we need to have the synanon groups; it's the only place where everyone is equal.

I commented on the amount of black-and-white thinking going on: if one does something because it's one's job to do it, then one can't also want to do it; if one does not have the power to influence certain events, then this automatically makes one more of a patient.

Patient co-chairman: Anyone object to the new seating arrangements? P: I like it.

48. *Friday.* A new patient was introduced; three more expected. Sponsors were sought.

At this meeting the group discussed the fact that the work committee had "fired" a patient from the work program. The committee had spent a great deal of time trying to get him to work; he refused to make up the work he had not done and did not show up at the morning work meetings. Some patients defended the "fired" patient, deeming the committee's action unusual, unfair (in that patients with poorer work records were not being so penalized), and its attempts to help the patient to work inadequate. Others reported their efforts to help the patient in question by working alongside him, efforts that had been rebuffed by him. Some attempt was made to explore the consequences of his having been fired; the clinical director made the point that less money would be allocated to the patient aid fund if other patients did not make up the work that had not been done. There was some reluctance to consider the possibility that others could do his work.

Statements were made by other patients that they did not like doing the work either; that the amount of money going to the patient aid fund as a result of their labors was infinitesimal compared to the fees they were paying; the patients actually found themselves more isolated from other patients as a result of the way in which they had been assigned to projects. There was an effort to clarify who was to blame, the patient who had been fired or the committee. The former's insouciance and provocation was clear in his contributions to the discussion; in addition, he was eager to accept the blame. Anger was expressed at the amount of time being spent on him, when he "didn't care." No one knew what would happen to him now that he had been "fired"; he had already been referred to the social problems council and put on probation by the medical director. Did the work committee's "giving up" mean that the whole community now gave up on him? A patient felt that he would envy the patient who had been fired if the latter got away with all this. Others chimed in to agree that they didn't like doing the work either.

I wondered if the work committee was in some way setting itself up to be attacked in the same way that the patient who had been fired had. For example, the committee at present seemed to be functioning in a way to avoid open discussion of its plans for expanding the work program, ignoring the grumbling that existed, and postponing consideration of the doubts people might have.

The meeting ended with a comment about a patient not at the meeting who was depressed and turning down offers of conversation and companionship. I wondered if the members of her small group, who knew her pretty well, might be able to get together and discuss what help the group might be. This was translated to mean the group's going off to visit the patient; that suggestion was rejected. It was also pointed out that the patient didn't like her small group. A nurse asked that people keep on trying, expect to be rebuffed, and not give up.

49. *Monday.* Two new patients were introduced.

A report was given on the film program selected for the year by the movie committtee; the chairman hoped there would be little objection, because there was little objectors could now do about the selections. There was some question about the number of "experimental" films, and suggestions for post-showing discussion and program notes. The cost of movies, the budget of the committee, the means of procuring films, and the suggestion (supported strongly by a nurse) that films be available on holidays, were all discussed.

A question concerning the number of days doctors took off for a particular holiday was not answered by anyone on the staff. P: "They are not allowed to speak!" A Blue Cross movie on the high cost of hospitalization was suggested. The discussion on movies ended with congratulations to the committee, and an uncomfortable pause created by some irrelevant remarks by a patient.

A nurse commented that a new patient was worried because everyone acted so well around the inn that she felt out of place; the nurse asked the group to reassure her. Some comments were made by patients that they all had bad times, too; that some patients were in their rooms during this meeting; that others had felt the same way when they first arrived.

A patient asked for further discussion about how other patients felt about the fellows' not being able to participate. A number of comments were made indicating that patients felt their control over the meeting was being taken away. A patient felt that many of the discussions at the meeting had been good, except for the times when patients become preoccupied with what the meetings are about and how they are organized. A patient asked the clinical director about his participation and how it was defined; he said he attended the meetings as a member of the community council and would speak up about anything that concerned the community if he could make a contribution. A member of the activities staff said he commented on activities but also on work since he had been sitting in on the work committee. There was an attempt by a patient to get the group to discuss the work committee proposal, but this was ignored in favor of further discussion of who has the power in the community, patients or staff. *P:* The staff has the power to make certain arrangements, but each patient has the power to stay away from the meetings or refuse to participate in them; thus the patients have the power to end the meeting. Uneasiness about my silence was expressed.

50. *Tuesday.* The group discussed the plans for expanding the work program. (The proposal, distributed about a month previous to this meeting, was designed to provide "real work" for the patient work force, making the work program responsible for all housekeeping work in the inn, shop, and nursery school; the grounds around the inn, shop, and nursery school; and dining room service—setting up for meals, cleaning tables. A housekeeper and supervisor of buildings and grounds would keep the work committee informed of work to be done and be available for advice and information. A maid and houseman would be continued in their jobs, for example, to prepare rooms for incoming patients and do the routine six-month cleaning of all rooms and the inn.)

The patient work scheduler announced he had resigned that morning at the meeting of the work committee, feeling he had doubts about the expansion of the work program and that he was not alone in these. He thought the incentive to work should be increased before increasing the work itself. In response to this, a patient said he couldn't respect hmself if he didn't work and elaborated the philosophy upon which the proposal was based: that patients should care for the areas in which they live, rather than depend upon others to take care of them. A patient retorted one could believe in this philosophy and still have doubts and questions. The staff representative to the work committee thought the scheduler had not resigned that morning and hoped he wouldn't

The supporters of the proposal made the following points. The community could now decide the conditions under which it wanted to live; if it wanted the grass to be two feet high, it could leave it that way. Patients would no longer be working in areas that did not have to do with their own lives and activities. The foreman would now be in charge instead of simply the middle man between his crew and a member of the maintenance or activities staffs. It was hoped that the work program would own its own tools instead of having to depend upon the tools of the maintenance staff, which were not always available. Six patients would be assigned to the dining room to work a full week once every seven weeks; this crew could then make its own individual arrangements for its work. It is better to be responsible for oneself, since then one can live in as sloppy a fashion as one wishes; the inn is too much like a hotel now.

The staff representative to the work committee suggested that the group seemed preoccupied with things that might go wrong, and how to punish people who wouldn't go along; perhaps it would make more sense to solve problems as they came up. He felt silence was assumed to mean opposition; why not assume it means assent? Work is therapeutic because a patient who is actively engaged in other areas of living can engage more productively in psychotherapy; there are important aspects of life other than psychotherapy, and work is an important source of learning and rewards.

There was some concern expressed about the possibility that in the new program people wouldn't be working as much together, that is, physically contiguous. An objection to the proposal was made on the grounds that it emphasized obligations to do one's duty to the community. A suggestion was made that the plan be put into effect by stages, starting with the abolition of the requirement for making up work missed, continuing with arrangement for willing workers to replace nonworkers in the interest of getting work done, and finally later taking over new work areas. *P:* The way people look at me I get the feeling they think I'm not *for* work; I am *for* work.

I wondered if it was difficult for people to ask questions about the proposal, because any doubts were interpreted as opposition to a moral view of principle.

P: I just feel that it is too much; the new plan makes me uncomfortable because it may just be too much work.

51. *Thursday.* An announcement was made that the housekeeper was complaining that towels were disappearing. A new patient was introduced.

A mimeographed sheet containing the new work program proposals was distributed. There was a series of questions and answers about various details.

A member of the activities staff wanted the shop to have its six-month cleaning on the same basis as the inn, by someone hired to do it; a patient replied that the assignment of patients to do this job had worked out well.

There was a discussion of room inspections. *P:* I like to keep my room in disorder; isn't that all right? *P:* Rooms have to be kept in shape for the next occupant. *P:* Are rooms to be kept like marine barracks? *Nurse:* The rooms have to be kept clean for a number of reasons; for example, the bathroom porcelain wears out and is expensive to replace. *P:* Dirt doesn't wear things out. *P:* Accumulation of dirt calls for more drastic cleaning methods, which eat into the porcelain. Comments about various cleansers. *P:* It all sounds like a television commercial for cleansers.

A patient argued for patients' doing the six-months cleaning too, right now; a maid means "I'm incapable of taking care of my own room." There were a number of objections to this; the suggestion was made that this be an option for a patient who wanted to do it.

After a series of angry interchanges, the silence of others was interpreted as anger. Some patients had stayed away from the meeting purposely, protesting the lack of participation of staff.

I noted that during the time patients were doing a competent job of coping with community problems, for example, the holiday weekend, anxiety had grown and reached a peak; when another patient performed an act of self-injury, the group simply became angry and refused to deal with her. More and more since then we have heard comments that what is expected of us is too much, we don't want to be bothered any more, we want to be "patients." Then the staff was blamed for making patients patients. Meanwhile, the group was ignoring that another patient had injured herself in the same way as the previous patients had done, that a patient had left the community under circumstances that concerned people, and that another patient had been depressed and had remained in her room a long time.

There were further comments about my "authoritarianism" and the fact that I had provided the patients with the model of the silent observer.

I commented that the patients were reaching for things to be angry about; for example, there had been a frequent repetition of three distortions of what I said previously: first, that it was my decision to have the fellows participate as observers—rather than the decision of the community program staff; second, that staff were not allowed to speak, although many were doing so; third, that nothing can be done by patients to alter a situation they don't like.

I was then asked for and gave further explanation of what it meant for a staff person to participate in the meeting in terms of his job in the community—that a staff person could contribute to any discussion about anything but would probably do so from the point of view of his own position in the community. I used the analogy of the team in which everyone can depend upon everyone else to do his job.

52. *Friday.* A new patient was introduced. A patient who slept dur-

ing the meeting was told by the patient co-chairman she shouldn't be there if she continued to sleep.

The plan to call a patient meeting, proposed by the work committee and to be acted upon by the community council, was mentioned; the purpose of such a meeting would be to discuss and vote upon the work proposal.

Q: Who will make the decision after people express their preferences about the area in which they want to work? *A:* It will be worked out by the foremen and schedulers on the basis of rotating people through different areas and previous records of satisfatcory work. *Q:* Who will complain if someone doesn't live up to his work obligations? *A:* A fellow worker, administrators of the work program, or the work crew—anyone feeling the effects of non-participation.

P: I am concerned about the dining room; the lawns can be left un-mowed and the individual rooms messy, but if the dining room gets dirty and the service poor . . . . *P:* Including the dining room jobs is crucial because anything not getting done will provoke immediate reaction; by the way, there weren't enough hamburgers at the barbe-cue. *P* (food representative): That has been a problem and I will take steps to take care of it.

A staff member pointed out that this exchange indicated that the community had in the community meeting a means for solving its problems about the work program on a day-to-day basis; if the new program ran into difficulties, we would hear about them and people could then act to correct them. We can't anticipate all the problems, but the potential for indignation in the room is a mechanism of self-regulation.

A patient commented that she didn't like the plan because it involved too much regulation. She was quizzed, and her answers attacked, somewhat relentlessly.

I intervened as a protector, noting that when people begin to express their feelings, they are immediately asked to defend them. I thought the fear, just expressed, of being "locked in a machine" should be respected. A staff person agreed, remarking that whatever was said about how the new plan would work was a fantasy since no one could know until it was tried. The group ought to get its fantasies about the program out since that was the way of testing it bit by bit. There is nothing wrong with fantasies; they are the start of all plans for action in reality.

P: I have a fantasy that there is someone or many on the staff (and among the patients) who are waiting to step in at the first sign of difficulty to say they knew the patients couldn't do it and that this or that new responsibility should be taken away.

The clinical director said there were certain staff people who felt the patients couldn't take over these responsibilities and carry them out effectively. But most of the staff feel the new plan needs time to work itself out and that a certain amount of disorder is part of that process.

Another staff person suggested that if someone wanted to know what the limits were and who the police were, he should let the place get really filthy and he would then find out.

P: I think the fantasy is that the new program will change the community; I don't think it will.

The staff representative to the work committee wondered if the objection to the inclusion of the dining room made earlier has to do with people handling dishes and silverware with dirty fingernails. This was denied.

There seemed to be general agreement, in response to a demand for another vote, that there was nothing wrong with having a new vote at a patient meeting, now that the issue had been discussed further.

WEEK SIXTEEN

53. *Monday.* An invitation was issued for people to join those working in the nursery school.

Discussion of the work program centered around the wish to have an experimental period, people's fears that they would be required to work longer than the now existing norm of one hour a day, and reassurances that if anything less time would be required.

A patient was asked about how she felt at her staff conference. *P:* I felt like I was on TV; there were so many doctors there and so many microphones.

A small group was asked why it had been unable to elect a representative to the community council. A nurse suggested that perhaps it was because the job was a thankless one; no one ever tells members of the community council that they do a good job.

I was asked to comment, since I was a member of the small group in question. I said that the high point of the group's thinking was the attempt to decide who was the sickest person in the group so that he could have the assignment since "it would do him good."

P: Why couldn't the person most qualified be chosen? Smiles.

A question was asked about relatives staying overnight; permission from nurses was required.

A patient brought up another who had twice inflicted self-injury upon herself; she's invisible most of the time; her door has a "Do Not Disturb" sign. *Nurse:* What do we do about a sign like that? *P:* I ignore them. *P:* A sign like that is the way the community used to be. The patient in question said that a sign like that meant she was sleeping: "I don't feel I'm invisible, but I do feel people don't care what I do." A patient discussed how isolated the patient in question was; even in the work program, she worked alone. *P:* Why hadn't the staff brought her to the attention of the group, as had been done with other patients? *Nurse:* The nurses goofed.

I wondered if the group assumed when the staff did not bring up such a situation it was because the staff didn't want it discussed. I also mentioned the concern about the return of a patient who had left the hospital, as well as about the staff's decision about a patient's staying.

The first patient announced she had returned as an inpatient; the second that the staff had decided he ought to stay. The clinical director discussed the staff's decision: it would be helpful for him to stay, even though he has been a problem in the community and was now being returned to the community; he was capable of working when he wanted to, but was not willing to share in the responsibilities of the community; the community could continue to try and work with him or could refuse to.

The patient in question spoke heatedly about being fed up with being the community scapegoat; he didn't feel he was the only one undercutting or finding fault with the work program; he went on to discuss the inefficiency of the work schedulers.

P: You won't have any more trouble with people being annoyed with your staying on here now that you've praised us all and told us how much you like us. *P:* You're not angry because of your failure to work, but because you've just discovered that there were some people who would have been glad if the staff had told you to leave.

54. *Tuesday.* There was a discussion of the relationship between the community council and the community meetings. Some members of the community council felt that the community meeting had taken over some of its functions; evidence of this was that fewer social problems were being referred to, or discussed by, the community council. A nurse thought this might be so because the discussions at the community meeting might be helping to take care of things before people became social problems.

I thought the concern of the community council was understandable if it saw itself primarily as a discussion group. In that case, the question would be why should we repeat a discussion here that has been held in the community meeting, or why should we discuss in the community meeting what it is our function and responsibility to discuss in the community council? Perhaps the community council would not feel so concerned if it saw itself as an action group. To the extent, however, that it found itself not able to make decisions, its morale would suffer.

There was reluctance to discuss the work program proposal in view of the fact that a vote would be taken at a Wednesday patient meeting. An expression of apathy and anger seemed to be related to a feeling that there was no way that things could be gotten done or events influenced by the community.

55. *Thursday.* There was some discussion of the fact that a patient with whom many were uncomfortable would be staying, following the recommendation of the staff conference. Patients directed comments at her, asking her to change the ways she had of annoying others, and to participate more adequately in the work program. A member of the activities staff suggested that she be invited to the next meeting of the activities committee in order to discuss her suggestion to prepare skits making fun of the hospital, which was greeted with apparent indifference by the group.

Following some comments about the few patients who were speaking, I commented that perhaps new patients come with enthusiasm but soon learn the way of life here from older patients and also then learn to teach this way of life to other new patients. New patients seem to be taught that suggestions for doing things don't go, that patients can't make a contribution to important decisions, and that the staff makes the important decisions—such as deciding to keep the two patients recently recommended by the staff conference to stay.

Another staff person spoke about the war going on in the meeting, which seemed to involve ignoring the purpose bringing patients and staff together; everyone who spoke in the meeting seemed to be told in one way or another to shut up.

56. *Friday.* A nurse opened the meeting by reporting the events of the previous night during which a patient had been drunk, angry, and extremely upset and upsetting to others. Another nurse reported that doors had been slammed so hard that paint and splinters were flying. People felt intimidated by his violence. There was some discussion about what might be troubling the patient in question, particularly in terms of his problems at home.

I commented that when people get upset we tend to think of the trouble coming from inside the person or from relationships with people outside the community. I suggested that it might be useful to the community if we might look at such events in terms of what was at that time going on in the community, some state of affairs that might contribute to such upsets.

There were some remarks about the patient's anger at the female patient with whom he had constantly been. A great deal of information emerged about how patients and nurses had cooperated and helped one another to cope with the distressing events of the previous night.

Toward the end of the meeting, objection was made about the assignment to the shop crew of a patient who did not participate in shop activities in preference to a patient who did so participate and also wanted to be assigned to that crew. When the scheduler said it was not his decision to make, I thought it probably was, that someone had to make such decisions; but that we hoped the person who had to make the decisions would hear about how people felt about such assignments at the community meeting, and could then take others' opinions and suggestions into account when making such decisions.

The meeting ended with the singing of "For He's a Jolly Good Fellow" and applause in honor of a staff person who was leaving the hospital.

WEEK SEVENTEEN

57. *Monday.* There was some discussion of the first day of the newly expanded work program. There was some indication that things were going well; the inn and shop looked good. The first two meals in the dining room had also gone well; the question was raised: "Are we going to be cooking our own meals too?" *P:* That is for the future. Laughter. No one had cleaned in one area, however.

The discussion shifted to a patient who had spent a good deal of money over the weekend. Other patients had sold her things or were trying to sell her some of their personal possessions. The issue was brought up by a patient who had sold her twenty dollars' worth of records. In the course of the discussion, she was advised by others how to handle her money and how to alter her behavior so she might receive the kind of attention and friendship that, it was assumed, she was seeking through money and other gifts.

I tried to clarify what approach might be taken to this problem: was it a problem of someone who had difficulty holding on to money? or a person being taken advantage of? or a patient who was "high" and spending impulsively in this abnormal state?

Toward the end of the meeting, a patient reproached the group for encouraging the patient in question in the kind of behavior people were now saying they did not like. She had come to a party wearing too formal dress; it seemed to him that many people had taken a sadistic pleasure in encouraging her to sing; she had a good voice but egging her on to twelve encores was like encouraging someone to jump off a roof or taking pleasure in watching an ex-champion boxer wrestle for fifty dollars.

58. *Tuesday.* A patient said that he had been encouraged by a nurse to bring up at the meeting that he was feeling bloody awful and as though he were going to explode. He had been desperately trying to sleep but couldn't and had finally awakened another patient who had sat with him until he fell asleep. People suggested participation in work projects or shop activities, and also discussed how he might seek out people to be with. He tried to leave the meeting at the end of this discussion, saying he was too tense to stay. I encouraged him to remain. He did so. At the end of the meeting, we shared the observation that although tense he had not exploded.

It was noted that people were cooperating with the dining room crew by bringing up their dirty dishes and carefully scraping and stacking them. However, the housekeeper was not sure what she should be doing or not doing; she was quite upset by the new program, as also the maids seemed to be. The head nurse said that maintenance people were always anxious during any period of change and suggested that patients be tolerant and understanding of them during this time.

A particular maid was talked about: her humbleness and obsequiousness. A patient bluntly suggested that she be fired; a number of other patients attacked him for his attitude. One told how he had found this maid on the verge of tears. He added that she wanted to be helpful but didn't understand exactly what was happening; she tried to do favors for patients such as fixing their beds, meanwhile saying, "Don't tell anyone or I will get fired." A patient likened impatience with the situation to rich people moving to a fancy neighborhood to get away from poor people; when the plight of poor people is brought to their attention, they feel they've paid money not to have this happen.

The superintendent of buildings and grounds was mentioned frequently as a crucial person in the situation. It was suggested that he be invited to the community meeting; this was countered by the information that he had been invited to a work committee meeting but had said he wasn't able to come.

I commented during the meeting (in response to a patient's saying that patients had a lot of power over what happens to other people) that patients occasionally caught a glimpse of the fact that they do have the power to influence events and people around them, but are apparently frightened by this power, the possible consequences of its exercise, and the responsibilities it implied, and apparently feel that sometimes it is better to be helpless.

59. *Thursday.* Three new patients were at the meeting. Some information about them was requested. An ex-patient appeared at the meeting, but objections were raised to his presence because of his possible effect upon the meeting, especially upon those who had not known him before; he left.

In response to a patient's asking about classes at a nearby college, another patient wondered whether a person who has only been in the hospital for a short time should be encouraged or allowed to spend so much time away from the community. The idea of preventing anyone from doing what they wanted to do was so obviously repugnant to the members of the group that he withdrew his comment.

There was some impatience expressed about the attention certain patients were receiving in the meetings.

A patient said she felt very despairing about what was going on in the community. A maid had come into the library while she was sitting there upset and had insisted that she had to vacuum immediately. The patient had gone to the housekeeper to ask her what the duties of the maids were. The housekeeper told her that she couldn't give the patient this information; that she gets her instructions from the superintendent; and that the patient should see him. Another patient pointed out that the patients had agreed not to bother the housekeeper but to go through the schedulers when such matters come up.

The same patient was disturbed about the situation at the nursery school; the patient who was assistant director was no longer coming, and it was difficult to get volunteers from the patient group to work there. She was also worried about the community newspaper, feeling she could not depend upon other patients for help with this. She was reassured by other patients that they would help her and told by them that she was exaggerating the difficulties.

A patient commented that people who are concerned seemed to be told over and over that things are not as bad as they see them. Is it possible that the group is not responding to their "real" concerns?

I wondered if patients were receiving conflicting messages. On the one hand, they are being encouraged to speak up about their feelings and to share their difficulties. On the other hand, people who do speak up are quickly told they shouldn't be feeling what they feel; it is as if anyone's misery is a burden upon all the rest; an effort must be made to get the miserable one out of the way.

60. *Friday.* Toward the beginning of the meeting, I asked where the nurses were. No one knew. I wondered if there was some crisis in the inn. Shortly afterwards, the head nurse came in and reported that a patient had taken an overdose of pills, had then come to the nurses and asked for help, had vomited up the pills, and was now all right.

The fact that this patient had been expecting a visit from her child that weekend and was very worried about the visit came out. She had evidently wanted her child to stay with her at the inn but was sure that other people would feel resentful or uncomfortable about this. People wondered how she had gotten this idea. Some comments had recently been made about the annoying behavior of some outpatient's children. A patient said he did feel some annoyance at the presence of children but would certainly be glad to keep such feelings to himself and put up with a little discomfort because of the importance to others of having their children visit.

There seemed to be a move to close the discussion off at this point with suggestions that people could reassure the patient in question about her concerns. I wondered if some people were not trying very hard to say that they do not get upset about things like children's being present, while others were trying very hard not to upset anyone else. Was being upset not acceptable around here?

A patient commented that he chose to face uncomfortable situations as a test of his ability to tolerate discomfort, but felt that other people in the group did not agree.

I wondered how long the patient being discussed had been worried about the visit of her child; it turned out that she had been thinking about this at least a week. I pointed this out as an example that apparently at least some patients felt it their duty not to let others know if they were upset or worried.

Others began to describe quite movingly their doubts and difficulties concerning their absence from their children, and the difficulties talking with children about being at the hospital. One patient said he wanted desperately to have his children visit him to correct any distorted notions they might have about "nuthouses" which they might have gotten from watching television. He wondered if parents could get together and arrange to have their children visit the same weekend so that the children would have something to do if they all got together. The fact that children make adults uncomfortable because they ask direct questions was discussed.

A patient said that he felt that anyone coming in from the outside makes this a better place for the time being, whether it be children, visitors, or speakers from programs. The head nurse said she thought the discussion had an underlying theme which related it to many other discussions: the theme of intruders, for example, the ex-patient who had appeared at the meeting recently, the maid, the visitors. She added that new patients also were a problem for the community.

Another patient said no one could help her with her feelings of guilt about her very young children. A patient turned to her saying, "Don't you do something desperate now. Give yourself and other people a chance and you may find that people can help."

Toward the end of the meeting, I commented that all hospitals tend to handle visitors differently. In a general hospital, for example, a visitor might sit at the bedside, a curtain drawn so other patients in the room could be ignored by or protected from the visitor. Some hospitals don't draw curtains and visitors find themselves talking to other patients in the room as well. Some hospitals only have visiting hours at certain specified times. At one hospital at which I worked we tried to arrange things so that the parents of patients could see one another as well as talk also to all the patients. I wondered if the community council perhaps could take up this issue and work out some arrangement which might make things easier for the visitors and for those who want to have guests; maybe, for example, there might be a day when all children would visit with some activities planned and even babysitting made available.

A patient said that was a good idea and that the community council would discuss it and perhaps report the results of the discussion in the minutes.

I said: "Why don't you tell us directly next week?"

The patient agreed to. Another patient came in to say that he thought this had been a good meeting.

At the end of the meeting I commented that the patient co-chairman had been very preoccupied for some time; it was apparently difficult for him at this time to take some responsibility for helping the discussion; I found things more difficult for me as a result and felt I needed help. The patient co-chairman said that he thought the problem he was having would go away soon. Another patient said that the rest of the patients could take more responsibility for keeping the meeting going.

PART II: IN THE BEGINNING

Change

The inauguration of the community meeting under the leadership of a relatively new staff member meant change.

The ultimate consequences of change could not even be guessed. Members of the staff themselves were angry, uncertain, skeptical, and divided. Faith in the benignity of future possibilities that might have arisen from a relationship to tried leaders was absent. Formulating in words the values of the process that had been initiated in the community meeting resulted in tentative commitments and also in fear and alienation. The initiators of change had to wait for the shared experiences of confidence, gratification, and solidarity, which would strengthen and maintain the first tenuous commitments, to come. Meanwhile, dread and apathy often overcame hope.

Change threatened existing values and normative arrangements. The immediate nature of that threat was soon adumbrated. Staff members were confronted by alien expectations, their positions altered; in some instances a staff member was displaced. The functions of staff groups and patient-staff groups suddenly seemed to shift from certain ground into a haze of shadowy doubt.

What did the sudden ubiquity of this word "community" and the alarming frequency of its concrete representation "the community meeting" portend? How important was "community" to become? More important than "individual?" That heteronomous values would have an increased potency, a greater opportunity for assertion and expression, seemed likely. How would the existing balance between heteronomous and autonomous values be affected? If consideration were increasingly given to the consequences of action for the community, what sacrifices might be exacted of, what limitations imposed upon, what claims made upon, individuals?

If the community's requirements for adaptation were to be met through greater openness and information-sharing, what would safeguard the individual's right to privacy? What potential assault upon his self-protective inclination to secrecy might he have to prepare to resist? If the community's requirements for integration were to be met through mutual help and by giving precedence at times to concern with the impact of one's behavior upon others over individual aims, what idiosyncratic wish, what imperative individual impulse, might have to go at least for a time ungratified?

No good comes without increase in misery. A greater group solidarity could not be welcome to an individual who was especially encrusted in and who treasured his isolation. In a congeries of separate, isolated individuals who actually take little notice of each other, except for going through certain conventional motions, not "belonging" troubles no one. No more than in a hotel is there anything to belong to. In a group of interacting, interdependent individuals, who share common

values and strive together to achieve common ends, the person who is
not a part, who cannot reach or respond to others, who cannot make a
contribution, cannot for long be regarded complacently by others or by
himself. He stands out. What he says or does jars. That he is "out of
step" and "out of tune" cannot be indefinitely ignored; but the awareness is painful. He may try to lead others away from the community;
success is uneasy and failure bitter. All this is as true for the staff member who has difficulty meshing his own efforts with those of others as
it is for the angry, suspicious patient encased in his own loneliness.
The development of a community inevitably means greater unhappiness for at least some patients and some staff; they cannot be blamed
for attacking it.

What were the states of the four subsystems of the community—
motivation, integration, adaptation, and consummation groups—during
the period of the first sixty community meetings? [3]

Motivation Group

During this period, with much misgiving I found myself as physician
and leader representing in the community certain ideals: those ideals
actualized in rational problem-solving processes of action or in the
collaboration of interdependent, mutually respectful patient and staff
groups.

Ideals are essential to animate a community. The dilemma is that
ideals are also easily corrupted: by single-minded, zealous disregard
of their consequences with respect, for example, to the actualization of
other ideals, or by expedient exploitation of them to achieve other ends.

When the ideal of the sanctity of the individual justifies gratification
of the individual's impulses at others' expense, or is used to conceal the
destructive consequences to others of the individual's self-seeking or to
protect the individual from the social consequences of his acts, then
that ideal is corrupted. (Somewhat over two years after this period, a
staff administrative representative to the community program became
alarmed that the secrecy of patients and their fears that their private
lives might be exposed would make detection and control of venereal
disease more difficult. In response to anxious query from two patients

3. For a theoretical formulation concerning the four subsystems in social systems,
groups, psychiatric hospital organization, and the therapeutic community, see
chapter one of this book, especially pages 17–20, and *Sociotherapy and Psychotherapy.*

about whether he would pursue this matter in the community meeting, he replied, "No." They then agreed to help him in the detection of cases. Having made this pact with him, one patient was overheard whispering to the other, "Great! Now we're in the clear!")

When the ideals of rational problem-solving or the welfare of the community justify expedient disregard of individuals, or are used by one group or individual to advance self-interests or vengefully to expose or embarrass another, then that ideal is corrupted.

When the ideal of the collaboration of interdependent, mutually respectful patient and staff groups justifies—in the interest of harmony—disregard for truth about either group or the situation in which they interact, or is used by one group to maintain its domination over the other, then that ideal is corrupted.

A community whose ideals are corrupted is itself corrupt. All its enterprises are overshadowed by the disgust of its participants at their own and others' cynicism. It is not difficult to imagine what life in such a community is like: patients and staff overlooking, accepting, making deals; the circumspect evasions and euphemisms; the doubletalk and lying; the sniggers in meetings and the scorn and mockery at midnight. No such community kindles the imagination or refines moral sensibility; its members possess no daring in their encounters with reality. Who among either patients or staff can be admired or respected, who can lead, in such a community? What happens to psychotherapy in such a community?

Watchfulness, the determination to "see," and the acceptance of the enmity of others are necessary if the apparently inevitable corruption of ideals is at least to be mitigated.

To my own distress during this period, these qualities were clearly limited in me. I had the usual desires to be safe, to be liked, not to upset others. Every time I was moved to say, "Look at what is going on," to protest zealotry, or to tear off some fabric of half-heartedness and insincerity choking discussion, the image of my own immediate reference group, my colleagues, their anger, their turning from me, as well as of the mute hatred in the eyes of patients apparently "validated" by the distrust of my colleagues, rose within me; the sense of my own isolation stifled and frightened me; more often than not I was silent or did not "see." I felt that to be shameful. Day after day, I wondered when my "being sensible" masked cowardice. In addition, however, I distrusted my own Circean ideals, for the love of which I might myself become fanatical; I watched lest I make use of my own ideals merely to advance my private interests. Such scruples, tormenting, preoccupying, and inhibiting me, were exacerbated by the doubts of others—and also kept me silent.

I wondered, I still wonder, if it is possible to possess moral sensibility and integrity, to avoid colluding in "deals" and the processes of corruption—without at the same time becoming pompously disapproving, self-righteous, and intolerant? It is true that one may love in another the manifestation of an ideal, but idealism is also a source of hatred—one may hate anyone who thwarts the realization of an ideal.

During the first sixty meetings, the ideal of patients' helping each other, not only helping those who were "misbehaving," but also those who seemed troubled or unhappy, became gradually more potent, presumably as a result of identification with psychotherapists and with a leader who was a psychotherapist. However, the resources of the community—knowledge concerning what help was needed, what means were available, appropriate, and effective in the social arena to help others—were not adequate to realize the ideal. (Psychotherapeutic "techniques"—at least, two-person interactions involving "interpretation"—proved inappropriate or inapplicable as a modus vivendi in the community.) Whenever resources are inadequate to realize an ideal to which people are committed, frustration and strain result. Since the ideal was not strongly institutionalized, attempts were made to discredit the ideal in order to relieve the strain. After initial attempts to cope with the problems of human unhappiness presented to it, the community withdrew its energies from commitment to realize this ideal, and its members sank into apathy.

The contagion of self-destructive acts occurred when the community was threatened with change. In such a period, anomie may increase markedly. Norms, being called into question, decrease in potency, usually before other norms have become institutionalized. It becomes increasingly impossible to depend upon a given response to one's behavior; nor can one know after a while what to expect of, or how to respond to, others. In the presence of a state more and more approaching normlessness, personal controls—especially those depending, as all do to some extent, upon social reinforcement—begin to collapse. The feeling, "It's no use," predominates. There is no reason to care about oneself or others.

Small groups, if they had been functioning adequately during this period, might have dealt with the strains between individual and community—individual disaffection and hopelessness—realistically and with some actual productive consequence. Individuals might then have been not only able to express personal tensions but, accepted and understood, might perhaps have worked out with others a set of meanings which would make sense of the changes and events taking place, and thus been able to find a way back into the community. But the small groups themselves, operating in a tradition involving other aims, were caught up in the threatening changes.

A change in the community structure leading to the feeling that one could no longer understand or depend upon anything or anyone in the community, inadequate community mechanisms for coping with individual tensions, the increasing loneliness of some outside the cohesive network of those beginning to commit themselves to new, incompletely institutionalized, values, the exacerbation of a sense of inadequacy in those who felt unable to meet new demands and expectations—all created pressures to get away from the community.

One way of getting away from the community during this period was to become intensely, exclusively involved in, and to depend completely upon, a pair-relationship.

The hypothesis to be considered is that the formation of pair-relationships of a particular kind—about to be described—is most likely to occur at a time of increasing alienation from community values, and that in such a social context when the hope for whatever is to be born from such a pair-relationship—often a utopian "closeness," intimacy, "always togetherness" with another, sometimes an affirmation of an idealized sexual prowess—is disappointed, as it must inevitably be, anger and despair are likely to result in self-destructive acts.

I imagine the typical process to be something like the following. People, lost in the community and alienated from its values, beginning to despair, seek hope for the future in an attachment to one other person. From this relationship, something wonderful is to be born. The two spend all their time together. No one else knows them. Nothing else much matters to them. They have little connection to anyone or anything around them. Sexual relations may or may not be involved, but are usually assumed by others to be involved. Because of the social context in which this relationship takes place, the pairing has no social meaningfulness, involves no responsible interdependence, no collaboration in achieving socially meaningful goals, no mutual obligations. The pair-relationship is a refuge from an intolerable social reality, and is largely divorced from that reality; the messianic utopian hopes bound up in the pair-relationship are doomed to non-fulfillment because there are no avenues in reality for their realization; no effort in reality would make sense. Sooner or later, one of the pair disappoints the other. Despair and rage commingle; a self-destructive act expresses both.

Although evidence is incomplete, for reasons having partly to do with the mal-integration of the staff during this period and the consequent difficulty in sharing information, there appeared to be some hint of a pair-experience involved in many of the self-destructive acts occurring at this time; allusion in the community meeting, of course, to any sexual element was always either indirect or on an abstract level.

Not until the sixtieth community meeting did there appear some suggestion of what a model for coping effectively with individual distress in a community setting might be like. Not until that meeting—concerning feelings about children who visit—was individual distress seen to be distress shared by others, arising in many individuals in response to a common situation and the facts of this particular community's life. Not until that meeting did evidence of such distress in an individual arouse, instead of a pseudo-psychological analysis of the individual as if the problem were all in him, an expression of similar concerns and feelings in others, leading to the visualization at least of the possibility of taking concerted collective action through an arm of the community organization, a representative committee, to do something about it.

Consummation Group

The ends competing for priority are expressive ends, adaptive ends, integrative ends, and motivational ends. Seeking such ends involves valuing and seeking, respectively, enjoyment, confidence, solidarity, and commitment. Put in another way, such ends involve the maintenance of, or an increase in, the value of an object of cathexis, an object of utility, an object of identification, or an object of respect (one that represents or symbolizes ideals or values).

During the period of the first sixty community meetings, all ends appeared to have much less potency for the community than the prepotent integrative end of coping with, diminishing, or mitigating the effects of, deviant behavior. The high value given to this end, the amount of attention to and concern with so-called "acting out" individuals, reflected, of course, the most strongly institutionalized values of this particular organization and community, which existed to help deviant individuals, the high level of enduring dispositions to deviance in such a community, one of whose basic criteria of selection for membership was the presence of such dispositions, and the high level of transient dispositions to deviance resulting from the continual introduction of new members into the community, who neither knew nor once knowing immediately accepted the specific norms of the community. In addition, the high level of such transient dispositions to deviance was considerably exacerbated during this period by changes in the community, which tended to undermine the potency of existing norms and the likelihood that members of the community would defend these or communicate them with conviction to new members.

Furthermore, during this period, commitment to the achievement of collective aims, necessary for the operation of the various community programs organized to achieve these aims, was shallow in comparison with the commitment to the achievement of what were regarded as purely individual aims. Again, this choice is consistent with the prepotency of the goal of treating individuals and the high value given to considering, first and foremost, consequences to a particular individual.

The programs (activities, work, community council, small group) were valued insofar as they were of help to, or good for, one particular individual or another. That what might be good for one individual might not be good for another or many others, that what might be good for many might not be good for one, were dilemmas to which people were sensitive but with which they did not explicitly cope. That individuals were, to some extent, interdependent in the quest for enjoyment, confidence, competence, knowledge, meaningful relationships with another, something worthwhile to respect, some ideal worth becoming committed to and seeking to actualize—and, in fact, the achievement of individual treatment goals—was only dimly and intermittently one of the shared perceptions of the group. That the various committees and enterprises were necessary means to create and maintain a social system in which individuals might achieve personal ends (which, in fact, they often shared with others, or at the least for the attainment of which they depended upon the response, active collaboration, or cooperation of others) was a view sometimes honored in discussion but less frequently in commitment to and participation in such committees and enterprises. More usually, individual activities and aims tended to be seen as competing with, different from, and in opposition to, community enterprises.

Work was not valued because of the resources made available through instrumental action for the achievement of some desired end, but because it was good for individuals to work. Activities were valued especially insofar as some individual was being creative by himself, usually as an alternative to participating in the turmoil of community life rather than as part of making a contribution to that life. The community council was valued to the extent that it helped an individual—

but not especially because of any effort to maintain or increase order in the community. The small groups were valued to the extent that individuals learned something from participating in them and especially from staff members about social intercourse, but were not seen as having any contribution to make to the state of motivational commitments in the community. Therefore, the dependence of other enterprises upon small groups coping with problems of commitment and alienation was not part of the thinking about small groups.

What this all added up to was that it was easy to mobilize interest in the community meeting for a discussion of a patient in trouble; it was difficult to mobilize interest in discussing the problems faced by any of the community programs or enterprises which represented efforts to achieve shared ends.

It seemed to me at this time that the most important way in which to increase commitment to community enterprises was to watch for signs of the wants, needs, and wishes that people in the community had, and then to make use of the community programs to gratify these. It did not seem to me that any social system could claim commitment and expect participation from its members, unless these members had clear evidence that processes in the social system resulted in gratification for them.

Many factors militated against this strategy. The community was perceived by most of its members as limiting rather than enabling individual gratification. Procedures for identifying the wishes of individuals or groups within the community were lacking or just beginning to be institutionalized in the community meeting. Making decisions about priorities for alternative or competing ends (needs or wishes) was difficult, especially because of the emphasis on individuality and strains arising in any situation involving preference for one person or group over another. Often a decision in favor of a particular person's or group's wish or need once made was not respected as legitimate; the total group could not be counted upon to be bound by it. Members of the group who did not share a wish or need of others could see no reason to support or strive for its attainment; no one seemed to make the connection between lack of response or apathy ("It doesn't matter to me one way or another") with respect to another's wish and that person's reciprocal not caring about one's own wish.

Enjoyment or gratification as a value was much depreciated in the community. Enjoyment tended to be tinged with guilt and defiance, and associated primarily with informal, illicit activities. The patients' "greediness" was suspect by both patients and staff, and instead of emphasizing planning, effort, and problem-solving as necessary pre-requisites for gratification, the staff tended to depreciate the wishes themselves on the one hand, or simply to gratify them benevolently upon utterance on the other.

The absence of cathected ends was also related to a sense of help-lessness and inadequacy: "It is better not to want what I really have no influence or means to bring about anyway." In order to alter this apathy, the patients' actual influence upon others, through the com-munity organization or patient-staff committees, had to be increased; such a change, of course, meant impinging upon the vested interests of various staff and patients.

One of the difficulties I felt most keenly in this period was the ab-sence of any staff group that regarded as its primary function cham-pioning enjoyment, fun, and self-expression—therefore, the importance of meeting wishes and needs—in the community. The activities staff, of course, felt responsible to contribute opportunities for self-expression, but did not generalize interest in classes, shop activities, or drama into interest in cathectic goals *in general*. So, for example, although the pet issue, while apparently having nothing to do with the activities program, did involve essentially an expressive end, no activities staff person (as part of his role as a member of the activities staff) felt any special commitment to the value of achieving this end on the basis of the gratification that might result.

Furthermore, the activities staff was primarily oriented to teaching skills; the acquisition of skills or the achievement of products was the value of concern rather than enjoyment, fun, or self-expression. In addi-tion, the activities staff was primarily oriented to teaching individuals rather than promoting, or participating in, group processes or collective efforts that might result in an increase in the level of gratification in the community as a whole.

The consequence of these preferences on the part of the activities staff was that the function of championing gratification as a value was abandoned to patients, who were then stuck with and often depreciated for representing the "id," while the staff represented not only the "ego" but a "superego" that frequently seemed opposed to wishes, pleasure, or gratification.

In general, also, at this time fears outweighed wishes in any collision between them. The fear of deprivation to others, if some should have pets, far outweighed the value of gratifying the wishes of those who wanted pets. The fears of inadequacy—that more would be expected of an individual than he could deliver—far outweighed the value of increasing the confidence and competence of those who wanted to reorganize the work program so that work, instead of being mere "keeping busy," might have a more meaningful relationship to desired ends. The fears of exposure, shame, ridicule, ostracism, or expulsion, or the loss of the individual in the mass, far outweighed the value of sharing information about specific deviant behavior in the expectation that sharing such information might result in steps increasing the order and solidarity of the community.

The technical problem, of couse, was, in the interest of achieving gratification, to allay fears by testing their reality, first in discussion of fantasied consequences of any proposed move toward a goal, then in planned and evaluated trials, and finally in decisions intended to cope with both unexpected and expected, undesired, actual consequences. Staff members were often unable to contribute to a process allaying fears, because the staff group felt stuck—by patients and staff—with the sole responsibility for caution and restraint in the face of the widely and certainly inaccurately perceived unfettered "id" of the patient group. Pretensions at studying a problem were usually not in the interest of "the wish" but often rather served the function of delaying action until it was so widely separated from the wish that was the original impetus that once the study was over no one cared any longer; or served the function of burying a problem in a committee or small group where it no longer would influence or disturb anyone else.

Adaptation Group

During most of this period, the work program was hardly mentioned in the community meeting. In essence, the work program had become the vehicle for resistance to changes occurring in the community program as a result of my entry into the community and the inauguration of the community meeting.

First, the threatening values of openness and sharing information represented by the community meeting were "put into," isolated, or segregated in synanon groups, where being honest was seen as a means to better human relationships (integration imperative)—rather than institutionalized as values of the entire community, in the interest of *understanding* the situation of the community itself (adaptation imperative). The staff representative to the work committee was drawn into participating in this process—which probably would have occurred in some form irrespective of his motivational dispositions—perhaps because such segregation also provided him with a protected area in which he could continue to function as leader as well as express his disaffection.

Second, regression to extreme black-and-white positions occurred: the community meeting is "mere" or "dishonest" talk and the synanon groups are "honest" talk; there are people in the community who don't want to work and others who are really dedicated to meaningful work. Taking such positions resulted in paralyzing divisions and fights, effectively thwarting the development of a workable consensus about new values or norms. Those for change, of course, were as ambivalent about and as much involved in the resistance to change as those against; zealous extremism in one direction can always be counted upon to mobilize fanatical opposition to that direction: result, stalemate.

Third, the apparent disagreement or split among members of the staff was exploited by the patients. The patient group was able to avoid coming to grips with its own ambivalences, value-dilemmas, and intra-group tensions in relation to change by becoming preoccupied with and—by taking sides—exacerbating splits in the staff group.

The following adaptation values were in intense competition with integration values: (1) that a patient should discipline himself, controlling tendencies to immediate discharge of anxiety, hostility, or desire for gratification, in the interest of achieving a task (*inhibition* value-orientation); (2) that interest in a patient's specific skills is what is relevant to a consideration of his role—what job he is assigned, what office he is elected to—in instrumentally achieving a goal (*restriction* value-orientation); (3) that a patient's actual or potential contribution to work, rather than his state of mind or degree or lack of lovability, is the crucial datum for a work activity (*doing* value-orientation); and (4) that *all* patients, regardless of personal status, should participate in work needing their participation and that such work should be evaluated by general criteria (*impersonal* value-orientation).

The informal patient group, the psychotherapy staff, and the synanon groups all emphasized the over-riding importance of relationships in which integration value-orientations were prepotent: (1) *discharge* (expressing feelings); (2) *expansion* (interest in the whole person); (3) *being* (who or what kind of person you are is more important than what you do); and (4) *personal* (informal personal relationships are more important than task-oriented interactions in the "formal" program).

The work committee itself was almost completely preoccupied with the state of the motivational dispositions of the members of the community, to the exclusion of concern with such problems as recruitment of workers from the available work-force or the mobilization of tools and facilities for particular jobs (adaptation imperative of the work program); or the establishment of agreement among patient and staff groups about criteria for what constituted satisfactory work performance and the organization of a work crew appropriate to a particular job (integration imperative of the work program). Since the work committee was not interdependently related to other community groups, such as the activities committee, it had to innovate its own ends and strive to attain others' commitments to these ends, or to assert that work was an end in itself, rather than focus upon organizing work to achieve ends generated by the life of the community and already cathected by its members.

The work values of the work program itself were strangely isolated in the community by their attachment to specific manual chores. No one represented these values in other situations with adaptation or work requirements. For example, when patients objected to the door's being shut during the community meeting or to required attendance at such meetings, no staff person as work leader in the community interpreted a shut door or attendance as necessary means for getting the work of such a meeting done more efficiently and expediently. Over and over again, other staff members and I were drawn into abstract discussions of general issues, rather than questioning the always existing discoverable here-and-now events in the community behind the interest in the abstract topic. Over and over again, other staff members and I tended to join patients in seeking general solutions to problems, or using automatically some means that had worked in some other situation in dealing with a present one, in preference to examining the details of each specific problem-situation and innovating the means for coping with it that would be precisely suitable to it.

This over-specification of work values to situations involving manual chores is another example of the confinement of values to specific activities or circumstances, such as I have discussed in connection with the activities program. What accounts for the apparent inability or unwillingness to generalize the relevance of values to a wide variety of activities or circumstances having common analytical components? The question of personal capacities aside, does this tend to happen when the social system might be threatened in some way by a genuine commitment to such values in many spheres? As we have seen, a commitment to gratification ends over a wide area would certainly impinge upon many vested interests and existing arrangements. If members of the staff had been wholeheartedly committed to adaptation values during this period, they would have had to face many unpleasant facts about authority relations and distributions of power, the realistic representation of which had been sacrificed to maintaining illusions about democracy and other ideological beliefs around which some semblance of harmony could be built, apparently in order to mitigate what must have been felt to be hopeless and unresolvable strains.

The effects of staff malintegration or discord upon patients may be specified, then, to be the result of a variety of mechanisms. For example, a staff person may cease to perform or may perform maladroitly needed functions because of the inner uncertainty inculcated by disturbance in his relation to a valued reference group of colleagues, or by value inconsistencies or incoherencies in the social system. Preoccupation and involvement with staff discord may make possible flight by the patient group from its own intragroup difficulties. The leadership, actions, or proposals of a disaffected staff person provide means that may be used by patients to defend, regressively or irrationally, against the realities producing strains.

The proposal for an expanded work program was tied to the synanon groups, and its fate therefore likely to be linked to the fate of those groups. The synanon groups might be seen as a means for establishing the ends of the work program—utimately, as with any revolutionary movement, the ends of the entire community—and winning commitment to these ends. The ends were embodied in the model of a residential community for the treatment of drug addiction (Synanon), which some patients and staff members had visited. That model included the values of helping oneself instead of depending upon the help of professionals; of mobilizing a fight reaction to a hostile, persecuting environment; of doing what one is told by other, more "mature" members of the community no matter if this be done without insight; of being confronted by and confronting others in "gut" language with the consequences of certain social behavior.

This change, too, then, came into the community from the outside—in this case, by contact with and diffusion from another social system, rather than by the introduction of a new staff member.

The fate of elements entering a social system depends in part upon their degree of congruity with other elements of the social system. If new values are introduced that seem or are in conflict with existing institutionalized values, part of the process of winning acceptance for the former may depend upon building ideological bridges between the new and old.

The synanon groups were based upon a model developed by and

for members of a different social-economic group, with different social and personal problems and resources, who eschewed psychotherapy. Acceptance by patients of such groups implied not only rejection of their own social-economic identity but a criticism of the hospital and its chief modality of treatment as well. Bridge-building would have been difficult, therefore, even if it had been attempted to any great extent (it had not); the lasting incorporation of such groups into the existing community would seem to have been unlikely.

Not learning from experience, not changing existing arrangements and procedures as new knowledge is achieved or in response to current exigencies, ultimately must result in the death of a social system; on the other hand, one must wonder, when there is too ready a change, if the social system involved is stably committed to any system of values. Certainly, continuous change in response to adaptation requirements is likely to impose great burdens on the integration of a social system; if change is valued, then mechanisms for coping with integrative crises and strains must be developed.

Interest and pleasure in change, in trying things out, in doing things differently, in examining critically and skeptically current beliefs and attitudes, were far from prepotent value-orientations in this community. Any real change, any step in a direction requiring a shift in value-commitments, typically led in this community over a period of time to strains. The reaction to strains almost always involved recourse to a fantasy or myth of a "golden age" when everything had been and gone well, an age embodying values now felt to be threatened. (The staff, having lost a series of significant leaders, was deeply immersed in this conception of its own past and the past of the hospital.) Invariably, some members of the group would call for a return to the ways and values of that lost age, and under this banner moves would be taken to modify and nullify as much as possible whatever changes had brought about, or were rightly or not held responsible for, current strains. Attempts to change the work program always had such a course.

On the basis of such considerations—the alien source of change, the difficulty of building bridges between the new and old, the inevitable strains resulting from an attempt at radical change, the inevitable reactionary movement in response to such strains—one might be able to predict the ultimate failure of such innovations as the synanon groups and the work program proposal linked to these groups. In the long-run, the failure or at least marked alteration of the community meeting itself might also be predicted, such developments depending also in this case upon the additional factor of the ultimate degree of integration achieved between the new member of the staff and the rest of the staff, and between the community program and the other enterprises of the hospital.

Integration Group

SOURCES OF INTEGRATIVE CRISIS

During the period of the first sixty meetings, three sources of integrative crisis were especially evident.

Intruders. The first had to do with the impingement on the community of "intruders." Intruders may have been especially threatening to the group because of rapid changes in membership and the group's lack of clarity about the nature of its boundaries. There was no unequivocal answers to such questions as the following. Who is a member of the community? Who belongs in the community meeting? What is the community? Why do people stay or leave? Any penetration in either direction of, or any challenge to, the community's boundaries threatened its total disruption, and was therefore likely to lead to defensive exclusion, that is, to attempts to render the boundaries relatively impermeable.

This was a period in which old staff were leaving, and new staff (fellows in training, for example) were arriving. A relatively new staff person was assuming a position of leadership. Changes in the community program (the community meeting, the work program proposal) challenged current definitions about what constituted the community. The largest turnover of patients in a nine-month period (this series of meetings starting approximately in the third month of this time span) had occurred in the month preceding the contagion of self-destructive acts; as has been discussed, the departure of old patients and introduction of new patients are major sources of strain and integrative crisis in the community. Community-wide, shared resources or mechanisms for welcoming and saying good-bye, and for educating a new patient in the ways of the community, were minimal and, for the most part, hit-or-miss, informal, and incapable of coping with an integrative burden of this size.

Concern with intruders was a continual theme in the community meetings: an intruder in a private room; the vandal-trespassers on hospital property; unwelcome, messy, illegally present pets; guests who come and eat up all the food. The fear that intruders would threaten

and deprive far outweighed any expectation that they might add resources or create new possibilities for gratification. Such an attitude to
the outside world, of course, conflicts with attitudes necessary for exploration of and adequate adaptation to reality.

On the whole, my own participation during this time (with the notable exception perhaps of the interventions concerning the "pet issue")
no doubt at times played into the defensive impermeability of the
group. In part, this resulted from my intention to help the group establish an identity, a sense of "who we are and what we're here for," and
in part from my own desire to exclude disorganizing intrusions into the
work of establishing the community meeting: for example, inundation
by a mélange of poorly integrated staff "interpretations" on widely different levels and with widely different purposes; or the inevitably disruptive casual participation of occasional visitors or irregular participants. My effort to exclude from the community meeting those who
had no meaningful role in relation to the task of the community meeting, as I understood that task and before that understanding was
widely shared, conflicted shockingly with conceptions of who belonged
to the community and created, of course, intense strains.

Strains emanating from psychotherapy. The second source of integrative crisis had to do with strains arising within the individual psychotherapy dyad: for example, the strains arising from separation of patient and psychotherapist over a holiday period.

Such strains, which occur as the result of a variety of vicissitudes in
the psychotherapy enterprise and the relationship between psychotherapist and patient, almost aways result in states of alienation or
deviant behavior in the community, since the community symbolizes
the values of the therapeutic enterprise. Such states of alienation and
deviant behavior are extraordinarily difficult to cope with in the community because their source, being in a private realm or privileged
sanctuary, is usually not identifiable, investigatable, or understandable
by members of the social system who are affected by them, "out of the
blue," so to speak, and who may rely only upon unrestrained fantasy
and irrational processes as guides to their interpretation.

Preoccupation with patient-staff relations, usually around some general issue or some representative, apparently trivial, incident, or an outburst of anger at a staff group or person at the community meeting,
seemed typical of community meetings either prior to or following a
holiday. Technically, one is tempted on such occasions usually by the
mounting passions to interpret the group process of the community
meeting; it is important to be able to relate that process to the reality

of the situation in which the community meeting takes place: for example, the separation of psychotherapists and patients.

During this series of meetings, around the time of a holiday there was a great deal of bitterness in the patient group about the amount of money the hospital charged and about the notion that doctors were at the meeting only to do their job, according to patients, instead of being really interested in patients as people.

Of course, such reactions may be understood in terms of the sharing by individuals of states of "oral" deprivation in response to separation. There seems to be a value dimension as well. Patient and staff groups are integrated around the shared value of putting the individual patient's welfare ahead of the professional's desire for personal gratification; the departure of the therapist on a holiday seems to be, or is susceptible to interpretation as, a challenge to the dependability (as far as the patient is concerned) of the therapist's commitment to that value position. Furthermore, the patient tends to approach the relationship with the expectation that it be characterized by the value-attitude *expansion,* that is, with the expectation that it will be like a family-relationship: there should be no limit to the therapist's interest in and obligation to the patient. Such an expectation is to some extent a necessary part of most psychotherapeutic processes, and cannot be tactlessly, completely unreciprocated. The therapist, while often experiencing some dilemma in this connection because of the necessity to have a very wide interest in almost any aspect of the patient and to relate to him as a whole person for the sake of the psychotherapy endeavor, nevertheless is constrained by his identity as a professional person not to carry his interest beyond certain ethical bounds and especially not to reciprocate pathological expectations of the patient. Therefore, the therapist tends to approach the relationship with the expectation that his interest in the patient, on the whole, will be limited by what is relevant to carrying out the psychotherapeutic aim and characterized, therefore, by the value-orientation *restriction.*

These conflicting expectations, of course, give rise to strain around such events as holidays and extratherapeutic contacts. If these group processes are interpreted solely in terms of the individual psychopathology of the members of the group, the value-dilemmas intrinsic to a social system whose prepotent aims are therapeutic, and the effects of an apparent betrayal of one or another of these values upon the members of, and their participation in, that social system, are likely to be overlooked. The hospital, which symbolizes certain value positions, may fall in the esteem and respect with which it is regarded if events are interpreted by patients to mean that crucial values are being betrayed by the hospital or its representatives; states of alienation from such values then ensue.

Intra-patient-group strains. The third source of integrative crisis had to do with strains within the patient group itself. At this time, individuality appeared to be a prepotent value. Supra-individual values, concerns with the welfare of the collectivity, were not only non-institutionalized but regarded as somehow opposed to individuality. The value of individuality seemed to imply that *discharge*, immediate gratification of impulses, or immediate expression of or giving way to feelings, should take place without evaluation of consequences; or if there is evaluation, consequences for the evaluating individual should always have priority over consequences to others or to the collectivity of which he is a member.

Members of the community had little identification with or concern about each other, but rather tended to regard each other at most as the means to personal ends. (Of course, to be identified as a member of a patient or hospital community was negatively valued; therefore, belonging to such a community and identifying with its members were rejected.) Even an expedient attitude toward others, a recognition that frustration of others' wishes is likely to lead at some other time to their frustrating one's own, was for the most part lacking as a basis for social integration; even the expedient "morality" of "I'll scratch your back so some time you will scratch mine" was absent.

The emphasis on individuality—in the sense that each pursues his own ends, without regard to others (except occasionally as means), and without obligation to cooperate or collaborate with others—was not actually an emphasis on respect *for* the individual. In the group life of the patients, not only did the individual have little respect for the wishes or welfare of the many and accord little legitimacy to collective decision, but there was on the part of the many little respect for the individual or for minority groups' interests or opinions.

What most people wanted at the moment decided many issues. The majority ruled, often without hearing out or trying to meet the objections of the minority. The assertion by an individual of objections or fears that might frustrate the wishes of others was not only not respected but regarded automatically as an affront and "making trouble," and likely to be "put down" or met with retaliation. A disaffected, uncommitted, antagonized minority, therefore, usually existed to sabotage majority decisions.

So, with reference to the pet issue, because "only a few" people's wishes were concerned, it was difficult to interest the group in solving the problem these people had in being separated from their pets. On the other hand, once the group committed itself to some extent to a consideration of the problem, the objections of those who feared having pets tended to be dismissed or dealt with as "troublemaking" or "quibbles." It often seemed as if, once the group allowed itself to become aware of a problem, it wanted it dealt with as rapidly as possible, no matter what the cost; the members of the group were unable to tolerate the tension and suspense of strains, disagreements, and negotiations long enough to permit adaptive problem-solving to go on.

I was careful not to interpret the apparent personal meanings that having pets had for various individuals or even the shared feelings about self that were externalized in the fantasies about and images of pets. I tried to confine my interventions to the level of the problem posed by the different wishes and fears that existed in the group with reference to pets, the intragroup strains resulting, and how these were coped with. In this case, there clearly seemed to be an effort by the patient group to deal with intragroup strains by denying their existence and displacing them into the realm of intergroup strains, that is, to make the issue one of staff-patient relations. Here, the medical director was provoked into making an authoritarian ruling, which could then be collectively complied with or rebelled against; in either event, the differences between patients on the issue could then be ignored. This kind of group process illustrates that viewing patient-staff relations in such situations *solely* as a one-way expression of the willful exercise of staff power over helpless patients may be simplistic.

Of course, staff participants such as myself were anxious about whether pursuing such an issue after the medical director had made a ruling would be perceived by him as undercutting or challenging his authority. Without mutual understanding of the goals being pursued and trust between the staff involved and the medical director, the patients' way of displacing their own intragroup strains into staff-patient relations could easily result in immobilizing the staff in the community meeting and thus make possible realization of the patients' covert intention to kill the issue.

DIFFICULTIES IN COPING WITH INTEGRATIVE CRISES

The major difficulty in coping with integrative crises in this community had to do with the ubiquitous lack of shared information about the "moral situation" by those who had to evaluate and deal with moral problems—that is, problems having to do with norms or the normative standards governing choice or action in specific situations in the patient-staff community, and in the informal patient community as that impinged upon the formally organized patient-staff community.

It is necessary for attempts at problem-solving that specific data be available to all members of both staff and patient groups about a particular situation: who is doing what with or to whom; what norms are thereby being disregarded or flouted. If such information is shared, the patients as a group are free to evaluate it, having to deal with all the differences in perception, value, and point of view within that group; the staff is free to evaluate it, having to deal, similarly, with its intragroup differences. Each group might then struggle to come to some internal agreement about what it would make sense to do in the light of such evaluation. Then both groups might negotiate and decide, in patient-staff committees such as the community council, upon action both groups—from their somewhat different vantage points, interests, and value positions—might be able to agree to carry out together.

In the absence of such shared information and such a problem-solving process, involving both groups, the only solution available was for the staff to announce what its values were, in general terms, not with respect to specific circumstances but rather with respect to such general phenomena as drinking or acting out. (Attempts, of course, to formulate such general over-all solutions often led to rather hollow statements, ridden with cant, and to thinking that was pontifical rather than sophisticated, that is, applicable in action or to problem-solving in a specific situation.) After such statements, it was hoped, patients would accept, identify with, or comply with so-called staff values—not as a result of any evaluation by patients of specific circumstances and specific consequences to themselves, to other individuals, or to the community and its valued enterprises, but because "the staff says so." Any staff position of this kind could, of course, be somewhat mindlessly accepted at face value or could be easily shot apart, if some patient had the mind to do so. In general, this way of proceeding, whether initiated by staff or patients, seemed to me to result in dependency by one group upon the other, or to futile cycles of—or concomitant—compliance and rebellion, rather than to shared participation by both groups in a difficult, complex, problem-solving process of the kind characteristic of the normative realm.

Why the lack of shared information? First, patients were frequently frightened that they would be attacked by other patients, especially if they "spilled the beans" or "squealed"; that they would be ridiculed or judged and condemned by other patients if they reported a socially disapproved action; that such a report might lead to discharge from the hospital; or that such a report might result, at the least, in a negative reputation, difficult to get rid of, no matter what change occurred in oneself, and determining people's response to one in widely differing situations and far into the future.

Second, there was widespread fear among both staff members and patients that the individual would be lost in, or dominated by, the mass; that the individual's right to privacy, and right to decide whether information concerning private areas of his life would become public knowledge, would not be respected; that individual autonomy with respect to personal decision and action in areas as far apart as going to school or work, on the one hand, and committing self-injury, on the other, would be interfered with; and that material belonging in individual psychotherapy—or revealed there—would be divulged to the group, even with, but most terribly without, the patient's consent.

Third, there was no organization making it possible for patients to evaluate such information independently of staff or to arrive at any proposal for action binding the patient group as a whole; such evaluation went on only informally and in segregated subgroups of patients. The staff, likewise, had no effective organization making it possible for staff members to evaluate such information and arrive at a proposal for action behind which the staff as a whole would agree to stand. The staff was literally unable to decide anything as a group, primarily because of great reluctance on the part of many, at different levels of authority and for different reasons, to delegate any individual member of the staff or small group of staff the authority to speak and act for, to represent, the staff after appropriate consultation. Consequently, every staff member spoke to the patients for himself alone. The patients were left to make what they could or wanted to make out of the mélange of statements, which certainly functioned to dilute the effective influence—but also possible dominance—the staff might have exercised if there had been a clear unified staff position with respect to particular questions. This situation also tended to paralyze everyone with respect to any course of action or intervention in such situations.

Most staff did not have confidence in the ability or willingness of the community council, for example, to cope with integrative problems in general or with specific cases of individual deviance. The community council, despite its patient-staff composition, was seen as a patient group. Neither nurses nor administrators saw the community council as the executive body representing both patients and staff, as their own organizational means for taking action through which they (nurses and

administrators) as well as patients should work to implement their
particular aims and responsibilities, and to whose judgments and decisions they as well as patients were subject. Nurses and administrators
often innovated their own actions, arrangements, and decisions with
respect to problems that were the province of the community council,
without either consulting with or reporting to that body. An interpretation of their behavior in these terms was likely to get the response:
"The patients are taking over; well, let them take care of it all by themselves, if they want to." Or the response: "That's my responsibility; I'm
not turning it over to any group of patients." In other words, delegation of responsibility for these problems to a group of patients and
staff, who would share such responsibility, was far from legitimized;
inconsistencies with regard to such delegation were seized upon by
patients to point out the "phoniness" of the staff, the helplessness of the
patients, and the justice of patients' washing their hands in turn of such
problems.

Because organizational means for responding to information were
inadequate, unused, or depreciated, when information was shared subsequent experience resulted in feelings of futility: that such sharing of
information did not lead to anything worthwhile. Disinclination to
share information thus tended to be reinforced. (Of course, in some instances simply sharing information and discussing it in the community
meeting were enough to alter perceptions and feelings sufficiently to
lead to change in individual behavior and thus in the problem-situation
of concern. To distinguish such instances from those in which further
action is necessary was part of the task of the representatives of action
groups functioning in the consultation process of the community meeting.)

The fears of retaliation, ridicule, condemnation, and damaged reputation, were, on the whole, justified by the facts of group life. Two
kinds of interventions were to be attempted to mitigate such fears.
The first was interference with, and interpretations of, such phenomena
in the community meeting, and provision by staff of models of other
attitudes toward people acting deviantly. The second was change in
the staff so that the threat of the ultimate sanction of discharge was not
resorted to immediately in all situations involving deviance; rather the
community council might develop instead intermediate, lesser sanctions, appropriate or intrinsically related to the particular deviance involved—for example, taking away the car keys of someone driving
recklessly, refusing access to a facility to someone abusing it, denying the privilege of showing visitors around the hospital to someone

acting in contempt of its institutions. The first kind of intervention was accomplished with some degree of success. The second met with much resistance, especially from the staff.

The factors militating against adequate organizational means for responding to information were struggled with by a variety of innovations and interventions. One was the attempt to establish a community program staff, which might represent and act for the staff in the community. Second was the attempt to clarify continuously the status of the action groups in the community as representing and acting for both patients and staff (not simply constituting patient groups with staff "helpers"), as having differentiated functions, and as responsible for taking action with respect to particular problems emerging and being discussed in the course of the review of current community life at the community meeting.

Coping with factors having to do with the relation of individual and community, with the dilemmas posed by the right to privacy, on the one hand, and the "need to know" if social problems are to be understood and responded to effectively with regard to the requirements of both individual and social system, on the other hand, was perhaps most difficult.

The staff on the whole, steeped in knowledge of the personality system, did not have concepts or a language with which to understand and discuss the community as a social system, rather than focusing only upon various individuals in it. For example, what went on in one individual leading to an upset was readily analyzed, but understanding and talking about a series of such upsets in terms of prevailing specific social conditions, arrangements, institutions (rather than in terms of the mere summation of fortuitously coincidental individual vicissitudes) were not easy. How an individual made use of a group to externalize internal problems or to displace feelings from therapist or family to the community was readily understood, but not so the use made of an individual by a group in rational, nonrational, or irrational social processes. Such concepts and a language had to be developed over time, not in leisure, but while immersed in the phenomena, struggling with urgent problems, and in the face of others' demands to make sense of what was going on.

Similarly, knowledge about social mechanisms for problem-solution (other than talking with particular individuals—whose behavior might simply be the manifestations of supra-individual social processes—or interpreting individual feelings and conflicts) was absent and had to be developed.

Without concepts relevant to understanding a social system and mechanisms for coping with social conditions rather than intrapsychic states, it was impossible to explicate what needed to be known about an individual for social problem-solving and what was indeed irrelevant (in this sense, purely personal) to such problem-solving. Agreements perhaps needed to be worked out between community program staff and therapy staff concerning the use of information about individuals shared by these two staff groups in their combined effort to understand the interaction between the two enterprises and ultimately between personality and social system, to understand more completely the individual patient from the point of view of his participation in both enterprises, and to understand the bases for different responses to the patient by members of the two staff groups having different foci of concern, aims, and responsibilities. (Such information was also shared because many staff members had overlapping membership in both staff groups.)

One such agreement might be that the staff member would use only the information that he received within the boundary of his own enterprise, that is, from the patient within individual psychotherapy, on the one hand, or from sources within the arenas of community life, on the other. The latter would include observations by, and communications from other than the individual therapist, but including the patient, to nurses, activities staff, the doctor on duty at night and over weekends, staff representatives to the various patient-staff committees, and other patients. Another agreement might be that the staff as a whole should be presented to the patients as a team, whose members communicate with each other, and each of whose members may use any information received as a result of such communication, with the interest of the individual patient in mind, in any task situation, at his own discretion. Either agreement has fateful, and both functional and dysfunctional consequences, for *both* the individual psychotherapy and the sociotherapy enterprise.

I would now suggest that there are certain kinds of questions about individuals the answers to which are relevant to social problem-solving.[4] Perhaps the knowledge that criteria exist, governing the performance of staff and patients in relation to a particular task, and that staff members are clear concerning the differentiated task with which they are concerned in any situation (concern with the intrapsychic or personality system, on the one hand, or with the social sys-

<hr/>

4. See the discussion of questions concerning individuals relevant to the tasks of various social enterprises in *Sociotherapy and Psychotherapy*, pp. 210–14.

tem, on the other) and with only that information relevant to that task, is what is actually necessary for mutual confidence to develop—rather than rules about who shall have or use what information when. Of course, answers even to these kinds of questions about individuals, which are neither esoteric nor irrelevant, and often public and readily available to at least some in the community, are not easy to get (for the whole group), attend to, or discuss. Wishes to conceal inadequacy, to protect illegitimate sources of gratification, to avoid negative sanctions, and to escape the complete social loneliness of the outcast that may be the consequence of the revelation of alienation from social values, all motivate barriers to shared access or attention to such information.

WAYS OF COPING WITH INTEGRATION PROBLEMS

The characteristic response to deviance during this period was for the group to assume that the problem was *in* a patient; to ignore the similar but concealed behavior of others and to act as if the deviant patient were the only one in the community feeling and acting this way; to regard current social conditions, problems, or processes as somehow irrelevant; and to try to help—that is, understand, instruct, and exhort—the deviant patient. Any shared problem in the social system, thus, was treated as if it were *in* one person in the social system. No one else admitted sharing the feelings or opinions of that person or complicity in his acts.

Frequently, the patient would continue perversely to behave unacceptably in the face of others' attempts to help him. Then, others felt rage, presumably because their efforts had been futile, rebuffed, rejected. The patient had proved himself incorrigible. Mixed with anger was always some evidence of envy of the supposed gratification the patient was getting either from the deviant acts—which others denied themselves—or from all the attention. Finally, the patients in their "helplessness" would turn to the staff to do something; the wish at this point that the staff get rid of the patient (discharge him) was ill-concealed. The "bad" in the community was in this way to be extruded.

Characteristics of another way of responding to integration problems. Although I might not have been able to state the following preferences explicitly during this early period, I believe they probably influenced my work. Outcomes of integrative crises should involve patient-staff collaboration based upon a real sharing of responsibility and authority especially by patient-staff groups; a shared understanding of the interaction between the vicissitudes of the informal patient group and the formally organized enterprises of the community; and a focus on the shared problems or dilemmas created by the conditions, tasks, and current exigencies of community life.

Patient-staff collaboration. Over the period of the first sixty meetings, there was some change in the degree of cooperation, at least, between patients and staff in dealing with integration problems: from the thirteenth meeting, when it was reported that a patient who knew another patient had committed an act of self-injury chose not to report the information either to the nurses or to the doctor on duty, to the fifty-sixth meeting, when there was a discussion about how patients and nurses had helped one another in trying to take care of a drunk, assaultive patient.

However, the nurses discouraged any formal collaboration between patients and nurses, such as sharing information during the change-of-shift nurses' meeting or (in subsequent months) having a patient on duty at night to help the nurses respond to situations arising then. In general, there was much less focus in the community meeting on patient-staff relations, especially on nurse-patient relations, than was warranted; there was little information about these matters and in part for this reason few interpretations at this level. This neglect was in part due, I believe, to the perception of the nurses' vulnerability as a group and as individuals by both patients and other staff, and by their desire to protect themselves and others' desire to protect them. On the whole, nurses preferred not to have their interactions with patients exposed in front of physicians, and seemed to feel that the nurses would automatically be blamed. They would reproach patients who tried to raise incidents illustrating difficulties in patient-staff relations: "Why didn't you discuss that with one of us personally?! Why did you bring it up at a meeting?!" They preferred to relate to patients informally rather than in patient-staff committees, meetings, or various community enterprises. To the extent that these were the work areas of the community, the nurses tended to be and feel left out, and they lacked a defined arena for the exercise of their skills. In addition, behind the scenes and in informal contacts, patients were able to exploit such preferences by seducing nurses into agreements that involved them in paralyzing dilemmas: for example, a patient would say to a nurse that he wanted to tell her about something upsetting him, but would not unless she kept it a strict confidence. (If she refused to make the bargain, she was not helping him; if she did make the bargain, she subsequently might find herself confronted by a social problem with respect to which she could take no action within channels provided for dealing with such problems.)

Over two years later, a patient who had been intimidating the nurses while in a drunken state at night turned his liquor over to them to keep for him ostensibly as part of his effort to keep himself from drinking. A week later the patient wanted the liquor back; on the grounds both that he was a minor and that he was a problem-drinker the nurses refused to give it to him and become accomplices to his further drinking. There was a roar of protest from him and other patients when he presented this action at a community meeting; the nurses had no right to withhold his property, especially without warning him that they would do so.

In the ensuing discussion, the following points were made and gained some acceptance among patients and staff. The nurses should not have made such an agreement in the first place; that is, agreed to keep his liquor on condition that they returned it when he wanted it, since that would prevent them from using professional judgment in the situation in which they were presented wtih such a request. The patients had to take some responsibility for their part in initiating such corrupt and impossible bargains. The nurses' refusal to return the liquor was in part a "last ditch" expression of their lack of confidence in the community council, which, on seeing this patient, had not discouraged him from resuming his drinking; on the contrary, the community council had positively sanctioned such a resumption as a matter of trusting him. The patients on the community council seemed willing to trust him to manage his liquor—without any evidence that such trust was now warranted but with some evidence that it was not—but were not willing apparently to share the responsibility with the nurses for coping with his drunkenness. However, it also turned out that the nurses had made no effort to present their point of view at the community council meeting through their representative, or to influence the discussion or decision of the community council, preferring apparently to work things out on their own with the individual patient rather than act through the community council.

Perhaps nurses should use their skills in interpersonal relations and their knowledge of the impact of the informal life of the patients on the formal community enterprises, and implement their concern for the maintenance of community norms, as members of the various patient-staff groups in the community program, and should work through patient-staff action groups especially when executive action regarding such problems as deviant behavior is required. The nurses might "get off the limb" they were on by turning the liquor over to the community council, which would then decide upon its disposition.

The issues then were the degree of confidence (especially felt by the staff) in the community council, the seriousness with which its responsibilities had been delegated, and the community council's willingness to assume these responsibilities in earnest.

Formal and informal community life. Although there were some hints that events in the informal life of the patient group were very much involved in the deviant behavior manifested throughout the period of these sixty meetings, there was almost no explicit discussion of these events. It is of little use in this connection to interrupt a group discussion with the comment, "The group is avoiding the 'real issue.'" I have noticed that often a staff person, including myself, makes this comment when he does not know what to make of the issue that is being discussed, when he is for some reason put off by it or cannot see its significance. It must be clear in the group that people are not going on "fishing expeditions" for "secrets"; there must be some indication about what kind of information about informal group life would actually be relevant to the task of the meeting.

Somewhat over two years after this period, there was an outbreak of venereal disease in the community. Clearly, something was happening in the informal life of the patient group that was relevant to a social problem and its resolution, but how was it to be talked about, especially without violating the privacy of individuals or indulging in mere gossip? A meeting to discuss the medical aspects of venereal disease for purposes of raising the level of knowledge in the community was organized and carried out by patients and staff with relative ease. But how was the group to get at the social meaning and social consequences of this outbreak?

The following sequences illustrate especially well the interaction between the informal life of the patient group and the formal community organizations.

At a community meeting, a male patient requested help in setting up a tea for a visitor; grinning, he pointed out that flower arrangement was not a man's job; a female patient volunteered.

It was announced that a poster hung in the game room had been taken off the wall and torn up, and that the activities committee bulletin board had been used to post obscenities. On the bulletin board, small group X was referred to as the "smut group" and the "necking group." (Actually, the female patients in small group X had for some weeks

ostracized the male patients in that group, for example, holding separate meetings from them.) Grim anger and a sense of hopelessness
were the response to these announcements.

The pet committee gave its report. Someone asked why the pet committee had a closed meeting. It turned out the meeting had been closed
in order to exclude one male patient the women patients on the committee did not want to have there, because he would "disrupt" the
meeting. Shocked silence greeted this news. The male patient involved,
who was in small group X, informed the community that the pet committee consisted largely of women from that group. People were out-
spoken in their dislike of using a meeting to deal with an individual in
this devious way.

Hoping to introduce information that would help the group adopt
a "study" attitude toward what was going on, I commented that I had
recently observed that while the community meeting patient co-
chairman for the first year and a half had been a man, during the next
year all the co-chairmen had been women, except for one man who
had been quite reluctant to run for the office. I wondered what people
made of this rather strange finding. (Actually, as I thought about it
after the meeting, the switch had taken place after a woman patient
had led a number of other women in a discussion scorning the patient
co-chairman as a "stooge" of the staff co-chairman; this "put down"
the men who had been in the office and apparently resulted in reluctance on the part of men to occupy an office that could be seen in this
way by the women in the group. I wondered then to myself to what
extent the feelings aroused by my pairing as co-chairman with a particular patient in the meeting, male or female, were affecting the work
of the meeting.)

The patients in the meeting began to contribute their own observations and researches. Although it turned out that the community council chairmanship had been rather evenly divided between men and
women, one man reported with some bitterness "research" he had done
recently resulting in the observation that of the seven patient members
of the community council, five were women, while during the same
period, of seven patients referred to the community council as social
problems, five were men. A number of men commented that some
women in the community were willing to analyze a man and tell him
what was wrong with him, but didn't want to hear anything back about
themselves. "So I just forget about what they say. Screw it!" Women
commented on the bitchiness and competitiveness of women and the

passivity and muscle-flexing of men in the community. A woman said she wouldn't want to be a man in this community; a man said he wouldn't want to be a woman in this community.

There were many comments about the role reversal in the community: men do women's work (housekeeping) and women do men's work (carpentry).

I commented on the widespread feeling by men that they are being "put down" by the women in various ways, and wondered what happened to the feelings of resentment about this. Perhaps the men get back at the women in the bedroom, where women can be depreciated by regarding them as trophies to show off masculine prowess.

During this time, there had been a gradual crescendo of stealing episodes. Money or liquor was taken mostly from the rooms of women in the community; there were also reports of strange nocturnal prowlings: doors being tapped or once locked found open. The community became quite hysterical about the stealing, forgetting all previous experience with it, accusing anyone who happened to be upset, and ultimately, immediately after one such episode, going around searching everyone's room. The latter behavior violated, of course, the value placed on the right of privacy in the community, and led to an angry reaction by many patients and members of the staff.

One suggestion during this time was to have the community "chip in" to pay back money stolen from any member of the community, as a way of representing the community's concern for the individual suffering such depredations. Another, on the theory that need for money was causing the stealing, was to create a community bank from which people in need of money could easily obtain it.

Interestingly, no one noticed the fact that the exacerbation of stealing had come in the wake of the outbreak of venereal disease and wondered what that meant; absence of attention to facts and investigative curiosity about them is, of course, rather characteristic of the mindlessness of many group processes. No one in the meeting showed much interest in investigating or knew how to discuss the social conditions that might be contributing to the exacerbation of stealing.

A subsequent community meeting opened with a patient's bringing in the door to his room and placing it on the floor to express his vehement opposition to any solution to the stealing which would involve better locks on the doors; he was for an open-door policy.

A patient then began to discuss his recent outburst, when he had smashed some windows and thrown bottles out of them. He then went on to discuss with intense emotion that he was upset because he couldn't reach people in the community, that the girls thought he was a "bastard" and he wasn't, that he had a lot of trouble in his relationship with one girl, and when she became angry at him she would go off to another fellow in the community. He stated emphatically that he was not angry at this other fellow, but that made things very hard on him. He also commented on how upset it made him to see one of the other men in the community continually "put down" by the girl that man was close to.

After some comments by others reassuring this patient that people were not angry at him because he had been so specific, a volleyball game held on the previous night was brought up. Some people had felt that there was something wrong with it; the play had been too rough; there had been too much determination to win. What emerged in the discussion was that one small group was playing together, feeling great solidarity, and having much fun. Others felt left out. (As nearly as one could infer, the discomfort at the volleyball game appeared related to showing-off by a group of men for the benefit of specific female patients, the exclusion of other female patients, and perhaps ridicule of male patients who were awkward in the gym. The show-offs and their intended audience seemed to be largely patients who might be perceived as involved in sexual activities in the inn.)

I commented that it is sometimes difficult to see others enjoying themselves, to feel envious and angry at being on the other side of the door.

These meetings give some hints about how to think about such a phenomenon as stealing in social as well as personality terms.

On the intrapersonal side, there are such factors as states of deprivation and anger, as well as either insufficiently internalized norms regarding respect for others' property, or internalized norms of this sort applicable only to certain groups and not to others. In addition, ego-disorganization may result in an individual's being unable to live according to norms to which he is ordinarily committed.

On the social or situational side, there are such factors as unequal allocation of valued objects in the social system (for example, women as sexual partners), an inequality held to be illegitimate; a heightened visibility of the fact that some members or groups of the social system have what is denied to others, brought about by the open discussion of sexual promiscuity and venereal disease; the possibility of ready illegitimate access to private possessions such as money and liquor; and the likelihood of escaping negative sanctions if one seizes such objects, because of the breakdown of community norms and the importance of permissiveness in the community ideology. (Similarly, the taking away of something formerly possessed, so that in relation to a previous state rather than in relation to another person one is deprived, may lead to an increase in such acts as stealing. An example is the apparent increase in reports of stealing in the community occurring when therapists leave for a brief holiday or to attend a professional meeting.)

The social or situational factors might be said to be the unique province of the sociotherapist and of a meeting like the community meeting; the intrapsychic or personal factors the unique province of the psychotherapist and the psychotherapy session. Obviously neither sociotherapist nor psychotherapist can afford to ignore a consideration of the set of factors of primary concern to the other.

What were the situational conditions at the time the reports of stealing increased? The information about venereal disease and the flaunting of pairings made it clear that sexual relations were available to some in the community and not to others. Furthermore, these sexual relations were apparently casual or promiscuous rather than occurring within a relationship characterized by fidelity and mutual obligations. A patient who observed a relationship such as the latter might feel a twinge of envy, but might also be able to deal with such a feeling by recognizing the other ties that bind the two persons involved. However, the patient who observed a promiscuous girl dispensing favors apparently without much inhibition was apt to feel all the more the sting of not being considered eligible even by her for such favors. He felt not only envious but "put down"—twice deprived, of physical gratification and self-esteem. His reflection was likely to be: "What's wrong with me that it's okay with her with all these others but not with me?" The deprivation of self-esteem was exacerbated in the community by the sense that the "girls" did not respect a man or value his company or his opinions in other informal situations or in formal meetings and enterprises; and that the women offered more aggressive leadership than the men felt inclined to offer. A female patient was likely to have similar feelings about her "sexy sister," who seemed to be so much more attractive to others than she was. Often, the difference in their behavior had something to do with the envious patient's sense of morality, inhibitions, or fastidiousness; the envy, therefore, tended to be mingled with self-righteousness.

What was desired (sexual relations) was in part held to be illegitimate, while at the same time to complain to someone of—that is, to make public—the lack of its possession tended to humiliate and shame the complainer further. Thus the envy being exacerbated in the community was difficult to ventilate or resolve; the envier in his envy was isolated and cut off from sources of support in the community.

At the same time, value placed on a homelike atmosphere, informal living arrangements, and ability to trust others, as well as some covert inclinations to tempt and provoke others by leaving possessions around, played a part in making illegitimate access to money and liquor in people's rooms easy.

One might guess that under such circumstances stealing might be likely.

One would expect the same result if one had a small group of people in a community flaunting great wealth, when other members were conscious of their limited means; if a patient or group of patients felt less esteemed than others because of a difference in education and socioeconomic background; or if some patients had access to opportunities—such as public office or contact with staff—that others were, as far as they are concerned, illegitimately deprived of. Certainly material goods matter, but what seems to matter even more in these situations is the deprivation of esteem or the symbolic deprivation associated with material deprivations. One cannot live, socially speaking, without respect.

With tension and competitiveness between women patients and men patients, with envy, a sense of deprivation, and hostility building up in some, the likelihood that community enterprises calling for solidarity, comradeship, and cooperation will be disrupted is high. The disruption of these enterprises itself begins a chain of further effects involving failure to solve community problems, therefore increasing deprivation in many areas, anomie, and alienation. Those who, because of the intrapsychic constellations mentioned previously, are able to express envy, a sense of deprivation, and hostility through stealing or other "mysterious" acts contribute to a widespread sense of confusion, suspense, and inability to depend on others.[5]

It is my opinion that a sociotherapeutic intervention in such a community should make it possible for the effects of phenomena in the informal life of the patients (such as promiscuity or casual sexual rela-

---

5. It is not to be supposed that such an interpretation must necessarily be communicated in these dry terms. As a matter of fact, this particular interpretation ultimately took the form of a parable—the story of the downfall of a utopian community—told by the sociotherapist to the group as all sat comfortably in front of a living room fire. The laughter, exchange of glances, and cries of recognition as the story was told did much to create a sense of the validity of the interpretation.

tions) upon other aspects of that informal life, and also upon the ability of the members of the community to work together to achieve shared ends, to become concretely visible to all members of the community. Only then can individual patients make the kind of evaluation of the consequences of their individual acts that is implied by the concept of responsible action.

The shared problems of community life. The third characteristic of this way of coping with integration problems—a focus on the *shared* problems or dilemmas created by the conditions, tasks, and current exigencies of community life, and the use of the community organization as means to deal with these—was not much evident in the first sixty community meetings. The preference was for focusing upon an individual and *his* problems, or upon the meeting itself. Certainly, an autoplastic preoccupation with the processes of the community meeting for its own sake, or with the internal processes of a particular individual, is usually *instead of* an alloplastic interest in the actual events in the day-to-day life of the community and in bringing about change in that community.

How does one enlist the commitment of young patients, alienated from society, suspicious of "phoniness," bereft of a sense that anything is worthwhile, wandering aimlessly from sensation to sensation? Certainly not by pontifical disquisitions on values, not by threats of expulsion, not by cautious evasions and safe silences, not by muddy thinking about social phenomena, not by sarcasm, not by jaded, disillusioned sourness, not by unwittingly entering into "deals" that make one an accomplice to deceit and hypocrisy. One attempts to hook onto the ideals that do exist in patients: the desire to change oneself, to be less "phony," to find some meaning at least in oneself; the desire for new experience; the longing to find something or someone to admire and respect; the feeling for community (symbolizing the sought values or ideals); wishes to help out, to share; response to the experience of comradeship; the fragment of chivalry and tenderness often existing in the most seemingly cynical patient.

Building a community in which such ideals might be realized, even recognizing its unattainable utopian nature, is an end to which people may commit themselves. To share and clarify the vision of such a community, and to demonstrate concretely and in detail that particular behavior interferes with the task-achievements and relationships necessary to bring it even partially into being, are the most potent mechanisms of integration.

But what a demand upon the members of a staff is implied by this proposed methodology: awareness; imagination; a feeling for the drama and meaning in details of everyday events; the courage, perhaps better yet the sense of irony, to bear the lapses, inconsistencies, breaches in one's own integrity; perspective, detachment, humor, steadiness, so as not to be swallowed in the moment, but also energy and engagement *now;* above all, perhaps, the capacity perpetually to renew idealism itself. It is nice to think about, but are such ingredients to be found in more than one or two persons for more than a half hour on an occasional day?

4. The Rebels against the Goodies

1

What shall we do about the black cat roaming around the inn? The black cat is "independent," and "does not belong to anyone." Its putative owner is not at the community meeting. How can we solve problems in community living when the people involved do not attend the community meeting? Why do certain people stay away?

I wonder if people stay away to express independence of the community? Or in response to the covert wishes of other members of the group that they should stay away, based on the feelings of these other members that the absentees would, if present, express negative attitudes toward the community which could not be coped with? (Is the black cat that which is unacceptable and does not belong within every member, which cannot be acknowledged by many, which is then displaced on to or represented by certain "outlaws" in the group, who are in fact then maintained as outlaws for this purpose by the rest of the group?)

The nurse has difficulty in this discussion (Monday, meeting 61). Her role-requirement to represent administrative disapproval of the presence of black cats conflicts with her role-requirement to attend to the interpersonal, to what the discussion means about the state of interpersonal relations in the inn, and to the consequences for these relations of one disposition or another of the black cat. Other members of the staff, feeling this uneasiness, begin to throw out suggestions, for the implementation or consequences of which they bear no burden of responsibility.

2

A patient, who has been a very active, resourceful leader in the community, leaves, optimistic about the future, tearful in his farewell to the group. Another patient becomes an outpatient. (Tuesday, meeting 62).

3

The group is split into the "goodies" and the "rebels." "Screw the goodies!" The group is divided about pets, about me, about the community meeting, about whether the community meeting is a social hour or has something to do with working on the problems of community life. If it is a social hour, someone might play the piano; attendance or lack of it would be inconsequential.

4

At a patient's suggestion, the nominees for an office in the community state their "platforms." This is the first time an attempt is made to discuss publicly the qualifications of different candidates for office (Thursday, meeting 63). Should a candidate, if elected, carry out his own platform or should he simply respond to the wishes of the group?

Difficulties in the election procedure lead to a call for action to solve these; the call for action is opposed on the grounds that the community meeting is for discussion not action. I comment that if the discussion is not acted upon by the action or executive groups in the community, when necessary, then discussion is futile. The group is divided about whether to talk or act.

5

An active attempt is made to cope with the feelings about a holiday weekend (Friday, meeting 64). Various activities are proposed; suggestions are made. I wonder if the activities committee might not organize to pick up, respond to, and try to meet such current needs.

Illicit activities are revealed: gambling; passing bad checks; borrowing money and not returning it. New patients appear to be at the center of such activities. I do not interpret the meaning of the appearance of this material, but, accepting that some needs are involved, push to see if these can be met within the formal organizational structure of the community: I wonder if the activities committee might organize bingo, for example. If the proceeds went to a scholarship fund, would the gambling be illegal?

This approach takes people by surprise. The "outlaws" are not sure they want to operate within the law. The director of activities tells me later she is startled by the conception that the activities committee might focus on meeting current needs rather than long-range routine

planning and focusing upon enduring projects. I think she is also
startled to have activities injected into a discussion about deviant
behavior.

Many roles are missing in the discussion. No one from the work
program raises questions about the relation between gambling and
failure to work. No one from the activities program wonders how to
meet the needs being expressed through action by the activities committee. No one from the nursing staff enters to respond to the challenging "outlaw" in a way that might mitigate rather than exacerbate his
isolation from the group. The administrative viewpoint that gambling
is not allowed is well represented by many members of the staff.

Similarly with the pet issue. No one from the work program volunteers to help organize the work that will be generated by the presence
of pets. No one from the activities committee responds in terms of the
wishes being expressed—for caring and being cared for—and how these
needs might be met through pets, but also, for example, through participation at the nursery school. No one from the nursing staff seems
concerned with the implications of having or not having pets for the
integration of the group, with the issues being suggested about the
difficulties in keeping rather than casting out the "unacceptable in our
midst," and with the problems of how the group is to care for patients
who want animals rather than people around them or patients who are
afraid of animals. The administrative point of view that pets are not
allowed is well represented by many members of the staff.

Staff solidarity seems to be based on the taking of similar, usually
administrative, positions or holding and expressing similar values or
sentiments, rather than on the interdependence of people making different kinds of contributions and holding somewhat different values,
based upon the fact that each has specialized differentiated functions
to perform. In the former case (mechanical solidarity or homogeneous
solidarity), consciousness is of the sense that "we are or feel the same";
in the latter case (organic solidarity), consciousness is of differences
and the sense of being able to depend upon each contributing something unique and essential.

6

A new patient reports that all suggestions he made over the holiday
weekend for activities were met with reluctance (Tuesday, meeting 65).

"Let's burn down the office building and parade with the doctors'
heads on spears!" At first, this is greeted as a "far out, unfunny" comment; gradually, different individuals are able to acknowledge anger

about doctors' taking the holiday off. (This is a good example of a group isolating someone as "psychotic" by refusing to acknowledge he speaks of feelings shared by others; by acknowledging such feelings, others include him as part of the group, not a foreigner in it, and the necessity for him to be "psychotic" in the group diminishes.)

(Is "*not*" having a good time on the weekend" revenge upon the staff, or an expiation for feelings of anger? Taking revenge depends upon being able to maintain the perception that activities are "what the staff wants," rather than what the patients want.)

A patient comes up to me after the meeting: "The new patients are ruining the meeting we have tried so hard to set up!"

7

The shop instructor needs help in setting up the art exhibit. "Is it our art exhibit or his?"

Silence at the meetings appears related to growing anger at staff, exacerbated by the holiday weekend, and at new patients who are making many suggestions ("Let's dress formally for dinner," "Let's have a current events group," "Let's all come out for basketball," "Let's dress informally in pajamas and bathrobe for Sunday morning breakfast") and behaving in ways felt to be different and unacceptable.

After heated discussion pro and con, for example, formality at just one dinner table, I wonder if it is possible to have one social arrangement suiting everyone's needs.

8

A new kind of meeting occurs (Friday, meeting 67). There is an attempt at the community meeting to solve a problem in community living involving relations between two groups: patients and nurses. The thermostat governing heat in the inn is locked; the nurses have the key. Some patients are uncomfortably cold; others are too warm. Finally, the patient group appears to agree upon a proposal that the nurses alter the thermostat so that it remains at 73 degrees. Will the nurses accept this proposal? The nurse present states she cannot make such a decision in the absence of the head nurse and that some discussion must be held with the night watchman who will certainly object to the proposal.

After the meeting the nurse is very upset, feeling she has behaved and been perceived as behaving incompetently because she did not feel she had the authority to respond positively to the proposal. Her disturbance communicates to other nurses who threaten to boycott the community meeting and community program staff meeting unless they get more support from me. The patient who made the proposal is told angrily, in an informal situation, by one of the nurses, to stop criticizing the nurses at the community meeting.

The staff, perhaps because of this kind of inner disturbance, seems relatively unavailable at this time to help, especially perhaps through participation in small groups, with new patients trying to get into the community, patients hoping for acceptance of their suggestions and ideas by others in the community, or patients trying to help other distressed patients.

It obviously would be of some advantage in a discussion like that about the thermostat for representatives of groups at the community meeting to feel they have been delegated some authority and the discretion to use it and that they may commit their groups to some action, especially such a minor accommodative one as this involving no change in general policy, rather than feeling they must always check back with their groups or sources of authority. However, this depends in part on the degree and nature of the integration of the represented group: whether understanding of policies and the considerations involved in the means of their implementation is fully shared; whether representatives are trusted with wide powers to commit the group or with only limited powers to follow its specific instructions; whether members of the group will give their consent and feel bound by the actions of their representative or will feel rather aggrieved and betrayed about not having been consulted first. In this hospital, traditionally, most representatives of staff groups and particularly of the administration acting in the community program tend to be given, implicitly if not explicitly, only limited powers to follow specific, previously agreed-upon instructions. This arrangement tends to foster behavior interpreted by others as rigid, evasive, and inadequate to novel situations calling for initiative and creative innovation.

Often, there is a dilemma. The choice is between, on the one hand, the impatience and apathy aroused by long delays and resort to formal channels in response to what seems to be relatively trivial matters best dealt with by informal agreement, and, on the other hand, the possibility that agreeing immediately to such a proposal would usurp the executive responsibilities of various action groups in the community, such as the community council, or unrealistically ignore or fail to prepare, or win the consent of, various absent individuals and groups who might be affected by or sabotage its implementation.

In this case, the nurses had the key, so presumably they had the authority to decide its use; interestingly enough, the nurses did not seem to feel that possession of the key did imply such authority; like most nurses in psychiatric hospitals, they experience a sometimes profound discrepancy between their responsibility and authority.

It probably would be adequate if not optimal, in a situation such as the discussion of the thermostat, if the nurse responded positively rather than hesitantly or evasively to the group, asserting at least her determination to see if the desired arrangement could be worked out through the community council, for example, where in the making of executive decisions both nurses and administration are presumably represented. (I wonder to myself if the nurses should possess this key at all; why not rather the community council, representing both staff and patients?)

9

Anger at the staff finds its focus in me (as after the fourteenth week, again following a holiday weekend) when I announce my coming vacation and recommend that my associate be co-chairman in my absence (Monday, meeting 68). Clumsiness results in my seeming to suggest the community council has the right to decide a staff assignment, rather than in my asking for support for the staff member, authority and responsibility for the assignment of whom ultimately rests with the staff group.

A new patient is reported to have suggested that the patients have a celebration when I go on vacation. (Tuesday, meeting 69.) There is a call for a patient meeting to decide upon acceptance or rejection of my replacement, and much anger when the community council decides upon his acceptance without calling such a meeting.

I point out that one issue the group is discussing is: are the members of the community council delegates of the patient group who are bound to act according to the wishes of that group, or are the members of the community council representatives elected by the patient group to represent the interests of the community as the judgment of each dictates? I make some comments about the presence of this issue in American history. As much as possible, I try to focus outward upon issues having to do with the life of the community as a social system and try to avoid inward-directed interpretations of feelings about me or processes in the community meeting itself. I would like the group to develop curiosity about the community as a social system, and an investigative attitude toward the issues that arise. I do not think that self-defense primarily motivates my approach, although it is difficult to be sure how much it enters; I think actually it would be easier to discuss in the group feelings about me, to interpret them, to explain them, even to defend myself. All of us then would certainly be on known ground.

10

In my absence, there is a stormy discussion about the community meeting (Thursday, meeting 70). Some patients are identified with me and the position or values they feel I represent: for example, it is important that everyone come to the community meeting. Other patients are identified with staff persons they feel have been displaced or excluded, whom they report as saying in answer to questions, "I have been forbidden to attend the community meeting." "Either all staff should be able to come and participate freely, or the meeting is just more therapy, and I don't want it." "Personal wishes and needs ought to take priority over the requirements to attend the community meeting."

11

Suddenly emerging in a community meeting (Friday, meeting 71) is the information that the patient who has become an outpatient two weeks previously is threatening suicide and has been telling other patients she was not permitted to remain in the inn because of "lack of funds." Two new patients have become deeply involved with her plight. "Where is the staff in all this?" "Why didn't a member of the staff go to see her?" One of the involved new patients tearfully reproaches other patients for not speaking in the community meeting, which is to help patients: "You've got a good thing here!"

12

The matter of the thermostat is worked out in the community meeting (Monday and Tuesday, meetings 72 and 73). The nurses agree to the proposal and work it out with the night watchman and superintendent. I intervene, when it looks as if this issue—which involves no change in policy—will be sent to a committee, to point out that the long wait in institutions between the expression of a wish and the response to it, the long chain of command through which it passes and often gets lost, contributes to apathy in such institutions.

13

A conflict is reported between movie and drama rehearsal schedules.

14

The distressed outpatient is discussed further. The emphasis is on the feeling that a doctor should have been there, in the absence of any criterion for the necessity of his participation, rather than on the community's providing help for the two patients who were trying to help the outpatient. (Feelings about these two patients, who are relatively new, are not expressed.) A second feeling that is expressed has to do with anger at the staff that the outpatient who obviously, it seems to the group, needs inpatient care was not permitted to remain an inpatient "because of money."

15

A conflict is reported between the scheduling of a basketball game by a new patient and a concert previously scheduled.

16

Disgust is expressed at the inappropriate action of a new patient.

17

A new patient who has worn pajamas and a bathrobe to breakfast on Sunday is reproved. I wonder if such a wish cannot be met at all in the community. The suggestion that the patient kitchen rather than the dining room be made available on Sunday mornings for those wishing to dress informally is rejected by some on the grounds that this would further divide the patient group. The issue is stated by a patient: "Are the preferences of the group to be imposed on every individual or can we accept differences in our midst?"

18

The director of the nursery school appears at the community meeting to request patient volunteers to staff the nursery school. I wonder if we can help the director by discussing conditions at the nursery school which might be keeping people from volunteering. The feeling that it is not a man's work, the experience of being thrown too quickly among children without preparation, and strains between patients working there and between patients and the director are mentioned; the latter factor is not discussed, but the first two are responded to.

19

Following a night of brawls during which a patient, drunk and upset, broke a number of things, the doctor on duty gives a detailed report of his experiences, and the head nurse reads the nurses' report of the twenty-four hour period (Thursday, meeting 74). (I have advised them to have such information available, despite my general reluctance to give detailed instructions to members of the staff about how to participate at meetings, rather than discussing the task of the meeting and their role in it, and leaving it up to them to find a way to implement these ideas. Some staff members have difficulty living up to the latter kind of expectation but are very effective if they know precisely what is expected of them in a particular situation. Of course, the difficulty with reliance on instructions is that what instruction is relevant to a particular situation is not often known in advance; the same instruction is often automatically followed in situations to which it is not appropriate, and a staff member—in the absence of a general grasp of community processes and his job in relation to them—is not able to innovate any participation that might be called for.)

Staff fears that there will be an outcry by patients protesting betrayal of privacy are not at all confirmed. (Apparently, the need for the information is clear to everyone.) In fact, some patients add events left out of the nurses' report. It is also reported that the distressed outpatient has injured herself and been admitted to a closed hospital.

Following this unprecedented shared communication of detailed information, it is possible for me to trace with the group how more and more people have been drawn into the upset centering around the outpatient, especially because their feelings and beliefs have been kept out of the community meeting rather than expressed and discussed.

The clinical director is able to discuss some of the hospital's dilemmas in relation to the outpatient, and gives some information which alters the perception of the outpatient as victim of the hospital's lack of concern. Obviously some confidence in the hospital is restored and there is a considerable diminution of tension during this meeting.

(The lack of confidence in the hospital and its staff, bred by encounters in the informal life of the community and by partial information that color perceptions of community events, ideally is a prepotent concern of the small groups, which may be alerted to such lack of confidence by community meeting discussions or report on such issues to the community meeting. The small groups at this time are not functioning adequately in these terms.)

20

A new patient is nominated for community meeting chairman (Friday, meeting 75). Should the rule against preconference patients' holding office be set aside? New patients do not know the community; they have not yet committed themselves to it. Anger at the new patient might keep people away from the meeting: "He will make the meeting his playground." He makes a "campaign pitch." Others come to his defense, accusing his accusers of retaliating for incidents which have occurred in the informal life of the group; these are alluded to but not reported in the meeting.

21

The kitchen is in a mess. (The state of the patient kitchen—that is, the extent to which people pick up after themselves or create a mess— seems to be one indicator of the integration of the patient group; strains in the patient group often seem to be reflected by mess in the patient kitchen.)

There is a lot of drinking going on. The activities committee is con-cerned that people should control their drinking and behavior at the next party, which is being planned and hosted by the entire activities committee.

I wonder if the group is afraid to respond to the behavior of one of the patients, whose staff conference is coming up, and who ap-parently—judging from hints in the discussion—has been responsible for much of the behavior being alluded to. The patient states he has been "busting up" and asks the group to make allowance for him.

PART II: CLIQUES

This material suggests some ways to think about the existence of cliques, splits, or subgroups in such a community.

Informal group-formations based on personal preference exist con-tinuously. At times, however, evidence of such group-formations is unusually visible, and the relations between such groups more strained, and the boundaries between them more impermeable, than usual. How is one to account for these exacerbations of clique-ishness—this inter-mittent sensitivity to who belongs to what group and to the prestige-rankings of such groups?

It is possible to distinguish levels of involvement or interest in the members of the community. These levels require different degrees of effort to maintain.

The first level, apathy, is non-involvement or lack of interest or con-cern in either one's personal condition or welfare or the condition or welfare of the community.

The second level, alienation, involves interest in one's personal wishes, but no interest in the condition or welfare of others and an evasion or rejection of the values and aims of others.

The third level, pairing, involves interest in one other, who is felt to be like oneself, especially in "being" or ascriptive attributes or qualities, feelings, sentiments, values. This is the level of narcissistic identification in psychotherapy, of pairs in the group.

The fourth level, mechanical or homogeneous solidarity, involves interest in a small group of others, who are felt to be like oneself, sharing the same qualities, feelings, sentiments, and values, and who are usually drawn together by personal preference in informal situations. This is the level of the clique. Acceptance into a group characterized by homogeneous solidarity is based upon who you are and what you are like, not what you can do or achieve; such groups are often perceived as exclusive.

The fifth level, that of alliance, involves interest in one other, who is recognized as different from oneself but who is depended upon to do something that makes a special contribution to an end desired by both; the bond, in fact, involves mutual reciprocal obligations and expectations of performance. This is the level of the psychotherapeutic alliance or, in the group, the reciprocally responsible couple related not only to each other but as a couple to some task involving relation to their situation.

The sixth level, organic solidarity, involves interest in others who are different from oneself and making differentiated contributions to an end to which all are committed. This is the level of the team and of interest in, and concern for, the condition and welfare of the community and its task-oriented enterprises. Acceptance into such a group depends upon the ability to make a contribution; such groups are often perceived as inclusive, but are also likely to be feared and avoided by those who feel inadequate to perform.

In a community consisting in good part of emotionally disturbed, self-preoccupied, narcissistic, deviant individuals, one might suppose that continual effort by staff and patients alike would be necessary to achieve levels beyond apathy and alienation—to get attention for, and caring about, what is outside oneself and different from oneself but to which one is related.

The level of pairing is common and may be a necessary transition in both individual psychotherapy and the community.

Because this community is small and traditionally relatively undifferentiated, its solidarity tends to be homogeneous rather than organic. Some consequences are that new patients tend to be excluded, giving rise to discontent and deviance; patients tend to judge each other in terms of qualities rather than capacities and competence; and tasks which would be facilitated by organization and differentiation of functions are not performed as effectively as they might be.

The most difficult levels to achieve and maintain are alliance and organic solidarity. The cathexis of common ends, the differentiation of functions necessary to achieve such ends, and the assignment of these as roles to particular individuals or groups (the division of labor), are necessary preconditions to the achievement of organic solidarity. These preconditions usually require some degree of renunciation of bonds based exclusively upon homogeneous solidarity—for example, the acceptance of difference, and of people on the basis of actual or potential performance rather than qualities, and impersonal rather than personal criteria.

Almost any inroads upon or exhaustion of the group members' energies or commitment to such a level may result in regression from the level of organic solidarity to the level of homogeneous solidarity— that is, to loss of interest in the community as a whole and in its formal enterprises and retreat into what is felt to be the "safer" clique. Tenaciously hanging on to the clique may be used also to protect against further regression to levels of locked-in self-preoccupation, alienation, or apathy.

The loss of task leaders; disillusionment in the community (the perceived failure of its enterprises or leaders to actualize the values represented by the community); continual demand for attention to integrative crises; or the steady all-out total-push expenditure of energy that may be involved in a task-achievement—all may result in a period of retreat to the level of homogeneous solidarity and, therefore, to an exacerbation of the visibility and impermeability of cliques. Cliques provide an opportunity under certain conditions for rest, for remobilization of energy, for renewal of commitment.

Because of the depletion experienced at these times, I believe, it is often then that patients look most intensely to the staff for input of resources and restoration of value-commitment; but this longing is apt to be expressed in terms of desire for informal contacts—or homogeneous solidarity—with staff. Furthermore, evidence that the staff is aligned with one clique—the established leaders, for example—rather than another inflames the strains between cliques and makes collaboration towards organic solidarity more difficult.

It would be interesting to study cycles of different levels of interest in a particular community: for how long and in what way is interest maintained at the level of organic solidarity?

As is apparent from the material presented, dominated as it is by the theme of reaction to new patients trying to "get in," cliquishness may also be exacerbated by the perception of threat from within. The clique becomes both a fight group to attack the threat and a flight group to dissociate oneself from it. The most common internal threat in a community like this arises from the entry of new patients, who are uncommitted to the community, to its values, traditions, and achivements, who are "not like the rest of us," who want to change things, who often introduce new provocations to and opportunities for deviance. The clique often becomes the stronghold from which to attack such deviance, isolate it, and dissociate oneself from it. The new members, rejected in their attempts to "get in," bitter toward the establishment and the existing leaders, give up trying to make a contribution to community enterprises, form their own cliques, often around deviance itself and fighting the establishment—thus, the "goodies" and the "rebels."

In a community whose chief mechanisms of socialization and social control have to do with the internalization and reinforcement of values and norms through identification and social responses, including respect and esteem, each clique legitimizes itself by convincing itself that it is really protecting the most important values of the community as it should be. The fights between such groups have the flavor of holy wars.

A complete account of a social phenomenon such as cliquishness, or of any social institution or social element, should probably include: (1) a statement of its manifest and latent *functions* in the social system, and its functional and dysfunctional, predicted and unpredicted consequences for the social system, and an evaluation of the adaptiveness or maladaptiveness for the social system of maintaining this element in the face of specific, varying situational exigencies; (2) a statement of its *structural* interrelationships, of its interdependent connections with other social institutions or elements it "goes with"; (3) a statement of its *historical* development and the particular, unique combination of factors involved in its origin and changes through time; (4) a statement of the *dynamics* of its relationships with other social elements, structures, or processes, with which it may conflict, compete, or be inconsistent; (5) a statement of its *economic* aspects—for example, the extent or intensity of value-commitments associated with it, or the resources allocated to it; and (6) the characteristics of personality systems and behavioral organisms that maintain, impinge upon, or tend to alter it. (This metasociological framework is, of course, roughly analogous to the metapsychological framework of psychoanalysis; these are not substantive propositions calling for empirical verification or invalidation, but simply ways of thinking about phenomena.)

To summarize, schematically and far from exhaustively, some functional or adaptive consequences of cliquishness for the community are: (1) the insulation against deviance the clique may provide its members; (2) protection of values against reckless change and casual situational vicissitudes; (3) the mitigation the clique affords its members of regressive tendencies to apathy, alienation, or pairing; (4) the possible renewal of commitment to values and re-mobilization of energy with which to actualize these that the clique may make possible; and (5) the support the clique offers members who seek to introduce innovation or change in the community. (These functions might be served within the formal community structure by small groups, if these groups were composed with an aim to achieving optimal homogeneous solidarity, that is, if these groups were homogeneous in crucial respects.)

Some dysfunctional or maladaptive consequences of cliquishness for the community are: (1) the exclusion of new patients, who are after all what the community is set up to receive (the acceptance of such patients ideally depending only upon their need for psychiatric treatment and their ability to contribute in some particular individual way to the community's enterprises); (2) the consequent exacerbation of deviance in these excluded patients; (3) the undermining of a wide base of consent for the actions or decisions of various groups; and (4) the interference by impermeable mutually rejecting cliques, which emphasize feelings and personal qualities as bases for selection or choice and tend to ignore task-contributions, with the development of the differentiation of functions and the organic solidarity required for complex task-achievements.

The last point describes an aspect of the dynamics of the relationship between cliques in the informal life of the community and the formally organized enterprises of the community. The clique is consistent with the high value placed in the community on feelings, personal qualities, private interpersonal relations, and the exercise of personal choice; it is inconsistent with the high value placed on fairness, openness to a variety of experiences and people, the need for open channels of communication for the sake of understanding and problem-solving, and the need for cooperation and collaboration between people who are interdependent in some way as members of the same community, even if not personally attracted to one another.

The clique is interdependently related to other aspects of the community structure: (1) age differences; (2) such living arrangements as seating possibilities in the dining room, the location of rooms, the size of the inn; and (3) the relatively great opportunity for informal activity compared with the minimal demands on the time and effort of members made by the formally organized enterprises of the community.

The historical development favoring the existence of cliques would have to include in a broad sense the origins of the present organization and the original aim of its founders to provide a small relatively undifferentiated group of patients and staff an opportunity to interact face to face; and in a narrower sense the history of contacts between the various members of cliques and the circumstances inhibiting or favoring clique-formation at particular points of time: for example, an excessive input of new markedly deviant patients (or staff) at a particular time.

Economic aspects of cliquishness have to do, for example, with the amount of energy available to maintain organic solidarity, and the degree of cathexis of shared ends and of the differentiated organizational means by which to achieve these ends.

A characteristic of personality systems affecting cliquishness, for example, might be the orientation to gratification; to the extent the personality system is oriented to gratification, it will be disposed to membership in a clique if that membership offers more gratification than participation in the formally organized enterprises of the community. Similarly, personality systems oriented to achievement may be less inclined, personality systems dominated by feelings of confusion, uncertainty, and incompetence more inclined, to participate in clique-formation.

5. The Fate of an Innovation

The fifteen community meetings 76 through 90 (weeks twenty-two through twenty-five) tell the story of the demise of patient service in the dining room. The material offers an opportunity to think about the factors determining the fate of an innovation in a social system.

Monday, meeting 76. I wonder if the group would like to hear something about the staff's thinking about a particular patient as expressed at a recent staff conference.

After considerable hesitation and uneasiness about this new procedure, and its energetic endorsement by the patient concerned, the information is reluctantly requested. The clinical director comments that usually a patient who has gotten into as much trouble during his preconference period as this one has does not do well here; he mentions the patient's drinking and negative attitude toward the community. However, the staff still feels a try is warranted, realizing that such a decision may impose a burden upon the community. The head nurse comments upon the patient's unwillingness to accept help from nursing staff and the number of people who get involved with him.

I add to this that the staff is concerned that other patients tend to join the patient as he gets further and further from what is real, which is no help to him or to them.

At the end of an ensuing discussion, a patient makes the suggestion that one community meeting a week be devoted to a consideration of the problems of individuals. Another patient points out that he has also been involved in weekend drinking bouts and the formation of "rat packs" of patients; why has this patient alone been chosen by the staff for discussion?

(The group is becoming preoccupied with individuals rather than with the community at the level of social organization and processes, and with deviant behavior to the exclusion of interest in other kinds of problems. I am being drawn into this.)

Tuesday, meeting 77. Various "rat packs," involving "triangles," jealousy, drinking, and patients upset about absent therapists, are discussed. My comments concern: (1) the likelihood that the community has resources to deal with situations it can come to understand as a result of shared communication of adequate information; (2) the tendency to locate problems and pathology inside an individual and to judge him rather than to study relationships and even more importantly the contribution of the social situation itself to such problems.

Thursday, meeting 78. Lengthy announcements about and arrangements for available activities, such as classes and bridge, seem to be used to defer a consideration of current problems.

The dining room work is mentioned as disturbing.

This topic is ignored in favor of discussion of a patient who has been drinking and destructive to property in his room. Various people ask why his liquor can't be taken away from him; gradually it becomes clear they are afraid.

I wonder if safety in the inn is not an issue: do people feel safe, as they have a right to feel in the community, from physical assault?

A patient comments that since the staff has decided this patient shall be treated here and lets him go on drinking, he himself, although frightened, simply keeps his distance from the patient being discussed. The fact that the patient has not been referred to the community council is discussed by various staff members as crucial. Is discussion in the community meeting replacing rather than facilitating action by the community council? What, then, do we have to depend on to keep law and order, since as a community we eschew locked doors, attendants, and other forms of coercion?

Friday, meeting 79. The activities committee has made plans for the weekend.

A patient is frustrated by her work in the dining room. It is annoying that maids paid to work there sit around while patients work. She almost dropped a large tray she was carrying, but no one of the dining room help made any attempt to assist her. A patient work scheduler points out that the dining room help have been instructed not to assist patients in dining room service during this "transition" period; they find this difficult, but have been told to give advice or answer questions, and not to lend a hand. Other patients present similar and different experiences with the maids. *P:* They are doing their job—working before meals, cleaning up after—and I am doing mine; they don't bother me.

I interrupt the discussion to report deliberations by the community program staff. (The community program staff agrees that the patient discussed at yesterday's meeting does present a threat to the safety of the community under certain conditions, particularly when upset about his relationship with a particular female patient, and then especially when drunk. Under these circumstances he is unusually suspicious of others. The nurses have been advised not to try to cope with him without male help when he is drunk. The community program staff does not feel that people who expressed fear in the meeting were just manifesting their own problems, as some suggested. The community program staff plans to discuss the situation with the medical director.) I go on to discuss the consultation functions of the community meeting and contrast these with the decision-making, action-taking functions of such executive groups as the community council.

The group is uncertain about accepting responsibility or admitting that its members have competence for dealing with the situation through the community council. The staff is reproached for letting the situation develop to this point. On the other hand, the opinion is expressed that the community council chairman should be required to come to community meetings, from which she has been absent, or give up her position. A patient reports that the patient whose uncontrolled behavior has been a source of concern said the previous evening that his therapist told him to stay away from all meetings in the community. Another patient reassures the group that he told her he was trying hard to give up drinking and thought he was succeeding. However, he is still drinking. A patient is afraid not only of physical assault but of the upset developing in the whole community in response to this patient. What is the staff going to do to see that he does not drink and to face the female patient involved with her responsibilities in the situation? He should be told by the administration what behavior is unacceptable and that if it occurs he will be discharged from the hospital.

I remind the group that it is part of the special genius of the community that patients and staff share responsibility for handling social problems through such an apparatus as the community council. (The community council subsequently meets with the patient; their discussion is reported at the next community meeting.)

Monday, meeting 80. The strained relations between the patient group and the superintendent, exacerbated by the patients' work in the dining room, are manifested in this and the following meeting.

A building inspector is due the next day. The clinical director expresses concern about furniture piled in the hallway; this is a violation of fire regulations. He hopes the furniture might get back into the room. A patient says: "Or into the attic."

I recount the series of events that has taken place to give an idea of organizational processes in a hospital. A patient requested that she be allowed to move her own furniture into her room and have the furniture there moved to the attic. The coordinating committee had taken some time to consider this request. The superintendent at the coordinating committee first stated that only maintenance staff members should be allowed to move furniture out of the patients' rooms, and at a subsequent meeting that the maintenance staff did not have enough men to do this and that patients should move their own furniture or that this should be done by a patient committee. The business manager disagreed, feeling that only maintenance staff members should move furniture in order to protect the furniture and the floors. Meanwhile, the patient had acted on her own, moving her furniture out into the hallway. The coordinating committee was unclear concerning whether the responsibility for moving furniture should be the community council's or the decorating committee's; the former tended to be seen as a patient committee likely to represent the wish of a patient to make his room as much like a personal home as possible, and the latter (chaired by the head nurse) as likely to represent the ideas of the staff about what rooms should look like over a long span of time.

I report my observation that the superintendent is more and more concerned about patients' taking over areas of living and upkeep at the inn, and is going along with this process reluctantly, and that patients seem to feel that it is very difficult to communicate to him directly; he has refused many invitations to attend various kinds of community meetings.

The suggestion that a group of patients get together and move the furniture is rejected because it does not solve the general problem. The head nurse has the key to the attic; she refuses to open the attic for this furniture. The clinical director represents the coordinating committee as requesting the community council to decide which patient (sic) group [1] is responsible for deciding when furniture may be moved from

1. Such a remark raises the question about the staff member making it: does he think of such groups as the community council or work committee as patient groups rather than patient-staff groups? Perhaps then he does not see these groups

a patient's room, tagging it, arranging for its removal and for its return when the patient leaves. The patient says she will move the furniture back into her room for twenty-four hours until the building inspector leaves. This is unacceptable to the clinical director, who points out that a fire hazard is a fire hazard whether an inspector is present or not.

I suggest that the community council may now have points of view and alternatives from this discussion to take into account in its deliberations. (It is eventually decided by the community council and coordinating committee that the special projects crew of the work program will take responsibility for moving the furniture, once the community council has given its permission for it to be removed.)

Tuesday, meeting 81. The group, led by the patient food representative, is incensed by a memo from the superintendent stating that there shall be no more club sandwiches served at the inn. The food representative reports her meeting with him as a "deplorable" experience. In answer to her questions, he said that was the way things were going to be and that he made the decisions. When she asked what was the point in her being food representative, he told her to report to the community that some people took too much food and didn't leave enough for others. She now comes to the community to find out how people feel about this decision. Loud hiss. The great beast! He's a fine one to talk about eating too much! He should be invited over to the inn for creamed tuna fish! The opinion is expressed that club sandwiches once a month is reasonable and there are various opinions about how many sandwiches should be permitted per person.

The director of activities comments that the superintendent is having his troubles with his staff since the institution of the new work program, including patients working in the dining room. The food representative offers the interpretation that he is reacting to the complaints of the dietary staff who are angry at the patients for taking away their jobs; she adds that she cannot blame the dietary staff for that.

The day of the club sandwiches is reviewed. Apparently there had been extra people in for lunch, there were not enough sandwishes prepared, and people had to wait around for the cook to make them. The head nurse reports that the cook is upset because his understanding based upon an agreement with a previous group of patients was that sandwiches should be prepared only as they were ready to be eaten to avoid sogginess.

---

as coping with responsibilities shared by patients and staff to be solved by collaboration between them as manifested in collective action taken by such groups.

There is a discussion of the job of the superintendent. The food representative suggests he has been left behind and has no idea of what has happened in the community during the last year.

People are no longer getting up for work and are suggesting that the whole work program be abandoned. The sponsors' committee is meeting now at 8:30 AM because that is the only time staff can attend; this is resented by a representative of the work committee, which is having difficulty getting people to work at that time. A patient comemnts that the real reason for the failure of the new work program is the work committee's failure to use the community meeting to discuss problems as they arise. A foreman reports that shop staff are complaining that the work is not getting done satisfactorily; patients are not working more than a few times a week now. A patient states she has such a strong distaste for working in the dining room that, even knowing her attitude is irrational, she had lost all interest in doing any kind of community work.

At this point, a patient interrupts to mention her concern about an upset patient. Another patient says that if an individual is upset, that takes precedence over any other issue. (Again, as so frequently happens, a switch from a group issue to a focus upon an individual.) The upset patient says her upset is not relevant to what is going on in the meeting; she doesn't believe anyway that any help is available in this community.

I point out that these exchanges are shedding no light on what the concern is; I ask if the nurse on duty last night or a patient there will tell us what happened. (Later, the nurse who was on duty that night and at the community meeting tells me she didn't answer when I asked for information: "I figured I'd just let the patient answer all the quessions.") The patient finally says someone had called her a name, that she had asked for it, but that she was upset about the different ways of seeing herself she was discovering, including in therapy.

I wonder why the group is giving this matter priority over the distress of people working in the dining room, the distress of the dietary staff, the distress of the superintendent, and the distress of the nurses trying to cope with the distress of the dietary staff.

A patient answers that she wants an upset patient to talk about what is bothering her before she does anything like hurting herself; she has learned that from these meetings. Another patient says she sees that when an issue comes up, the group switches to discussing an individual.

(I am very edgy about my intervention. I wonder to myself if I intervene to protect the upset patient from the group. I am uneasy that other staff will criticize the community meeting for sabotaging the work program by not discussing its problems in the meeting. I am aware that there is the usual anger at therapists for missing appointments on the following day, a holiday; the group may be using the upset patient, who is reacting to her psychotherapist's impending vacation, to express this anger. I wonder if I am moving too quickly; it's as if the group says to me, "As soon as we learn something from the meetings and try to implement it, you're off on another tack." Nevertheless, the main point is probably that the distress of an individual is felt to be more important than any group issue, and the distress of an upset, "acting out" patient more important than the distress of any person trying to do his job and finding out that for one reason or another in this community he cannot. To ask the question, "What is it about this place, this society, that makes for difficulties for individuals?" seems to many to absolve individuals of responsibility for their own behavior because "the community is to blame." I think though that much individual behavior *is* a consequence of social organization or disorganization, of social structures and processes, despite the narcissistic wound that is inflicted if one accepts this view of oneself. Far from absolving an individual from responsibility, I feel that such insights make it possible for an individual to behave responsibly and more consciously in relation to the social forces impinging upon him, rather than simply to participate unconsciously in social processes under the illusion that whatever one does is a manifestation of individual "will" and "autonomy" or that one is exempt from the domination of social sanctions, norms, values, and beliefs one can always see clearly enough influencing the behavior of others. There is no autonomy without knowledge, and that includes knowledge of group life and the nature of one's participation, including at times involuntary sharing, in it. Yet, of course, it is true that such insights can be used not to keep one's head in the midst of social processes but as an excuse for losing it. Especially if this kind of rationalization is a consequence, knowledge indeed may undercut whatever order there is in the social fabric.)

Thursday, meeting 82. No one showed up for work in the shop this morning. When a patient tried to wake others, he was met with excuses and refusals. One problem is that work is done by various people at different hours rather than all trying to work together at the same time. *P:* I overslept. *P:* I was out late and put a sign on my door: "Do not disturb, especially for community work." People are saying they don't give a damn about community work and that if they want to sleep in the morning no one can do anything about it. *P:* I disagree with the view that when a person is upset and can't get out of bed, he should ignore these feelings and go to work anyway. *P:* Some people get upset four or five times a week; others hardly ever. Two patients were out until 4 AM although they both knew they had community work the next day.

The work committee only hears rumors but doesn't know what people really feel. "We don't know, perhaps there are only ten people who don't like to work in the dining room and thirty who feel it is a fine place to work."

Pressure builds for a vote soon. *P:* "I want to know to whom I am talking. I want to know what will happen with my discussion."

The inauguration of the work program is reviewed by the clinical director; he discusses the change in atmosphere from one in which there were no obligations or responsibilities, a hellish atmosphere, to one that is consistently better as more work has been added. It is important for patients not to be waited on but to take over responsibility for taking care of themselves. Although staff at first feared a work program would make it more difficult to treat more disturbed patients here, actually the obligation to do a certain amount of work has proved helpful to disturbed patients. Probably a hospital should be set up on a full self-service basis. If people have doubts about the value of this from their experience, let's hear them.

Work in the dining room was instituted in part because there was not formerly enough work for everyone.

People are getting more tense now that the time for decision about the dining room service is approaching. *P:* I don't show up for work because I'm lazy. *P:* I don't know why I dislike dining room service so intensely, but I hope it is eliminated; mealtimes should not be interferred with.

P: The work program is a program for idiots; I rake the same leaves each day because no one, patients or maintenance staff, carts off the piles of leaves; the dining room service makes sense; I would like to work there all the time. Maybe those who want to work in the dining room area should be allowed to work there, and those who prefer to work elsewhere allowed to do so; let the roster of dining room workers be made entirely from those who enjoy working there, and let this be their contribution to community work.

P: I haven't enjoyed working in the dining room much; I got sulky answers from the pantry staff and decided I could either get annoyed with them or start kidding around; I decided on kidding.

P: I don't like being told that I'm not allowed to go into the kitchen. *P:* That is a rule. *P:* Once I tried to go into the kitchen to get my grapes; the maids stopped me, saying no patients were allowed. *P* (sarcastically): You should have told them this is your home.

P: My trouble is that I tried to meet everyone's preferences; some people don't want to work on weekends, others don't want to work at breakfast, and I ended up with all the work no one else wanted to do; somehow, working in the dining room ruined my whole day; I kept worrying about having to be there, and that interrupted other things I wanted to do like work in the shop.

The meeting ended with a discussion of the refusal of the business office to give any more petty cash to the activities committee for evening snacks because the record of expenditures was incomplete and confused.

Friday, meeting 83. The meeting opens with a discussion led by the chairman of the activities committee on plans for the coming weekend. Mention is made of the opening of the current production by the drama group.

Then there is further discussion of the dining room service. Suggestions are made that all patients do dining room service in pairs one meal a week; that only patients who want to work there be allowed to work there; that the dining room be another area in the work program with a regular crew occasionally rotated; that maids not be left standing around in the dining room; that maids be kept for weekend breakfast service; that the first person up for breakfast on the weekends set up for everyone else; that patients take over the cooking of the meals also. Some complain they cannot depend on other patients to show up and give a hand when someone is unable to work; others report a contrasting experience. *P:* Working in the dining room is menial work, but I don't mind it too much. *P:* I hate it! A patient says that when she worked there the maids told her they wanted their jobs back, and that she told them that would be fine with her. A representative of the work committee reports that money earned by the patients for the patient scholarship fund has more than doubled since the inauguration of the new program. A patient says he does not like to be challenged to do work when he doesn't feel like doing it; and that furthermore the problem with community work is that necessary tools are not available to patient workers; on grounds work, for example, he has to rake leaves because the maintenance staff refuses to make available a more efficient machine.

During the course of the discussion it is reported that the superintendent has transmitted a complaint by the kitchen staff made to him that a tray of desserts had been left in the pantry and never gotten to the dining room. *P:* Since there are no snacks now, sometimes dessert trays are taken to the patient kitchen and eaten later. *P:* Why should the kitchen staff care what happens to the desserts! (It turns out that leftover desserts are eaten the next day by staff.) *S:* There is money allotted for snacks. *P:* Patients pay for desserts just as they pay for snacks.

I have the sense that the work committee is encouraging a discussion of feelings and attitudes as an end in itself, or perhaps in the hope that opposition to the dining room service will turn out not to have much support. There is no evidence that the work committee plans to make use of any suggestions in its own thinking. When I comment during the meeting that it would be helpful to the group to know what the members of the work committee have made of the comments they heard at the previous meeting, that their thoughts shared now might help to give some direction to the discussion, I am told that members of the committee want to hear further opinions. The request for still further discussion is repeated during the meeting.

At the end of the meeting, I try to make something of the material so that people do not have the feeling that they have not been heard by anyone; the kind of statement I make would better have come from a representative of the work committee. I comment that people apparently would like to work where they have a preference and with people they choose; I wonder what it is that prevents thinking in terms of patients' volunteering for jobs and dividing up the work according to preference. A second difficulty seems to have to do with the sense that patients have of the inn as in part at least their "home"; this conflicts with experience of it as part of an institution with areas like the kitchen that patients are not permitted to enter and tools they are not permitted to use. A third difficulty has to do with the strains between the patients and maids who work in the same area but do not talk to each other; each group complains "upwards" to its own leaders. I explore a bit the notion of patients as employees, not simply consumers, the psychiatric hospital being an example of a complicated kind of organization where a group paying for services cannot simply consume services but has to work and contribute effort and participation within and as part of the organization to get what it is paying for.

Meetings 84 through 90. I am away during these meetings.

This period begins with a report that three patients have committed identical acts of self-injury. The low morale of the community is attributed to the current production of the drama group. (One of the patients was fired from the play; the play is depressing; a character in the play commits the same act of self-injury; two members of the cast have been unable to listen to one another; the play involves no catharsis.) The low morale is also attributed to the start of the community meeting (the head nurse points out such episodes occurred before there were community meetings); the absence of therapists, who are sick or away; a belief that acts of self-injury are the way to get help and attention from others; a contagion among people.

The superintendent is reported to be too busy to attend a meeting with the patients. Twenty people are not getting up for work. Work involving growing things (the greenhouse) is going well; work in the shop and inn, housekeeping work, involves no rewards for individuals; the shop and inn are "places of destruction rather than creation."

Will therapists have extra appointments to make up the ones missed because of a forthcoming holiday?

There is increasing pressure to vote on the dining room service, and a call for its elimination. A patient volunteers to set up a permanent crew of nine people who want to work in the dining room; he has them lined up; the offer is ignored by the work committee.

Alternatives are outlined by a patient: maids and not patients, some patients and not other patients, or all patients working in the dining room. A suggestion is heard with increasing frequency from one or two patients that all meals should be cooked by the patients in addition to the dining room service. Some attempt to object to this on the grounds that the sanitation department would not approve it, a belief that others say is not true.

There are reports that maids are being nasty to patients and that patients are being nasty to each other in the dining room.

Cases of mononucleosis are reported by the clinical director; these are attributed in the discussion not only to kissing but to dirty utensils in the patients' kitchen and dining room. A set of silverware, china, and cooking utensils has been stolen from the patients' kitchen. Suspicion falls on outpatients who use the patients' kitchen or appear there; the head nurse especially expresses this suspicion. She is told by one patient that even if this were so, patients would not reveal it, because of the feeling that outpatients are not getting what they are entitled to. This results in a discussion of a proposal that outpatients be entitled to more meals at the inn.

The work committee decides to submit to the pressure for a vote; but offers no alternatives except to vote "yes" or "no" on a continuation of the patients' working in the dining room as presently set up.

No one at this time is willing to run for work scheduler. A patient who has been at the hospital some time expresses resentment that the group has preferred to elect new patients who know nothing about the community for these offices. The office is not sought because of the resentment such a person has to bear for assigning work and trying to get people to work. Elections tend to be popularity contests rather than to involve issues of relative competence.

Objections are stated to having to work alone rather than with others; to the expectation of greater amounts of work from patients during a time hospital fees have gone up; to the absence of incentives and sanctions; and to the intolerance by some of the feeling that some people some days are too sick to work.

On a day before a holiday, the patients meet together and vote to end patients' working in the dining room.

At the next meeting a patient is reproved for painting a mural on a wall of the inn; she agrees to wash it off, but says it was painted in anger at what has been lost in turning the dining room back to the administration. P: "Why did we rush into it?" There is now enough work in the community for about half the patient group if these patients work no more than a half hour a day. Not working is a way to express anger; there should be other ways to express anger; there should be more immediate, direct responses to the anger of patients. This all started when the medical director disregarded the recommendation of the social problems council and did not discharge the patient who refused to work. That started the feeling that people do not have individual responsibility for their behavior; their not working is somehow the community's problem not theirs. S: But the attitudes of this patient who refused to work are now shared by very many in the community, and perhaps were at that time too.

PART II: THE FATE OF AN INNOVATION

That an individual will express his anger by refusing to work or evading work obligations or that not working is a manifestation of individual anger are psychological hypotheses about community phenomena. Most explanation in the community is at this level.

"What about community organization or disorganization, structures or processes, results in such angry states in individuals?" is not asked; the assumption in this individualistic society tends to be that every individual anger is idiosyncratically determined.

Why is an individual who is angry able to get other people who are angry, perhaps for different reasons, to join him in refusing to work

or evading work obligations? Why are individual states of anger manifested by a collective refusal to work or evasion of work obligations
at a particular time rather than by some other phenomena?

The form of a hypothesis that is social rather than psychological
would be something like the following: the nature of the social system—its structures, organization, goals, values, norms—interacting
with a particular situation (including not only cultural systems and
other social systems or subsystems, but the personality systems and
behavioral organisms of its members as well) leads to a variety of
functional and dysfunctional effects, including the refusal or evasion
of work obligations. Such refusal or evasion results in social disorganization, which inevitably frustrates the goal-seeking of groups and
individuals, resulting in strains between groups and individuals, and
anger and tension within individuals. Angry, tense individuals are especially prone to deviant behavior. The increase in deviance results in
increasing social disorganization, with the subsequent "vicious cycle"
effects noticeable in the material reported.

Characteristics of the social system which are linked in some way to
the fate of an innovation, as illustrated by the reported material, will
be described under the headings of the four subsystems or components
of a social system: motivation; integration; consummation; adaptation.
(As a review of the material itself reveals, the process as it occurred
was not analyzed or discussed in these terms by or among staff and
patients. Ideally, such analysis or discussion of similar processes might
lead to greater sophistication in staff and patients about what must be
considered, understood, and anticipated, in order to attempt effectively
to bring about change in a social system. A social system by its very
nature contains conservative factors—for example, the interdependence
of its elements, the institutionalization of its values and norms—militating against change and tending to return the system to a former
state in reponse to every effort to change it, as well as factors, such as
internal strains, facilitating change and responsiveness to situational
exigencies and conditions. The institutionalization of a positive value-
orientation toward change—adaptation, technology, innovation, progress, achievement—or of a negative value-orientation toward change
associated with the prepotency of positive value-orientations toward
being, harmonious arrangements, sacred traditions, order, and integration are among the most potent factors facilitating or militating against
change, respectively.)

Motivation. The survival of an innovation depends upon its consistency or compatibility with existing elements in the social system:

particularly, the consistency of values implied by the innovation or explicitly linked with it, and the norms which it generates, with the values and norms institutionalized in the social system.

The value linked to work in the dining room is "taking care of oneself" rather than "being taken care of"—"doing" rather than "being." This value is certainly consistent with values of psychotherapy and the treatment enterprise, but it does conflict with the patient's initial expectation that he is in the hospital to be taken care of—feeding being an especially emotionally invested vehicle of care. Careful work with new patients is, therefore, especially necessary; the disruption of this expectation is likely to lead to a sense of deprivation relative to what is expected, and a sense of deprivation is likely to lead to deviant behavior. (Notice in this connection the hypersensitivity to the absence of staff who are ill, on vacation, or away on a day's holiday; the stealing of kitchen equipment; and the feeling that outpatients are not getting what is coming to them—the reparation suggested being to make more meals available to them!)

The relative lack of formal attention to new patients and their induction in the organization is, then, a factor contributing to the failure of the innovation. So, also, is the fact that leaders in the work program, determined to separate "work" (as a meaningful activity in itself) from "therapy," and the "patient role" from other roles such as that of "worker," do not build an adequate bridge or emphasize enough the link between the values of the treatment enterprise itself, to which presumably everyone in the organization has at least a minimal commitment, and the values of the innovation.

Furthermore, the dining room service tends to be regarded by all as a token symbolic of "taking care of oneself," but not in reality involving in a meaningful sense for this particular group "taking care of oneself." A discussion of this point, of course, takes us into a consideration of what kind of work would be meaningful for this group in this situation with its particular membership, having a particular location and future in the society at large, matters which have been considered elsewhere in these pages.

Emphasis on the impersonal (everyone should share alike in the dining room work) is also explicitly linked to the innovation; this conflicts with the emphasis in the community on the personal (the irregularity and frequency of hours of dining room work interfere with someone's personally valued activities; those who want to work there should do so and others should be exempt from such work if they prefer). The emphasis on the impersonal conflicts, in fact, with the existing arrangements in the work program, in which every other assignment is made largely on the basis of personal preference rather than requirements for workers in an area.

Whether or not the impersonal "everyone must do it" is so central to the innovation that such a value needs to be insisted upon quite so vehemently especially in the beginning, when the innovation is being planted and has not yet taken root, is a matter of judgment. (That it is so insisted upon probably is related to the fact that the innovation grew out of a "revolutionary" movement to change the community as a whole; see previous discussion of the synanon groups.)

One may form the hypothesis that, other things being equal, the more zealotry characterizes adherents of an innovation, the more opposition is likely to be aroused; defeat, even temporarily, of such aroused opposition is likely to require the use of coercion, if coercive power is available. If not, then zealotry, through the reaction it exacerbates, must itself be counted as one of the factors leading to the failure of an attempted change. If coercive power is available, its use will tend to mobilize covert opposition over a period of time, be costly, and thus in the end involve either defeat or marked compromise of the innovation. In this connection, the following are noteworthy: the apparent lack of concern by the work committee with minority objections ("we are not sure that the majority objects; perhaps *only* ten people object"); the failure of the work committee to modify its position in response to opinions and feelings expressed by others or to offer the group alternatives (based upon proffered suggestions) other than acceptance or rejection of the innovation as it stands; the insistent suggestion by those apparently intending support for the innovation of ever more radical innovations at the height of the opposition to what is already being tried ("patients should cook all meals as well as serve in the dining room").

The dining room work requires also, as all work does, a high value on inhibition or discipline rather than discharge—a tolerance of strains and problems—even more so during the period of its inception when difficulties are likely to be greatest. Discharge mechanisms and the support of discipline as a value-orientation are then especially required; but small groups, as set up, do not appear adequately to provide for tension-discharge or to support the value of discipline. For long periods of time, also, current difficulties with dining room work and feelings about them are avoided in the community meeting, an avoidance which the work committee at least goes along with, if it does not indeed—out of fear of opposition based in part on the perception of the lack of staff solidarity—sponsor it.

In the end, leadership in the work program, apparently losing heart, succumbs to an insistent demand for "action"—for a vote—when feelings are at their most intense, without helping the group to plan, to foresee consequences of various actions, or to formulate alternative proposals prior to such action. The attempt to hold off a vote is seen at this time by this group—which tends to prefer discharge to inhibition under almost all circumstances—as a refusal to let people express their rightful will; discipline, inhibition of discharge, thought, are far from institutionalized values in the community. To this also leaders in the work program have, perhaps unwittingly, contributed, by condemning wholly the "talk" of the community meeting, for example, in favor of getting out and "doing" something, and presenting these as opposing rather than complementary processes.

The loss of heart by work leaders may be understood in part from the statement of a staff person, who says in a community program staff meeting, "I refuse to fight any longer for the proposal. I find I am fighting everyone in the place, and I am tired of it." So the staff representative to the work committee is often silent and sometimes absent during discussions of the dining room service in the community meeting.

It is the rare staff representative who can represent the values and norms linked with and generated by an innovation consistently and steadily, so that others may respect him as the representative of these values and identify with him as the model of the norms involved, in the absence of solidarity with his colleagues. In the absence of such solidarity, his leadership is likely to be inconsistent, to waver and vacillate; in the end he sits by, lonely, sickened by his isolation, beset by self-doubts, angry at his colleagues, almost hoping that what he has created will be destroyed—so he may be done with it.

(The perceptive reader will recognize that many of these and subsequent points and hypotheses are applicable to a consideration of the introduction, vicissitudes, and difficulties of the community meeting as an innovation, also being described in these pages.)

In addition, the inconsistency of the values and norms linked to or generated by the innovation with those of important groups to which staff and patients belong outside the hospital also have a bearing upon the fate of the innovation. Most of the patients come from a socio-economic group in which the valued role-expectation is providing jobs; taking away jobs from people who need them conflicts with this expectation. (Despite surface manifestations of rebellion, the patients tend to accept the values of their families and class, especially when they are able to remain unaware that their behavior has its origin in such values.) In this connection, one wonders why the first step has to be all or none; why patients and dietary staff cannot work together side-by-side for a long time, with no hiring of new kitchen staff perhaps, but no threatening of the positions of the staff already hired. To be sure, this would not end difficulties posed by the fact that patients perceive themselves as not needing these jobs in the same sense that others in the extended community do need them.

Integration. The greater the degree of organization and organic solidarity of one group in comparison to another, the more power the first group has either to effect change in, or to reject change emanating from, the second group.

The administrative structure of the hospital—led by the superintendent and involving hierarchically ordered maintenance and dietary staffs—is more organized than the community program, and successfully, if covertly and passively, able to subvert an innovation emanating from the community program. The community program staff, in contrast, is split; the patient group is split; and the various enterprises of the community program are far from perceiving or acting in terms of their interdependence. The community program is, therefore, unable to sustain an innovation against outside hostility.

As the ratio of *the organic solidarity between the parts of a social system to the homogeneous solidarity of a part of the social system* increases, the greater is the likelihood that a change requiring collaboration or cooperation between that part and other parts of the system will survive.

Since the innovation depends upon collaboration or cooperation between administration as an enterprise (the staff members of which are experiencing in these circumstances of threat a heightened sense of identity and shared interests) and the community program as an enterprise, the relative lack of organic solidarity between these two enterprises makes it likely that the innovation will fail.

Note in connection with these hypotheses the difficulties in patients' getting tools from the maintenance staff; the way in which patient work such as raking leaves is nullified by lack of cooperation between patients and maintenance staff; the strained relations between maids and patients; the actions taken by the superintendent arousing the anger of patients.

The work committee acts as a group with a high degree of homogeneous solidarity, but there appears to be little organic solidarity between the work committee and other enterprises in the community program with which this committee must collaborate if the innovation is to survive. Under such circumstances, the work committee appears to other groups as a threat, as an elite imposing unwelcome programs, rather than as a depended-upon differentiated part of a common enterprise.

Since an innovation is likely to cause strains within and between groups and individuals in a social system, the likelihood that the innovation will survive depends upon the effectiveness with which such strains are faced and mitigated as they arise. This effectiveness, in turn, is a function of the degree of organic solidarity in the social system, that is, the extent to which each part of that system acts to perform its unique and necessary functions, upon the performance of which the functioning of other parts as well as the achievement of the aims shared by all parts depends.

During the period of this innovation, the work committee is not making use of the community meeting, neither bringing problems to it nor responding to its deliberations. The relation between the community council and community meeting is such that the community council appears to have abrogated its function of dealing through action with deviant behavior and to have suspended even usual sanctions; the community meeting, which is ill-equipped to cope by itself with deviant behavior and has no action apparatus with which to cope with such behavior, appears to have arrogated community council functions to itself. The community meeting is so swamped with consideration of problems arising from deviant behavior that it can attend to no other requirement of the social system. The work committee, in a society in which "courts" and "law" have apparently ceased, is unable to plan or carry out work in the presence of unchecked deviance and growing anomie. The small groups do not focus upon what in community life causes and maintains tensions within and between individuals, do not take action with respect to these tensions as they arise, and do not come to the community meeting prepared to ask for help in coping with such tensions, to work them out when necessary with the members of other small groups, or to act as a resource to the community in dealing further with such tensions as evidence of them appears in the community meeting. The small groups do not perceive themselves nor are they perceived as executive or action groups in this sense, with particular specialized community responsibilities. Therefore, in the absence of effective social mechanisms for mitigating tensions, these tend to build up and to result ultimately in deviant behavior.

Consummation. The survival of an innovation depends upon: (1) the shared perception that it contributes or will contribute in some foreseeable time to a shared cathected end; (2) the position of that end in a hierarchy of ends, when the attainment of some of these is postponed or sacrified by the innovation and its consequences; (3) the intensity of cathexis of that end; and (4) the ratio of the actual level of gratification attributed collectively to the innovation to the actual level of deprivation attributed to it. (The intensity of cathexis of a shared end is defined not only by the degree of effort that will be expended by each member—individual or group—against obstacles to attain that end, but also by the extent to which such cathexis is shared by different elements—individuals or groups—of the system.)

That working in the dining room will actually lead to the desired state of affairs in which patients take care of themselves is itself widely questioned: there is no indication that the administration has any intention of relinquishing its control over this realm, so that patients are likely to end up performing an isolated, menial part-task, in connection with which they are kept out of the kitchen and feel demeaned. Even those patients who have intensely cathected the end of "taking care of oneself" (and there is much ambivalence in, and there are wide differences between, patients with respect to such cathexis) see no opportunity to share in the entire process of obtaining food, preparing it, as well as serving meals—each step involving decision-making as well as routine chores—and therefore no opportunity to take the managerial and creative roles with which they are identified, or credit for or pride in the achievement of a final satisfactory product or outcome.

Cathexis of the end of that state of affairs in which patients take care of themselves does not compare in intensity with such ends as: (1) the achievement of maximum personal gratification (the pursuit of personal activities and doing what one wants whenever one wants being widely perceived as sacrificed to the requirement to work regularly in the dining room at an onerous task); and (2) the reduction of interpersonal strains (which are, indeed, exacerbated by the fact that a patient's failure to work adequately in the dining room leads quickly to frustration and deprivation of others in a realm, such as eating, so freighted with emotional meanings that such frustration and deprivation are even more intolerable than usual).

Adaptation. The survival of an innovation depends upon the shared belief that it will not threaten, but enhance, a system's relation to its situation—the availability and mastery of resources in that situation; and the shared belief that benefits accruing to one part of the system will not endanger the adaptation of the entire system.

The innovation of patients' working in the dining room clearly disturbs the relation of the community program to administration, which is a source of many needed resources—money, food, tools, facilities; furthermore, administration demonstrates its ability to cut off access to such resources. (The unavailability of trucks or other tools involved in leaf-raking, the decision about club sandwiches, and the decision to withhold budgeted funds from the activities committee, whatever the justification or lack of it of such decisions, illustrate the possession of this power.)

Such an innovation may also disturb the relation of the hospital organization to the extended community of which it is a part by withholding jobs from members of that community depending upon such jobs or believing they have a right to them. This bears upon the whole question of the relationship between a tax-exempt organization and a small community, whose financial resources are limited, and the strains developing between them over whether the existence of the organization, in balance, involves economic deprivation for the community or contributes to its welfare.

Part of the hospital's relation to its situation also has to do with its financial circumstances. A rise in living costs has necessitated a rise in already relatively high fees. What implications does this have for the ability of the organization to compete with similar organizations and to survive in the long run? There is no confident belief by either patients or staff that the innovation will contribute financially to the hospital by saving money and making it possible to reduce fees or to forestall further increases in fees. The suspicion is that in the long run it will prove wasteful and inefficient, and, therefore, whatever its supposed immediate benefits to patients, maladaptive as far as the entire organization (and its continued ability to serve patients) is concerned. (How, indeed, is particpation in a maladaptive process likely to benefit patients? What delusions must be maintained to sustain the belief that it does?)

Confirmation or lack of confirmation of all these kinds of beliefs and the level of confidence in the results of such investigatory processes are important aspects of the adaptation subsystem's contribution to the fate of an innovation.

6. A Crisis of Confidence

During this three-month period (weeks twenty-six through thirty-eight), a series of events contributed to the development of a crisis of failure of confidence in the hospital and its staff, followed by a number of different attempts at recovery.

The time span of three months as a meaningful unit for examination is itself suggestive of a number of problems, even excluding those involved in attempting meaningfully to order and carry out research investigations upon such phenomena. In long-term individual psychotherapy, of course, no experienced psychotherapist attributes great significance to an isolated event, session, or even week of sessions without some sense of its place in a process requiring a much longer time perspective to evaluate. However, in a community, each episode of upset, disorganization, program failure, or deviance, is likely to be responded to by staff and patients as if it occurred de novo and in vacuo, unrelated to anything happening before or afterwards in the community, random sparks and idiosyncratic eruptions from individual personality systems. The community, presumed to be a relatively unchanging *given* of structures and qualities, a more or less dependable instrument which reacts to these "bolts from the blue," is set the task of struggling one after the other with sudden, unpredictable "catastrophes of nature." But it is the very nature of continuous processes of the community as a system that are involved in creating, giving meaning to, or determining the response to these "bolts from the blue." These processes cannot be understood in terms of isolated events but only by studying patterns of events over time. Such recurring patterns are quite recognizable in different years and do not lose their essential character despite the fact that meanwhile individual patients have left and arrived and one staff member has been replaced by another.

The dysfunctional effects of feedback of information to the organization, in the community meeting or in various staff meetings, about each event as it occurs include: (1) overreactions to isolated events; (2) distorted evaluations of how things are or how the community is doing, which are then used to "make points" by various vested interests or to sanction negatively or harass participants in the process, interfering thereby with the skill and evenness of their performance; and (3) premature interventions or emergency measures the consequences of which have been inadequately anticipated.

Perhaps one of the most crucial contributions a sociotherapist in an organization might make is to provide a longer time perspective than may be possible for those struggling at any one moment with particular dilemmas, who are required to *do* something *now* to meet a specific system-imperative, and who are dependent upon the response of groups in which they are participating to be able to do something. These, of course, are the very conditions militating against detachment, rational thought, and a creative yet objective grasp of the total situation. If the resolution of difficulties is to involve the participation of rational egos in rational problem-solving, then often the most important thing to do in a time of turmoil is to be alert and to wait for there to be a shared perception and evaluation of the situation by those involved in it; the perspective contributed by the sociotherapist may make such patience possible at least some of the time.

Not that this is a counsel of passivity. In my experience, when there is a process involving loss of confidence in the hospital and its staff and programs—with sequences of alienation, deviant behavior, disorganization, the failure of programs and therefore the failure to meet certain requirements of the social system as well as certain requirements of its various members, and the development of further loss of confidence—intervention meant to interrupt this process needs great skill and tact. Such intervention comes best at a time when the members of the social system have come to the point of sharing recognition of the state of affairs to which the community has been brought and—on the basis of the recognition of the unpleasant consequences accruing to everyone and the even more unpleasant if not disastrous consequences anticipated if the process is not reversed or halted—determining collectively to bring about recovery. (That time comes when consequences are perceived to be widely distributed rather than incurred by a segment of the community.) At this time, the nature of leadership is especially likely to influence events, for example, the choice of means brought to bear to bring about recovery. Until this point has been reached, the most effective interventions—from the point of view of rational problem-solving—have to do with helping to bring about such collective recognition and evaluation by blocking attempts either to deny the existence of what is happening or to ignore the connections between behavior and events, or to exorcise magically the "badness" that is felt to be somewhere in the community by investing it in one individual and driving him away.

What brings about loss of confidence in a hospital? Confidence in an organization depends ultimately on the extent to which there is the perception that the leaders of the organization consistently represent the ideals of the organization in their actions and that the ideals of the organization are being actualized by the attainment of its primary aims. Hospitals are particularly vulnerable to such crises because of the difficulty in evaluating the extent to which a hospital is actually achieving its goal of curing patients. (Thus, also, the emphasis on respect for its professional leaders as a basis for confidence.)

Confidence in a hospital is therefore likely to be based upon secondary, tangible indicators: the prestige and reputation of the staff, indicated in part by published research, in part by the number of professional visitors who come to the hospital for consultation and to learn, in part by the number of fellows drawn to the hospital for training; the lack of turnover especially among the most valued staff—staying represents a vote of confidence; a full census—a "full house" represents a vote of confidence; the lack of acting out among patients—such acting out represents "something wrong"; participation by patients in various programs—such participation represents "things going well."

Of course, none of these indicators bears a necessary direct relationship to the adequacy of treatment; some—such as the quietness of patient behavior—may be inversely related to the adequacy of treatment over a certain range.

Crucial events in creating a crisis of confidence include: (1) the loss or discrediting of respected leaders; (2) the failure to attain a goal to which staff and patients have become committed, especially if it is perceived to be related to the primary aims of the hospital and actuated by a desire to fulfill important ideals of the hospital. The latter might include the failure of a project in the community or the necessity to send a patient to a closed hospital or to discharge a patient who could not be helped by the hospital.

Crucial factors in exacerbating a crisis of confidence include: (1) the simultaneous occurrence of a number of events tending to create such a crisis; (2) the departure of patients who have no faith that the hospital can help them; (3) the failure of mechanisms of social control to cope with the deviance, withdrawal, lack of participation, and disorganization resulting from the loss of confidence.

WEEK TWENTY-SIX.

During this week, there is evidence of the community's reaction to the failure of the dining room project. Bitterness is a residue (Monday, meeting 91).

P1: We voted out the dining room. *P2:* What do you mean—we? *P1:* The community. *P2:* Eighteen people in the community.

P: How long before maids can be hired to do the work? *P:* The superintendent will need four to six weeks. *P:* Maybe the vote should have been taken a week after the program started if we have to wait six weeks before it can be given up.

P: Why did you set up the tables this weekend when you objected to the dining room service so much? *P:* I didn't mind doing it with [another patient]; we were first at meals; what I really objected to was the way it was handled—shut up and let me finish what I was going to say!—the way the vote was put off; I refused to work there because that was the only protest that could be made.

The first response to the question "Where does the work program go from here, there now not being enough work?" is a call for a detailed system of stringent sanctions against those refusing to work, one patient in particular being singled out. (This is the beginning of a movement to cope with reactions to the failure of the dining room project by singling out particular individuals to represent the "badness" so that it can be gotten rid of.)

It is noticed that attendance at the morning meetings, where daily adjustments in work assignments are made, has fallen off considerably. Assertions of the obligation to work and take responsibility for the administration of the work program are countered with the demand that a worker get something back for his work, that there be some attention to incentives and rewards.

At the next community meeting (Tuesday, meeting 92), there is an announcement that many staff will be away to attend a professional conference. This is followed by a discussion of the present confusion in procedures for elections; all memory of how elections take place seemingly has vanished from the group. A file containing all such information that was to have gone to the community council chairman has disappeared. In that file is also a letter the medical director had once written about therapists making up therapy appointments missed for any other reason than illness or national holidays. A coming holiday is mocked as surely not a "national" holiday. Objection is raised that some therapists make up appointments missed because of the conference; others do not. It is moved to make the day the staff is away a work holiday for the patients also.

The work committee announces that henceforth people not working or missing the morning meeting will be referred to the work committee. There is an argument over whether or not referral to the work committee takes precedence over any other appointment including a therapy appointment, as is true of referral to the community council.

A great deal of anger is directed at the work committee; I wonder if some of it reflects feelings about the therapists' being away. A patient says that the patients pay for their therapy appointments and should get them; another patient comments sarcastically that the fees being paid for the cancelled hour are being used for the therapists' travelling expenses. *P:* If the therapists may make individual decisions about therapy appointments, then patients may make individual decisions about whether or not to work.

I comment that members of the patient group speak as if individual hours with their therapists, rather than the entire program of the hospital, constitute all the "good" they have paid for. I also question the tendency to retaliate by having a miserable time as though this screws things up for anyone else more than for those retaliating.

At a subsequent meeting (Thursday, meeting 93), it is announced that a patient is upset and in his room; I question the idea that this cannot be discussed because the patient is not present, since concerns of the community are involved.

An older patient runs for the office of work scheduler because "the work program is in such a bad state it's a challenge to work with it." An outgoing scheduler—also one of the older patients—speaks heatedly about the rejection of elected leaders by the group, wishes the whole work program could be thrown out so people might experience what it would be like without it, and calls for "rules like in the army": work is something that should be done because it has to be done.

Another patient gives another meaning to the idea "has to be done" by pointing out the value of a person's setting the table because he wants to eat.

There is a lot of talk about the formlessness of the day, despite rebuttals concerning all the available activities; a call for more structure is in the air. A number of people say that there should be rules about this or that. *P:* The group has experienced a breakdown in structure; there is nothing to lean on; there should be *no* new ideas now; the work program should be made to function. (This is the initial statement of a reactionary credo: let's go back to the way it was before—a credo which is to gain momentum and influence over the next weeks.) The call for structure, rules, and "going back" is countered by suggestions by some patients of ways to increase individual gratification, as though this indeed is being threatened: let's have a highball hour after dinner so people will not have to go elsewhere to drink; let's organize skiing and bowling.

I wonder if the community perhaps is in a state of shock over the rejection of the dining room service. The group seems determined not to examine feelings about this rejection, whether of loss, guilt, or relief. I comment also on the evidence I see for a beginning breakdown in the way things are organized, and confusion in the arrangements for carrying out business beyond the boundaries of the work program: for example, conflicts in scheduled meetings, making it impossible for people to be where they are needed.

The patient who had been singled out for not working now bursts into a defense of himself: "I am not in a conspiracy to destroy the work program." He goes on to say that people live like slobs all day and think they can make up for it by working one hour in the morning.

The patient running for the office of scheduler asks the clinical director if it isn't true that more patients can be treated at the hospital because of the existence of the work program; the clinical director replies at some length about the history of the program, the doubts about whether expecting patients to work might lead to being able to accept fewer patients for treatment, and the lesson of experience which proved that many patients can now be treated here, because of the work program, who otherwise could not have been.

At the last meeting of the week (Friday, meeting 94), when many of the staff are away, a number of patients report that liquor has been stolen from individuals and that food has been stolen from the refrigerator. There is a general rallying around planning actively for the weekend and a list of thirty-six possible activities for the weekend is compiled.

WEEK TWENTY-SEVEN.

There is some discussion of snow-plowing (Monday, meeting 95). Patients object to not being allowed to use the snow-blowing equip-

ment: it's foolish to shovel by hand what can be handled by big equipment. Response to this is a report from the coordinating committee,
transmitted by me, that the superintendent observed patients had apparently been unprepared for the first big snow. (A quite frequent pattern in the meetings is that, when patients criticize staff members or
staff arrangements, the staff responds with some criticism of patients.)

There is a lengthy discussion of a poem a number of patients had
written together over the weekend; some object to its "bad taste" and
"obscenity": the patients who had written and distributed it have, in
fact, been referred by a patient to the community council as social
problems. I wonder what the social problem is. A number of staff say
they found the poem clever and humorous and congratulate the writers
on expressing the feelings involved in words rather than acts. The au-
thors of the poem say they wrote it to cheer people up over the weekend and were pleased when people reacted with laughter.

There is some confusion that the staff has not responded as expected,
with disapproval. There is objection to a movie that had been shown
over the weekend: too modern and upsetting.

I wonder if the reaction to the poem might express the fear of some
kind of breakdown in community mores because the structure of the
community is felt to have been weakened by the failure of the dining
room project: a fear that things are getting out of control, and that
there are no clear limits on what goes and what does not go and no
traditions to be relied on.

A nurse comments that the poem and the movie coming together
were just too much. She thought part of the poem was clever, part of
it disgusted her, and part of it she considered just "sick." (There is
usually a marked difference in the methods patients use to "nurse"
each other when upset and those preferred by nursing staff.)

After a discussion of the fact that many people were upset over the
weekend, I wonder if the feeling is that the staff and the "good guys"
(the "responsible people") had been outvoted by the "rebels" and "outsiders" in the community; and if there is shock and alarm over this
turn of events, and concern about whether it represents a direction in
which the community is going—especially since many now seem to be
ready to consider the point of view of people thought of as "rebels" and
the possibility that they might have something valuable to say about
the way the community is run.

There is considerable uproar after this statement, no one wanting to
acknowledge membership in either group.

Tuesday, meeting 96: The preoccupation with getting the "rules" in order continues; a committee reports it has begun work on revising the community book of rules and policies. A patient says that at school the rules had to be memorized and that students were then quizzed on them. There is laughter. An older patient thinks that the first part of this might be a good idea. A patient challenges the idea of writing a statement of the rules when no one is obeying them anyway; the chairman of the committee says that he is going to work on the rule book—it's no concern of his what happens to the rules after they are drawn up. (This sort of statement gives some idea of the ritualistic element in the preoccupation with rules.)

There is much anger over a community council meeting, in which members of the community council had tried to find out the facts behind a patient's being out of her room all night without having informed the nurses of her whereabouts. The council members are accused of idle, evil, morbid curiosity. The patient involved says somewhat defiantly she is not going to tell anyone anything; she claims to have been too upset to tell the nurses where she was going; a nurse replies that her behavior had apparently been planned since her bed had been made up to look as if she was in it. Another patient says she had done this for the upset patient, who should not be blamed. There is some attempt by staff to help the group define what might be expected of a referral to the community council under these circumstances.

This is interrupted by a patient questioning the "goings-on" at the neighborhood tavern: a girl working there crying; the bartender dancing with guests. The tavern is supported by some patients as a fine, upstanding one; the questioning patient is attacked as hypocritical. Patients are questioned by other patients concerning what they find at the tavern they do not find at the inn. There is heated argument with accusation and counter-accusation.

My comments concern the fact that despite the fact that the community is made up of all kinds of people, the discussion is primarily in terms of "right" and "wrong," "black" and "white" absolutes, and there is in the discussion no attempt to look at any facts and no reasoning.

Thursday, meeting 97: The community is now attempting to recover from the failure of the dining room project by a reactionary movement comprising the reestablishment of the old ways of doing things, the tightening up of rules, the stringent sanctioning of deviant behavior, and the location of community problems as "badness" within deviant individuals and their expulsion. It is unlikely that this movement will work, if for no other reason than the defiant reaction it is exacerbating, with concomitant splits in the community along polarized opposites of "good" and "bad," "right" and "wrong." The staff itself has not yet had time to recover from the strains that have been exacerbated by the failure of the dining room project, so that there is as yet no leadership confidently drawing the group's attention to the problems within the community and hospital organization, involving complex intergroup relations, and offering possibilities of tackling these directly. The loss of confidence in staff resulting from the failure of the dining room project is still at such a height that it is unlikely such leadership would be at this time followed even if it were offered.

Now a new blow hits the community. It is announced by the clinical director that the medical director—who with some ambivalence has recently been referred to as the "god who never appears" (one might suppose, that is, the sacred personification of the values of this community)—has had to be hospitalized because of a serious illness. A nurse has also gone to a hospital for diagnosis of what appears to be a serious illness.

A nurse says something of her experiences with upsets the previous night; she thinks the upsets emanated from events at the neighborhood tavern, about which she would like to know. Her request leads to a rather frank, detailed report of the circumstances leading to a number of patients' having been caught up in a fight with the bartender. There is an attempt to discover why patients did not leave the tavern when they saw that trouble was developing. A patient says he was provoked because he thought the bartender was regarding him as a "crazy mental patient." Others remained to help him.

The question is again raised by a patient: what is it about the inn that makes people want to leave it and go out for drinks at 11:30 at night? (Such an exodus to external communities is commonly associated with a breakdown in solidarity in the inn.) One consequence of the night's events is apparently widespread absence from work the following morning. It is reported also that a number of people are upset; there is a lot of drinking going on.

There is some discussion of the happy and unhappy experiences patients have in the town. Patients express concern about difficulties they anticipate in trying to rent apartments in town. I comment on the difficulties any newcomer has in moving to a small town.

The discussion of the community's relation to other groups in its situation, perceived to be in part unfriendly, apparently draws the group together: "The enemy is outside." Externalization of internal threats and strains is, of course, a common way of dealing with them. It is noteworthy that I participate in this process rather than observe it. The meeting ends on the note that the discussion has been rational, that patients have been of help to each other and see how to be of more help to each other should such circumstances arise again.

Friday, meeting 98: Plans are made for the holiday season, which is approaching. After a somewhat hypomanic discussion of many activities, there is some disagreement about the color the backstairs are being painted. Black is suggested for the rug. Do maintenance men or patients tear cigarettes into pieces and grind them into the rug? Who is putting banana peels under the cushions in the living room? Further comments about the rug: it looks like the kind of rug one finds in funeral parlors.

Responding inwardly to the hypomania and such cues as "black" and "funeral parlor," I wonder about the fact that there have been no comments about the medical director's illness. P: Patients don't want to think about the Great White Father being in trouble. P: The clinical director assured us there is nothing to worry about.

I comment that the staff is quite concerned.

There is a discussion of the possibilities in connection with the medical director's illness, and the arrangements for covering things while he is away. P: I'm glad there are community meetings now; a year ago, when there were none, patients would have heard nothing about any of this. P: I agree; prior to the community meetings, patients never heard anything unless there was a major crisis. A request is made that the group be kept informed.

WEEK TWENTY-EIGHT.

Monday, meeting 99: A number of missing items are reported. It is planned to send a plant to the medical director from the greenhouse with a note from the patients wishing him a speedy recovery. The patient kitchen is in a mess. No use putting things away because it's always in such a mess. Arrangements for a group outing to have dinner and see a movie are worked out.

There is a long, serious discussion, attempting to diagnose why there are so many dropouts from classes set up in the activities program. Lack of expertness by class teachers in organizing discussion, the varied backgrounds of the participants, the fact that people are unclear what the class will be about or like when they sign up for it, not liking the teacher or the way the class is handled, the special problems patients have in studying and reading, are all mentioned as factors. One patient says that he doesn't like to commit himself to classes because he feels that he is being left out of other things people are doing; it would be easier for him, he thinks, if everyone were taking classes on a special "class night."

I wonder if some special teaching methods might not be required in the activities area. (The need for special skills in teaching people who are for the most part college dropouts and who have difficulty concentrating and trying to meet expectations they feel incompetent to fulfill, and the contribution that attention to group processes and solidarity might make to these problems, seem to me quite clear from the discussion. How nice if an activities staff and activities committee would make use of such a discussion in their thinking about, and functioning in, the activities program!)

Tuesday, meeting 100: More missing articles are reported. I urge the group to try to understand the development of the phenomenon of stealing at this time. The group recalls previous episodes: the threat one patient made to put poison in the beer he kept in the refrigerator; the call for fingerprinting; the requests for better locks. Comments are made about the general demoralization of the community and the lack of trust patients have in one another; in this connection, the failure of people to help with community work, the lack of respect for the community council, and the increase in drinking, are mentioned.

An argument ensues—with considerable defensiveness by people who think they are being attacked as problem drinkers or are edgy that someone is going to do something about their drinking—about whether or not drinking is a problem. Do nurses and patients differ in their evaluation of the facts? What are the facts? Has social drinking or solitary drinking increased? Is drinking that has always gone on now going on more in the open? Individuals begin to discuss their own reasons for drinking: nothing else to do; feelings of tension becoming intolerable. That various staff, especially nurses, have been talking about imposing a ban on drinking is one possible reason people find it difficult to discuss drinking openly enough to see what the facts are.

Thursday, meeting 101: There is a discussion about the impending visit of a former patient and the uneasiness aroused in some by it, particularly the indefiniteness of the proposed length of stay as a guest in a patient's room. What will happen if she gets upset? What precedent is being set? Is she coming for a visit or for care? It is suggested she stay in the inn one or two nights and then find a place to stay in town. The head nurse makes it clear that that is her decision about the matter, to the apparent relief of the discussants.

The meeting concludes with an announcement that a patient is leaving the hospital, some discussion with her about her plans, and a consideration of nominees for office—their qualifications and the difficulties some are having. One of the nominees says that he is interested in making it possible to exempt people from work and to have the program a voluntary one.

Friday, meeting 102: There is a long discussion about an "outsider" and what the community can do to help: this outpatient is reported to have neither a job nor to be going to school, to be hanging around the inn, and to be having a destructive influence on an inpatient (who might otherwise be succeeding better in relating to the community) by encouraging her not to do her work in the community or attend community meetings. (Again, as in meetings 97 and 101, the group unites to consider dangers from without.) There are a series of suggestions concerning how to help her, including that she be referred to the community council and that she take advantage of activities available to her as an outpatient. There is some concern about whether or not lack of money has resulted in the hospital's discharging her to be an outpatient before she is ready.

I comment on the impact of outpatients on the community and wonder if the community council might consider further what actions and policies might be indicated in connection with the relation of outpatients to the inpatient group.

WEEK TWENTY-NINE.

Monday, meeting 103: Snack money has been stolen. Money has been stolen from someone's wallet. Phonograph records are missing. It is suggested that people avoid leaving tempting items around. Locked doors are rejected as a solution. Someone reports cookies missing and someone else confesses eating them. A nurse comments on the miscellany missing and suggests the group try figure out why these things are being taken. One theory: people borrow things with the intention of returning them. P: People "borrowing" don't go through people's coat pockets. P: Why shouldn't people just ask someone, to borrow money?

I mention that in a discussion by the community program staff the idea emerged that stealing occurs in outbreaks at certain times when there are widespread feeling of deprivation in the group.

P: The group is probably feeling deprived at this time because of the medical director's illness. The holiday season is also mentioned; many people remember that there seem to be outbreaks of stealing with each holiday. *P:* Let's get rid of holidays right now; let's make an announcement: no more holidays! The stealing reported when many of the staff had gone to a professional conference is also mentioned. It is also pointed out that a certain amount of stealing is probably always going on but only at certain times is it reported.

There is a call to bring in investigators from the outside. I remember that the reason for the rejection of this idea previously was the cost of such an investigation, which no one seemed willing to underwrite. This is confirmed by the clinical director.

People who steal are encouraged to talk to a nurse, to the community council, to the small groups, and to the community meeting to explain what happens and what they feel, and that if such talking takes place trust in the community's desire to help will grow. *P:* I trusted someone with my car and the trust was abused. *P:* Every time someone talks at the community meeting, he gets pounced on.

I remember times when people did bring such things to the community meeting and did not get pounced on.

P: Perhaps stealing is a way of expressing individuality; someone might want something offered the whole group, like the snack money, to get something he felt entitled to, not through a committee, but in his own way.

Toward the end of this discussion, I suggest the group might have a research assistant to keep track of the reports of stealing and when they occur.

The meeting ends with a discussion of a patient party, planned by the entire activities committee; there is some agreement that such parties are best because more people work on them.

Tuesday, meeting 104: The community council initiates a discussion of what is involved in the status of being an outpatient. Do outpatients need as much contact with the hospital community as possible? Should the outpatient be as independent of the hospital community as possible? There is some discussion of the outpatient in trouble who has been seen by the community council: again, there are questions about whether or not the staff hasn't made a mistake in discharging her or whether this decision was based on her financial assets.

I suggest two alternatives for discussion: one, the plight of the outpatients at present and what to do to help them; two, the hospital community at present and what needs to be done to reorganize it so that patients are adequately prepared for leaving the hospital, perhaps to become outpatients. For example, a patient who becomes an outpatient should have learned how to take care of himself: how to prepare his own meals; how to get himself to bed on time, so he can work the next day.

There is discussion of the differences between being an outpatient in a large city with job and school opportunities readily available and the likelihood of contact with the hospital community except as an out-patient minimal, and being an outpatient in a small town where it is difficult to make other friends and there are relatively few job op-portunities.

I comment that in the view of the community program staff, one problem is that staff recommendations are not communicated directly to the community but transmitted by the patient involved, who, almost without exception, tends to distort these recommendations when com-municating them to other patients. For example, a patient who cannot be helped here often communicates to other patients that he doesn't need help at all; other patients are able to see that such a patient does need help; that perception arouses doubt about the staff.

Uneasiness is expressed about divulging any information from a pa-tient's staff conference to the community.

The director of activities changes the subject from this touchy mat-ter, and comments that in her experience outpatients make better use of the activities facilities when they are outpatients than when they are inpatients.

I change the subject again, remembering a comment by a patient, that upset patients, who use the time of the doctor on duty, should have fewer hours with their therapists—and less upset patients more hours. I wonder if there is some truth in this not intended by its proponent, in that the general misconception seems to be that the sicker one is, the more one needs to see the psychotherapist, whereas actually psycho-therapy is a kind of exploration that requires people on the whole to be at their best in order to participate in it. States of acute distress are more likely to require good nursing care than psychotherapy.

P: Actually when I am feeling and doing better I do get more out of my psychotherapy; my doctor and I have discussed that when I am most upset, I tend to withdraw from the community, but that's when I really need the community the most. *P:* Perhaps we could apply this thinking to the question of being an outpatient; perhaps an outpatient should be someone who needs less nursing care.

Thursday, meeting 105: This meeting before a holiday consists of some announcements, kidding, charades (one on the word "community"), jokes, and a "study of communication": whispering a message around the room and seeing how transformed it is in the process.

WEEK THIRTY

Monday, meeting 106. The meeting opens with silence and unresponsiveness to all comments and queries. The nurses report the weekend had gone well, that more people had remained in the inn for the holiday than ever before, that things had been handled "family-style," and that patients were of much help to each other. People had tried to keep their upsets under control, and now perhaps everyone is tired.

A discussion ensues about the fact that a patient had secreted overnight guests in her room and lied to the nurses about having them. The nurses feel they were made fools of. A question is raised about the propriety even in a "home-like" atmosphere of mixing sexes in one room. There are expressions of anger that the patient ignored the rules; she should be punished for this. There is some discussion of whether or not "outsiders" are disturbing: one is reported to have been helpful; on the other hand, people do not like to encounter strangers in the hall late at night. *P:* This places owes patients at least that much security. *P:* I don't care who has guests as long as they are in some other wing. *P:* The issue of guests is like the issue of pets; one or two is all right but a half dozen makes life intolerable.

A patient speaks with great emotion of being awakened by the guests, being unable to get back to sleep, and becoming so tense and upset that she needed medication; she had no intention of putting up with this any longer.

(Again, it is the outsider or intruder who is the problem.)

Tuesday, meeting 107: There is some discussion of discomfort due to excessive heat in some of the rooms; the nurses agree to change the thermostat setting.

A patient has brought an iguana from home and wants to know if there is any way he can arrange to keep it. Does the rule about pets apply to iguanas? What is basically lacking in this community that someone is forced to bring in an iguana? Laughter. An iguana may grow to six feet. Keep it at the shop. The shop instructor refuses because the cage would be too large. Keep it in the bathtub. There is a rule against that. There is no reason to respect any rules; if you want to do something against the rules, you can do it if you don't bring it to public attention. Keep it outside. It needs a constant temperature of 75 degrees. Joking about the heating of rooms. Keep it in the greenhouse. It isn't hot enough. Something can be rigged up for heat. There isn't enough room.

The patient is urged to bring the iguana into the meeting. He does so. A number of people express fear. It looks like a rejected prehistoric creature. It's beautiful. Give it to some staff member. I don't want to give it away; I want to keep it. Does it have a name? Puff.

I comment that rules can be considered solutions of problems: a rule solves the problem automatically by informing people what is allowed and what is not. Such a view of rules does not make allowances for the expression of individual needs or for differences arising in different situations. Are goldfish, iguanas, dogs, and cats all the same? Rules, on the other hand, might be viewed as guideposts, informing people that there is a problem in this area, so that a departure from the rule called for by individual circumstances needs to be discussed and consequences considered. This view of rules makes for less efficiency, but also less chance that a rule is used to close off more than is necessary.

There is further discussion of people's fear of reptiles, of not wanting even to pass the door of a room in which the iguana might be. *P:* I don't want the iguana here; I'm not alone; other people are just not speaking up. *P:* I'm tired of people who don't speak up always getting their way.

What will you do with the iguana if you are not allowed to keep it here? People can eat it. (It is interesting to remember Freud's discussion of the totem animal here.)

P: I've heard that many people buy baby alligators and flush them down their toilets; now they have found a good habitat in the sewer system of New York City; I don't believe the story, but one or two sewer men have been reported missing.

P: We have to live by rules; one exception cannot be allowed because there is then no way of stopping everyone who wants to keep a pet. *P:* You keep your motorcycle in the shop, although that's against the rules; like everyone else, you want rules with no exceptions, except where you are concerned. *P:* Your fear of making an exception is like worrying about crossing the street because you might get hit; no one would ever do anything.

I suggest that the patient involved explore with various executive agencies in the community, such as the activities staff and the community council, about what, if anything, might be possible as far as the iguana is concerned. The problem of the iguana is not solved, but in discussing such issues, we learn about one another and the difficulties we have in living together.

(Again, the dread "outsider": in the form of a frightening reptile. There is a persistent effort to locate the community's difficulties in one of its members who can be expelled, or in an outsider who can be kept out or extruded. The iguana seems to represent what the group finds unpleasant about itself: its underground life; its negative values. The staff is challenged provocatively and at the same time appealed to: what are you going to do about this aspect of us?)

Thursday, meeting 108: The meeting opens with a discussion of a party to be held that holiday weekend. The head nurse cautions about the use of candles during the festivities. There are agreements about taking responsibility for this not becoming a hazard. People are re-assured they don't have to come dressed formally, although some pa-tients plan to. There is an argument between those who want "rock and roll" and those who want symphonic music.

The work committee reports its consideration of a proposal that the hospital hire a coordinator of work, so that there will be some con-tinuity in the work program, and work will be a more important part of the patients' life at the hospital. Included in this report is the view that patients cannot be in charge of organizing work. The plans en-compass not only chores that need to be done, but also the possibility of paid work for patients.

There is some discussion of this report, but the subject is changed three times: once to concern with obtaining and repairing a pinball machine; once to concern with breakdowns in the movie projector and the possible cause of these; and finally to the concern of the head nurse about the current interest in guns and the refusal of the nursing staff to keep them any longer for patients. The staff representative to the work program objects to this change of subject and advises the nurses to take care of the matter themselves; the work issue is of more concern to most people. There is a debate about which subject should have priority. It is settled when two patients express their concern about two other patients' getting their guns from the nurses, and wav-ing them about. One of these patients says they were cleaning the guns. Another one of these patients is asked why he keeps doing things that frighten other people. There is disagreement about whether or not to cater to people's irrational fears. P: Why don't you keep your guns at home? P: I want you to get those guns out of here. P: The inn is my home; why shouldn't I keep my gun here? The President's assassination is mentioned. Someone mentions the assaultive behavior of a patient

and says if there had been guns available at that time he would have fled the inn.

I comment that the issue sounds like a question of deciding between allaying some individuals' fears and fulfilling others' wishes, but that information concerning why this has become an issue now—when it turns out, upon questioning, that the nurses have been keeping the guns for three months—is missing. I ask if one of the patients hasn't been telling everyone that he plans to kill himself.

The patient blandly admits that this is so. The other patient defends himself against the allegation that he has been encouraging this patient's self-destructiveness; he feels the interest in guns is healthy and that all the two of them have done with the guns is shoot at empty tin cans.

Another patient says that she knows what the one patient is trying to do for the other, because the former has confided in her that he is trying to show the other how dangerous a gun can be. Others agree they can see how this patient was trying to help the other by going out shooting with him.

I comment that it seems that one patient is trying to help another who appears to be in serious difficulty. I wonder if under such circumstances a patient might not want to consult with the staff. The patient had tried to do his helping without any collaboration with staff, who meanwhile were concerned about the situation and making their own plans about how best to deal with it. I emphasize the value of intergroup collaboration in coping with such problems.

WEEK THIRTY-ONE

Monday, meeting 109: Mess is reported in the patient kitchen. No one cleans up after evening snacks. Who is responsible for cleaning up? The pool table has been taken apart and cue sticks broken. Fruit has been smashed against the wall. Glass has been broken and scattered in the TV room; glass has been found in the cushions of chairs in the TV room. There is a new hole in the table in the patient kitchen and a new gouge in the table in the living room.

Solutions offered include: locking the patient kitchen; taking the patient kitchen off the work program assignment list so that people understand they have the responsibility to clean up after themselves; withdrawing snacks for a time.

I comment on the fact that no names are mentioned and there is no attempt to find out who have been littering, messing, and destroying.

Patients comment that they know who is involved, but expect that person to speak up.

As an experiment I mention matter-of-factly knowing who broke the glass in the TV room and give the name of the patient, suggesting that until we can discuss such concrete facts as a group, little problem-solving can occur. The patient mentioned admits the deed, says he cleaned up after and did not scatter the glass, and that he was "pissed off" at the time.

In response to the claim that people do not know who has done these things, I comment on the fact that people live very closely together, do observe what is going on, and that various people know at least parts of every situation; these parts can be put together at the community meeting.

Members of the group object to mentioning names because of the amount of anger about the acts; it is impossible to discuss them matter-of-factly. No one is about to run the risk of making enemies in such a small community. There are references to "squealers" and "squealing."

P: But everyone in the community has done something like these kinds of things at some time.

A patient contrasts the acts with the success of the party over the holiday, which had involved many patients working cooperatively together; maybe people don't want to admit that they can have a good time and work together.

I wonder about the assumption that it is always the same people who do "terrible" things and always the same people who do "useful" and "helpful" things

A discussion follows concerning whether or not putting cigarette butts out in milk bottles in the kitchen is a "terrible" thing.

I comment on the differences in the community about what is tolerable; such differences have to be taken into account in order for the group to live and solve problems together.

(It is possible that feelings of anger have been exacerbated by the holiday season and the inevitable disappointments and sense of deprivation associated with that season. That the anger is acted out upon the group's physical living space suggests that the anger is at the hospital and its staff.)

Tuesday, meeting 110: A patient who has decided that she has an eating problem wants help from the community: people should not talk to the patient about food or diets, should stop the patient from eating when necessary, should not kid about this matter.

I wonder if the group is being asked to collude in an individual's

self-delusions. This comment is followed by much discussion about
the meaning of over-eating, about eating as an addiction, and about
what might be helpful in dealing with such an addiction; people accept that the problem is real. (Is this patient discussed with such interest because an eating problem represents the hungers and sense of
deprivation shared by many in the group?)

A patient is being referred by the work committee to the social problems council because of his long-standing problems with work and because, whether he works or not, he has a demoralizing effect on others.
It is supposed that the social problems council will be listened to with
more respect than the community's agencies, such as the work committee or community council. (Respect and esteem for the community
and its agencies, and for the values it represents, have been steadily
declining since the demise of the dining room service.)

I interpret this move as "passing the buck" to the staff to solve a
problem which belongs to the community; I point out there has been
relatively little attempt to discuss this problem in the community meeting, and that there is no way to know at this time whether or not the
community is in fact incapable of coping with it.

Ignoring the patient or leaving him out of the work program is
declared by various patients to be impossible, because *so many other
patients* would envy a patient who did not have to work. (It is clear
that a shared problem is being "put into" this one patient, in the hopes
that it can be solved by doing something to him.)

I interpret the wish of the community that the social problems council get rid of the patient altogether or influence him by some "magical"
powers. I take the position that this is a problem for the community,
that the community must find some way to deal with the patient involved, and that if the community wishes to solve it by getting rid of
this particular patient then the community itself must decide that he
can no longer be tolerated as a member of it.

Some patients give testimonials about the value of work; the patient
in question declares that working in the community has no value for
him—he has a job outside the community and knows how to "work."

(I fail to inerpret the process of splitting "good" and "bad" attitudes
toward work, as though this ambivalence is not shared by all, trying to
locate the "bad" in one individual, and then trying to get rid of it by ex-
pelling him.)

Thursday, meeting 111: A patient confesses to damaging the pool
table. Another patient says that he has damaged the kitchen table and
has agreed to take the table top to the shop to repair it.

The staff representative to the work program observes that major renovation is going on at the shop and wonders why the shop instructors did not contact the work committee for help with this project. A patient's comment indicates that the shop instructors want the job done in a hurry and, by implication, do not believe that patient workers would be able to accomplish that. Some patients are giving occasional help. The kind of work being done requires skilled workers; patients, who cannot be expected to have such skills, are helping by keeping the shop clean through the work program. The director of activities reports that the shop instructors have had bad experiences calling on the work committee for workers in the past. A patient comments that the shop instructors want to be independent from the rest of the hospital program. (Lack of confidence in, and respect for, the community programs are exacerbated by the lack of integration of the staff.)

The group turns to discussing the phonograph records that are missing; and then to discussing the desire of a patient to transfer from one small group to another. I bring up the latter problem in a request for consultation with the entire group before this is discussed by the small group staff. Various people mention the frequent changes of staff in the small group in question; the automatic reactions of its members to each other, their incompatibility and unhappiness with the group. Suggestions are to disband the group or to constitute it a "melting pot" for all the dissatisfied members of other groups. The patient wanting a change attributes the desire to the fact that the clinical director has left the group; he was the "column" holding the group together, a "father figure," a teacher. (His leaving the group is related to the burden of other responsibilities, which have increased with the medical director's illness. This connection and the fact that the group is responding to the event of the medical director's illness and its consequences are not pointed out.)

The function of small groups, changes in them, and disagreements among staff about them are discussed by the group. The synanon groups are seen as competing with the small groups. There is a move to get staff members to "square off" and explain their differences at the community meeting. One patient says he cannot tolerate the idea that the staff is not united; another patient interprets the focus on the staff as a way of avoiding community problems. Which of the staff is the more "evolutionary" and which the more "revolutionary" is debated, with different patients having different impressions.

Friday, meeting 112: It is announced that a patient has inflicted injury upon herself. The group is at a loss how to discuss this, especially in the face of the unwillingness of the patient to discuss it.

I wonder if the comings and goings of patients are not having a profound impact on the community: two recognized leaders are planning to leave soon; a patient, who has been treated at the hospital for some time has been advised by the staff to transfer to a closed hospital; a patient is becoming an outpatient; other patients are thinking about becoming outpatients; the staff has only a limited amount of time for outpatient work; there is competition among patients about this; in addition, new patients like the one who has injured herself are coming into the community, and do not know what the community stands for and what will or will not be accepted; her act is part of the current disorganization—the increased drinking, apparently for sedation and to make contacts with others possible, and the use of proscribed drugs. I wonder why such information as the fact that the patient who had injured herself and another patient have been recently using proscribed drugs is not brought to the community meeting. I discuss my distress about the failure of all efforts to make it possible for patients and staff to share information at the community meeting so that processes in the community might be better understood; neither group seems willing to join in such communication.

I am challenged to tell who was involved with the use of drugs and how I found out. I am hopelessly drawn in, and see no way out but to give this information. Immediately, there is a stormy reaction, since my information comes from a therapist; it is his understanding, conveyed previous to the meeting to me, that the patient had agreed to the use of the information in the community meeting, but the patient denies that this is so and acts shocked and betrayed.

I comment that a patient is not treated by one therapist but by a team consisting of the whole treatment staff, and that it is necessary for therapists to consult with other members of the staff in the interests of the patient's treatment.

The patient who injured herself says she has never discussed this drug-taking with her therapist, considering it "too unimportant." I describe this as evidence of the community's failure to help her become aware of what the community is all about.

Other patients are upset that the patient was seemingly not consulted before this information was given at the community meeting. It is clear that many patients think of the therapist as providing a sanctuary where any deeds can be reported without consequences. The incident is used by the group to justify not discussing individuals in the meeting, because it is "clear" how "hurt" they may be by such discussion. A few patients discuss how harmful it can be for a patient to keep secrets from a therapist. I am asked to justify my behavior.

I say that I think the community should choose between living auto-matically according to rules or living by reason. To live by reason, the consequences of actions must be investigated and understood: the meaning of what people do and its effect upon themselves and others. The goal is learning.

(This meeting is disastrous from a number of points of view; I am drawn into a process by which the community is able to ignore its own dilemmas in problem-solving and to see me and the therapist associated with me as deviant and responsible for the problems of the community by betraying sacred values. Technically, one way to avoid this is to use in interpretation only information that is given within the boundaries of the meeting itself and not to be drawn into giving other information oneself. That I do not stick to such a procedure has partly to do with my alarm about the state of disorganization the community is in and my concern about future developments; partly with my sense of miss-ing roles, of a vacuum that is not being filled by other staff members. In addition, this meeting contributes further to the loss of confidence in and respect for community leaders; the debate that goes on in the in-formal life of the community between my supporters and opponents in-cludes many attacks upon the integrity of both myself and the therapist associated with me. Because the staff itself is divided and its solidarity low, contacts of patients with other staff tend to inflame rather than off-set their doubts. This process reaches a terrible climax when the patient involved, who has for some weeks heard his own therapist attacked by others, and in addition become involved in a number of situations that cannot be described here, inflicts injury upon himself two times, one after the other, despite the efforts of all to mitigate his self-destructive behavior. It is important to note that this meeting occurs at a time when the community must assimilate the apparent failure of the hospital to treat a patient successfully who has been in the hospital a long time but who is now being sent to a closed facility; and when patients are ex-pressing their lack of confidence in the hospital community by seeking to escape from it by becoming outpatients and then further losing con-fidence in the hospital because of the perception that allocation of out-patient time is being accomplished unfairly or inconsistently by the staff. The community has now entered a winter of despair.)

WEEK THIRTY-TWO

Monday, meeting 113: A new blow: the superintendent has died over the weekend. The new patient who has injured herself is being sent to another hospital. The social problems council has recommended to the medical director that a staff conference be held to review the situation of the patient who is having difficulty working in the work program. The patient asks that people tell him how they feel about him, because he does not believe he is so disruptive as a few have made him appear to be. He does not believe he is responsible for the downfall of the work program or that he is the leader of the "beat" patients. There is some discussion about how he has disrupted work.

I wonder whose social problem we should discuss: the patient's or all those whose feelings about work are so precariously balanced that the patient's challenge can upset them. I also think that for the first time we are hearing about the actual consequences of work's not being done: for example, the state of the washroom.

Tuesday, meeting 114: A patient sends a written message to be read at the community meeting about the patient who has been sent to the social problems council. " . . . other members of the community who have not taken part in parts of the therapeutic community are being completely ignored. How about the conspicuous people that continually miss community meeting, or the people that don't bother with small groups? Are these people leaving no effect on the community or do we continually pick on [another patient] because he has become a community mascot for blame? Can one person have a bad effect on a program? Or perhaps we should ignore the ten or fifteen people that always miss meetings? Are we being fair to the individual? It is my opinion that we are not being fair, but if I am wrong, I'll apologize. If the community meeting isn't important, I'll apologize. If there isn't more than one person having a bad effect on the community programs, I'll apologize. I ask that [another patient] remain a community problem. Certainly no one's problems involving the community cannot be solved by the community, no matter how big or tiresome the individual problem may be, and if I am wrong as to that, I'll apologize."

P: Others are interested in the community and still trying hard to fit into it and go along with it; he is against what the community is trying to do. P: I don't think he is being scapegoated. P: I am fed up with the fact that all we can do is approach this problem, get angry, get to the point of doing something, and then back away. P: I think he is serving a useful function in the community, like myself, by challenging its programs, but his behavior has gone on too long.

I comment on the feeling that there can be no exceptions; I also wonder if one of the things that makes this patient so intolerable is his continually putting his finger on the "sore spots" of the community.

P: The whole community has been moving in a direction of working together and of setting up meetings and programs which will make it possible for individuals to affect one another and to examine their effect on one another; we are concerned not to allow isolates to hold on to the position of being outside the community and that is what he is doing and rejecting all these ideas and in a sense pushing the community to be something different from what it is trying to be.

(The "holy war" is not about the work program alone, it is clear, but about the ideals of a therapeutic community itself; the ambivalence about these ideals is being dealt with by the formation of groups of "holy warriors" and "infidels.")

P: But others are isolates and we don't do anything about them. *P:* I was talking about the direction that the community has chosen to take; I didn't mean we are there already or that it is working perfectly. *P:* I think we ought to tolerate someone who objects to doing community work because I have never liked doing it either and can't see that I personally get anything out of it.

(The struggle is in part between self-interest and an orientation to the interests and welfare of the community as a whole. Many patients have no conception at all of committing themselves to anything unless it is in their immediate interest to do so. Recognition of supra-individual values might be an important output of community life to the superego or ego-ideal of the individual patient.)

There is much sarcasm and quarreling.

I wonder about the kind of community this should be and what kind of patients should be treated here. Should the hospital turn down patients who find it impossible to conform to the community's expectations? Can the community find some way to include patients who, because of the kind of person they are, can only come around slowly to the realization of what concern for others and cooperation with others involves?

P: Not everyone can be treated here. *P:* I am not in favor of a "shape up or ship out" community.

Candidates for the position of community council chairman discuss their positions on these subjects.

Thursday, meeting 115: A patient is planning to leave the hospital against the advice of his therapist and the staff, because he doesn't feel that he can be helped here; the patients at the community meeting attempt to dissuade him.

In connection with feelings about this, I invite people to share feelings they have about another patient's being sent to a closed hospital. Questions are asked the staff; there is some explanation by staff members of the circumstances leading to the staff's recommendation. Feelings about the unpredictability of the results of psychotherapeutic treatment, and the fact that psychotherapy is not completely scientific, and that emotional problems are not as specific and tangible as physical illnesses, are expressed.

P: I packed to leave once when another patient was sent to a closed hospital; there is a sense of failure on everyone's part; we all feel we might have done something differently that would have helped the person to stay.

P: I think of the hospital as the greatest place and all other hospitals as no good or at least not as good; it troubles me when someone is being sent away.

The staff representative to the work committee interrupts to say that the meeting makes him uncomfortable. Why is it being used to explore fantasies? It sounds like a combination of a wake and group therapy. There is a lot that needs to be done and real life problems calling for action.

P: What do you mean by real life?

A: Listen to the sound of the sanding machine; that is something going on in real life.

P: I feel it is important to discuss fantasies; it helps to think about what is going on and what it means to live together; I don't know what the result of today's meeting will be, but I feel that what is happening is good.

I comment that there may be a connection between the shaking of confidence in the hospital as a result of the staff's decision to recommend that a patient be sent to a closed hospital, and the impulse arising in others to leave the hospital because the hospital can't help. The thought that a hospital and its staff may be fallible is experienced as very threatening to a group that needs to feel that the place just can't be wrong in any way.

Friday, meeting 116: One of the patient leaders of the community announces that this is his last meeting; he is leaving the hospital. He obviously is having intense feelings about his departure. He doesn't want to talk about it and in fact leaves during the meeting.

The community council proposes that outpatients be allowed to eat Sunday meals at the inn, if there is advance information to the kitchen of their coming. The clinical director is asked to comment; he says, essentially, that if a patient needs continued contact with the inn, he should remain an inpatient; outpatients do have access to activities and facilities such as the shop but should not need room and board or nursing care.

One of the reasons for the new proposal, according to one patient, is that if outpatients feel they are getting a "fair deal" from the hospital, they might be less inclined to walk away with linens and silverware.

The patient who was discussed yesterday reports that he has changed his mind about leaving for the present.

There is some discussion about the disadvantage that doctors are at who do not attend the community meetings as far as knowing what is going on and understanding it is concerned.

WEEK THIRTY-THREE

Monday, meeting 117: There is a discussion about impending visitors to the community meeting. The director of activities asks that the program committee not plan on using the shop for its programs without first contacting the shop instructor, since he is greatly surprised there will be a jazz concert at the shop the following day and feels there will be a lot of work involved in getting the shop ready. There is a discussion of skiing plans.

P: What is the purpose of these meetings? P: I've been here a long time and I still don't know. P: The purpose is to discuss general community problems. P: The meeting is sometimes used when people want to discuss problems they are having. P: The work committee, community council, and activities committee use the meeting to talk over their plans with the community. P: This is the one time of day that the entire community gets together.

P: A gloom has settled over the community. P: It's different here during the winter. P: It's colder. P: I have to get away from here this time of year. P: In the warm weather people can get out and do things, but in the cold weather there is nothing to do.

P: What has the staff decided to do about the patient referred to the social problems council because of work problems?

I comment that the matter is still being discussed by the staff. I wonder if there are not solutions that might be worked out in the community.

There is some exploration of why it is so disturbing to the community when someone does not do community work, although there is no such reaction to nonparticipation in other important programs, such as therapy, small groups, community meetings. A patient has said that she doesn't participate in community activities because other things are of more interest to her: is this a valid position?

Tuesday, meeting 118: There is an argument about whether or not the special projects crew did clean the shop that morning in preparation for the concert. An announcement is made that the administration has decreed that there shall be no drinking by minors at the concert.

A patient asks for help from the community: she is trying to break off her relationship with an older male patient; she is trying not to drink heavily; she may be irritable and would like people to understand.

The work committee unanimously has suspended the patient having work problems from the work program. The conditions under which he may reenter the program are given. The committee does not wish to discuss this at any length, because the feeling is that he has been discussed too much already.

Should the money to fix the pool cues come from the activities budget or should they be repaired by members of the community?

There is joking about bowling games, ping pong, and a number of private jokes.

I comment on the edginess in the meeting and wonder if it has to do with feelings about the information revealed in a previous meeting about a patient by myself and the patient's therapist. I wonder if we might formulate some policy about what is appropriately revealed in the community meeting.

On the whole, comments indicate acceptance of the necessity and advisability of staff members' communicating with each other about patients, and there is little inclination to proscribe any material as too private to be discussed in the community meeting. The patient who had been involved says he thinks what was brought up was important to bring up for the sake of the other patients' understanding why their behavior was an issue of this kind of community and how it affected themselves as well as other people. There is much agreement that before a therapist reveals at a community meeting information received from his patient, he should talk this over with his patient.

Thursday, meeeeting 119: There are announcements concerning consequences of the superintendent's death and medical director's illness. The staff representative to the work committee has been asked to look into the question of a closer coordination between the maintenance function in the hospital and the work program. Because of the medical director's illness and the death of the superintendent, there have had to be many staff reassignments; staff members are taking over new administrative and teaching responsibilities and time has had to be freed to enable other staff then to spend more time in the treatment of individual patients. Time devoted to training has therefore had to yield for the present to these pressing requirements. One immediate consequence is that the fellows in training will no longer be expected to attend the community meeting as a group.

There are several reactions: the patients have no say about what happens around here; the patients and staff are drawing farther apart, and this in the face of the recent requests by patients that more staff attend community meetings; the patients resent that such decisions are simply announced rather than talked over with patients first; the staff have stopped coming to programs sponsored by the program committee and perhaps should cease to be invited to them; the doctors are probably glad to be relieved of the burden of coming to these meetings; that there will be fewer doctors at the meetings—only one or two—indicates that these have been intended to be therapy meetings all the time.

It becomes clear that many fellows wish to continue to attend, and they are invited by patients to revolt.

My comments are in the direction of asking the group to think about the people who need to be at the meeting because of their jobs or their roles in the community program. Nurses, for example, from this point of view might be more crucial to have attend than therapists who are not working directly in any of the programs or on any of the committees. There is a disparity between the intense feelings aroused by this change and the actual effect the change is likely to have on the achievement by the community meeting of its purposes.

Friday, meeting 120: Visiting doctors attend this meeting. A patient discusses her plans to leave. *Nurse:* You've been just like one of the family and we'll miss you. *P:* Lots of luck. A patient accepts the feeling of many that he should be the shop foreman although he lost the election by one vote.

A nurse brings up the fact that people seem to be drinking for purposes of sedating themselves. In addition, about a fourth of the patients are now taking sedation. Why are patients not using the hospital and its facilities, including the nurses, instead?

The harmful effects of taking alcohol and barbiturates combined are mentioned. Disturbances in the relationship between patients and nurses are brought up by one patient as a topic to be discussed; the topic is dropped. The nurses are particularly concerned about one patient, about whom many patients are also concerned, who seems to have developed a problem with drinking since she came to the hospital. Is drinking a way of life at the hospital? Isn't drinking at parties better than drinking alone in one's room?

I wonder what it means about the community itself that a patient who apparently did not drink before coming here has now developed a problem with drinking. I am told that it is because the patient has become twenty-one while at the hospital that she has started to drink. A nurse comments that the patient had some upsets involving drinking before she became twenty-one. *P:* She's one person who doesn't want to be helped.

P: Drinking is a perfectly normal social activity, helping one to be relaxed and friendly and to feel good. *P:* If you feel good when you start to drink, you feel better later; if you feel bad when you start, you feel worse later. *P:* When I drink when I am upset, I only become more upset. *P:* One time I got very drunk before a rehearsal; I realized later I probably did that to bet out of the play, and that was what happened: I was fired. *P:* I drink in order to feel comfortable when I am all alone in my room. *P:* Speaking as "your representative for recreational drinking," I feel good when I go to the tavern each night, have my customary number of drinks there, and return feeling good, no worse, no better than when I left. *Nurse and others:* How many drinks? *P:* More than once you've gotten drunk enough to worry a lot of people about what was going to happen next. *P:* I just get louder. *P:* I get scared of you when you drink. *P:* People shouldn't be expected not to go out and have a drink just because someone else might get frightened. *P:* I live my life for myself and drink when I want to for my own reasons and the fact that someone else is affected is never going to change that. *P:* That's what everyone feels. *P:* Not true; some people care about what effect they have on others.

I comment that we hear of the importance that people place on acting above all in their own interest. Leaving aside for the moment the question of the effects on the community, however, is the drinking actually in patients' self-interest, from the evidence we have from today's discussion?

This discussion is interrupted by a patient who wants to consult with the community about what to do about the pinball machine, which has been declared by an expert to be beyond repair.

WEEK THIRTY-FOUR

Monday, meeting 121: The weekend has been particularly upset and gloomy. A year ago, one patient comments, small acting out occurred such as patients' writing on walls; now, these acts having been discouraged, only major acting out is available to express distress. A patient has inflicted injury upon himself over the weekend. A meeting was held on Sunday, at which a good deal of anger was expressed about this act, and two proposals were made: a formal contact with the nurses to improve relationships between nurses and patients; a weekend community meeting.

P: People in this community put on faces; you never know when anyone is unhappy until he breaks a glass or something; people don't talk to one another when they're unhappy; if they did, these self-destructive acts might not happen. *P:* When we want to tell how we really feel, there are no words. *P:* Weekend community meetings might give the community a sense of being together on weekends; people can plan things to do at such a meeting and hear how things are going with everyone; the meetings can be held without staff. *P:* Attendance doesn't have to be required; these could be informal meetings.

At this point, a suggestion is made that what is really needed is a swimming pool. (The proposal that some formal arrangement be set up to improve relationships between nurses and patients is ignored by both groups; one has the impression that the patients decide that it might be better to depend upon facilities than upon staff, who have seemed to be so unreliable.)

Other suggestions are made for small parties over the weekend. A proposal is being explored that part of the earnings of patients from their participation in the work program go to an activities fund instead of to a scholarship fund for patients who need help in remaining at the hospital.

There is a protest about the Sunday meeting. It had gone on too long and left people feeling upset and angry. *P:* The Sunday meeting was like all other meetings around here—useless.

The clinical director, who had chaired the Sunday meeting, says that he too thinks it was a bad meeting; he had noted the group was very angry, but he could not get hold of any thread during the meeting.

I wonder what the people who called the meeting had in mind for it to accomplish.

The chairman of the community council says he called the meeting because a patient had injured himself and people were upset; the meeting was for the sharing of information to get at why people were upset. Explanations for the distress include: many patients are leaving; staff are planning to leave at the end of the year; the weather makes it tough because people are thrown together more. There is a request for information about what doctors are leaving at the end of the year and what new doctors are coming.

I comment that the community is having a rough time, undergoing a number of losses and changes: the superintendent's death, the illness of the medical director, the loss of patient leaders who have been discharged, the withdrawal of fellows from the community meeting, my withdrawal from a small group, the anticipated loss of doctors at the end of the year, the experience of what seemed to be a betrayal of confidence. I note that the patients had suggested at a previous meeting that the fellows revolt. Perhaps, the patient who injured himself is leading a revolt of the patient group. How effective is such a revolt? Does it effect the changes actually desired?

The wish to revolt is hotly denied.

I also mention the comments reported from the Sunday meeting discussion about the "lack of supports in the community structure" and the relations between nurses and patients. The issue seems to center on trust or faith in the hospital and its staff.

P: What I learned this weekend is that this is a community in which nothing is worth the effort.

Nurse: The patients are aware there is only a limited amount of nursing care available; this weekend half of the nursing care had to be given to the patient who injured himself; that meant there were only two nurses with whatever additional nursing help they could muster from the doctor on duty and other patients to devote to all the other patients; that spread the nursing care pretty thin; people may have been inclined to act up in order to claim their share.

A patient raises the question whether the doctor on duty at one time was actually unavailable. The circumstances giving rise to this report are explained.

I refer the matter of weekend community meetings to the community council and the matter of additional weekend activities to the activities committee (in an effort to mitigate feelings that discussions in meetings never go anywhere).

Tuesday, meeting 122: Various announcements about activities are given: a meeting of the activities committee; a concert; the awarding of a prize for the winner of a ping-pong tournament; entering a one-act play in a drama festival. *P:* We are sure to win, because this is a very dramatic community.

The work committee describes the undertaking of three projects, which will mean that patients can be hired to do meaningful work: renovation of the stage and backstage areas; painting the back hallway of the shop; finishing the work benches and construction of cabinets in the carpentry areas of the shop. Patients who are seriously interested in working on these three projects may now apply for these jobs. Three people are needed, two of whom should be men. The three people will be hired by the staff representative to the work committee and the patient schedulers, according to such criteria as skill and previous work records. At least two hours of work every morning will be expected. There will be no pay for the jobs since no money has been budgeted for these renovations. People who are hired will not have to do chores. The staff representative to the work committee plans to work on the projects himself and will be working on them whether or not other people join him. Unskilled people will have an opportunity to learn skills.

There is some discussion on the design for the stage and backstage, with some disagreement that the drama director has the best design. The problem is that the stage area at present is dangerous to the actors; the work will involve laying down boards over the stage. Opinions are expressed that the drama group should pay for the renovations out of its budget.

P: This is unlike me, but all I heard before this meeting was that everybody was angry and, boy, wait until the community meeting! Well, what's happened to all that anger?

P: I'm angry at the hospital; after yesterday's discussion, I assumed everyone knew that [another patient] was in trouble and that somebody knew what had to be done about it and how to do it; now he has hurt himself again; I wonder what all the people who are supposed to be taking care of things have been doing; I don't know what to expect next and I'm frightened.

P: This is an open hospital and everyone has to put up with people getting upset. *P:* Everyone has come here because he was in trouble; "nutty" behavior has to be tolerated.

Head nurse: I just came back from being away a few days and find this such an intensely angry place that it makes me want to pack up and take off for the South Seas; if I find it intolerable after one morning, I can't see how anyone else could have tolerated living with it over a weekend.

P: If the hospital cannot be changed, then he will have to leave; in a closed hospital someone in his state would be under constant observation, and his instruments for hurting himself would be removed. *P:* I have complete faith in the staff and their decisions; they must know what they are doing keeping him here; despite what is happening, I think he is being helped here; there hasn't been a suicide here for years. *P:* One would be too many. *P:* Are people waiting for someone to be killed before doing anything?! *P:* A few suicides for a hospital might be a good sign, an indication that the hospital is willing to take risks rather than restrict individual freedom. *P:* I've been trying to understand my own anger; I feel it has something to do with my realization that I can't be of help to anyone. *P:* You actually increased everyone's tension by running through the halls screaming. *P:* We can see how tension spreads by contagion. *P:* I just want everyone to know I don't have it in me any longer to help anyone and I don't want to be told by anyone that people have to be helpful to one another; I tried to help [another patient] when he wouldn't work and all I got were sarcastic answers; this is the same kind of thing with someone else.

(The ideals of the therapeutic community are being attacked as unrealizable; the sense of their unattainability justifies abandoning them. The staff is being attacked for standing by and not being helpful; there is steady pressure for the staff to take over and abandon all effort at a community involving shared responsibilities. There is a dim sense that change in the community is an alternative way—instead of doing something *to* an individual—of coping with these problems; but the only change that seems conceivable is to make the community a more restrictive one; that this alternative is not acceptable seems to justify abandoning attempts to cope directly with the structure and processes of the community itself. The attempt to change the community represented by the work committee's projects is not even perceived as related to the present problems of the community. This perception is certainly absent because in part it requires change in the way of life of a number of people rather than in the way of life of one or two defined "impossible" deviants.)

P: I want to hear from [another patient]—what are you trying to say? *P:* My acts are my statement. *P:* Do you feel you're being helped here? *P:* Yes, I think I'm getting a lot out of being here. *P:* You don't seem to realize the effect you have on others. *P:* I do realize this and, however foolish it sounds, I want to say I'm sorry. *P:* When a person is having a difficult time, no apologies are necessary. *P:* I do think an apology is called for; people shouldn't feel they have failed me by not being able to help me; many people have spent time with me; others have tried to come up and talk with me; I'm in too bad shape now to accept anyone's help. *P:* Do you know what's troubling you? *P:* I don't, and I hope to find out in therapy; the staff will be meeting soon to discuss me.

I comment on the wide range of feelings among staff and patients about what is tolerable in the hospital community.

P: Someone has to make a decision and that will be the hospital's position. *P:* He has made it clear that he is a suicide risk and since this is an open hospital, he should leave. *P:* I don't want to hurt his feelings but since he has injured himself twice in such a short period of time, after a long time in which he seemed to be doing well, I want to talk to him or ask him what he needs or be of some help to him or sock him in the mouth or something—I can't stand this feeling of being helpless; I want him to stay here and I want the hospital to try to help him.

P: I want one thing clear: is it your intention to commit suicide? *P:* No, that is not my intention. *P:* That's all I want to know.

P: I know what the cause of my anger is; I have many thoughts of killing myself and solving my problems that way, and I fight against these; now here is someone saying that's the easy way out; I know I'm not the only one who has such thoughts and his acts arouse fear in a lot of people. *P:* I agree; the anger people are feeling covers up their despair.

P: I know what he is trying to say: that he is angry at everybody and "what a bunch of shits" everyone in the community is; maybe that's projection. Laughter.

P: I think people are trying to cover up their anger at him and I think he should know how angry people are.

I wonder how such an expression of anger will help, since it has not helped after the first act to prevent the second; I note what I sense to be some self-righteousness on the part of others.

P: I just want him to know one thing; I can't take the experience again of having the nurses come up to our floor and carry him out with his boots in their hands.

Wednesday, meeting 123: The clinical director and I call a special meeting, he to discuss the administration's position on whether or not the patient can remain at the hospital, I to communicate some of my thinking on the causes of the current state of tension in the community and some implications for possible change.

The clinical director says he has met with the patient, who has serious doubts about his ability to control himself; he would like the patient to remain, but if he has to be sent away, it will be done in his interests, not to get rid of him or out of anger at him. This will be a crisis period for him, if he should stay for a while, and his therapist will have the job of finding some way of helping him get through it.

(The therapist is being asked, essentially by the whole community led by his own patient, to demonstrate that a member of the staff does indeed care, has the ability and willingness to help, and will prove reliable and persistent even in the face of hatred and despair. It may be noted here that the patient is not discharged or sent to another hospital, but does continue his therapy in this community for many months.)

In response to the clinical director's comments, there are a number of disclaimers that people are angry at the patient. *P:* I don't think there is any anger at him now; this can be proved if people are asked to raise their hands to show if they're angry. *P:* I was "damn angry" before but feel no anger now.

I comment on the "wave of anger" that has swept over the community. What makes communities like this one reach the point where this happens? The response to this kind of self-injury is particularly intense; somehow it is seen as an act humiliating others and making fools of everyone, somehow expressing lack of respect either for oneself or others. I speak of the "dynamite" in a community like this of using sexual relationships, alcohol, or drugs, self-destructively or with destructiveness toward others; such behavior arouses intense anger, which may then be acted out, arousing even more anger. Relationships between patients and therapists involve strong feelings, including anger at times; and such feelings may be noted and exacerbated by other patients wittingly or unwittingly. I note the probable effect upon patients of hearing their doctors gossiped about in the community as "untrustworthy," "tricky," or "power hungry." These are statements about a doctor's character, and, if true, would mean he perhaps should not be treating patients here. On the other hand, nurses, doctors, patients all may blunder. I also comment that the community's only recourse when it tries to solve problems is to do something to an individual—usually get rid of him. Perhaps we ought to think about the possibility of, and what might be necessary for, changing the community itself. The action committees have the responsibility to think about the way they function and what they wish to accomplish in the community. The work committee is active, but seems to be out of touch with the feelings of the community. The community council seems to avoid taking any action; might not the community council respond to people who are considered social problems with limited sanctions that fit the nature of the person's behavior, so that the only penalty available is not such an extreme one that there will always be reluctance about its use? I give as an example taking car keys away from someone who is driving recklessly, or making certain facilities unavailable to people who abuse them or do not help to maintain them, or confining someone to the inn who is getting into trouble when he leaves the inn.

There are comments indicating that any kind of restriction of individuals by the group will only make people angrier, but also that it would be good to have the community set limits on some behavior that causes trouble in it. Some are worried that the community should not restrict individuals, because that would take away from people the obligation to exert personal controls. In response to this kind of position, I wonder about the acceptance of the use of sleeping pills, which to some extent involves abandoning one's personal controls in favor of chemical controls. What will the community do, when the relative unavailability of personal controls is part of the situation it must cope with?

Thursday and Friday, meetings 124 and 125: I have no notes on these meetings. During this period, it is announced that the synanon groups are disbanding.

(This series of events demonstrates well the difficulties in formulating cause-effect propositions about social phenomena. Any phenomenon is an outcome of both what a social system is—its values and norms, the ends it is seeking to attain and the way it is organized to attain these, the strains arising from within—and the situation of that social system. The latter includes the availability of resources, facilities, media, opportunities, the current relationship with goal-objects, the conditions to which the social system must at any particular time adapt, its capacity for such adaptation and the nature of its mechanisms of adaptation, and the strains arising out of the interaction between the social system and its situation. In any given social system at any particular time, either the intrinsic nature of the social system or the characteristics of the situation impinging upon it may be given greater weight as determining specific phenomena. In addition, the consequences of a particular combination of autonomous and heteronomous factors in themselves will have consequences which may alter the social system or its situation or both in particular ways, these alterations in turn having further consequences. A social process, then, cannot be conceived as linear, but rather as a complex network of branches, each fork of which represents a state which contains within it alternative possible consequences, some of which are realized and some of which are not, depending upon the relative weight of immanent developments and external interventions. You cannot attribute a particular outcome represented by an outer branch to the fork existing far behind a series of forks, although in some sense there is a connection between them. Given a system of such complexity, the strategy of trying to order the phenomena by abstracting certain patterns of events and typical processes, recognizing that no concrete phenomena are going to match exactly such ideal types, and that the phenomena cannot be described by propositions concerning the relationship between two variables or even the interaction among a number of variables, seems to me a good one. Similar methodological problems have, of course, been faced by the investigators of any complex system, the noteworthy example being the psychoanalytic investigation of the personality system. It has often seemed to me, as a result of such considerations, that the struggles and models of sociology may have more relevance for psychoanalytic research than those of positivistic experimental psychology.)

PART II: RECOVERY

Given a process of social disorganization, some steps leading to recovery are:

1. a *shared* perception, perhaps brought about by some dramatic event symbolizing the state of the community, that "things are really bad," that the consequences of this deplored state of affairs, recognized as the result of many contributions, are widespread and accruing to all, and that "if things get worse, an intolerable disaster will occur";

2. the availability of leadership that intervenes in the direction of thwarting unrealistic solutions or those destructive of community aims or values, for example, isolating someone as "the problem" or "getting rid" of someone as a solution; leadership that intervenes, with evident confidence that at some point, with effort, order will emerge from chaos and knowledge from uncertainty, in the direction of helping the group to define and face realistically the actual situation of the community and the internal strains within it combining to produce dilemmas and experiences *shared* by all members of the group; leadership that intervenes to mobilize and rally resources available in the community, including its formal apparatuses and agencies for problem-solving and meeting imperatives of the community as a social system;

3. *shared* efforts, with differentiated contributions by different individuals and groups having different functions to perform, to change not an individual but the community's mastery of its situation or the nature of its adaptation to what seems unalterable in that situation, or to change the community itself—its norms and values, the ends sought, the degree of commitment and adherence to these, the nature of the arrangements or the organization of efforts to achieve community aims, or the degree of realistic recog-

nition of the intrinsic dilemmas and consequences of, and inconsistencies between, institutionalized norms and values.

Some of the "seeds" of recovery, already apparent in the material,
are:

1. the intervention by staff leaders at a time of crisis (meeting 123);
2. the invitation to a therapist, to which he responds, to restore
the community's confidence in the staff by demonstrating fidelity,
reliability, and the power to "rescue";
3. the new work projects offered by the work committee, with
the implied suggestion of a new way of organizing community
work;
4. the disbanding of the synanon groups, with the possibility
created thereby for an increase in the solidarity of both the staff
and the patient groups.

The disbanding of the synanon groups again raises the question of
what degree and kind of solidarity of the staff group are required to
maintain the confidence of the patient group and to make the achievement of patient-staff community enterprises possible? Are not differences allowable? Holding the same position or expressing the same
sentiments do not seem, most of the time, particularly crucial. Organic
solidarity, however, does seem to be crucial. Staff members may differ
or be different when it is apparent that they share bonds based on common values and commitment to common ends, and that their differences arise out of the different roles they occupy or jobs or functions
they perform and the differences in interests, values, and skills required
by these roles, jobs, or functions—each of which, however, is perceived
to make a differentiated, necessary contribution to the actualization of
shared values and the achievement of common ends. In such a framework, conflicts over priorities at any particular time, competition for
resources, different points of view or ways of looking a the same thing,
and an emphasis on different kinds of actions, interests, or values, are
inevitable and can be accepted, as long as there is also a legitimized, institutionalized apparatus for integrating, or, when necessary, settling or
resolving, such differences. When no such apparatus exists or the operations and decisions of such an apparatus are not accepted by all
parties as legitimate, or when differences are crudely expressed and
perceived as mutually exclusive polar opposites and the definition of
the "moral" situation is that if one staff member or group is chosen as
"right," the other must be rejected as "wrong," or when indeed differ-

ent staff members or groups are committed to different ultimate ends, then loss of confidence in one or the other—and ultimately in the hospital itself—and social disorganization are likely to supervene.

We may, also, ask at this point, what is the nature of the recovery offered by the new way of organizing work. The community has suffered the strains of experiencing the discrepancy between its ideals, including its work ideals, and its resources to actualize these ideals. One solution is to create a subgroup, an "elite," led "in person" by a staff member, who acts as a model for identification; the elite subgroup will then represent the achievement of such ideals for the whole community. This may "work" for a time by reducing the experienced strain. However, especially in such a small community, subsequent developments are likely to include envy of the status and achievements of the "elite" by the many; rejection and isolation of those few who are perceived as special and perhaps as preempting the opportunity for certain satisfactions by many others (no matter that these others may be less capable at a particular time of a sustained commitment to a work enterprise); and ultimately a refusal by the many to cathect ends commitment to which might generate meaningful work for the "work elite" to carry out.

The next step is to be the development of a special "job unit" of "real workers," who are hired, expected to meet certain work-requirements, and who do achieve individually certain skills and satisfactions. The members of the job unit are not widely perceived, especially by other patients, as acting for others in the community or making a contribution to it. The special projects of the job unit are seen as extraneous to or actually competing with the wants and ends generated by community living; the "glamor" of these projects further depreciates and reduces commitment to the community chores.

Partly as a result of what is learned from this experiment, an attempt eventually (over a year from the time being described) will be made to create a work program with the following characteristics.

1. Work is generated by the life of the community: the wants, needs, and aims of its members, which receive collective commitment. Work is supported by such institutionalized values as "taking care of oneself," "doing things in the real world to bring about results one desires," and "being concerned for the welfare and enterprises of the group of which one is a part." Putting on a play, building a new game room, and maintaining valued facilities are examples of ends that meet felt needs and wants, and require instrumental action and collaborative effort to achieve.

2. The work committee is not responsible for mobilizing commitment to work as an end in itself or to the desired ends requiring work to attain, but depends on other community agencies, such as the activities committee and activities staff, to mobilize commitment and energies available for work as the result of the cathexis of an end that work will make possible; the community council, and the nursing staff working largely through the community council, to cope with deviance and disorganization interfering with work achievement; and the small groups, and small group staff (including nursing staff) working largely through small groups, to cope with strains within individuals, especially those arising from community life, which may otherwise result in alienation from those values supporting work and withdrawal from or active disruption of work.

3. The work committee becomes responsible for technical rather than "moral" problems: developing arrangements for work or an organization of workers best suited to a particular task; developing criteria for work-accomplishment about which various interested groups may come to an agreement; mobilizing resources—including personnel with particular skills for particular jobs, as well as facilities or equipment; and keeping the entire community aware of the consequences of the actions of specific groups and individuals for the accomplishment of work necessary to attain ends to which the community is committed.

One of the most interesting aspects of this later development is how it, like all noble experiments, is compromised and corrupted, not only because of the opposition of those who with every difficulty hanker for the way things were in the "good old days" (one might say, "when we were in Egypt"), but, more basically perhaps, because the support required to bring about change in the established work program comes as a matter of apparent necessity where most strain exists: from those who see the development as a possible vehicle for the overthrow of the community-oriented aspects of the established work program and for the expression of their own extreme self-oriented values, and who visualize a volunteer work program in which no one is required to participate and in which anyone can work anywhere and at anytime and for as long as he personally wishes, no matter what the work-requirements are.

WEEK THIRTY-FIVE

Monday, meeting 126: The meeting opens with announcements about a bridge tournament; the date inspection stickers are needed on cars; the loss of a pair of boots. *P* (angrily): I don't mind when my things are borrowed because I've always assumed they'll be returned; now, I'm not going to trust anyone. Instead of silence, suggestions are made concerning where the boots might be.

A patient reports that he is making arrangements to give the iguana to someone living outside the hospital. (On the one hand, this might be seen as an action symbolizing the community's belief in the magical efficacy of the expulsion of "badness." But more importantly at this time, it is experienced by the group as someone being willing to respond effectively to the wishes and distress of others, as someone, in other words, caring about others; such caring, when it is expressed in deeds, is likely to be part of a process of recovering solidarity.) There are a number of comments about how to keep the iguana alive while moving it, including the suggestion that it be wrapped in a blanket.

The heating system failed at the greenhouse over the weekend; most of the plants died. Staff and patients discuss how a signal light might be set up to warn of a drop in temperature.

A nurse explains in answer to questions that the fire alarm had gone off over the weekend because of a faulty valve; he is reassuring about how well the alarm system is working, and humorous in his account of people's reactions. The head nurse is asked if there have ever been any serious fires. No, a few small fires in wastebaskets, some burned sheets and blankets, but always caught in time. The head nurse comments the hospital has been lucky. A patient suggests there ought to be more fire drills.

A memo, which has gone out from the medical director and clinical director, is now discussed; it states that the community has the responsibility for deciding when it can no longer tolerate the patient who has difficulty doing community work and who was referred to the social problems council, and that the administration will respond to further referral of him by a community agency by discharging him.

A patient asks if this will really be enforced. It ought to be, because the patient should help the community as the community tries to help him. *P:* Perhaps now that the uncertainty about what will happen to him if he doesn't work is over, he will not be such a problem for the community. *P:* The next time he is referred, the community will mean business. *P:* I don't want that responsibility and I'm sure there are many others who feel as I do. *P:* How will the decision be made? *Clinical director:* By the community council, on the basis of discussion at the community meeting.

P: I wonder what it is that the community cannot tolerate in him; other people don't do their community work; he could be seen as helpful to the community by bucking and criticizing it.

I encourage people to think out in advance what it is specifically that is objectionable and what steps might be taken to deal with a continuing problem, rather than to act impulsively "to get rid of somebody" when feelings are high and there is a sense of emergency.

Essentially an assertion of community norms and values is now made by a number of people. (This collective ritual appears to be a necessary part of the process of recovery, mobilizing and reinforcing commitment to such values and norms. The timing of such a ritual is important, if it is to be effective.)

It is difficult to maintain one's own intention to work in the face of someone else's refusal to work: that is the problem. It is not fair for someone to use facilities he doesn't help to maintain.

The patient in question responds that he understands it will help others if he works, but that working one hour a day in the community has no meaning for him.

The staff representative to the work program says that the question, "What's in it for me?" makes the issue a psychotherapeutic one. The work program is not for psychotherapy. Patients who had originally wanted the work program wanted it because they were fed up with the self-absorption and narcissism of their lives, with thinking constantly about what other people were doing for them. What these patients had wanted to do was something for and with others, working at a common time, and earning money that would benefit other patients. (Presumably, the contrast being made is between giving priority to consequences for oneself or giving priority to consequences for the collectivity to which one belongs. If I were the speaker, I would not want it to appear that I am dissociating psychotherapy—a prepotent enterprise and source of community values—and the work program.)

P: I am willing to cooperate with others in doing what makes sense to me; I was happy working in the dining room when that was part of the work program. P: It makes sense to keep the inn the kind of place people like to live in .

I suggest that is the essential meaning of the work program: to get things done that people want to get done, rather than the traditional reasons of helping people to get up in the morning or to have a group experience.

This is objected to by the staff representative to the work program and a patient, who suggest that getting things done is not an adequate reason to work because hired help can do the work more efficiently than patients.

(The memo of the medical and clinical directors, while doing nothing to undercut the notion that *one* patient is "the problem," does enhance commitment to the community and its agencies by indicating that these agencies do share with staff groups the responsibility and the authority to act, and that in fact these agencies represent the staff group as well as the patient group, since what is done collectively through them will make a difference to and be binding upon both groups. The fact that community agencies can represent the community and take action with respect to individuals in it in response to the community emphasizes the interdependence of patients—at least with respect to mutual obligations and sanctions, although not so directly with respect to being allies in achieving shared cathected ends. An increase in the perception by patients that they are indeed interdependent may lessen their dependence upon staff.

However, since the memo is in the form of an ultimatum, it is a foregone conclusion that the ultimatum will be tested by the kind of patient who is involved at this time, and that eventually he will be discharged. This expulsion, too, is a collective ritual, having perhaps not so much the function of punishing the deviant or rehabilitating him in any way as asserting and thereby strengthening the commitment of others to the community's values and norms. When the need to mobilize and reinforce commitment is great, because of strains, widespread disorganization, and growing alienation within the community, the collective intention to carry out such a ritual has a compelling, driven quality and is indeed difficult to circumvent through any kind of reasoning.

Are such processes as these inevitable in meeting the motivation imperatives of a social system? Adaptation value-orientations to empirical means-ends relations, to what works, to cognitive standards, seem irrelevant or, when called upon, seem to interfere with motivation requirements, for the meeting of which the relevant orientation appears to be to the meaning of events and objects in terms of a system of values and the institutionalization of those values.)

Tuesday, meeting 127: A patient has left the hospital and written his therapist that he will not be returning. Questions confirm that he has left against medical advice. *P:* It's a shame; he came here angry and left angry. The question is raised whether the college psychiatrist will hold it against the patient that he left against the staff's advice.

I turn this concern into a discussion of the concerns many people have about whether or not they will be re-admitted to college after having been in a mental hospital. Various patients recount their experiences and expectations with respect to returning to college. The speculations about the future remind patients about betting going on when various famous people are dying. *P:* If that's the way the world is outside, who wants to go there?

Another patient says with some feeling that the patient who left needed the community's help, but was quiet and therefore ignored, whereas all the meetings and conferences had been held to discuss a patient who made trouble for everyone. Whom do we want to spend our efforts on? Is the person who yells the loudest the one who gets the biggest share of the cake?

P: The "cake" is what the doctors have to offer the patients, and doctors only have so much time to give to patients. *P:* A person has to learn to ask for help. *P:* Not being able to ask for help may be the person's problem. *P:* I can understand why no one would help a person lying still with an unseen broken bone and why a lot of people would rush to help a person raising hell about his broken bone. *P:* He did ask for help in many ways. *P:* He was a funny kind of guy who never spoke. *P:* He won't be missed because we didn't know him when he was here. *P:* A lot of people have left the hospital under similar conditions and done fairly well. *P:* He did get the necessary attention here; a community meeting was devoted to him, and he talked about his problems in small groups. *P:* He was a hard person to get to know because he was always so angry; I guess it's my fault I couldn't take his anger; he was likeable when he wasn't angry. *P:* Is this a wake? (Three patients leave during this discussion.) *P:* This is getting to be one sad place. *P:* This is the kind of thing that goes on here all the time. *P:* Little things go on here all the time, but we shouldn't have to expect so many big things. *P:* People are wondering what we should have done to save him. *P:* He may not have been mad at the community; maybe he was mad at his therapist. *P:* Maybe we should talk about what we should do next time when someone gets the feeling he isn't being helped in this community. *P:* Everyone is guessing; no one has any information about what he was really feeling.

I wonder what the evidence is for the assumption that the patient had not been helped while in the community.

P: His feelings of hopelessness and lack of trust in the hospital are shared by every patient here; maybe I'm speaking only for myself. *P:* These are normal doubts everyone must have in a situation like this.

Two announcements from the community council: two patients are going on drinking bans and want the community to know so people can help them. There is a debate about whether or not individuals are responsible for each other in the community. A battle is reported to have taken place in the patients' kitchen, as a result of name-calling: that's what it's like to live here. *P:* I am going to have a rough time this afternoon, and if anyone planning to hang around is willing to talk to me, I would welcome the company. *P:* There are many small ways in which people can begin to show consideration for one another; I wish people would begin to think about these rather than the big things that might be done to help someone. *P:* I agree; I also think if people took some responsibility for their own behavior, this place would be a better place to live in.

(The departure of the patient, on the whole, is not defined as evidence of the failure of the hospital to help but as arising out of his own characteristics. Perhaps there is some relief that some of the anger has left the community. There are moments when it is recognized that members of the group share the same problems, concerns, and feelings. There is a drawing together in the face of difficulties with a feared outer world. There is a willingness to consider taking small actual steps rather than to rely on messianic hopes. Members of the group appear to be resolving to try to change their own behavior, at the same time asking for help from others in accomplishing and maintaining such changes. There is some consideration of the possibility that help is available from others than doctors. Persisting strains are indicated by the fact that four patients have left the meeting before its end; there is evidence of bitterness that help is not justly allocated among the members of the community, who are competing for it.)

Thursday, meeting 128: Poor attendance at the activities committee is reported. Those attending school are urged to let the work schedulers and nurses know their schedules. Thirty dollars is missing; a patient considers it likely her own absent-mindedness was responsible. There is a discussion about whether or not the hospital accepts patients who have problems with stealing. The evidence is that it has. What does a doctor do when his patient tells him that he has stolen something? Different therapists differ. Therapists in the past have suggested that patients speak to the persons from whom they have stolen something, or bring it up at the community council.

There is a growing movement in the meeting to pull the community out of its doldrums by taking specific steps. The director of activities emphasizes the importance of patients' attending the activities committee's meetings, so that their suggestions may influence the allocation of its funds. The possibility of patients' going skiing together in groups is explored. *P:* Perhaps the reason people don't attend the activities committee is that a low point in the feelings of despair sweeping the community has been reached. (I have the impression that the diagnosis of the "low point" is usually made by someone in the group after it has, in fact, passed and the group is experiencing the beginning of recovery.)

I pick up a book the co-chairman has in front of him and comment: [The co-chairman] has been reading *The Decline and Fall of Practically Everyone.* There is laughter and a noticeable diminution of tension.

People seem to enjoy their misery and hang onto it, or at least people get stuck in it and act as if they are trying to see how much misery they can stand. New people come into the community with enthusiasm; then the community responds in a way to kill their enthusiasm.

There is a request that the hospital's car be made available for transporting patients on weekend excursions like skiing trips. The director of activities agrees, after some challenges, to explore this possibility with the business manager.

I comment on the various solutions attempted to better life in the community. For example, locate the source of trouble in one person; make efforts to get rid of that person. So far, that has resulted in the discharge of one iguana. Another kind of solution is to try to get the staff to take over and solve the problem. I wonder if referrals to the social problems council, and now the request to the staff to provide transportation, are not examples of that kind of solution.

When I am asked for suggestions, I interpret that also as an example of turning to the staff.

P: Let's have only three community meetings a week and two instead of one small group meetings. There are groans and a chorus of objections.

The patient asking me for suggestions then reports on the liveliness of the shop: the building and personal projects going on. Others comment on the fact that the shop is a stimulating place and that getting involved in even little projects perks up one's feelings. *P:* It isn't necessary to do anything there; having coffee with other people is a help; you may find youself just picking up a piece of paper and starting to draw. A number of difficulties in the way of patients' participating in shop activities are mentioned: renovation going on may interfere with carrying out personal projects; a shop instructor pretends to be interested in patients' ideas, but he is really only interested in his own.

Others modify this latter comment to indicate that the shop instructor will let you carry out your own project on your own, but is not interested in other people's ideas about his own projects.

I wonder about the many other things people might also enjoy or be enjoying; a number of these are mentioned, including work on the play. Why are people reluctant to mention the things they enjoy doing?

Friday, meeting 129: The director of activities announces she is delighted that one of the group's problems is solved; the shop instructor has agreed to take a group skiing over the weekend, using his own station wagon. There is silence, and she wonders if she has brought bad news rather than good news.

(My own reaction is that a member of the staff has volunteered to help the patients. I question this in my own mind for two reasons: (1) the patients are not thereby encouraged to rely upon their own resources and to depend upon one another—if they do not discover that they can be sources of satisfaction for one another, their incentive to cooperate with each other is lessened; (2) the help comes fortuitously and with almost magical ease and swiftness upon the heels of the wish, rather than through efforts involving the community's own apparatus for solving problems, so that instead of learning to make use of organization to solve problems, patients are encouraged to believe that the expression of a wish is enough to bring about its gratification and to depend upon the benevolence and generosity, and therefore the moods, of various individual staff members. However, perhaps I am too puristic in this position. During a process of recovery, everyone is stimulated to "pitch in and help." Why not members of the staff also?)

I wonder how the shop instructor has come to agree to do this. The director of activities says that she asked him and that he would be reimbursed for the trip. Perhaps, she then thinks, the cost of the trip should be shared by the activities committee and activities staff budgets.

There is some discussion about whether transportation is the problem; it seems to be rather that people lack enthusiasm, prefer to do things on their own, or don't like to make decisions or plans for tomorrow. There is a comment implying that there is nothing to talk about at these meetings. I comment that if people express a wish one day and it is gratified the next, then what problems indeed can the community have to discuss.

The head nurse annouces that a nurse has volunteered to drive patients to a play in a nearby town.

A study committee has been formed to consider the problems of the work program. I wonder if this is a way to solve the problem or get rid of it; a study committee has no special magic to get at facts people do not want to discuss. Other patients report their experiences: study committees mean a lot to the people participating in them, but somehow become isolated from the community and do not affect others or result in action that is followed up.

There are a number of comments about the amount of criticism that goes on at the community meeting, compared to the shop, for example.

The staff representative to the work committee agrees with my doubts about the value of a study committee. He is concerned about the number of meetings. People at one meeting talk about what has happened at another. He would like to see the community get rid of all this talk. (These comments tend to confirm the perception of the community organization as involving "mere" talk, rather than as a means for solving problems and achieving ends. Interestingly enough, the comments immediately lead to a burst of nostalgia about the way the hospital used to be during the time of its founder thirty years before.)

P: In the old days, the group would take a walk for an hour in the morning and an hour in the afternoon; I think everyone would feel a lot better around here if people took walks rather than attended meetings. *Clinical director:* In the old days, people went to the shop for an hour in the morning and an hour in the afternoon. The staff representative to the work committee tells a story about how in the old days patients would be driven to the top of a mountain and then unloaded and told they would have to walk back.

(One "solution" to strains is to cathect an image—often a myth—about "the ways things used to be," and to believe that if the group could only reproduce that "golden time" all would be well. Of course, such a reproduction is by the very nature of things impossible, so that the image or myth is used primarily to criticize the present, which again by the very nature of things is always relatively unsatisfactory, at certain times more than at others. It is fascinating to see how a patient who has cathected such an image is quietly ignored or disregarded as long as most people feel things are going reasonably well and are committed to the social system and its ideals, but as soon as strains, crises, anomie, and alienation increase the same patient becomes a seer, whose words are heeded with respect. Parallels are apparent in every society. The increasing ascendancy of such a viewpoint occurs with the failure of realistic here-and-now problem-solving processes.)

There are a number of comments about the use of humor to relieve tension, which does nothing to change the situation; people don't want to bring facts into the meeting because facts might change the situation. *P:* As far as I can tell, people don't want the situation changed. *P:* People act in a way to insure there will be no change.

I comment that perhaps getting rid of discussion is not a solution, but that understanding why talk does not lead to action in the community might be helpful.

The staff representative to the work committee says he is not just for action but for a more appropriate balance between talk and action.

P: I agree there is too much talk.

Clinical director: The community council's thinking about the study committee was that perhaps people might find it easier to talk in small groups than in large groups. The staff has found that a small group may focus the issues so that a large group can discuss them.

WEEK THIRTY-SIX

Monday, meeting 130: A patient, who has accepted the nomination for work scheduler, sends a letter to the community, to be read by the staff representative to the work committee at the community meeting:

"There's always talk about an individual's regression but now I wish to express what I feel is a community regression. This place is back into a state in which it was when I first came here over a year ago; not as cool but just as pathetic.

"We are back to where sickness is the guide by which we direct ourselves in our daily involvements. It seems that to be visibly depressed, anxious, and/or angry is the big thing. We are promoting our own structural and self destruction. All the incidents that have come up recently are our fault because it is all of us collectively that make up the atmosphere in which we live.

"What kind of an atmosphere is it anyway? It is an atmosphere that caused [another patient] to want to leave and not to feel he was even able to tell us or talk to us about it. Not even his closest friends.

"It is an atmosphere that allows and in a sense encourages [another patient] to twice [hurt himself] within a period of a few days.

"It is an atmosphere that many times has made [a female patient] not want to stay and, later on, I feel was a contributing factor in her [hurting herself].

"It is an atmosphere that allows us and encourages us to sit around on our selfish tender asses day and night and discuss (rather than do something about) who is upset and 'How can we flip-out tonight?'

"There isn't one of us who has an ass so tender it can't survive a damn good kick.

"We live in an atmosphere that is shit and it is the fault of every damn one of us so let's every damn one of us do something about it and not tomorrow but right the hell now. Let's all of us grow up a bit and throw away these teething-rings of depression.

"With sincere apologies for not being able to be here,

"This is hypocritical I know but please don't disregard this because of that. I sincerely believe this."

P: I agree; something has to be done right now; if you're feeling low and stare at the walls, you find yourself climbing the walls. A patient discusses the possibilities for new kinds of relationships in the community.

The director of activities says that the opportunity to do useful and constructive things is available in this community and in the cultural life of the extended community around it. *P:* That involves transportation, which is not available. *P:* When I hear statements like the activities director's, I think somehow I am being accused of not taking advantage of all the things being done for me. *P:* The shop instructors have been too busy to give me any instruction all the time I've been here; for a month, nothing but a renovation of the shop has been going on. *P:* Why shouldn't we deserve the things we are offered? We pay for them. The staff representative to the work committee wonders if the money actually comes out of the patients' own pockets; maybe this can be a place where by our own work we can make it possible to reduce the fees.

A nurse reports that the nurses have decided to work in the following way. If a patient comes to a nurse and says he has a terrible thing to tell but wants the nurse to keep it a secret, the nurse will not agree to keep it a secret because the nurses's first responsibility is to respond to the knowledge in whatever way might be in the patient's interest.

A patient had agreed to do a poster and then quit. People should do little things like say hello. There are a series of comments involving disagreement and criticism with almost anything that is said.

I comment that any time anyone makes a suggestion, someone else says no; it is easier to tell in this group what *not* to do than what to do.

P: I wish staff members would be helpful in their comments. *P:* People always seem to be looking for a personal meaning in activity before they get moving; looking for personal meanings, they do nothing.

I comment that the suggestion that people find ways of being active rather than sit around and be depressed as a solution to some of the existing problems was supplemented by the activities director's pointing out opportunities available in the community. I wonder if the response to her contribution is, it is not our shop, it belongs to the shop instructors. In addition, no one seems to know whose work program it is.

P: People get upset because of what is going on inside them; no opportunities for being active can do away with that fact. *P:* A person can either give in to his feelings of depression or work against them.

Tuesday, meeting 131: People are invited to a program in town. A patient apologizes for getting drunk and spraying the contents of a fire extinguisher around the patients' kitchen and on various people; people thought it was funny; she thought it was funny; later, she realized it wasn't so funny, thinking about why she is here; she plans to keep tighter control over herself and has given her liquor supply to the nurses.

(What seems to me absent in this emphasis on the need for self-control is a positive goal, which people want to join together to achieve and for which it makes sense to control one's behavior. An assertion that it is good to control oneself is an abstraction unrelated to concrete ends and just as likely to result in proscriptions against "fun" and "liveliness" as against destructiveness. Or the end to which such a value-orientation is supposed to contribute remains intangible, something about "atmosphere" and a "better place," rather than a specific cathected end for the attainment of which postponement of discharge makes sense, but which also promises some eventual discharge and gratification. Or the consequences of discharge are minimized or exaggerated but never specifically examined. Self-control in the interest of achieving ends is rarely the issue in this community, which seems to swing rather between being "for having fun, no matter what the cost" or being "against any pleasure, no matter how harmless"; splits in the group often seem to occur to represent these positions.)

P: I would like to express my agreement with yesterday's letter; I think this community stinks and, until it changes, I have no intention of sitting through any more of these meetings. He walks out. *P:* I am getting tired of all these dramatic entrances and exists. *P:* If he doesn't like the way things are going, he has an obligation to stay and help change things. *P:* What he has done is like leaving a sinking ship during a time of distress and going to sit out in a lifeboat, instead of helping to pump out the bilge; that's the surest way to insure the ship will sink. *P:* It's the surest way to sink the lifeboat, too.

Questions are asked about why a patient has been referred to the social problems council, since that's "passing the buck" and it obviously did no good when the previous referral was made. *P:* The important thing is to help her, not the work program. *P:* Why does it help her to work rather than to stay in bed if she doesn't feel well? *P:* Staying in bed hasn't helped her. *P:* The staff representative to the work committee told me I made a commitment to participate in all the community programs when I decided to stay here; I wasn't aware of it and had certainly never been asked to do so. *P:* That is true of me, too. *P:* Why can't work be seen as a person's problem? We might set up a be-kind-to-animals program but that would not mean that there wouldn't be people who hated animals or couldn't stand to be near them.

There is some discussion of the proposal to have a staff person hired to be the coordinator of the work program.

P: I would like to see the community discuss individual people and what they are going through.

P: My class has been discussing Roman law; for years, Roman law was devoted to solving each individual problem as it came up; it made a big advance when it applied some general principles to the problem of law; individual cases then came under these principles; maybe here we spend too much time trying to work with each individual issue, rather than formulate a philosophy that would apply to everyone.

I comment that various aspects of community life, requiring people to work and solve problems together, inevitably create strains between different groups. It might be helpful to use this meeting to find out about these strains and see what might be done to resolve them. Asked for an example, I mention the strains created within and between people by the efforts of people to do certain jobs in the work program.

The patient referred to the social problems council comes in at this time and, in answer to questions, says she doesn't know what would help her. Another patient says that he has found growing favor for the idea of having more small groups, in which it is easier to talk, and fewer community meetings. (Again, the phenomenon mentioned under the discussion of cliquishness of the move toward smaller group formations during times of strain. In part, such a move seems at this time a rejection of the aims of the community meeting, which seem to some impossible to attain and to others to threaten their extreme self-orientation or to "rub in" their inability to function at a level of solidarity with a group of people, and in part a wish to escape from the strains in the community, which are most visible in and perhaps represented by the community meeting where there is an attempt to explore them. Perhaps, without disrupting necessary structures a move toward small groupings might be employed technically in the service of realistic coping with rather than flight from strains.)

P: How long has the hospital been this way? *Staff member:* Since

19—, when the medical director came here. *P:* For two weeks. *P:* The community is always upset in cycles. *P:* I got here just in time for the crest! *P:* A small committee should be formed to study the organization of the community.

I wonder why the community meeting should not be a study committee to look at the strains in the community. For example, we would probably see that one of the causes of strains in the work program is that new people are always coming into the community who don't know how things are done here; attempts are then made to "bring them into line."

There is the observation that new patients seem to participate well in the community programs until after their staff conference and the decision to stay; then they relax.

In further discussion, I comment on a second source of strain in the work program: its administrators strive for universal participation. This inevitably results in difficulties when the program is faced with people who refuse to work or who say they want to but can't.

P: The patients on the work committee are willing to let those who who want to work, work, and to let those who don't want to, not work; the staff on the committee insists on universal participation. *P:* There are only two staff members on the committee and five patients. *P:* It doesn't make sense to outvote the staff, because they are the ones who know the therapeutic benefits of expecting people to work.

There are comments that the community meeting is the community's problem: its discussions are directionless and cause tension.

Thursday, meeting 132: A good activities committee meeting is reported, demonstrating, according to the director of activities, how many creative ideas can come out of a number of people working together. Arrangements are made so that a bridge tournament does not conflict with a typing class. Someone asks if anyone is going into town; he would like a ride; he is offered one. There is much joking. There is a good deal of conjecture about who might be playing music in the library; it turns out that a patient has left a record on so the meeting would have a background of "harmony." There is general agreement expressed by some patients and, with coaxing, a nurse that tension in the inn has decreased; one or two people are still upset, but on the whole group is relaxed and feeling better.

(One is skeptical of a change that is not based on any objective change in the group's situation or internal characteristics.)

A patient announces he is quitting as work scheduler. His problems with drinking are discussed with him; members of the group offer various suggestions for the treatment of the drinking, ranging from "a drug that makes you sick if you drink" to hypnotism. A patient who has given up drinking successfully is mentioned; he says, "You can stop drinking if you want to stop, but nothing helps if you don't."

The characteristics of the scheduler's job are discussed. He has to bear sarcasm and challenge about "his" work program. His job should be to organize the work, not to get people to do it. The job would be easier if everyone supported the work program.

I wonder if people disagree with the work program as a whole; it seems more likely that objection is to specific and perhaps relatively minor aspects of it. There is agreement. The present atmosphere of co-operation and support among workers at the shop is mentioned.

A patient asks what has led to the recovery of the community. Two alternative theories are offered by various patients: warmer weather; and the efforts of a lot of people to reduce the tension.

P: Do the staff really feel the hospital would suffer an important loss if the work program were abandoned?

I assert that all the staff agree that psychotherapy is best carried on in an environment which offers realistic opportunities for work and activities. Disagreements which occur have mostly to do with what is the best way to achieve such an environment and, compared to the agreements, they are relatively minor.

Perhaps we should drop the program for a time to see what it is like. With the community always changing, it would make more sense for the people who have had the experience working in the program to maintain its traditions and explain its values to new patients. Will the program ever see a time when it is supported by one hundred percent of the patients? There will always be patients who will object to the program or not be able to work in it.

Comments are made about the difficulties small groups get into. Reassurance is given. Small groups run into trouble from time to time and always come out of it. *P:* My group has been in trouble ten months. *P:* There is still hope for your group. Maybe a group might be split up or its members rotated among other groups. It's important for the groups to have the same people. *P:* I had trouble with my group at the start and finally became comfortable in it only because I got to know the people after a time. We shouldn't try to change the structure of the community every time we get into trouble.

There is some discussion about whether or not staff members squelch such suggestions as having a study group or having a meeting with the entire staff.

(The note of optimism seems related to expressions of agreement and reassurance. The comments suggest that tension in the inn is related to anomie, to lack of solidarity, to dissension, antagonism, and intergroup strains—rather than directly to the degree of upset of particular individuals or even to the number of upset individuals. A decrease in strains in the meeting is probably related to the explicit reduction of expectations: the acceptance of the impossibility of achieving total commitment at any one time. Upon the basis of expressions leading to homogeneous solidarity, the group is able to turn its attention to problem areas such as the work program and the difficulties of individuals and even to discuss the characteristics of an office rather than an individual that lead to difficulty. There is a renewed call for a study group. However, there is as yet in the meeting almost no analysis of the details of a problem. There are relatively few hypotheses about the nature of problems, based on evidence, and on the basis of which plans might be made to cope with them. At this point, an apparent homogeneous solidarity and tension-reduction seem to be ends in themselves. The stability of such solidarity and what, if anything, such solidarity is seen as relevant for achieving are not apparent. If tension-reduction and the maintenance of homogeneous solidarity are not seen as ends in themselves, then the question becomes: what degree of organic solidarity is necessary to maintain collaboration and cooperation in the presence of the inevitable strains associated with problem-solving and achievement—and how can such a meeting as this contribute to the development of that organic solidarity? Does the group have to go through cycles of periods of attention to building solidarity and coping with individual strains or reinforcing individual learning followed by periods of task-achievement and adaptive problem-solving, which draw upon what solidarity and learning has been created, but create in turn new intergroup strains and individual tensions? Can any kind of study function be performed in such a large intergroup meeting? How?)

Friday, meeting 133: It is announced that there will be a community meeting over the weekend for those who can use "spiritual encouragement."

There are plans for trips together. Why should we not visit other hospitals? A staff member discusses the possibility of an exchange of drama productions with another hospital. (Does the group now turn outward on the basis of a felt strength to relate to the ouside world, to flee from community strains, or as a device to reinforce homogeneous solidarity? Many months later, the drama group does put on a play in another hospital. Seeds are planted in the meeting; one does not know when they will take root and grow.)

The proposal made by a patient that the hospital hire someone to operate a job procurement agency for patients and expatients is raised for discussion. Perhaps, because the obvious hopes of the patient making the proposal for himself arouse reactions which neither staff nor patients feel can be expressed, the discussion is somewhat edgy. The plan should not be mandatory for patients. Why should local employers cooperate? They have an obligation to the unemployed labor force in the area. The only jobs available in the area are menial or labor, which do not require union membership.

P: I've been thinking about organizing a baby-sitting service. *P:* Do you think people want mental patients taking care of their children? The fact that many patients have done baby-sitting is reported. There is more to needing to work than the money. Do people in town know how much patients pay to be here? There is a discussion by patients and staff about strains between the town and hospital, expressed for example in towns-people's feelings about the hospital's being a non-profit organization which does not have to pay taxes.

(Skepticism and lack of support for the proposal threatens the solidarity of the group. Almost immediately, there is a move to picture the world as hostile, which visibly draws the group together again, but around a potentially mal-adaptive definition of the situation.)

Thinking that many might be able to cathect the end of improving relations with the town, and that such an end may provide an incentive for collective effort, I wonder if patients could not think of ways to contribute to the town that would mitigate existing strains. This fails to strike a spark. The clinical director, apparently to reassure the group, asserts the inevitability of (and thus the futility of attempting to mitigate?) "town and gown" problems and resentments of people with less income toward those with more; moreover, he points out that the town is aware of the contribution the hospital makes to the local economy in money spent and people employed, and that in fact once after the war, when it looked like the hospital might be in trouble, a strong movement developed in the town to try to raise funds to support the hospital.

Perhaps because relations with the external world no longer seem to be a problem at all, a patient now begins to focus on relations between patients and staff: what does the staff do about proposals made by patients? Was a former patient's proposal to have follow-up studies ever considered by the staff? The clinical director discusses attempts to carry out such studies and their associated difficulties.

Perhaps because of having been reassured that there is no problem in relation between patients and staff, the group returns to the theme of the hostile environment, this time citing stories of patients who were fired when it became known that they were mental patients, and speculating on the reluctance of employers to hire mental patients.

Patients comment that people who have had treatment make better employees because they have done something about their illness and that people with handicaps often make the best, most motivated employees in jobs for which they are suited. Such comments lead to the recognition by one patient that the patient group's self-image is: "We are a bunch of paraplegics!"

Staff comments focus on correcting distortions in patients' stories, changing the perception that the environment is unfriendly and that prospects are hopeless, and stressing that what matters in getting a job is a person's abilities, confidence in himself, and whether he presents himself as "ill" or as a person who can do the job.

(Such comments, by altering the definition of the situation, also of course reduce incentive to consider the proposal for a job-procurement agency, to the extent that interest in it is related to people's fears about the difficulties in getting outside jobs.)

WEEK THIRTY-SEVEN

Monday, meeting 134: I comment that the current issue of the patient paper is an excellent one, and mention some things I especially enjoyed. There is much agreement. *P:* The issue is the first one that reflects a new collaborative effort.

There are announcements of "lost" or "missing" sums of money.

The director of activities says the nursery school will have to be renovated if it is to continue in operation. She mentions its contribution to the town and to relations with the town. Some patients have found a career developing out of their participation there. She says, some staff are wondering if the nursery school is as much an interest of the current generation of patients as of previous ones.

There are persistent suggestions that the money be invested in a swimming pool for patients. *P:* How about having patients assigned to work on the new nursery school building and having the money that they earn applied toward a new swimming pool. A patient suggests that patients help to build the new swimming pool and the money earned be applied to rebuilding the nursery school. *P:* The definition of the use of the nursery school by the town and its importance as a public relations project doesn't make me want to work there. *P:* It isn't really an activity, because once you sign up you have to come regularly, because children are involved, whether you feel like it or not; that's work.

A patient brings up the tension, distress, heavy drinking, people passing out cold, and the shouting and hysteria of the weekend. The difficulty is located as starting on Friday night and getting progressively better, as a result of various people's efforts, over the weekend. The head nurse and a group of patients attribute the difficulties to a party held Friday night. *Head nurse:* Patients have been talking about helping one another; now they were doing it—in the wrong ways. The nurses on duty had not known what to do; *their* help was refused by so many patients. Discussion suggests the perception that the nurses had been as upset as the patients.

Members of another group of patients insist the the party had actually helped people who were upset and that efforts had been made to stop people from drinking so much by the party-givers.

Head nurse: Intoxicated people are not in a position to ask for or receive help. *Doctor on duty:* I had the feeling nurses were being ignored by the patients.

Where is the staff in all this? Doesn't anyone on the staff care what is going on or plan to do something about it? Someone is going to bump himself off! The medical director is not around because he is ill, and the clinical director is not around because he is so busy.

The clinical director says he is sure that patients and staff are feeling the effects of the medical director's illness. He explains his own activities. He wonders if there should be a ban on drinking; he feels probably not, but also wonders why the group at the inn has not come to the realization that the drinking was making life intolerable for the people who lived there and making the hospital the kind of place a therapy staff does not care to run.

Another staff member favors a ban on drinking: no one can study the causes of tension while people are getting drunk and passing out.

With much feeling, the following points are made by patients. There are no longer any rules in the community. The rules still on the books are disregarded. There are no longer rules about drinking or community work. The committees are out of touch with one another and refusing to cooperate. The work committee is reluctant to refer patients to the community council. The work committee and activities committee have not elected representatives to the community council, so that the community council's functioning is compromised.

I comment that the group seems to be split, with various factions competing with each other as the ones who are helpful and want to make a contribution to the community. Following a request for a statement of opinion and feelings about the nursery school, people suggested building a swimming pool. I assume that these people were as concerned about the future of the hospital and what might be helpful to patients as those who were concerned with renovating the nursery school, but the discussion simply sounded like different groups fighting, each considering the other as not concerned about the patients or the hospital. Probably, both patients and nurses over the weekend were sincerely trying to be helpful, but the discussion sounded as if these groups competed with each other. We are all trying to make the hospital a better place in which to live and work, but no group, neither patients nor nurses, and no other single group, can do this alone. Every group—including various patient and various staff groups—probably makes some mistakes in trying to do the right thing as its members see it. What is necessary is collaboration among these groups in accomplishing what is important to all of them.

There is a renewed call for a meeting of the entire patient and staff group to discuss the "alcohol problem." (Such a meeting is desired as evidence that the whole staff is concerned and cares.)

Tuesday, meeting 135: The work committee announces that it feels it is an agency of the entire community and is now asking the community what suggestions it has, what it wants to do, and what it wants the work committee to do. As a matter of fact, however, the work committee uses the meeting to try to deal with a patient who doesn't "believe in the work program," and who says the program is obnoxious to him and that he can no longer participate in doing chores he detests when he can see no benefit to himself. Efforts are made to get others to tell this patient how much difficulty he causes them (especially the foremen and work schedulers); that people must do what is required for the work, however obnoxious; that the patient is talking "bull"; and how important the work program is to patients and to the hospital. P: When I don't get up for work I don't get to therapy appointments or to any meetings. P: Let's hear from others how his not working affects them. P: The library has been a mess this weekend; that's what happens when people don't work.

P: The community must choose among a volunteer work program, a compulsory work program, and no work program. P: I feel there should be a work program. P: You want a program for everyone else!

I comment that I understand the importance of talking about patients' not working, but wonder what would happen if at least as much time were spent discussing the people who work well, who make a contribution and perhaps should receive some recognition for it.

I am told by one of the most zealous members of the work committee that I don't understand the seriousness of the problem.

P: The strongest supporters of the program are those elected to run it; they are rewarded by the community; their reward is the chance to complain about the people who don't work. *P:* That's no reward! Patient leaves the room sobbing.

P: People should be rewarded by having vacations from work. *P:* That implies work is so bad one should be rewarded by not having to do it. There is a call for the old system of requiring "make-up time" from those who do not work. *P:* I'm for the program, although I don't know why it helps people; everyone who has left here better has been a person who has gone to therapy, done his community work, and attended community meeting.

I comment on the two views: one ought to work because work helps the community and one ought to carry a share of what it takes to make the place comfortable; one ought to work because working helps one personally. The latter view includes the possibility that a particular patient might declare that the program is of no help to him individually. *P:* We have to have both views, because if a person rejects one, "you can hit him with the other!" Laughter.

A patient makes what has come to be the usual plea to the clinical director to tell everyone how awful it was in the days when there was no community work. He does so.

P: Once, when patients didn't work, they were not permitted to have therapy hours.

(The work committee does not actually use the meeting for "consultation." There is no effort to elicit suggestions and different views and to consider these seriously; rather, the effort is to define what view is "bad" and to mobilize the community against it and to define what view is "good" and to mobilize the community for it. Attack mobilizes counter-attack. Those who feel right also then feel unappreciated.

The following day, apparently in the interest of unity, a meeting is called of the entire staff and patient group. The clinical director has made a plea for unity to the staff: let's act together as a unit and show our concern. The staff sits silently through the meeting, with the occasional exception of a staff member's encouraging an analysis of the causes of tension. There is widespread disappointment in the meeting. Staff comments later indicate splits in the staff: a fellow says, "I didn't talk because I'm a fellow"; some staff members feel they have been represented by members of the community program staff to patients as "not interested in the community" or resent recommendations from members of the community program staff.)

Thursday, meeting 136: There is a discussion of plans for the long holiday weekend coming up. There has been no meeting of the activities committee, because only two patients showed up. *P:* I don't want to hear from [another patient] that the reason why people are on the activities committee is because they like to complain about other people not attending meetings. *P:* I won't accept your challenge but we can call each other by our first names. *P:* I'm sorry; what the activities committee is experiencing is the same as what the work committee and community council are going through. There will be no more snacks, because the accounts don't balance and the patient responsible cannot make them balance. (No one, including members of the activities committee, offers to help him.)

A suggestion is made to have a tea for the staff and their families. There is an argument about whether to have a party with liquor—a "bash"—or a tea.

The head nurse is concerned about who put the hole in the plaster in the library wall behind the curtain, apparently last Tuesday. Some giggling.

A patient makes a suggestion that the weekend might be a good time to get away. *P:* Those of you who will be driving better drive slowly because of the holiday weekend. *P:* Imagine anyone driving slowly, away from here. *P:* That comment is stupid; it just increases tension.

There is further discussion of the possibility of a tea. *P:* "I'm not going to work on any goddamn tea!" There are jokes about tea ceremonies and fans. The suggestion is made that a sign be put on one patient's door, "purity," and on another patient's door, "sin." *P:* I know which party everyone will go to!

I comment on some experiences of my own which would lead me to think that in a very large inn a party involving everyone might be organized that would include a variety of activities and meet the needs of many different groups.

There are some suggestions along these lines.

There is some discussion of the patient-staff meeting. A staff member is asked to elaborate his comment that the patients and staff sat at the meeting like "two different groups, who remained two different groups." There is some exploration of the uneasiness at the meeting. I wonder if it is related to a fear on the part of some patients that other patients will use a meeting with the staff to impose a drinking ban upon the community.

There is a complaint that the community meetings were supposed to provide a chance to get together with *all* staff to hear what staff members think. Groans. *P:* Don't bring that up again!

(It is clear in the meeting that some patients, feeling in the "right," turn to staff for support of this self-perception, and want to be allied with staff as representing the "good" against those other patients who are "bad.")

I comment that perhaps such a meeting together is the next development. The task of bringing patients and staff together in a collaborative, working relationship is similar, perhaps, to finding a way to have a party a number of different groups can enjoy.

Friday, meeting 137: A report is given of the state of the community: people are remaining in bed; few are doing community work; people decline nominations for office. The head nurse leads a discussion of the suggestion that another patient-staff meeting be scheduled. The hoped-for benefits mentioned by either patients or staff: bringing patients and staff into a closer relationship; bringing in structure when the patients feel helpless to remedy a situation in which, it seems to some, all rules are being ignored. I assume that perhaps a truly collaborative relationship is desired, rather than one group's desiring to depend upon another; and encourage the group to think about what it would like to see accomplished by such a meeting.

A number of people comment that they are not listening to the discussion. P: There are empty rooms; I hear the staff is afraid of accepting patients now because of the terrible state of the community. There is an objection to these agendaless meetings, where anybody says anything off the top of their heads and there is no logical order in the discussion.

WEEK THIRTY-EIGHT

Tuesday, meeting 138: The work committee announces a series of decisions, which involve "going back" to the way things used to be. To be reestablished are: make-up time; vacations; the expectation that people, without exception, will work, and those that do not will be referred to the work committee, then to the community council, and then to the social problems council. No alternative proposals were considered.

The interpretation of these decisions by some is that now the threat hanging over a patient is that he must work or be kicked out of the hospital; the individual will have to conform out of fear.

P: We have to admit that the new work program has turned out to be a big failure. P: I think it was an experiment worth trying; the thing I don't like about these new decisions is that they seem to imply a stand against further experiments in the community, especially those that might fail.

A patient leaves, returning with a statement, which he reads, trying to present the argument for an individual-oriented work program, one primarily concerned with helping individuals to find themselves, rather than one existing primarily to perpetuate the positions of the members of the work committee. *P:* I agree that the work committee has a heavy investment in the program, but I don't think it acts simply to protect or perpetuate itself. *P:* The work committee acts like it owns the work program. *P:* I'm quite willing for the community to do away with the work program; I would have felt some relief if that had been what people wanted, but it wasn't. *P:* I voted yes, but I don't know why. *P:* The staff representative to the work program had raised his hand first and everyone had to follow.

(Recovery has been in the direction of reaction, in the direction away from change and back to what seems in retrospect to have offered some security. The uncertainty, the ambiguities, the misunderstandings created during this time of change and attempts to institutionalize reliance on attention to the current situation and processes rather than timeless formulas, are, for the time being, experienced as intolerable; retreat has been sounded.

Among patients' comments at the next day's patient-staff meeting are the following: "In the past several months, patients have been told repeatedly that they have virtually unlimited powers in determining the structure of the community and the direction in which it will move, that they need only to talk it over together, decide what they want, and institute appropriate action. They have seen this to be the case. They have, in fact, been told they must decide not only what they can tolerate, but whom. This seems to me to have led to a great deal of testing of every existing structure and flaunting of every rule. As yet nothing has stood firm and the result is a tremendous feeling of unease and personal unhappiness. Is this a desirable or necessary step to something better? I do not know."

Patients feel that responsibility is a burden, perhaps especially because they have little evidence that it is genuinely *shared* with staff in a collaborative effort to achieve the aims of the hospital through joint patient-staff committees. To some extent, the lack of solidarity of the patient group and the lack of solidarity of the staff group contribute to the failure of the development of meaningful collaboration between these groups or to any cathexis of an end shared by both groups, toward the achievement of which it is generally agreed these painful changes will contribute. The changes wrought by innovation can be tolerated to the extent that there is hope, to the extent that periods of unease and disturbance are seen as transitions to a state of affairs generally felt to be desirable.)

Thursday, meeting 139: The meeting is characterized by active participation by the staff representative to the work committee and by the amount of light bantering exchange between patients and staff. Plans for a volunteer, individual-oriented work program are solicited by members of the work committee from the "deviant" members of the group. Many suggestions are made: allow for activities such as going to school, making tapestries, writing music, or doing something useful for the community other than chores; consider assigning work projects to small groups, because members of long-term crews develop a sense of responsibility for one another. A patient is asked why she didn't clean that morning. She says she was too tired but will clean the front hall right after the meeting.

Doubt is expressed that if "creative" activities are considered fulfilling work obligations, any chores will get done.

The staff representative to the work committee encourages freeing thinking so that any kind of plan may be considered, and suggests that various patients and staff members write up their plans.

Director of activities: you can't depend on a volunteer plan to get any work done; music isn't work.

I wonder humorously that she, of all people, who knows a great deal about music, doesn't consider music work.

I comment that there might be some way to encompass both chores and creative activities in the same community, the problem being that no one wants to be chosen as suitable for the former rather than the latter.

The staff representative to the work committee says that in his experience you can't predict in advance who will consider what creative or who will be attracted by what kind of work.

Having to clean the men's john is something that anyone would find a chore! Even writing music involves chores. A person can tolerate chores if he sees some meaning in what he is doing. The joke of "musical toilets" as combining creativity and chores is much elaborated.

P: The dining room was one area where people seemed to enjoy working together and enjoyed the work, too.

I comment that I have never fully understood that project's being voted out when a number of people indicated they were willing to do this work. I wonder if the demand that everyone work there had contributed to the demise of this project. I am told that people would not have been willing to work there week after week. The first tour of duty was an adventure, the second difficult and burdensome, and the possibility of a third dreaded.

P: I am now convinced that the only reason people here refuse to work is because they are lazy and spoiled. Applause.

I comment that people who don't work may be adhering to one of the important values of the community. In a community dedicated to psychotherapy there is inevitably a high value placed on self-development, self-interest, and self-fulfillment. The value of working for the sake of a group to which one belongs is another value, felt by some to conflict wtih the first.

P: I think the expectation to do work symbolizes being told what to do by others, and that makes it repugnant.

The staff representative to the work committee suggests that sometimes people can begin to "go through the motions" and to work even before it makes sense to them to do so because they are told that this is the kind of place we have and the kind of place we like it to be.

The mess being made by cats at the shop and the wish that one or another cat be gotten rid of are discussed.

Friday, meeting 140: People are not filling out their preference sheets for work. There are missing articles, including some valuable ones. *P:* I am looking at a piece of sheet music, which says, "The Well-Tempered Clavichord," and having the fantasy that someone will sit down and play this music, and the whole community will become well-tempered and people will begin to trust one another. Suggestions for locks to rooms or locked boxes in rooms are rejected by patients because of the risks of suicide or because such suggestions imply people will never be able to trust one another. A patient objects to discussing the "causes" of stealing, because it sounds as if people are justifying it. A staff member lists three alternatives: (1) remind people to be careful about their possessions and assume that people who steal are working this out in therapy; (2) develop group trust enabling people to work out stealing problems with others in the community; (3) have the staff investigate stealing and discharge the culprit when they find him.

People will never discuss such behavior in meetings because they will inevitably be labelled "thief."

Two images of a desirable community are contrasted in the discussion: one, a community in which people respect each others' privacy and possessions, do not go into each others' rooms without permission, and do not borrow things without asking; two, a "family" home, in which there are no locks on the doors, and people feel free to borrow from one another.

The meeting ends with questions about discussions at staff meetings. What is said? Might minutes become available to patients? Might a patient representative attend staff meetings?

(Again, the theme of stealing is associated with a sense of longing for contact with the staff, in fact, with a wish to abolish boundaries between the two groups—which exists also in the fantasy of the "family" home with no doors. The complexities of community life lead to a wish to depend upon the staff to solve problems, or for contact with the staff that magically will resolve problems, at a time when the staff seems, because of organizational changes and the withdrawal resulting from strains in the staff group, to say nothing of death and illness, less available than ever before.)

7. When Nothing Happens

This period (meetings 141 through 160) was quiet.

The morning meetings were discontinued.

A senior staff group started evaluating the community meetings.

Attendance at the community meetings decreased. Typically, many patients sunned themselves on the porch while the meetings were going on. Various explanations were offered concerning the decrease in attendance: not much is happening; there aren't so many problems; no one makes any effort any longer to bring people to meetings; the responsible leaders come, others do not (this did not hold up on an examination of the evidence); people who have been "put down" or discussed at the meeting do not return (evidence was contradictory and equivocal); there is a letdown after the patient-staff meetings; the staff is evaluating the community meeting and perhaps the meetings will not be continued; discussions at the meetings have no consequences; it's up to the staff co-chairman to improve the meeting.

Those who continued to attend—and there was a steady attendance level, but not by any means always involving the same patients—were, on the whole, tactful. Many people seemed sleepy or preoccupied. Both staff and patients paid many compliments—for example, for the drama group's current production—and emphasized agreements with others. (Frequently, people who were complimented were not at the meeting to hear themselves praised.)

The medical director was reported to be better; a patient said, "I knew nothing could happen to him!"

Relations between the community council and the community meeting were reported as "good." A letter from a previous patient to the community was read: doing well.

Impatience with the "slow discussions" led to efforts to start a discus-

sion group that would include only those who want to discuss and—
like the synanon groups—leave out the "dead wood."

A game of "Murder" was played enthusiastically in the evenings.

A patient was elected work scheduler who was not achievement-
oriented, took the antithesis of the zealous "back to rules, back to structures, back to the good old days" position, and was often in personal
difficulty; this patient could be depended upon to have a tolerant easy-
going attitude toward work problems. I took this opportunity to encourage the group to explore what the election of a particular person
at a given time might indicate about the state of the community. The
hypothesis was offered by a patient that the group was reacting against
the previous scheduler, who wanted "structure," and was now swing-
ing in the opposite direction. There was always some implication, also,
in this and subsequent discussion that patients were chosen for office
as a way of "helping" them, integrating them into the community, and
mitigating their deviance or withdrawal; members of the group often
had an uncanny sense of the person who was ready to take responsibility despite outward appearances to the contrary and who could be
"reclaimed" in this way. There was a definite disinclination to select
people impersonally and according to previous performance.

Some problems presented themselves: for example, what to do about
movies for the rest of the year since the movie committee had over-
drawn its budget; what to do about this-or-that work problem. Any attempt to work out alternatives and move toward selection between
them aroused impatience and inevitably the irritable complaint: "I
don't want to talk about [movies, the work program] anymore; do we
have to keep talking about it!?" Alternative proposals considered with
reference to the "movie problem" were to show two expensive films,
using the remainder of the budget and cancelling two months' programs; to show five cheap films; to request more money from the coordinating committee. Although the director of activities stated it was
not likely that the coordinating committee would supplement the budget
in the absence of an emergency, it was clear that the group was for
that solution and expected to make such a proposal to the coordinating
committee through the activities committee. (Eventually, the coordinating committee did supplement the budget.)

In a discussion about stealing, I wondered about the possible relation between the casual attitudes about property (which was abused,
neglected, or left lying around), money, budgets, and keeping receipts
and an orderly record of expenditures, and the incidence of stealing in
the community.

A patient arrived whose hypomania was intolerable to members of the group. An attempt was made to explain some of the community norms to him, in response, for example, to his professed preference for mess and disorder, but the group appeared almost too tired to persevere, perhaps too conflicted about its values to assert them, but more giving the impression that the disturbance and bother primarily were unwelcome. The patient was very soon sent to a closed hospital.

There were some arguments about old, familiar matters. For example, transgressions of the "midnight rule"—patients should not visit in each others' rooms after midnight—by two male patients aroused concern especially in a particular nurse. Whether the nurse's concern about what the two patients were doing together, the nurse's implicit response to the isolation of night duty, or the nurse's compulsive determination to see rules enforced was primarily at issue was never clear. However, the response of the group was that both the nurse and the patients had upset a desired equilibrium. It seemed clear to most people that such a rule had to be "on the books" and, for the most part, respected. Internal functional effects included cutting down noise so others could sleep; making it possible for some patients to use the rule to resist group temptations and lures at night when resistance was low; and—what was never explicitly discussed—also avoiding the exacerbation of envy and frustration in others by provocative, flaunted, apparently sexual activity. External functional effects were represented by the clinical director especially: the maintenance of the respect of the extended community for the hospital. It also seemed clear to most people, however, that an attempt to enforce such a rule strictly would mobilize unmanageable strains in this community and require a degree of policing and intrusiveness incompatible with its basic values. Like many similar social norms, the rule could not be enforced to the letter without dysfunctional effects, but neither could transgressions of the rule be tolerated without dysfunctional effects. The destroyers of such an equilibrium, which took a great deal of tact, discretion, and the exercise of judgment to maintain, were zealots on either side: those who wanted to expose "hypocrisy" and "inconsistency" and get rid of the rule altogether, and those who wanted to see it absolutely enforced. The group criticized the nurse for enforcing the rule too zealously and the two patients for "loving to argue" rather than just saying, "thank you," when the nurse approached them, and going off to bed. Deviance in the direction of any extreme that disturbed the peace tended to be regarded with ill-favor during this period.

Problems to which the group was sensitive and which tended to be noted with relative frequency were those located in "other" groups or "elsewhere": a young person living in town who was in trouble and needed "help"; the bartender, who was behaving strangely; the people in the business office or maintenance department, who were accused of creating unconscionable delays when their help was required to trace missing magazine subscriptions, to repair a broken phonograph or laundry equipment, or to purchase a new movie projector. (It was impossible to determine to what extent procrastination and disagreements within the group contributed to these delays; there were innumerable incidents of a member of one group's "just missing," "misunderstanding," or "being unable to get together with" a member of another group.) There was, also, during this period some interest in sending money to help a nurse who had gone to the South to help build a church there. There was much discussion about whether movies shown at the shop should be open to the townspeople, with fear expressed about elements of the town "who might come and make trouble"; there was no evidence offered for such an expectation.

Efforts were made throughout this period to get various individuals to prepare proposals concerning a new work program for a meeting of patients and the entire staff. No action was contemplated for such a meeting; neither the patient nor staff group prepared itself by trying to arrive at some consensus before the meeting to support a particular proposal and try to persuade the other group to accept it. What existed was a kind of faith that meeting with all the staff in itself would result in something "good."

What occurred at the community meeting with reference to life in the community tended to support the notion that talk about interpersonal difficulties at the meeting might be helpful. A male and female patient had a "fight"; the details were aired at a community meeting (following a community meeting in which there was much silence and desultory conversation, the "fight" apparently then having been on patients' minds but not mentioned). Some thought it was too private a matter to be discussed at the meeting; but the view that the discussion was justified by the widespread fears of the male patient's impulsive, assaultive behavior and the garbled versions circulating about what had happened was generally accepted.

In a subsequent discussion this patient broke down and cried; I noted to the group that this meeting marked the first time someone had experienced and expressed a good deal of feeling without rushing out of the room, but had instead sat it out and participated in the discussion.

Toward the end of this period, the work committee, following suggestions made at the patient-staff meeting announced the following decisions: foremen will be elected by their crews rather than "at large"; a plan for vacations has been adopted; a personal gardening project proposed by a patient will be sponsored and supported by the work committee as a legitimate part of the work program; and the work committee will report each week to the community meeting and respond to the suggestions and opinions expressed at that meeting. There was some grumbling about the work committee's arrogating executive and legislative powers to itself, but on the whole this way of working and defining the relationship of an action committee to the community meeting was accepted.

A "Latency" Period

It is especially important to try to account for periods when "nothing much" seems to happen. Commitment to the active achievement of goals through persistent effort certainly seems at first glance to have been at a low level during this period, if it can be said to have been present at all. Like Holmes' response to the "dog that barked at midnight," curiosity may be as much aroused by the absence as by the presence of a phenomenon.

In addition, achieving perspective with respect to such periods is important because activists among both staff and patients find it difficult to endure such periods, and are likely to become impatient and discouraged, to reject the group, and, if influential, to define a situation for everyone as "bad" that may, in fact, have many functional aspects. In this connection, it is important to remember that the definitions of situations themselves, especially if these come to be accepted and shared by members of a group, appear to have significant further effects, including the production of behavior that is likely to confirm the definition giving rise to it.

In Bion's terms, one might cite these meetings as evidence of a group's acting on basic assumption Flight.[1] I do not find this an adequate classification of all the phenomena. The term "flight" seems to me to have, as ordinarily used, a pejorative quality, usually implying dysfunctional effects for the system. Moreover, the fact that intergroup,

1. W. R. Bion, *Experiences in Groups* (New York: Basic Books, 1961).

not simply small group, phenomena are involved tends to make one hesitate to apply such concepts without considerable qualification.

I have been many times through similar periods. The experience has a quality I associate with the small pilot light on the gas range: a group "keeps a small fire going" for everyone during times it does not seem to be needed, against the day when it will again be brought into use. However, this metaphor too suggests that indeed "nothing is happening" that bears fruitfully upon processes of goal-attainment.

Why at least does the staff not make use of the meeting as an intergroup arena in which to diagnose the strains or requirements of the various groups involved? Are the patient and staff groups caught in a peculiar cycle of dependency and reaction to it: one group seeks the other to meet its needs; the second group, inspired to help and rescue, responds; the first group, inevitably disappointed, attacks; the second, feeling called upon to do what it cannot do, draws back; the dependent longings of the first group are exacerbated by the withdrawal of the second and again the first group seeks the second? Is this a quiescent period following disappointment and disillusionment, or involving preparation for the next fruitless mating of the two groups? Perhaps. One problem with such a model is that no element of it provides for progression out of this equilibrium cycle.

The Alternation of Task-orientation and Restoration

Why have processes of detecting the ends to be attained from an examination of current interactions in the situation, and of responding to the necessity to attain such ends through appropriate collective action, apparently slowed? Is a lack of commitment to such a process, or lack of understanding one's role in it, or lack of a shared conception of the meeting in terms of such a process, at issue? Or are the means for taking collective action so inadequate or creaky, or do they involve so much delay, that the incentive for detecting needs about which one can do little has diminished as a consequence? Probably these factors play a part, although one might expect such a goal-attainment process to go on, somehow, even in the absence of self-conscious participation or a perfectly adequate machinery for achieving ends. That, at least, would appear to be part of the meaning of the idea that ends are inevitably generated by the life of the community.

Suppose we return to the assumption that achievement of ends or work (in this sense) and harmony or integration are to some extent incompatible; that every examination of interactions in the situation results in some strain; that every attempt to meet requirements or satisfy needs or wishes paradoxically also results in some strain; that perhaps even attempts to resolve strains somewhere in the system inevitably result in additional increments of strain somewhere else in the system (it being necessary then to follow the strains in an investigation from one location to another in the system or in systems bounding it).

Then, as Parsons, Shils, and Bales,[2] for example, have suggested, adaptation, goal-seeking, or task-orientation should alternate with periods of rest, restoration of the internal condition of entities of the system, restoration of integration between entities of the system. It is as if there is a certain amount of harmony or integration and value-institutionalization and learning "credit in the bank" which is drawn upon during periods of work and which must be replenished following its expenditure in work. (Actually the credit is not simply used up but new strains and problems are created by task-oriented processes, requiring more or different kinds of integration, learning, or commitment.)

The evidence in the community meetings during this period suggests that the end generated by life in the community and selected for attainment is the institutionalization of motivational commitment to the community meeting itself and the community it represents; that is, motivation group processes predominate.

Certainly there seems to have been a marked preference for maintaining states of harmony rather than for attempting to do anything. The staff shared this, preferring, for example, to give additional money to a budget rather than to "make waves," even in the interest of teaching the value of making an effort to achieve goals or the value of recognizing that one must select among ends rather than assume that all ends are gratifiable; and preferring also to praise rather than to point out problems. Patients contributed; from the point of view being explored here, even staying away from the meeting for a brief period might have had a functional aspect: removal of members who might otherwise have caused trouble. In addition, a patient leader was chosen who eschewed achievement in favor of "human relations."

What then might have been occurring during this "latency" period, to use Parsons' term, was a process of institutionalizing the values of the community meeting and its legitimation in the hospital organization; to this process, other ends were subordinated.

2. Talcott Parsons, Edward Shils, and Robert Bales, *Working Papers in the Theory of Action* (New York: The Free Press of Glencoe, 1953).

Then we can understand both the "flight" from the meeting and the demonstrations in it of "what has been learned so far"—for example, the use of the meeting by action committees and individuals to share information and achievements, make announcements, and, in general, consult with others—as if by these demonstrations what has been learned so far becomes consolidated.

Relevant, also, is the dissolution of alternative structures to the community meeting—such as the synanon groups and the morning meetings.

The significant event was going on outside the community meeting; it was as if all the group waited for its consummation. That event was the evaluation of the community meeting by a senior staff committee, which, of course, did not conduct a cognitively oriented research investigation but rather a process of legitimizing the community meeting as part of the organization by a respected group representing that organization.

Almost a year to the day after the inauguration of the community meeting, the committee issued its report. While deploring the staff strains resulting from the "authoritarian" means by which the community meeting had been created (primarily the lack of adequate consultation with, and consent by, the entire staff), the members of the committee stated: " No one has proposed that [community meetings] be discontinued: they seem to have found a place in the general structure and their usefulness seems to grow. Hence they should continue . . . . Daily meetings permit continuity, and some member can bring up unresolved problems that perhaps others would like to sweep under the rug . . . . The format should be that of taking up the problems that have arisen since the last meeting, and any plans or projects that are under foot and need discussion . . . . The meetings have been likened to a good daily newspaper which reports the facts accurately and headlines the urgent news, dispels rumors, and has a policy of free discussion which urges expression of all views. The meetings can be a place where consensus and a problem-solving culture can be built up, which in turn provides an underlying base on which to proceed when a real crisis erupts. The frequency of meetings permits this kind of development, and also more rapidly orients new patients to the group and its methods. It would be hoped that this procedure would evolve to the point that the group's wishes and needs are not stalled or delayed but will be facilitated, putting an end to the all-too-frequent sequence of enthusiasm, frustration, and disillusionment, with a feeling that nothing can be done and that in particular the staff tends to sabotage things.

Problem-solving would be applied both to the needs and wishes of the community and to individual or group disruption of the community—strictly a group function. (It is noted that the carrying out of such functions definitely increased the ego functions of the individuals participating.)"

Shortly after, a very important visitor, a highly respected, well-known scholar and teacher, attended a community meeting in my absence. A patient member, obviously expressing the widely felt awe, asked him to address the group. The patient co-chairman, with calm certainty about the nature of the enterprise upon which he and the group were embarked and its legitimacy, stated (to the surprise and delight of the visitor), "No, that is not the purpose of these meetings, that's not what we're here for."

The Disposition of Values

There is still another way to view phenomena observed during periods when "nothing happens."

It is difficult to escape the impression that different groups, or groups at different times, differ in the way in which they dispose of values by processes of internalization and externalization. At this time, it is impossible to be other than vague and tentative in the formulation, because elucidation of what is involved would require a careful study of the symbol-making function in groups: how symbols—object-representations and ideal-representations—are formed and combined; what determines to what vehicles or concrete entities such symbolizations become attached.

It is important to note that, in the frame of reference in which these experiences are discussed, values always involve a choice between alternatives; "value" means preference for one orientation over another. Values are dichotomous. If one aspect of a dichotomized value is internalized in a personality system or institutionalized in a group, the alternative which clings to it by implication must be disposed of.

Normatively we might say that in a "mature," differentiated group, each value-alternative is allocated to the subsystems (structures or processes) to which it is appropriate. (Such an arrangement obviously has survival value in enhancing the functions represented by each subsystem.) The system includes all values in some relationship to each other indicated by the nature of the relationships among its subsystems. Values are not black-and-white, eternally mutually exclusive antagonists, but are perceived as appropriate to different functions, aims, or types of action. Choice between these functions, aims, or types of action and the values appropriate to them depends upon both current exigencies of the situation in which the system is located and the immanently determined requirements of the system. Short of such a mature differentiation, every group, characterized by a certain pattern of allocation of effort to various subsystems, and struggling to avoid the disruption of the group from internal strains or from failure to achieve aims resulting in the loss of necessary objects or resources in its situation, disposes of opposing values in a particular way.

For the sake of convenience, all values will be dichotomized, with respect to the orientation and standards of the members of a particular group, into an accepted alternative (positively cathected) and a rejected alternative (negatively cathected). What, then, are the possibilities for their disposition?

1. Neither the accepted alternative nor the rejected alternative is internalized by the members of the group or institutionalized. Both alternatives are attributed to, assigned to, or represented by concrete entities or vehicles external to the group. That is, both are externalized. Such concrete entities may be, as in the typical case, other groups or social systems, as well as in special cases reconstructed "historical" entities considered to be part of the past of the group itself.

In the material we have just been considering, other groups represented for the community both the accepted values of the community (the therapy staff, for example) and the rejected values of the community ("unacceptable" elements in the town, for example).

Processes of action in such a group are, then, likely to include primarily attempts to achieve contact with the group representing the accepted values (faith in meetings with the entire staff, for example) and attempts to flee from or fight the group representing the rejected values (the impulse to avoid outsiders, for example). Such a group may be particularly prone perhaps to make choices determined by fear, and to be preoccupied with problems of separation from desired social objects. To the extent such a group is not committed to the actualization of its own internalized or institutionalized values, it appears to be relatively passive and to give primacy to heteronomous concerns and response to objects in its situation rather than to achievement of its own inner-determined aims. The members of the group seem to have little solidarity and the group as such seems to have little value for, or to be little respected by, them. In such a group, often, nothing seems to happen.

Such a formulation may be a way of conceptualizing what underlies some aspects of Bion's fight-flight group.[3] These processes also appear to be homologous to the *phobic* ego's flight from the externalized rejected object and attachment to the externalized accepted object.[4]

2. The accepted alternative is internalized or institutionalized; the rejected alternative is externalized.

Processes of action in such a group are likely to include energetic, zealous attempts to actualize internalized values, perceived to be absolutely "right," and to destroy social objects representing the opposed, absolutely "wrong" values. Such a group is likely to be cohesive, grandiose in its aims and self-image, and self-righteous in its attitudes toward, suspicious of, and antagonistic toward, other groups.

Such a formulation may be a way of conceptualizing what underlies some aspects of Bion's fight-flight group as well as the messianic fervor of Bion's pairing group.[5] These processes also appear to be homologous to the *paranoid* ego's externalization of the rejected object (hostility, suspicion) and internalization of the accepted object (grandiosity).[6]

3. The rejected alternative is internalized or institutionalized; and the accepted alternative is externalized.

Processes of action is such a group are likely to include the acting out of a negative self-image, and dependence upon and over-estimation and idealization of an external group. Examples might include some actions of a patient group and its relationship with a therapy staff; some actions of a minority group and its relationship with an oppressive majority; some actions of a deviant group and its relationship to the establishment.

Such a formulation may be a way of conceptualizing what underlies some aspects of Bion's dependency group.[7] These processes also appear to be homologous to the *hysterical* ego's internalization of the rejected object (conversion reactions) and externalization of the accepted object (idealization of the loved object).[8]

4. Both the accepted alternative and the rejected alternative are internalized or institutionalized; but there is no allocation of values (regarded neither as permanently accepted nor as permanently rejected alternatives) to appropriate differentiated subsystems, functions, or aims.

3. Bion, op. cit.
4. W. R. D. Fairbairn, *Psychoanalytic Studies of the Personality* (London: Tavistock Publications, 1952), pp. 28–58.
5. Bion.
6. Fairbairn, pp. 28–58.
7. Bion.
8. Fairbairn, pp. 28–58.

Processes of action in such a group are likely to include an intense emphasis on autonomous concerns and the unfolding of the immanent potentialities of the group with relatively little interest to spare for relations to other groups. Opposing values are represented fortuitously and fluidly by various individuals or subgroups which appear to form and dissolve primarily in the interest of being able to represent such opposites. The group appears hesitant or paralyzed in action attempts to achieve aims through relations with its situation, because the group tends to be immobilized by internal strains. The response to any suggestion is likely to be: "Yes, but . . . . "

These processes tend to be homologous to the *obsessional* ego's internalization of both the rejected and the accepted object and its efforts to expel the former and retain the latter.[9]

9. Fairbairn, pp. 28–58.

8. Outputs of the Community Meeting

The community meeting is primarily concerned with adaptation and integration outputs to the community and to the action or operational groups (small groups, community council, activities committee, work committee) and resource groups (activities staff, nursing staff) comprising it. The community meeting, since it operates primarily on the adaptation-integration axis, gives primacy to organic solidarity—bonds between people and between groups within the community meeting are based upon making differentiated contributions to a shared end. (Smaller groups, even action and resource groups, and certainly informal groups, which operate on the motivation-consummation axis, are more likely to be concerned with or characterized by homogeneous solidarity—bonds between people within the group are based upon sharing the same qualities, feelings, sentiments, and values.)

Adaptation outputs of the community meeting include:

1. cognitive representations of the situation, including the relationship of the community to the organization and to the extended community of which it is a part, or definitions of reality in terms of verifiable empirical knowledge, especially for the sake of mastery or the mobilization of needed resources (to the adaptation subsystem);

2. expressive symbolizations of the situation or definitions of—or reactions to—reality in terms of gratification-deprivation actualities or potentialities (to the consummation subsystem);

3. evaluation of the situation in terms of a system of norms (to the integration subsystem);

4. evaluation of the situation in terms of a system of values, recognition of states of alienation from or commitment to institutionalized values, or interpretation of events of their value implications (to the motivation subsystem).

Integration outputs of the community meeting include:

1. examining alternative means to achieve a given end, according to cognitive standards of validity, empirically verifiable truth, efficiency, and expediency (to the adaptation subsystem);
2. examining alternative ends to pursue or wishes to gratify, as well as considering the implications for one end (including its possible sacrifice) of the commitment of means or resources to the attainment of another end, according to appreciative or aesthetic standards of appropriateness, taste, or ultimate desirability (to the consummation subsystem);
3. examining alternative norms to be institutionalized, according to evaluative standards, specifying criteria of right and wrong in terms of consequences to the community, some group or individual part of the community, or the organization or social system of which the community is a part (to the integration subsystem);
4. recognizing the competition of various values, value-orientations, value-positions, or systems of values, within the community (to the motivation subsystem).

With respect to motivation and consummation outputs, the community meeting also:

1. is an object symbolizing the therapeutic community itself, representing the values of that community for all its members (so that a process increasing respect for the community meeting as a symbolic object increases commitment to or respect for the institutionalized values of the therapeutic community);
2. provides an arena in which various action groups can seek community-wide commitment for a course of action decided upon by the action group, that is, commitment for a particular selection of means, an end, a norm, or a value-position chosen from among the alternatives considered in the community meeting;
3. indicates to action groups what ends are most salient at a particular time and refers problems or goals-to-be-achieved to appropriate operational groups for decision and action: what needs or wants doing (to the work committee); what wishes are pressing for expression or gratification (to the activities committee); what norms are required or need to be supported through mechanisms of social control of deviant behavior (to the community council); what strains, within what individuals, are being mobilized, espe-

cially by events, decisions, and processes in the community (to the small groups);

4. provides an arena in which various action groups may reward individuals and groups with general recognition and esteem for their efforts and contributions toward the attainment of shared goals.

Adaptation Outputs to the Adaptation Subsystem

1. *Week 44, Monday, meeting 116.* A research associate presents knowledge about the factors involved in stealing from a research report about embezzlers he has been reading. Embezzling seems related to: (1) the necessity in a social system to be able to trust people in certain positions without having to put limits on such trust that might impede essential activities; (2) the existence of a financial problem for the embezzler he does not feel he can share with others; (3) the fact that techniques for embezzling are learned necessarily as part of the position the embezzler occupies; (4) the rationalization of their activities by all embezzlers so that these do not seem to them to be stealing or to involve dishonesty.

The second and fourth factors are thought to be relevant to stealing in the community. Do we create conditions conducive to community members' sharing their needs with each other? Do we too readily accept rationalizations of community members' deviant behavior?

2. *Week 45, Thursday, meeting 167.* Hiring a band for a party will cost more than is available in the activities committee budget. Can the rest of the money be raised through contributions? How much money is left in the budget? Contributions for the party are volunteered.

3. *Week 45, Thursday, meeting 167.* A report is given by a patient of his meeting with a repairman. He gives a detailed description of the way to use the phonograph to avoid breakdown in its functioning. A number of people comment that they hadn't had this information. It is suggested that a list of directions be posted near the phonograph.

4. *Week 45, meeting 168.* Volunteers are solicited to help host the Saturday night party. Volunteers are solicited to help clean up after the party. A request is made concerning whether anyone has a microphone or loudspeaker or knows where one can be obtained for use at the party. Suggestions are made as to how such equipment might be obtained, and someone volunteers to obtain it.

5. *Week 46, Tuesday, meeting 169.* An attempt is made to understand what factors contribute to making the job of scheduler an undesired one. The scheduler is caught in the middle between the staff

people in various areas who complain that work in the shop, nursery school, inn, or on the grounds is not getting done and the patients who resent efforts by schedulers to get them to work.

Adaptation Outputs to the Consummation Subsystem

1. *Week 44, Tuesday, meeting 162.* A suggestion made that people who are doing good work as well as those in difficulty be mentioned in the community meeting—because this would give a truer picture of the situation (adaptation output to integration subsystem)—is apparently rejected by some patients, not on the grounds that such information is irrelevant, but on the grounds that such recognition is apt to become a gratifying end sought for its own sake. It is said that adequate performances should be simply expected from everyone and not rewarded or the absence of such performance blamed; adequate performance should be its own reward.

On the whole, I take the position that perhaps reciprocally giving and experiencing such gratification is necessary to maintain desired performance in the community. Some people apparently refuse to work no matter what attention they receive and some people work impelled by an inner "motor" without regard to the response of others; these seem to be in the minority; most people have mixed feelings about working and their inclination rather than disinclination to work is supported by the sense of gratification that results from recognition of their contributions.

(Underlying the opposition to community-wide recognition seemed to me to be the fear of being blamed for inadequate performance; the fear of the envy mobilized by hearing some patient singled out for such recognition by staff members; the fear of being unjustly rewarded for what is felt to be a very minimal performance undeserving of praise.)

Following this meeting, for weeks there is some care taken in the meeting by many patients and staff to mention with appreciation the contributions of people in various offices.

2. *Week 45, Thursday, meeting 167.* Because there is a holiday on Monday and no therapy, we should have a lively, unusual, and if necessary more costly party with a band on Saturday. *P:* When I heard the band for the first time, I was very depressed, but then became very happy: instant happiness!

Adaptation Outputs to the Integration Subsystem

1. *Week 44, Monday, meeting 161.* It is reported that a patient got into a fight while drinking, away from the inn. There is an attempt to

find out to what extent the patient has been drinking around the inn. The patient has sent in his resignation as special work-projects chairman. Does all this indicate that he is "in trouble"?

(Deviance is automatically evaluated in terms of the intrapersonal state of the individual rather than in terms of his relationship to the norms of the community; deviance in this community tends to be automatically attributed to illness or to intrapersonal motivational factors. That is, there tends to be an automatic assumption that a person who does not behave in accordance with the norms of the community does not wish to do so, or cannot do so because of intrapersonal deficiencies or conflicts, and that a person who behaves in accordance with the norms of the community does so because he wants to or because of the absence of intrapersonal deficiencies or conflicts.

That a person may desire to behave in accordance with the norms of the community but be unable to do so because of situational factors is not considered. Such situational factors include, for example: (1) incompatible expectations facing an individual having two roles or statuses in the community—ill patient, effective community member; member of formal therapeutic community, member of informal patient subgroup; (2) the incompatible or competing demands made of the occupier of a given role.

That a person may not desire to behave in accordance with the norms of the community because of factors other than intrapersonal deficiencies or conflicts is also not often considered: for example, relative deprivation or lack of access to means to achieve accepted ends; or lack of cathected goals arising, for example, from a rapid change in goals due to changes in circumstances.

That a person may desire not to behave in accordance with the norms of the community, but nevertheless behave in accordance with them, due to situational factors, is also often not considered. Such situational factors include: (1) the likelihood that desired generalized rewards such as others' approval and esteem are consequent to behaving in accordance with norms; (2) the likelihood that negative sanctions or deprivation are consequent to deviance; (3) the relative lack of opportunity to behave deviantly.)

2. *Week 44, Tuesday, meeting 162.* A wallet is reported stolen. The hypothesis is formulated by the patient from whom it has been stolen that the thief took it to provide himself with identification in order to make obtaining liquor as a minor easier. (The wallet is subsequently found: the patient refuses to clarify the circumstances under which it was found "away from the inn.")

3. *Week 44, Thursday, meeting 163.* A patient has committed a self-

destructive act. Her present condition is reported to the group. An attempt is made to discover the circumstances leading to the act. A patient reports that she talked to him about her suicidal thoughts shortly before committing the act; he did not report this conversation to anyone, including the nurses. The act is attributed to the patient's feeling rejected by the community and to pressures from parents experienced by the patient.

A patient objects to all the stories going around about his calling a patient names and attacking her verbally about her sexual behavior with other patients. He reports various conversations he has had at various times with different people about his relationship with this girl and her relationship with other male patients, and how others have overheard and misinterpreted. A letter from one of the male patients involved to the girl who has been self-destructive is reported by him; according to him, she felt mistreated by him and was trying to retaliate. He accuses her in turn of mistreating another male patient.

There is a discussion about the way messages get carried from one person to another in the community, being considerably garbled en route; people then respond strongly to the distorted version.

I discuss the following factors in the situation: (1) information is not shared until things have "blown up" and nothing can be done; it is discouraging to talk only about what might have been done to prevent the crisis rather than being able to anticipate and abort it; (2) individuals carry messages to one another that inflame the situation and exacerbate difficulties; (3) there is no mechanism for collaboration between patients and nurses in coping with crisis situations, and no consultation by members of either of these groups with members of the other.

4. *Week 44, Friday, meeting 164.* I wonder if it might not be helpful to have the nurses and patients plan a party together, since both groups are facing a "rough" weekend together. I ask the head nurse what help she thinks the nurses would like from the patients that weekend. No answer. A patient points out that it has been suggested many times in the past that a night meeting between patients and nurses would be helpful to the community in anticipating upsets. I comment that apparently some patients would like to be of help should some difficulty arise. I ask the head nurse how nurses are likely to feel about working with patients who want to help out. She is noncommittal; perhaps that will be all right. I inquire about what night nurses will on duty that weekend and whether or not they will hear about this meeting's discussion. The head nurse indicates that can be arranged.

(It was almost two years later, following a discussion of a night's up-

set in which patients—who had left the nurses to cope on their own
with a drunken patient but were also very critical of the nurses' way of
managing the situation—were faced with their own responsibility in
such situations, that a group is set up of patients who are willing to
serve as patient-nurses to work with nurses in dealing with upset
people and crises at night. It took this long, and the departure of many
nurses and the arrival of new nurses, before patients were willing to
accept formally sharing with the nurses the responsibility for coping
with each others' upsets and deviant behavior, and this long before the
nurses were even willing to consider establishing a formal alliance with
the patients rather than with the therapy staff to cope with such problems.

Perhaps the crucial event bringing to everyone's attention the lack
of integration of the nursing group in the therapeutic community was
the resignation of a nurse—during this period two years later—who was
widely suspected of stealing liquor from patients' rooms. This nurse had
been an isolated, rejected individual.

Following this event, the nurses indirectly appealed to the therapy
staff and medical director a decision of the community council, to make
drinking in the game room possible. Their objection was to the permissiveness of the rest of the staff. They had not been required, however,
to articulate this position in the community council itself, to make specific suggestions based upon such a position, or to negotiate with other
groups represented on the community council—so that the ultimate decision would reflect a variety of values, including their own: the need
for structure and some degree of external control; the high valuation
placed on patients' internalizing certain norms and governing their own
behavior in accordance with these without external sanctions from the
staff; and the needs for gratification in a social, recreational setting.

If the views of different groups are seen as representing requirements
of the social system, rather than as absolute black-and-white value
alternatives, then within the community council itself, negotiation,
give-and-take, and the requiring of every group to make specific objections and proposals rather than express vague emotional rejection or
withdraw and sabotage, may be part of the desired processes.

What prevents nurses' participating in such processes? Why are
nurses reluctant to relate to the patients as a group and collaborate
with them to achieve common ends? The following factors seem to be
involved.

1. Intragroup: (a) The head nurse prefers to act herself within the
community program rather than delegating to other nurses respon-

sibilities within that program. Other nurses are left out. Not only do they then not "understand" what the program is all about, but they feel that the head nurse, who performs a different role from theirs, and who, of course, then cannot act as their role model either, does not really represent their interests and views in the community program. (b) Nurses, while they are autonomous in the sense of being left pretty much to themselves to innovate their own role, are not organized, in the sense of being able to work out together common values, points of view, and required skills, having some intrinsic relationship to the understood, shared, unique purposes of their own group. Each nurse, then, must speak in every situation as an individual; it is never clear what intervention by a nurse is appropriate and competent; the nurses as a group are of course at a considerable disadvantage in negotiating with other more organized groups.

2. Intergroup: (a) The nurses, on the whole frightened of the patients, prefer an alliance with the therapy staff to an alliance with the patients. But the nurses' role in the community program requires them to negotiate and collaborate not only with members of the community program staff but, together with members of this staff, with the patient group, especially in patient-staff committees and enterprises. (b) Integration of the nurses and other staff groups is poor. There is some ambiguity about whether or not the nurse is primarily a sociotherapist operating in the community program, or an assistant of the therapist in dealing with his individual patients. The therapy staff tends to define the role of the nurse in the former way; most nurses, except the head nurse, probably visualize their roles in the latter way; as a matter of fact, the allocation of their time and effort to person, place, and activity is more in accordance with the latter definition than the former. That, even as sociotherapists, their unique role contribution is unclear to themselves and to many others, means that they are often left to innovate their own role according to their own wishes and fears rather than according to task-requirements, and that then they have no objective criteria for performance upon which to base a sense of competence.)

5. *Week 45, Tuesday, meeting 166.* A new arrangement is being set up for the work of the grounds crew, modeled after the job unit. A member of the maintenance department will supervise the work, and people will be required to sign up for at least two hours' work a day and will be formally hired and, if necessary, fired.

6. *Week 45, Tuesday, meeting 166.* The patient business office is a mess. The library is a mess; people leave phonograph records lying

about without covers or put them in the wrong covers; someone has abused the phonograph, which is not working.

7. *Week 45, Tuesday, meeting 166.* Work at the greenhouse and nursery school has been excellent. At the shop and on the grounds, large crews are being assigned for work that one man might do in a short time. Many people are not showing up for work in these areas. *P:* That's not true; people are doing a fine job on the grounds crew.

8. *Week 45, Tuesday, meeting 166.* The coordinating committee has approved the proposal that outpatients be invited to any Sunday meal. The way this will be aranged is discussed.

9. *Week 45, Thursday, meeting 167.* Thirteen dollars is missing from the activities committee cashbox which had been in the drawer of the chairman. People suspect that he has made a mistake in calculating.

10. *Week 45, Friday, meeting 168.* The shop has not been cleaned; no one is showing up for work.

11. *Week 45, Friday, meeting 168.* A patient complains that nurses were not available at the inn the previous night; they were at the office building next door for an hour; emergencies are always possible, and one does not know when one is in the making. *Head nurse:* We were only the distance of a phone call away. *P:* Two patients were upset and wanted to contact a nurse but weren't able to.

Adaptation Outputs to the Motivation Subsystem

1. *Week 44, Friday, meeting 164.* A patient writes an open letter to the community about his feelings of respect for the community and his commitment to it.

"It has only been recently here that I felt that I could drop any role I have been using as a defense and be myself. I feel that this has been made possible by this community and therapy. The freedom to be myself has not been the effort of one person, or even a few, but rather the feeling I have gotten by living within this community. It is true that there are many conflicts, and there are those with whom I don't get along as well as I wish to, but, in general, the entire community is the finest bunch of people I have ever known.

"I realize that at times I have fought the community, and refused to be a part of it, but this was due primarily to the fact that I was afraid if I did drop the role I was playing, I would be hurt and depressed. I think that with any group of people, this would have been true but with a community who understands hurt and depression, and feels these emotions often, these feelings are much more easily dealt with than they could be anywhere else, or with any other group of people.

"For the first time in my life I'm able to admit to myself and others that I do have feelings and for this, which I feel has been made possible by this community, I can only offer the most appreciative thanks."

At the same meeting, it becomes clear that a great deal of anger and tension has been mobilized in the community. People seem "high" and many are not sleeping. Some are angry at the patient who has been self-destructive, or worried about how to receive her on her return. Some are angry that a patient has been fired from the play for not showing up at rehearsals. Some are angry and embarrassed that patients' sexual interpersonal relationships have been so openly alluded to in the previous day's meeting. An ex-patient's intended visit that weekend also has aroused concern. There are many camps and factions; people are taking sides and supporting the divisions that have been created. People leave the meeting at various points in this discussion.

2. *Week 45, Tuesday, meeting 166.* A patient resigns as scheduler, another as special work-projects crew foreman, the first because there is not enough work for the scheduler and the patient prefers to be a worker "like everyone else," the second because he sees no sense in such projects as throwing logs through a basement window for storage.

3. *Week 45, Tuesday, meeting 166.* Does getting out a literary magazine or newspaper depend on the leadership of one person or can it be done by a committee?

The existence of a literary magazine or newspaper depends upon the interest and contributions of the patient group; if there is no such interest, there will be no struggle to put out a literary magazine or newspaper.

People express interest in writing; their contributions are welcomed. *P: I* don't want to hound people for contributions. *P:* People need a little push. *P:* People need some appreciation for what they do.

4. *Week 45, Thursday, meeting 167.* A patient refuses to run for scheduler because of difficulty in obtaining community support for someone with responsibilities. He cites the difficulty in getting people even to express their wishes concerning the showing of Sunday night movies.

5. *Week 45, Friday, meeting 168.* The scheduler says that people are not showing up for work, that he has no intention of doing anything further about getting people to work, that if everyone wants people to

work then everyone may do something about seeing that they do; he no longer **will**.

6. *Week 46, Tuesday, meeting 169.* There are a number of people refusing nomination for scheduler, most of them on the grounds that the job is a burden rather than a pleasure, because the person holding it gets no support or help from others in the community.

A patient volunteers to be scheduler when no one will accept the nomination for the office. His offer is questioned because he tends to take on a lot of responsibilities and then to give them up.

7. *Week 46, Tuesday, meeting 169.* I question that the job of scheduler can be made free of problems and difficulties. Problems are inherent in positions of responsibility which involve dealing with two different groups. A number of patients complain that the difficulties are too great in comparison with the rewards; there is no extra pay. I mention increased respect and esteem. There is a discussion about the fact that schedulers are not respected; they have no prestige.

A scheduler is upset that a patient who has not been working has been referred by the work committee to the social problems council; it is the understanding that the next time he was so referred he would be discharged from the hospital.

What is it that makes working on the job unit so satisfying? Is it just because people know they will be fired if they don't work?

People on the job unit attempt to describe what makes the work so satisfying. Others (perhaps envious of this elite) tend to want to cut off what they are saying or to depreciate it. There is a heated discussion about excusing these workers from chores that others are expected to do. This is countered by staff comments that these people are not really needed to do the few chores.

I wonder if the experience of working in the job unit is satisfying because a job done well is recognized there. A patient speaks of having buffed the floors in the basement and of having been so proud of this that she had called people to look at the floor.

8. *Week 47, Monday, meeting 172.* A series of grievances are expressed by patients living in a particular wing, concerning a patient's noisy, inconsiderate, disturbing behavior: her loud speech; her giddy discussions; her door-slamming; her inordinately loud playing of her phonograph. The patient reacts furiously, stating she had never been welcomed by the people in the wing, excusing much of her behavior as "symptoms" or as justified by the inconsiderate behavior of others. She is planning on leaving the hospital and wants one more chance,

now, to tell everyone what they have done to her. They have turned her experience into "shit!" She storms out, slamming the door.

I comment during the ensuing discussion that it is difficult for a group to influence the behavior of one of its members, especially in times of upset and crisis, who has never been welcomed into, or helped to feel a part of, the group.

Integration Outputs to the Adaptation Subsystem

1. *Week 45, Thursday, meeting 167.* Where should the party be held? The game room: the people living over it will be disturbed. The shop: no liquor is allowed at the shop. Beer was once served there, but not to minors. The TV room: too small.

Integration Outputs to the Consummation Subsystem

1. *Week 44, Friday, meeting 164.* Facing a rough weekend, the group discusses whether or not to have a party. Do people want to drink? Is it better to have them off drinking separately or all together? It is suggested that a special community meeting might be held Saturday to plan activities for the weekend and to base the decision on whether or not to have a party that night on how people are feeling that afternoon.

2. *Week 45, Tuesday, meeting 166.* What kind of literary magazine or newspaper is most desirable: one made up entirely of patient contributions or one including material by others than patients?

3. *Week 45, Thursday, meeting 167.* Do people want the free movies that are available for Sunday night showing or not?

4. *Week 45, Thursday, meeting 167.* Plans for a Saturday night party, including a rock-and-roll band, are discussed. Objections are raised concerning the noise of the proposed rock-and-roll band. Why don't people who like quiet parties make an effort to plan the kind of party they like? The Halloween and Christmas parties were planned by those who like quiet parties.

I comment about the importance of "give-and-take." People try to rally others to their wishes, but then are the very ones to reject others' wishes when their support is asked for these. There is a lot of enthusiasm for the party by some. Perhaps such enthusiasm should be welcomed and encouraged; it is so rare. Then when another wish comes up which requires the support of those wanting the party today, for example, for another kind of party, they will give it.

5. *Week 45, Thursday, meeting 167. Head nurse:* Shouldn't money be contributed to the Cancer Fund rather than to a party?

6. *Week 45, Thursday, meeting 167.* How should money remaining in the activities committee budget be divided for the rest of the year?

Integration Outputs to the Integration Subsystem

1. *Week 44, Monday, meeting 161.* A patient wants help in refraining from excessive drinking while around the inn, but does not want interference with his going elsewhere far from anyone at the inn when he wants to drink. (A norm concerning excessive alcohol intake is "relevant" only around the inn. It can be evaded only by going elsewhere. "Going elsewhere" protects the community, rather than the individual, from some of the consequences of his drunkenness.)

2. *Week 44, Monday, meeting 161.* Staff and patients disagree about proposals to make meals available for outpatients. Patients accuse the coordinating committee of unconscionable delay in responding to a proposal that outpatients be invited to more meals; the clinical director does not even remember such a proposal's coming to the coordinating committee from the community council. The suggestion that patients invite outpatients for meals prepared by patients in the patient kitchen is rejected by them. It is clear that the patients feel that the staff treats outpatients like "stray dogs" and does not adequately feed them.

(The norm desired by the patient group is one that legitimizes receiving gratification directly from staff. The establishment of such a norm is seen by the patients also as a means of enhancing the integration of the inpatient and outpatient groups. The norm desired by the staff group is one that encourages independence of the outpatient group from care at the inn and thus discourages the integration of inpatients and outpatients—presumably for the sake of the outpatients, primarily—and that encourages the inpatients to take some responsibility for providing the means of gratifying their own wishes.)

3. *Week 45, Tuesday, meeting 166.* Various suggestions are made to deal with the fact that the patient business office is in a mess: lock up the office; lock up the mimeograph machine.

4. *Week 45, Thursday, meeting 167.* What time should the party start and stop? *P:* People should be able to get to sleep at a reasonable hour. *P:* We should be able to hear the band for the full time it is hired for.

Clinical director: The party will have to stop at midnight because it is illegal for a party to run into Sunday in this state. *Nurse:* The music should stop at 11:30 so people have a chance to quiet down.

Who should be invited to the party? After some discussion, it is agreed that only people who have some connection with the hospital should be invited. An objection is made: anyone who wants to come should be invited, but people who misbehave or cause trouble should not be invited again. It is agreed that a person who is alleged to have something to do with illegal drugs who has been invited should be asked not to come.

5. *Week 45, Thursday, meeting 167.* There is a discussion about whether or not to nominate for scheduler people who don't come to the community meetings, because such absence would interfere with their doing a good job as scheduler.

6. *Week 45, Friday, meeting 168.* Staff and patients disagree about what is to be expected of nurses. Patients, on the whole, feel that nurses should be available in the inn at all times to help cope with emergencies or upsets. Staff, on the whole, feel that nurses, in order to be able to function well, need time to meet together, to learn, to discuss their work, to get additional training. There is agreement that the nurses should let the patients know when they are going to be out of the inn, next door at the office building. There is some attempt to explore in what situations a patient might get help from another patient and in what situations a nurse would be necessary.

I ask what the group can suggest that might make it possible for nurses to have time to meet together, and learn necessary skills. The main suggestion is to have a substitute nurse available for such situations; in general, patients reject the idea that they can take care of themselves during such times and bitterly complain that asking for help is difficult enough, that nurses ought to make it easier to get help, that a patient shouldn't have to worry about whether he fitted the category "emergency" or not. The idea that patients can help each other is rejected because patients get angry when someone around them gets upset. The suggestion that there be a night meeting between nurses and patients is again referred to the community council.

I wonder what the head nurse has made of the discussion and how it has affected her thinking and plans. She states that she has been thinking that there is nothing wrong in expecting patients to rely on themselves or one another for an hour.

(A number of people are surprised to be reminded that the coming Monday is a holiday. The sense of deprivation has led this time, perhaps usefully, to a direct discussion between a patient group and staff group concerning differences in normative expectations.)

7. *Week 46, Tuesday, meeting 169.* A number of patients feel that the schedulers should not be concerned with getting patients to work, because consequences accrue only to the patients themselves. Why do schedulers develop the feeling that they are responsible for carrying out the patients' contract with the hospital? The work committee feels the community has two alternatives: a work program which has people's support or no work program at all.

Integration Outputs to the Motivation Subsystem

1. *Week 45, Monday, meeting 165.* A debate begins which lasts for some meetings concerning the firing of a patient from the drama group because he hasn't attended rehearsals but went to the races instead. That values are at issue is suggested by the fact that the discussion can be understood as a conflict about means, ends, or norms, all of which are governed by values.

Some patients feel that, in deciding about the wisdom of the norm and the necessity of adherence to it, consequences for the individual patient should be given highest priority: if he benefits from being in the play every effort should be made to make it possible for him to get his part back, whether or not he has failed to attend rehearsals. Other patients and the drama director feel that consequences for the play itself and the achievement of the drama group should be given highest priority: if a person does not do his job in the drama group, then, since other people depend on the performance of that job, he should be replaced.

A similar issue revolves around the replacement of the patient by a citizen of the town: the town person is considered by the director the most capable person for the part; some patients feel that, in the selection of personnel (a resource or means), patients should have priority, no matter what their competence, because the purpose or end of the drama group is not, according to them, primarily to put on a good play but to benefit individual patients. The drama director and others take the position that if putting on good plays is not the primary goal of the drama group, patients will not benefit by participating in it.

A patient points out that the issue is the same in the work program: is the purpose of the work program primarily to get needed jobs done as effectively as possible or to do therapeutic good to individual patients?

Ultimately, competing value-orientations are at issue. The drama director represents the value-orientations of selecting people for roles on the basis of what they *do*, not who they *are*, and *impersonally* (anyone residing in the town, including patients, with certain skills) rather than *personally*—giving preference to those in a particular relation to herself (that is, *her* patients). She also requires attitudes in herself and others of *inhibition* (evaluation of consequences, losing the role or ruining the play) rather than immediate *discharge* (going to the races whenever one feels like it), and *restriction* (interest in and response to a person in his specific role as an actor) rather than *expansion* (interest in and response to a person in any role or aspect).

Essentially, then, the drama director, in contrast to many patient members of the group, gives primacy to instrumental action (work) in achieving an expressive end (the play) and to the adaptation values appropriate to such action (doing, impersonal, inhibition, restriction) over the integration values (being, personal, discharge, expansion) favored by others and especially dominant because of the prepotency of integration values arising from the primacy of the integration or therapeutic aims of the hospital. That most staff and patients (with the notable exception of the drama director) consider the drama group an activity (implying presumably the primacy of expressive action) rather than work (the primacy of instrumental action) adds to the considerable confusion about what value-orientations are appropriate to participation in it. (Of course, work and activities both involve instrumental action. They are best distinguished in terms of the end pursued. Work involves instrumental action in the pursuit of a utilitarian end: something useful. Activities may involve instrumental action in the pursuit of an expressive end: something pleasurable.)

9. The Pet Issue

Discussions of pets—the possibility of changing the rule of "no pets," the disposition of the black cat, the arrival and departure of the iguana—had occurred during the first half of the first year of the community meetings, as reported in previous pages. Following the removal of the iguana, there was no discussion of pets or the pet rule at community meetings for eight-and-a-half months, except for a single reference to a dog that was purported to be tearing up papers and contributing to the messiness of the grounds; the owner denied the truth of these accusations: "He used to do that sort of thing, but he doesn't any more."

During all these months, the community program staff had worked to achieve the following.

1. To distinguish between a psychotherapeutic and a socio-therapeutic enterprise, and to make interpretations consistently about the community as a social system, its aims, and the intergroup and intragroup strains—the conflicts of interest, purpose, and value—interfering with, and affecting the nature of, solution of community problems, rather than to focus in the community upon intrapersonal conflicts, individual neurosis, transference, or psychopathology.

2. To alter the attitude toward specific norms or rules, from one involving the perception of them as traditional, sacred objects—the only possible objectification of basic values—to one involving the perception of them as the product of negotiated agreements between groups to solve specific problems at specific times, which may be reconsidered and perhaps, although not necessarily, altered

Richard Spahn, Research Associate, whose observations and notes have been invaluable to me, was especially helpful in organizing this material as the situation or circumstances and the needs of these groups change, in the light of shared new information, new wants, or the availability of new skills or other resources.

3. At the same time, perhaps somewhat paradoxically, to alter the status of norms and values as external objects imposed by external authority, to be evaded or complied with as expedient, in the direction of a status of internalization within members of the group, norms and values therefore no longer requiring external sanctions to maintain—this alteration to be accomplished not only through processes of identification and respect or esteem but also through processes of shared experience and examination of the consequences to the community and to its enterprises of departure from such norms or alienation from such values. (Essentially, the effort with respect to norms and values was to substitute the internalization and institutionalization of generalized value-orientations for prescriptions or proscriptions of specific acts.)

4. To interact with patients in a relationship characterized by mutual collaboration in achieving common purposes, and to influence primarily through example and idea rather than by the exercise of authority or by domination through false or distorted representations of reality—but at the same time to avoid abrogating that authority and responsibility required for the effective performance of certain functions.

5. As part of this endeavor, to structure situations to include explicit available alternatives or choices and to clarify the values intrinsic to these and the consequences of one or the other of these, always explicitly distinguishing between the personal preferences and individual vested interests of staff members and the value-preferences intrinsic to their professional role and specific tasks in the hospital community, and avoiding undue defensiveness or the idealization of the staff.

6. To make it possible for different groups of patients and staff to discover and express their wishes and the fears associated with various wishes, such expressions to provide the basis for processes of problem-solving and goal-attainment.

7. To thwart attempts to get rid of, as rapidly as possible, tensions and strains, involving the collision of different wishes and fears, by "passing the buck" to an external authority, to and against whose decision the group may then submit and rebel without recognition or resolution of actual differences *within* the group itself, and to thwart the use of such external authority by subgroups

of the community to justify ignoring, deprecating, or crushing the wishes of any other subgroup.

8. To encourage the formation of interdependent bonds among community members, by demonstrating that the collective agreements and action of community members are necessary for solving community problems, achieving community aims, and meeting various felt needs, so that members are motivated to solve problems involving each others' wishes and fears and to turn to each other in doing so, rather than to ignore such problems in favor of a primary concern with satisfying or rebelling against an external source of normative or coercive authority (the administration or therapy staff).[1]

9. To institutionalize a problem-solving process involving the explicit statements of specific wishes and fears, negotiation and give-and-take between groups, and attempts to understand and to meet by some specific measures, insofar as realistically possible, both the wishes and fears of various groups; rather than a process involving vague, stubborn objections, withdrawal, covert sabotage, or meeting wishes without regard to the existence of fears, or sacrificing wishes in order to allay fears.

10. To bring about a perception of rational organization as the means necessary for such problem-solving to occur.

In the fourteenth month following the inauguration of community meetings, the community council hears with reference to the rule prohibiting pets in the inn that, according to the latest "cat census," only two patients have cats in the inn. In the meetings of the community council during this time, the following discussions take place.

P: The last time the community council talked about the pet rule it was felt to be unenforceable; however, the head nurse had said that pets could not be tolerated because of the damage they inflict on rooms. Should the problem be taken to the community meeting?

Nurse: Before taking it to the community meeting, the community council should first get the facts straight about whether there is room to compromise. According to the medical director's last memo on the subject, there are to be no pets in the inn at any time. What do you do when you have unenforceable rules? Who is going to enforce the pet rule? *S:* Pets represent a genuine conflict of interest between those who

---

1. For a discussion of what constitutes the therapeutic community and what is external to it, in terms of a theoretical analysis of psychiatric hospital organization, see *Sociotherapy and Psychotherapy*, pp. 119–168.

like animals and those who don't. *Nurse:* A memo should be sent to the medical director asking for clarification of the rule and the possibility of its amendment in the future.

The community council decides to stand behind the pet rule until some changes are made. A motion is made and carried unanimously that those people who have pets in the inn will be referred to the community council as social problems.

Later community council minutes refer to six pet owners or "guardians" in the inn.

At a subsequent community council meeting, it is reported that the situation of pets in the inn has become so serious that the head of the maintenance staff plans to take the problem to the coordinating committee. The community council wishes to try to enforce itself what seems an unenforceable rule. At this time the rule states that no pets are allowed in the inn at all. To take care of the immediate problem before the staff steps in, the community council asks two patients to send their cats to outpatients to take care of, and asks another patient to keep her dog outside.

The community council tries to find a way of altering the pet rule to something more acceptable to all the community. One suggestion is a pet room in the basement. A patient should have only one animal and any pet would have to be cleared through the community council: no elephants or rhinoceri. If the owner doesn't conform by keeping the pet in the basement, the pet will have to be sent away. Furthermore, any damage done to the inn will have to be paid for by the owner. It is decided to take these suggestions to the community meeting for discussion.

At the meeting, it is reported that a cat, who seems to belong to no one, has been wandering around the inn, starving and making a mess. The comunity council considers him to be an SPCA problem. The community council votes to notify an outpatient, his present guardian, to get him out of the inn, or the SPCA will have to be called. The community council decides that if the rug in the west wing cannot be cleaned, the outpatient should be asked to pay for it. Another patient will investigate ways to clean the rug to avoid this.

On a Monday in the fifteenth month at the community meeting, the community council chairman announces that the council will be discussing a proposal that pets be permitted in the hospital. She explains that the proposal will allow pets to be kept in the basement of the inn, with their owners responsible for their behavior and for any damage the pets might do. There are no questions or further discussion.

On the next Tuesday, it is reported at the community meeting that a patient has decided to look for a new home for her cat. The chairman says the community council is pleased that this problem is solved. Nothing is said about any proposal.

At the community council meeting on the following Monday, it is decided that the pet rule is to be strictly enforced. Two cats are to leave within two weeks. The dog has a two weeks' period of grace, in view of his owner's affection for him, pending a possibly more acceptable solution to the problem.

The two-week moratorium for the cats is offered in a different spirit from the two-week moratorium for the dog. Apparently, support for the rule, however hard-hearted it seems, is going to lead to the eviction of the cats. At the same time, there is a hope for a revision of the rule in order to enable the dog to remain. The basement proposal has disappeared.

At the community meeting on the following Tuesday, the community council chairman wonders if something new can be worked out about pets. Perhaps the owner of the dog can be made an exception to the rule because her dog is really no problem: "Actually he is clean." The difficulty is that the owners of cats have expressed resentment of this proposal.

P: The general feeling in the community council is that the "no pet" rule is a good one but some people feel that perhaps it does not have to be a blanket rule; those who have pets already obviously love them, and understandably it would be hard for them to give up their pets.

In the discussion that follows, there are a number of comments in support of the community's rules, with statements from patient members of the community council that they have agreed "to stand behind the nurses in their efforts to enforce rules." At the same time, there is also a tendency to agree that "no one is going to go around looking for violations."

P: The principal reason for this rule is that some people object to pets. *P:* And some people do not. *P:* We heard yesterday at the community council that hospitals can have pets and still pass inspection.

P: I hope that the community council will be able to work out some policy which will have built-in protection and respect for those who object to pets. *P:* No pets is the only way to protect those who object to pets. The patient who owns the dog says, "Why don't we admit we don't dare challenge the staff because we depend upon them too much?"

At the community meeting on the following Monday, the community council reports that the patient owning the dog refuses to be an exception, and is planning to present a pet proposal and also planning to contact someone at another psychiatric hospital to learn something more about their policy regarding pets kept by patients. In subsequent weeks, there is much anger at this patient for refusing to allow the group the way to a rapid solution: make her an exception and we don't have to worry about the problem any longer. Objection is subsequently raised about her proposals that the set of rules would involve too much administrative effort by the community council.

At the community meeting the next Tuesday, the community council chairman reports that the council did not have enough time to talk about pets.

In the sixteenth month, the entire community receives copies of the pet rule revision proposal which the patient who owns the dog had presented to the community council two weeks previously.

The proposal follows. Although it includes a number of specific suggestions, it tends to leave most of the difficult decisions to the community council, decisions that will have to be made before the revision of the pet rule can go into effect and decisions that will have to be made on an on-going basis in the future. The proposal suggests the formation of a "pet committee" but does not conceive of this committee as taking the administrative burden off the community council. Its task is to be "supervision and inspection of rooms as a preventative to damage."

REVISION OF THE PET RULE

Considerations:

1. Type of pet allowed.

All patients wishing to have pets would have to have the approval of the community council; if the pet is, in the community council's opinion, unsuitable owing to size, type, poor conduct, irresponsibility on the part of the owner, the community council shall have the power to refuse the pet's admission into the inn.

2. How many pets will be allowed in the inn at one time?

In order to insure that the inn isn't overpopulated by pets there shall be a maximum number of pets allowed in the inn at one time. The number shall be decided upon by the community council. No patient shall have more than one pet at a time. The community council may wish to install a waiting list.

3. Where would pets be allowed?

In order to take into consideration that there are people who do not like pets, or who do not wish pets to be in the inn, no pets shall be allowed in public rooms. A dog on its way to its room shall be leashed if necessary. No pets would be allowed in the east wing.

4. No pre-conference patients shall have pets.

5. Should pets be allowed to live in the inn?

The community council shall decide whether a pet is suitable to live in the inn. If *any* pet disturbs those near it at night the pet should not be allowed to stay in the inn. If the pet is not clean in its habits or is destructive to inn property it should not be allowed to stay in the inn. Kitty litter shall not be dumped on the lawns.

6. What conduct is expected of pets and of pet owners?

If any pet is unduly disturbing, its case should be reviewed with the community council. Since pets are not to be allowed in public rooms, the conduct of the pets would be based on the amount of disturbance it caused in its room and on the way there too. If the noise or disturbance occurs too frequently the community council shall have the power to dismiss the pet from the inn.

If an owner shows irresponsibility in caring for the pet to the point of disturbing people, this should be pointed out to the owner by the community through the community meeting or by individuals. The community council shall discuss the problem as it sees fit. If the owner seems to be incapable of caring for the pet in a responsible way after a warning, the community council shall suspend the pet from the inn. The owner may apply to the community council for readmission. Irresponsibility should be broadly defined: everything from neglect, to cruelty, to general disturbance.

7. Should the community council consider the therapeutic value or harm to a patient with a pet?

I think not. It can and should, however, tell the patient that the community is disturbed by his behavior in connection with the pet.

8. Supervision and inspection of rooms as a preventative to damage to be made by a pet committee.

At the community meeting on the next Thursday, the patient who owns the dog reports on a telephone conversation she has had with the associate medical director of another psychiatric hospital. The following information about the other hospital is offered for the group's information.

1. Pets are allowed in all buildings, but they are not allowed in public rooms. 2. There are no restrictions as to the number of pets in the hospital, or the number of pets per patient, or the type of pets. 3. The pets may stay in the patients' rooms. 4. Problems which come up are dealt with on the halls themselves. There is no committee which deals with problems about pets. 5. The lack of cleanliness has never been an issue. Where there are pets, there are problems. The problems seem to be worth it. It is felt that those people with pets benefit from the experience. Pets bring people together.

During the sixteenth month, at the community meeting on Monday, a patient reports that her father visited her this weekend and brought her dog along. The family cannot keep it at home any longer. She wants the community to know that she hasn't brought the dog here in defiance of any rules. She plans to keep it at a local kennel. She would like to bring it on the grounds on occasion because she is in the process of training it. *P:* I hope she will be allowed to train her dog on hospital grounds; a too strict enforcement of the rule may force her to spend more time away from the community than she should.

That day, at the community council meeting, two patients are concerned that pets cause discomfort to patients as a result of their noise, odor, and damage to property. The patient who owns the dog presents her proposal to allow pets. Another patient points out that her disliking a pet in no way means that she is attacking its owner. The pet iguana is cited as an example. A motion is passed to have all patients vote whether they are *for, indifferent to,* or *against* a proposal to reconsider changing the pet rule.

At the community meeting on the following Thursday, the results of the vote on the question whether the community is in favor of considering proposals to change the pet rule is announced. There are thirteen votes for, thirteen votes against, and four votes registering indifference. The clinical director's immediate comment is: "That settles it!" I comment: "You mean we have agreed to disagree?"

I then ask if the community council considers the vote a resolution of the problem. The community council replies that only thirteen people have voted for further consideration of the pet rule, which is hardly a majority. I then ask: "What do we do with those thirteen people—bury them?"

The community council chairman then says that the community council has taken its own vote on whether to support the proposals. "We voted eight to two against. However, we didn't want to take the responsibility for killing the whole issue. That is why we passed it on for a community vote." She then adds: "I myself used to be completely indifferent about it but now I am completely against pets. I am so tired of talking about it."

I then comment that I am not sure why the community should accept a resolution which is in fact a lack of resolution. I then ask the community council chairman if she can explain why the community was asked to vote before it had a chance to hear and discuss the specific proposals.

P: The community should also have a chance to hear what the head nurse said at the community council meeting—that all of the inn rooms will have to be redecorated if pets are ever allowed, no room can have a rug, all floors will have to be covered with linoleum.

I agree that it is important to hear the head nurse's ideas. If they're specific, we can find out what the nurses object to about pets and what would have to be provided for in order to get them to accept pets. Similarly, for the same reasons, we should hear something more from those patients who voted no. Why did they vote no? What would get them to change their minds?

P: Good luck to you.

There seems to be some general agreement at the end of the meeting that it will be helpful to the community council to hear some further discussion of the pet issue before the next council meeting.

I take note of the "genius of American political life" which makes it possible for society to draw together after a conflict over issues. I then suggest that a committee in this community has the job of discovering the kind of consensus that will draw people together and enable all persons concerned to come to terms with a decision.

I speak of the community council and its work on the pet issue, suggesting that the committee has fled from the responsibility to lead, apparently because its members cannot face and deal, in any constructive fashion, with their own feelings about accepting or rejecting pets. Instead of coming before us with some thoughtful, reasoned decision, for or against or somewhere in between, a decision that might bring general support, the council has brought us "grandmothers' tales" to frighten children, such as that every room will have to have linoleum floors, and that inspectors will descend upon us from outside and raise objections. The council might have sought to understand the reasons for opposition to pets and to attempt to deal with such opposition with specific proposals. How do you deal with an issue when some people say yes, and some people say no? What is needed is for those who say no also to say what would change their minds. Maybe those who say no are only saying that they won't scratch anyone else's back because theirs has not been scratched. I cite some examples of this from current discussion about interpersonal encounters. Whatever the objections are, however, if they are stated, the people who say yes can then try to meet them.

Maybe the split is not between those who say yes, and those who say no. Some time ago, the head nurse said at this meeting that she personally would enjoy having some pets around. Now she raises objections. Maybe the real splits are within ourselves, not the splits between us. I know from conversations with the staff that many of them are mixed in their feelings about pets. Without acknowledging and facing these mixed feelings, we will never be in a position to influence each other.

P: We will never change some people's minds.

I comment that it is part of the belief upon which we base our therapeutic work that, through reason and understanding, people can change.

P: People in this community have a stake in not getting what they said they wanted; I put a sign on my door in very small letters saying, wake me up. When they don't come to wake me up, I get furious at everyone. I voted against any reconsideration of the pet rule at the community council meeting because I was angry with [the patient who owned the dog]. We had the way out, to give her special permission; then she ruined it.

A staff member says he thinks the fact that he is tired of the pet issue has influenced his decision to support an immediate vote by the community.

The community council chairman says that she knows that she has been irrational throughout the discussion of the pet issue at the community council meeting. I'm afraid of animals; I think almost everybody on the community council is. That is why we wanted the community to vote, to be fair.

The clinical director says he agrees that the discussion at the community council has been irrational to a large extent. The undercurrent was a fear of animals.

The community council chairman adds: I think we can do better.

At the community meeting on the following Monday, the community council chairman reports that, on the pet revision vote, two more ballots had been cast than there were members of the community around at the time.

There is no indication of any interest in determining the direction in which the voting was affected. There is general agreement that this was a terrible way to get one's way. The words "scandal," "villainy," and "culprits" are used. Smaller voices attempt to account for the discrepancy as oversight, error, or informal proxies.

The community council chairman says that the community council plans the appointment of a committee to study the pet issue. I comment that I've caught on; if you want to kill some issue, send it to a committee; it's a standard procedure.

P: It's not true. He defends the study committee that has been set up to evaluate the work program. *The community council chairman:* Don't just criticize us, make another suggestion.

I suggest that the community council hold on to its responsibility to work out the pet issue. There are at least two questions that I think would be better considered in the community meeting or in the community council than in any study committee. Can the community, with any real sense of comfort, proceed to work at this time to make a change, which the medical director has explicitly opposed, during a period in which he is ill and cannot personally engage in any dialogue about the wisdom of such a change? (This may be an even greater concern of the staff members on the community council than of the patients.) What about people's fears of animals? What does it mean to acquiesce to these fears or to ignore them? The way we talk about and face such questions influences what kind of community we build.

P: Why can't some rooms be set aside for pet owners? This might be possible but these rooms would have to be furnished differently. Does differently mean worse? Why shouldn't pet owners be willing to make the "sacrifice?" Who would want to live in or near a "zoo room?"

If we let down the barriers, there is no way to keep the situation from getting out of hand. What does "out of hand" mean? Too many animals? Yes, including pet rhinoceri.

Pet owners will have to keep their pets confined to their rooms, and that is cruel to the pets. *P:* No, what a pet experiences as cruelty is the prolonged absence of its master.

We have to remember that this a hospital. *P:* But some hospitals allow pets; some do not.

The people who want pets are not interested in the welfare of the community. Their attitude is selfish. The people who don't want pets are selfish. The people who want pets are just as interested in the welfare of the community as anyone else. Why should people who want things be allowed to get their way?

I wonder why shouldn't we want people to get their way? We are facing a choice between fears and desires. Perhaps the most useful question is whether we can solve problems by asking people who want things why they want what they want and how they plan to go about getting it, while asking those who don't want these things if anything could make them change their minds. I comment that one of the things at issue is people's love for their pets. Should we build the kind of community that helps people avoid encounters with the things they fear, or should we build the kind of community that helps people achieve what is necessary to meet their needs, and in addition a community that gives a high value to feelings of love?

A week later the community council puts the pet issue in the hands of a pet committee.

At the beginning of the seventeenth month, the pet study committee issues a report. From the report, it is obvious that the committee does not see its job as proposing solutions or suggesting any basis for agreement. It does, however, attach to its report one piece of evidence, which seems designed to counter one of the arguments against pets.

THE PROS AND CONS OF HAVING PETS IN THE INN

Pros:
1. Source of pleasure.
2. Develops a sense of responsibility—feeding, walking, grooming, etc.
3. Forming new friendships through pet-owners getting together; people who like pets get together.
4. Help in putting personal problems to one side.
5. Help people to get over fear of animals.
6. Help in getting to know people outside the hospital community.
7. Good exercise for owner—walking, playing, etc.
8. Helps develop creativity and imagination—training, teaching tricks.
9. Help in overcoming isolation—pet friendships can lead to making friendships with people.
10. Can help in letting off steam by running and playing with pet.
11. It's nice to have a pet to love.

Cons:
1. Odor, noise, damage.
2. Difficult for people who do not like pets.
3. Too confining for the animals if kept in rooms all day.
4. Damage to the gardens; dog messes on the lawns.

5. Animals bring more animals.
6. Danger in the parking lot—dogs chasing cars.
7. Concern about what to do about owners showing lack of responsibility and neglect.
8. Concern about the age of the pet—training puppies, kittens ruin rugs.
9. The head nurse feels that no one takes care of cats—kitty litter not changed every day; cats destroy furnishings. She thinks the line should be drawn between cats and dogs. There is a lot of evidence of the damage cats have done—torn curtains, torn rugs, and stench.
10. Furnishings would have to be different if cats were allowed— no rugs, no frills on chaises or chairs, etc.

An addition to the report from another psychiatric hospital: for the most part the rooms are furnished in much the same way as the inn rooms. The rooms are carpeted and decorated as well as ours.

SUBMITTED BY THE PET COMMITTEE

A few days later, the patient-owner of the dog prints and distributes to the community copies of the other hospital's pet regulations. Over and above the confirmation once again that a psychiatric hospital can permit pets if such were its preference, this paper indicates what kind of specific measures are required to meet the anticipated difficulties.

In the next community council meeting, the patient-owner of the dog feels that the community has lost a certain degree of interest in the pet proposal. The committee has been seemingly ineffective and unable to present a conclusive report. She herself has presented four papers on the subject including the pros and cons of pets, a report from another hospital on pets, a listing of the pet regulations there, and her own revision of the present pet regulations here. Another patient proposes having pets on a trial basis for one month. The clinical director reminds him that the pet restrictions are already an established administrative policy which will have to be rescinded.

At a community meeting a few days later, following a report from the community council, a patient says that she has heard that the owner of the dog is almost ready to drop the subject and go back to living "on the borders of the rule." The pet owner replies that she is getting "an odd response" from everyone; "I have decided not to be the only one interested in changing the rule."

P: I would still like to see the rule changed, but I agree about the response; I cannot cope with both statements: get the staff to agree first and the patients will state how they feel; get the patients to agree first and the administration will state how it feels.

The pet owner: I feel that every time I have done what someone has asked me to do in the way of research and suggesting concrete proposals, I am told to go and do more. She is complimented on her hard work, good research, or excellent proposals. The community council chairman says that the community council supports the research.

P: Does the community council support the proposals?

Chairman: I don't know.

P: I suggested that the community council go ahead with an experiment, a one-month trial, and was told that this couldn't be; someone still has fantasies of the place being overrun by dogs.

I ask: Who?

P: I suppose the medical director.

Clinical director: It is true he is against pets messing up his house or the inn but I know he is willing to listen to any sensible proposals, although there is no guarantee that what the community thinks is sensible will seem so to him.

I comment that there are two things that might account for the "odd response." For one, patients may not want to go ahead with the discussion of the proposal because the head nurse has hinted that the rooms at the inn will have to be changed in some way. For another, and this probably involves the feelings of both staff and patients, people may sense that this is the time, at least for a while, to "cool" it. When a significant staff person is ill, for example, the medical director, and cannot be directly involved in discussions which would alter or challenge his previously strongly held position on some issue, it might be felt to be more considerate to postpone working on that issue.

A few days later, the community council chairman reports that the community council has agreed upon a procedure for handling the proposals about changing the pet rule. She emphasizes that this procedure is something other than the proposals themselves. The plan is first to get a list of decorative and furniture changes that will be required if a room is to house a pet. This list will be submitted by the head nurse and then approved by the community council. Next, the community council will solicit suggested amendments to any proposals for changing the pet rule. The community council will then approve or disapprove the amendments. A final plan will then be submitted for community referendum.

A majority vote will decide the issue once and for all. If there is a vote in favor of a pet proposal it might influence the medical director to approve such a plan.

The pet owner: I am no longer sure whether I am more in favor of dropping the issue or pursuing it; I resent not being asked to participate in the community council discussion yesterday.

Community council chairman: There is currently one cat in residence and one dog that goes in and out of the inn but doesn't sleep here.

Later in the month, the head nurse indicates the modifications of rooms that would be necessitated by having pets in them. She thinks the floors would need to be covered by vinyl, the furniture upholstered in tough fabric, and the rooms provided with scratching posts. She thinks having pets will just add on too much headache to the already big job of running this place.

One idea suggested is to charge persons wishing to keep pets a given sum payable in advance.

Two patients still have their pets even though the deadline for both of them to move them out has passed.

At the next community meeting, the head nurse speaks of the "nurses' suggestions" for the conditions under which two or three patients might be allowed to keep pets legally. The community council chairman observes that the pets currently in residence in violation of "our too strict" rule are both well-behaved animals. She describes the sequence of steps required to get any proposal approved by the medical director, probably taking at least a month, as "our working-through procedure." The suggestion about a given sum payable in advance is described by a patient as "posting bonds."

P: Approve three patients' having pets and everyone excluded will be provoked into bringing in an animal.

P: Responsible behavior on the part of pet owners might be an alternative to trying to make the environment pet-proof.

P: The most important influence on the behavior of an animal is the way his master relates to him.

P: Everything really depends on the way a pet owner supervises his pet.

A patient suggests that the pet plan include the setting up of a pet committee, a group of everyone who has a pet to supervise each pet owner's supervision of each pet.

Late in the month, two proposals are considered and combined by the community council. A few amendments are added and the resulting proposal is given a unanimous vote of approval by the community council with the clinical director abstaining.

The plan that the community council has approved for a community vote is read in a community meeting at the end of the month. It is mentioned that the proposal had been unanimously passed by the community council with the clinical director abstaining because, according to him, the proposal confused him; the head nurse had declined to review the proposal on the grounds that her position was clear—her declining had been accepted by the community council.

In the ensuing discussion, five additional suggestions are made for possible inclusion in the proposal. These are: (1) female pets should be spayed; (2) all pets should live in one room of the inn; (3) one common room, perhaps the game room, should be made available to pets so that they can be together indoors; (4) pets, in transit between individual rooms and the outdoors, should be kept on leashes; (5) rooms with pets should be inspected at least once a week.

The first and fourth suggestions are included in the revised proposal presented for a vote.

P: At this point, anyone who is still concerned with his fears of animals is talking about pure fantasy.

P: I agree that the proposal meets the objections about fears about pets; it satisfies me completely.

P: Just thinking about what should go into the proposal and feeling that it might be accepted now has been useful to me; if the proposal is accepted, it will enable the pet owners to evaluate the personal meaning of wanting to keep a dog or a cat; I am reconsidering my wish to keep my dog in terms of the effect this might have on my ability to spend time with other people and to do other things.

I comment that whatever the outcome of the vote on this pet proposal, the work on it reflects a great advance in the community's ability to tackle complicated issues.

The vote on the pet proposal is held at the beginning of the eighteenth month. The inn is decorated with posters, urging votes for and against. For professionalism and humor, the posters against pets have a decided edge. They are signed: C. R. A. P.—Committee for the Remedy of Animal Problems. The burden of these posters is that a vote against pets is a vote against odors and messes. Fight crap with C. R. A. P. There is a good deal of banter and an uproar of animal noises during the voting.

The final vote is rushed into the following community meeting: pro—18, con—12, abstentions—2. The proposal follows.

> The following proposal to have pets in the inn is based on several kinds of responsibility: of the individual for his pet; of the pet owners as a group to help each other fulfill their obligations;

and, finally, of this group to act on and respond to community feelings. The privilege of having pets in the inn cannot work unless the pet owners work to make the community feel free in living with the added complications.

1. A committee of pet owners and a nurse and a community council member (to be chosen by the community council) will enforce the pet rules and be responsible to the community council. The community has the right to expect this committee to carry out its duties without creating undue tension or hard feelings.
2. There is a limit of six pets in the inn.
3. One pet is allowed per person.
4. Dogs may spend the night in the inn at the discretion of the pet committee based on size and behavior.
5. Hamsters and other unusual pets will be allowed at the discretion of the pet committee.
6. All pets must be housebroken.
7. No pre-conference patients may have pets.
8. No pets will be allowed in the common rooms.
9. Pet owners must change the litter boxes once a week per directions, and in a specially designated garbage can.
10. Pet owners must provide scratching posts.
11. A $150 to $250 deposit will be required before the pet is allowed to stay in the inn. The amount will be set by the head nurse according to the value of the room.
12. If a room needs more than usual refinishing or cleaning, the patient would have to pay the room fee while this work is being done.
13. There would be a special room inspection by the pet committee at room inspection time, to check for damage.
14. The pet committee will receive referrals and suggestions from members of the community. If the complaint persists for two weeks there would automatically be a discussion or personal referral to the community council. From there it could be brought back to the pet committee for action or the community council could take definite action at that time.
15. The pet committee is responsible to the community for assuring constant care for the pets and consideration for other people's comfort. This implies that a pet owner who is constantly irresponsible will be asked to remove the pet from the inn without argument. The pet committee must have the

support of the community meeting and the community council in these decisions.

16. The new pet rules, as a privilege granted by the community, will be subject to revision and review once a month.
17. Patient seniority will be the basis for originally acquiring pets, and these original pet owners will be the members of the initial committee.
18. Subsequent granting of the pet privilege will be based on a waiting list similar to the room change list.
19. All female pets must be spayed.
20. All pets must have had their shots.
21. All pets must be carried or on leashes when going through the inn to and from patients' rooms.

One month after the vote at the community meeting, the community council chairman reports that at the community council meeting she had "asked about the pet rule, er, pets"—

P: Pet proposal!

Chairman: Yes, the proposal is on the medical director's desk. He's read it. The clinical director and the head nurse want to speak to him about it but they haven't found the time for an appointment.

Minor amendments are suggested by the medical director toward the end of the nineteenth month, almost two months after the community's vote. During the following month, there is much squabbling as the community council tries to incorporate these new amendments. No one seems interested any longer in working on the proposal; no one, in fact, expresses any interest in having a pet. When the amended proposal is finally approved by the community council a month later (at the end of the twentieth month), there is little rejoicing; it is almost as if, after such a long delay, people have forgotten what the whole matter is about; so there can be little satisfaction in the achievement. As a matter of fact, when the approval is announced, a number of new patients want to know what that is all about.

10. Subsequent Developments

One might expect, following the year during which the community meeting was becoming institutionalized, months characterized by its *use* for specific achievements with reference to community life. A review of some achievements of the second and third years of the meetings tends to confirm this expectation. Examples follow.

1. *Thirteenth month.* The examination of the community-wide pattern of medication—chemotherapeutic and sedative agents ordered to be given on request of patients—actually requested and received by patients suggests that shared social processses, rather than merely the idiosyncratic vicissitudes of individual personality systems, significantly determine increases and decreases in the intake of such medication. This hypothesis leads to a discussion of taking such medication as a way of life and its consistency or lack of consistency with the aims and values of the therapeutic enterprise. An attempt is made to agree upon a brief moratorium on the taking of all such medications; there is intense conflict over this proposal. The discussion results in a heightened awareness of such phenomena and the institutionalization of a weekly medication report from nurses to the community meeting. As is true with so many innovations like this, the report becomes ritualized, a mere routine, and finally ceases to be given; no one after a period of time—most crucially perhaps, including the nurses—regard such a report as relevant to his job or seems to know what to do with it.

2. *Eighteenth month.* Cycles of tension with concomitant increase in the intake of chemotherapeutic and sedative medications are studied in the community meeting; the hypothesis is formulated that peak periods of tension and medication-intake coincide with the final stage of each drama group production. Apparent in the discussion are: strains experienced by drama group members during periods of demanding work; the difficulty that "stars" have participating in, or

returning to, the mundane work-a-day world and the resentment they have toward others who do not seem to appreciate their special needs; the jealousy and sense of deprivation of other community members who feel "put in the shade" by the "stars"; the tendency of drama group members to renege on other responsibilities in the community and to withdraw from other community enterprises and from relationships with other than drama group members, resulting in an increase in social disorganization and anger in others; the occurrence of increased drinking by drama group members during rehearsal and post-rehearsal hours. Apparent results of the discussion are: some increase in flexibility as far as holding drama group members to other responsibilities during periods of peak effort with regard to a production; some increased effort by drama group members to keep up with their other responsibilities during a production or to return to these responsibilities as promptly as possible following the close of a production; a self-imposed drinking ban by members of the drama group during and following rehearsals and for the period of the production.

3. *Eighteenth month.* The group discovers that a previously unidentified person who has been stealing can be named in the community meeting. A guess based on shared knowledge is followed by an admission. Such disclosure is not experienced as personal or collective disaster.

4. *Twenty-first month.* The patient group challenges a staff plan to renovate the shop, which has not involved consultation with the patient group. Discussion of this plan reveals strains among various activities groups—for example, crafts, painting, drama—resulting in part from competition for space. Negotiation among these groups ensues, affecting the final plans for renovation of the shop. (Later, the drama director begins to attend the community meeting regularly; other members of the activities staff continue to express preference for non-attendance at the meeting.)

5. *Twenty-second month.* The alternative of planning and carrying out projects to raise money, rather than turning to the coordinating committee for it, is considered. (Eventually, the coordinating committee decides to allow the activities committee to make choices concerning expenditures within a limited budget during a given year on the basis of current exigencies and needs, rather than insisting that every amount be irrevocably earmarked for given purposes at the beginning of the year.)

6. *Twenty-second month.* "Role-playing" or dramatization of a small group meeting in the community meeting is used to explore with a

small group the difficulties it has been having for which it has asked help from the community meeting. The role-playing results in a lively discussion with many insights and suggestions.

7. *Twenty-third month.* Role-playing a coordinating committee meeting is used to explore fantasies in the community meeting about what a coordinating committee meeting is like. Understanding how a staff group functions is seen as necessary in order to enter into effective negotiations with it. Later, the community program staff enacts a meeting of its own at the community meeting, dispelling to some extent strains related to feelings about supposed staff withholding or secrecy.

8. *Twenty-third month.* Staff and patients tend to perceive synchronously the need for controls to cope with current disruptive "acting out" and the demands of these groups for such controls coincide, resulting in a more prompt subsiding of deviant behavior and fewer strains between patients and staff in achieving this integration aim than usual.

9. *Twenty-fourth month.* Patients wish to hold the community meeting on the lawn outside. Some staff members object, claiming that conditions there, such as noise, will not facilitate work. The outcome of prolonged negotiations on this matter, including an experimental period of meeting on the lawn, includes: clarification of the purposes of the community meeting; the presentation of the alternative values involved and consideration of their consequences, rather than simply living out a power struggle; and a clarification of the rights of each group to make decisions for its own members, with decisions affecting both groups requiring negotiation between them.

10. *Twenty-fifth through thirty-first months.* Patients enter into prolonged negotiations with staff concerning the building of a new facility desired by many patients. Patient-staff groups study what is required for such negotiations and become increasingly clear about the values at issue in the differences between and within the patient and staff groups. Although the proposal is ultimately rejected by the coordinating committee, the learning involved is ultimately used to resurrect a proposal for a game room in the inn, which might meet needs within the community identified in the previous month in a discussion of what patients seek who spend much time at the local tavern in preference to the inn or the activities of the community. This proposal is presented effectively, with much advance planning, and accepted by the coordinating committee with reasonable dispatch, while interest is high. During the building of the game room, there develops some increasing awareness of the importance of organization, organizational channels, and differentiated roles, as means in achieving complex tasks, as well as of the

interdependence of various groups in making such achievement possible. The strains associated with such learning are indicated when a patient sells some old pianos in the inn without "going through channels"; the indignant reaction of the administration and the ensuing uproar serve both to underline the impatience and irritation with the organizational means that confine and to demonstrate their necessity. A New Year's Eve party is planned for the grand opening of the game room. Both patient and staff groups become aware of their differences, which include differences in roles and differences between generations, making planning a party including both groups a tense, difficult matter. The party, however, at which members of both groups share their pride and satisfaction in a joint achievement, is to all appearances one of the most successful and joyful ever held at the inn.

11. The Sociotherapist's Use of Social Theory

In these pages, I have presented a sociotherapist who brings an orientation to the situation or social system rather than the personality system as the object of analysis and intervention. His interpretations (and in this chapter let us focus on this particular kind of intervention) are, ideally, informed by his awareness of group processes, including intergroup relations; and his knowledge of the covert or unconscious, and often shared, meanings groups and organizations or their parts have for the individuals participating in them, and of the covert aims group members share, which determine to some extent their relation to one another, to their leaders, to other groups, and to the tasks that presumably they have joined together to achieve. The ultimate goal of the sociotherapist's interpretation is the resolution of intragroup and intergroup strains interfering with the attainment of various group ends generated by the requirements of community life in the hospital or militating against the institutionalization of the treatment values constituting that community insofar as it is therapeutic.

It would not be in the spirit of this book now, in conclusion, to make claims for, to sell, such an approach to the treatment of patients or to advance reasons for preferring it above other approaches. (In any event, the place of the sociotherapy enterprise in any organization whose goal is the treatment of psychiatrically ill patients, and its relation to other enterprises within that organization, have been detailed in a previous volume, *Sociotherapy and Psychotherapy*.) Here, let us conclude instead by examining what are the difficulties, the dysfunctional as well as functional effects, in making interpretations in the therapeutic community in a social-theoretical rather than psychological frame of reference.

Most commonly in the therapeutic community meetings of many hospitals, a personal, a psychological interpretation of events—for example, an analysis in the group of the characteristic of a particular patient which provokes a certain response from others, and perhaps of the intrapsychic causes of such provocative behavior—is given and is likely, I believe, to have certain dysfunctional effects. Such interpretation plays into tendencies in members of the group to disown feelings or covert aims; these are projected into one member, who is then seen as having the problem; in rejecting or extruding him, the other members of the group defend against the presence of the problem in themselves. The individual, who must bear the burden in himself of what belongs to all, begins to exaggerate his own propensities, becomes disorganized, and feels caught up in behavior experienced as uncannily outside his control.

Furthermore, a psychological interpretation tends to ignore the impact of the situation upon individuals; and the participation of individuals in collective processes in which affects, beliefs, values, and aims are shared, often unwittingly. It may thereby encourage the sometimes prideful, sometimes painful illusion in individuals that their social behavior is idiosyncratic and personally determined.

Finally, being interested in the individual rather than in the social in a hospital may mean at times focusing on the wishes or distress of one individual at the expense of attention to arrangements or conditions affecting the possibility of many other individuals' actualizing values or achieving aims important to them.

The tendency to perform a psychotherapeutic function—that is, to focus upon an individual's transference reactions, intrapsychic conflicts, or interpersonal style—when a sociotherapeutic function is appropriate (for example, when a therapeutic community meeting is apparently used for psychotherapeutic purposes to investigate a particular patient's personality system or the intrapersonal sources of his distress or action) may exist because of confusion about the task facing the group. Such a tendency may be exacerbated by the absence or denigration of the skills or knowledge required to perform a sociotherapeutic function; by a defensive anxiety-motivated abrogation of the sociotherapeutic task, when the exposure of "touchy" social situations is required; or by commitment to a psychotherapeutic orientation as most prestigious or as representing personal, individual, humanist values in an increasingly impersonal, mass society. (The latter formulation, it should be pointed out, involves the fallacy of viewing individual and social as concrete incompatible entities.)

Of course, understanding psychological systems is important in attempting to understand social systems since these are interpenetrating

systems. For example, even in identifying social structures, shared
values and purposes, and the availability of resources or existence of
constraints, as determining agents, one must also take into account the
meanings these social facts are likely to have for individuals with
certain personality-constituents, the extent to which values are internalized in personalities rather than external facts expediently adapted
to, and the condition of individual personality systems making possible
or militating against various knds of participation in social processes.[1]

As I hope has become apparent in the previous chapters of this book,
an interpretation in a social-theoretical framework may have useful results. It may alter community members' shared perception of a social
situation with respect to its significance for the treatment enterprise
or the actualization of treatment values. It may mitigate the effects of
simplistic, right-and-wrong side-taking by tracing the dysfunctional as
well as functional effects of adhering to any cherished value, or by
revealing the strains resulting from attempts to actualize two values
that are in some ways incompatible. It may clarify the nature of the hospital organization itself, so that such organization may be used more effectively as a means for the accomplishment of shared goals. It may
increase integration of the community by leading to awareness of the
reciprocal impact of the requirements of community problem-solving
and the shared anxieties and available capacities of its members, as
well as the reciprocal impact of the formal organization and the informal life of the group.

However, it has also become apparent in these pages that there are
difficulties in, and even dysfunctional consequences of, interpretation in
a social-theoretical framework.

First, such interpretation requires information about what is happening in the social system: how are individuals and groups performing
the tasks required for the solution of the primary functional problems
of the social system? That means revealing incompetence or deviance.
Both staff and patient members and groups have a vested interest in
collusively defending against the exposure of either incompetence or
deviance. Collusive defenses include silence, blurring roles so it is
never clear who is responsible for what, making it possible for individuals to shift between multiple roles when any role becomes associated with difficulty, positively sanctioning in the name of equali-

1. For a discussion of the function of psychological theory in the explanation of
social phenomena, see Talcott Parsons, "Psychoanalysis and the Social Structure,"
Essays in Sociological Theory, rev. ed. (Glencoe, Ill.: The Free Press of Glencoe,
1954), pp. 336–47.

tarian ideals reluctance to exercise or accept authority, and segregating, in the name of privacy, the informal life of the group from its formal organization so that the reciprocal impact of one upon the other cannot be investigated.

Second, social-theoretical interpretation makes the individual aware of his often unwitting unindividuated involvement in what is social; that act of awareness itself is an individuation from the social. The fear of standing alone, rather than safely merged with others, on the one hand, and, on the other hand, the narcissistic injury of discovering that one has unknowingly been participating in a social process while under the illusion of privately willed action, motivate resistance to any requirement for individuation, including that represented by the interpretation. This resistance may take the form of an individualistic objection to the social-theoretical interpretation as involving impersonal reduction of the individual to a mere case illustration of a social process. (Needless to say, interpretations which reify the group, which represent group processes as simply the summation of individual feeling-states— "the group is angry"—and which fail to specify the concrete contributions of individuals to a social process and the meaning such a process has for them, may especially exacerbate this kind of opposition.)

Third, the sociotherapist who makes an interpretation cannot escape his role as a type of leader in a social process. This becomes especially apparent in the therapeutic community, whose ideology often is a vehicle for rationalizing hostility towards and distrust of authority or leadership in any form, at the same time that it is organized to disguise and diffuse such hostility. Staff members may avoid becoming the targets of such hostility by eschewing and sharing authority; and both patients, who are dependent upon the staff, and staff members, who may feel occasionally uneasy that they are being intimidated by patients, often defensively idealize their relation to one another in the name of equalitarianism and democracy.

To the extent that leadership is a leadership of involvement—for example, mobilizing the group's commitment to shared ideals, rallying the group to the defense and aggressive actualization of such ideals, or inspiring the group to pursue some desirable state of affairs—it may arouse, especially in those with uncertain or defensively impermeable ego boundaries, anxieties about the loss of self in the social, the sacrifice of the self to the collective, and the submission of self to the domination of the social. Group members sharing these anxieties will attempt to discredit such a leader. They will seek out, and, if they can, exploit, his inconsistencies. They will provoke him to declarations of intention which they then can attempt to thwart. They will try to make him doubt himself or drive him into rigid postures. They will caricature and oversimplify his beliefs, and anti-leaders representing contrary beliefs will be raised to oppose him. His leadership will be fought in the name of individualistic values, calling for freedom from any restraint, discipline, or obligation that might interfere with the pursuit of self-interest wherever it may lead. Most subtly, he will be treated with awe and respect, perhaps made a deified historical figure in his own time, while the values he represents are ignored in everyday life.

Similarly, to the extent that leadership is a leadership of individuation—requiring differentiated, complementary, integrated performances and adaptive recognition of, and response to, situational exigencies—it may arouse guilt over, or fear of punishment for, deviance, or anxieties about incompetence or inadequacy. Since the cognitive interpretation of the sociotherapist is part of leadership in the service of integration and adaptation, it manifests and requires individuation. It will, therefore, tend to meet the fate of all such leadership: group members may become confused, ignore the interpretation, or attack the interpreter, who will be made to feel he has been callous, clumsily hurtful, or blunderingly incorrect, or that he has violated the group's most sacred values or betrayed its past golden age.

Of course, any kind of leader by his own dispositions, out of his own anxieties, or because of lack of required skills or resources, may behave in such a way as to collude with the members of the group in the destruction of his particular leadership function.

Fourth, interpretation as a cognitive-adaptive activity presupposes commitment to change, to innovation; such commitment is always limited in a social system, because change threatens existing arrangements and the satisfactions associated with these, and knowledge, which is necessary for adaptation, and leads to awareness of the need for change, nevertheless arouses anxiety about its unknown consequences. The pursuit of knowledge and the implementation of change are always in tense relation to, and constrained by, commitments to harmony, stability, and known gratifications.

Finally, we come up against a factor that has not to do with the anxieties created by requirements of the social system for individuation and involvement and the defenses against these, nor with attempts to protect vested interests in existing arrangements, but with the very nature of society itself. A subtle dysfunctional effect of social-theoretical investigation and interpretation was illustrated, for example, by an increase in cynical social behavior following the revelation in a community meeting of the existence of venereal disease in the hospital community. Exposing the workings of a community to cognitive scrutiny may undermine its status as a sacred or numinous object symbolizing a shared value system for which it commands respect, allegiance, and active commitment.[2] The sociotherapist who examines the community must be aware that his cool cognition, however much it may serve adaptation, is always in inevitable conflict with requirements in the social system for nonrational commitment to ultimate values. Interpretations exposing deviance and ineptness, while true, may nevertheless undermine the order of, and confidence in, the community, and lose its support and cooperation. (On the other hand, lying and hypocrisy—which, of course, may represent examples of logical, expedient behavior—may expose the community and its enterprises to the effects of concealed deviance and ineptness as well as undermine respect for it.)

To the extent that the stability of the community, the involvement of its members in processes of action required for the solution of its primary functional problems, depends upon nonrational respect for, or faith in, the community as numinous object, the cognitive attitude always represents some threat to it. An interpretation may explain loss of confidence in a community or loss of respect for the values it symbolizes; it usually cannot, in and of itself, restore such confidence and respect. A cognitive interpretation may invite individuation; it does not, in and of itself, inspire involvement. The imperatives of adaptation, integration, motivation, and consummation, of individuation and involvement, are in fine balance, one against the other. For mitigation of the social disturbance caused by interpretation in one direction, however great its contribution in another, the sociotherapist as interpreter depends upon both his own tact and skill and the counterbalance provided by the participation of other types of staff leaders in the thera-

---

2. Pareto has stated that there is no necessary coincidence between social utility and scientific truth. Nonrational belief and ritual are essential for man's morale and commitment and for mobilizing the energy to overcome obstacles to achieving desired ends; the equilibrium or stability of the group depends on the sharing of nonlogical sentiments and values. Science, which simplifies, which analyzes, which is concerned with logical, causal, verifiable, means-end relations, and which is never normative and can never determine the choice of, but only the means of attaining, ultimate goals, gives rise to doubt and skepticism; and may, at a particular time, be destructive to the values, beliefs, and rituals essential to a functioning society. See Raymond Aron, *Main Currents in Sociological Thought II* (New York: Basic Books, 1967) and Talcott Parsons, *The Structure of Social Action* (New York: The Free Press of Glencoe, 1937).

peutic community, and the variety of types of intervention other than interpretation they provide.

In this final chapter, then, let our main emphasis fall on various kinds of difficulties or dysfunctional consequences of interpretation in a social-theoretical frame of reference, for skill in implementing the view of sociotherapy presented in this volume depends in part on a steady awareness of these difficulties and consequences.

First, such interpretation tends to reveal incompetence or deviance, against the exposure of which both staff and patient members and groups have a vested interest in collusively defending.

Second, social-theoretical interpretation makes the individual aware of his own often unwitting unindividuated involvement in what is social; anxiety about individuation motivates resistance to such intervention.

Third, the sociotherapist who makes an interpretation is a type of leader in a social process and will therefore become the target of the group's destructive response to leadership and the demands leadership makes of membership for involvement or individuation.

Fourth, interpretation as a cognitive-adaptive activity presupposes commitment to change, which is always limited in a social system and in tense relation to commitments to harmony, stability, and known gratifications.

Finally, a subtle dysfunctional effect of social-theoretical interpretation has to do with the very nature of society itself. Exposing the workings of a community to cognitive scrutiny may undermine its status as a sacred object symbolizing a shared value system for which it commands respect, allegiance, and active commitment. Mitigation of this effect requires other kinds of (but complementary) interventions and therefore presupposes a degree of organic solidarity among staff leaders, at least, in a hospital community that is rarely to be found.

Let the aspiring sociotherapist, then, who has read and perhaps been influenced by this sociotherapist's journal consider himself warned.

Appendix A
A Note on the Work Program

The following note on the work program may give a picture of the kinds of issues that were debated around the conduct of the work program in many staff discussions, even squabbles, which were intense yet unclear, and in which zealous assertions vied with doubts and cautions. Statements, even apparently technical ones, had the ring of avowals of faith and belief rather than the more matter-of-fact tone of empirically testable propositions about means-ends relations. "Patients who come to the hospital must work in the work program! That is the commitment they make when accepted for admission." "Is it good for a patient to pressure him to participate in work when he is not yet ready?" "What shall we do with a patient who will not work?" " 'Talk' and more 'talk' with such a patient is just a foolish transfer of psychotherapy to the social realm; what matters in the community is what the staff *does!*" "It is good for a patient to work; a patient should be 'active' rather than 'passive.' "

The author had been reading the work of Parsons and his colleagues,[1] and felt with obvious exhilaration that, using social system rather than personality system theory, he could now understand something about the arguments. The issues were not trivial; neither were they easily resolvable. But they reflected universal value questions, dilemmas of any social system, and could be clarified by making necessary conceptual distinctions.

The note gives a glimpse of the strains related to the different foci of concern, essentially the different values and aims, of the psychotherapy

1. See Talcott Parsons and Edward Shils, "Values, Motives, and Systems of Action," in Parsons, Shils, et al., *Toward a General Theory of Action* (Harvard University Press, 1951; Torchbook ed., New York: Harper and Row, 1962), Parsons, *The Social System* (New York: The Free Press of Glencoe, 1951), and Parsons, Shils, and Robert Bales, *Working Papers in the Theory of Action* (New York: The Free Press of Glencoe, 1953).

enterprise (individual personality system) and the therapeutic community (social system). Are consequences to one or the other to have priority, and under what circumstances? Is a subsystem of the therapeutic community program to be organized and evaluated in terms of its output to the individual personality system or to the therapeutic community as social system? Strains, even embarrassment, also arise from the following factors. Although the psychiatric hospital is a modern organization committed to achieving goals through the use of empirical knowledge, and although therapy staff members of such a hospital regard themselves as professionals using scientific knowledge and abstaining from moral evaluation, nevertheless knowledge is incomplete and inevitably ideological beliefs and commitments to societal values fill the gap between the end sought and the decision concerning how it is to be achieved. The ends themselves are ultimately cathected by nonrational processes. Participation in any social system necessarily involves taking a stand with respect to moral questions— choosing, for example, between the consequences of any process of action to a part of the system and to the whole system.

Note on the Work Program

There seem to be two kinds of questions that need to be considered in relation to the work program: the first being that of the *value-orientation* required of its participants; and the second having to do with problems of *deviance* and *mechanisms of social control* to prevent or correct such deviance.

Value-orientation. Because the influence of the value-orientation encouraged by individual psychotherapy in this setting (the extent of such influence being related to the crucial role of psychotherapy in accomplishing the goals of the hospital), many patients approach the work program feeling a positive obligation to be *self-oriented* rather than *collectivity-oriented.* That is, the patient in considering the consequences of alternative behaviors in relation to this program is likely to give primacy to the consequences to himself and his own self-interest, rather than primacy to the consequences to the collectivity, that is, to others and to the group as a whole. This is a true dilemma, involving polar opposites, *not* a continuum, since the choice in each *specific* situation must be to give primacy to one value-orientation or the other in case of a conflict between them.

Both orientations seem to be in a continuous struggle with each other in any discussion of the work program. For example, patients will argue

on the basis of the values of individual psychotherapy that self-fulfillment, self-improvement, personal "meaningfulness," autonomy and
choice are primary values in deciding upon participation in the work
program. The work program in this framework is, to paraphrase one
patient, like the medicine that the doctor orders for a patient as part of
his treatment, and participation should be governed primarily in terms
of whether or not the doctor and the patient think it would be good
for the patient to participate in the work program. (In some cases, such
arguments seem to be offered by a patient who wishes to use accepted
values to attack an aspect of the community program from within—
as a member of the community rather than an outsider.) In contrast,
there is an emphasis on the work that must be done, and the consequences to other people and the community in general if the work is not
done. The value here is likely to be stated, "if you live in a place, and
there are things that need to be done to make the place liveable, then
everyone needs to share in this work."

Both value-orientations involve difficulty for the work program. In
the first, the patient can easily make an argument in terms of his lack
of interest or ability in doing manual work, or his positively motivated
efforts in other areas—for example, school, painting or writing, theater,
outside jobs—as a reason not to participate in a common work program
based on self-orientation. "It is good for others, but not for me." In a
self-oriented work program, voluntary participation—that is, a program
in which lack of participation is not negatively sanctioned—is "logical,"
since participation ought to be primarily on the basis of whether or not
an individual's self-interests are indeed served by participating in the
work program. On the other hand, those who argue from a collectivity-
orientation have difficulty because they bump up against the crucial
self-development values institutionalized by individual psychotherapy,
mentioned previously, as well as against the somewhat embarrassing
facts that the work program does not have "enough work" to do and
that it is not indeed necessary from the point of view of the organization for such work to be done by patients.

Deviance and mechanisms of social control. There are two kinds of
questions. The first, what types of deviance are negatively sanctioned?
The second, what mechanisms of social control are in general utilized
to achieve participation in the work program?

If we regard all types of deviance [2]—including *compulsive performance* (dominating others, compulsive enforcement of rules), *compulsive*

2. See Parsons, *The Social System,* pp. 249–325.

acquiescence (submitting to others and perfectionistic ritualistic observance), *active alienation* (rebelliousness and incorrigibility), and *passive alienation* (withdrawal and evasion)—then we see that certain problems may come about because of the *positive* sanctioning of one kind of deviance (compulsive performance or acquiescence) along with the *negative* sanctioning of other types of deviance, particularly active alienation, which involves aggressive attack on social objects and group values.

Now, as a matter of fact, deviation in the direction of compulsive performance and acquiescence also creates much difficulty for the work program. For example, efforts to enforce rules compulsively have an impact on individuals already in a state of alienation that is likely to make them more alienated and thus to increase the amount of total deviance in the community rather than the amount of participation in the work program. Similarly, compulsive acquiescence results in token performance that is often seen as sabotaging the program. However, compulsive performance and acquiescence are rarely if ever publicly negatively sanctioned.

In addition, the rewards and penalties, positive and nagative sanctions, may not be in optimal balance in the community. Negative sanctions sometimes seem to outweigh in frequency and intensity the positive response to desired behavior, despite knowledge from psychotherapy and learning theory about the importance of rewards to reinforce desired behavior. The result is that a good many people seem to know what *not* to do, a relatively inactive position, but not many people know what to do and those who do know what to do are frequently in a state of frustration and low morale because of the lack of the expected positive response for desired performance.

Those individuals who deviate in the direction of compulsive conformance are made very anxious when the individual who is alienated is punished; such anxiety results in an increase in compulsive performance and acquiescence and thus in an increase of deviation in this direction, with consequent difficulties for the work program. In addition, the emphasis on negative penalties, of course, creates tremendous strains in the community, placing a high value on secrecy in order to avoid such penalties, which makes communication and problem-solving difficult, and tending to have the effect of extruding the deviant person from the community or pushing him further and further into an isolated position (rather than of socializing such an individual or drawing him away from the deviant position back into the community).

The desirable aspect of negative sanctions is apparently felt to be that *other* people are thereby discouraged from participating in deviance. In terms of resocialization, however, such an emphasis on negative penalties is likely to lead to failure with the alienated individual, which weighs heavily on a community whose primary goal is treating illness.

One attempt to relieve the resulting strain is in terms of seeing the deviant person's behavior as not the result of illness: he is responsible for such behavior and may through an effort of will prevent it. This is the usual criterion in a society for criminal deviation as distinguished from illness deviation. Another attempt is to define the goals of the hospital, implemented through admission and discharge procedures, as restricted to apply only to certain kinds of patients and not to others.

Part of the difficulty with providing positive sanctions may have to do with difficulties in finding what rewards would actually serve as rewards in the community program. Pay, extra therapy hours, and vacation have all been suggested. (Therapy hours seem to have many of the scarcity and reward characteristics money has in the culture as a whole.) For reasons not yet altogether clear, but which appear to be quite complicated, approval and esteem, usually the most potent societal rewards, do not seem to be brought effectively to bear. Some possible factors, each requiring particular coping techniques, are: (1) informal groups reward deviant behavior and negatively sanction behavior valued by the dominant group; (2) expected response, negative or positive, is inconsistently or is not forthcoming; (3) negative or positive response is given by members of the group whose attitudes are not valued as highly as those from whom such response is not forthcoming; (4) individuals who are deviant in the direction of alienation are insulated from approval or disapproval by their very deviance—"I don't care"; (5) disapproval is given without friendliness or without finding a basis for solidarity with the deviant individual, without necessary permissiveness, without adequate rewards, or without avoiding reciprocation of the deviant individual's inappropriate expectations—driving the individual into an even more deviant position; (6) expectations are inherently ambiguous—the individual is expected to do as much as he can, but then how much is that, and how can malingering be distinguished from incapacity?

One problem may have to do with some uneasiness on the part of staff about using the creation of *solidarity* (support), *permissiveness,* in conjunction with the *refusal to reciprocate t*he patient's inappropriate expectations, and conscious manipulation of *rewards,* as mechanisms of social control, ostensibly because such mechanisms are associated with individual psychotherapy "and the community program is *not* psychotherapy"—despite the fact that such mechanisms of social control in somewhat different forms are necessary for coping with deviance, especially severe deviance, in any social system and are ubiquitous in social situations other than that of individual psychotherapy.[3]

Instrumental and ideological beliefs. There is a distinction that must be made in addition to the one concerning *value-dilemma* (for example, self-orientation versus collectivity-orientation).

A patient deciding whether or not to participate in the work program orients himself to the situation not only in terms of specific *value-dilemmas* but in terms of a particular *system of beliefs.* The distinction that I think might be helpful here is that between *instrumental beliefs* and *ideological beliefs.* Parsons[4] divides belief systems into *existential beliefs,* which include those of science (empirical) and those of philosophy (non-empirical), and *evaluative beliefs,* which include ideologies (empirical) and religious ideas (non-empirical). Given a goal, and primacy of cognitive interest, one is concerned with *instrumental beliefs,* that is, those contributing to the solution of the problem of predicting the consequences of specific actions for goal-attainment. *Instrumental beliefs* are obviously then existential, empirical beliefs. However, one's interest might not be in goal-attainment primarily but in *integration*—of either an ego or a collectivity. In this event, one orients one's self not to instrumental beliefs but to evaluative beliefs; in the empirical realm, these are termed *ideological beliefs.* In the case of an instrumental belief, one is concerned with determining the *truth or falsity* of the belief by cognitive standards. In evaluating an ideological belief, one is concerned with establishing the *rightness or wrongness* of the belief in terms of moral rather than cognitive standards. A belief is ideological insofar as it implies a requirement of commitment in action; the acceptance of such a belief is treated as a moral obligation. An important question in relation to an instrumental belief would be: will a certain action lead to goal-attainment or not? An important question in relation to an ideological belief would be: is an action necessary for the integration or welfare of the group (others) or the integration or stability or an ego? Commitment to an ideological belief, then, is usually an aspect or condition of membership in a group or a prerequisite to peace of mind for a personality. It may be concluded that

3. Parsons, pp. 249–325.
4. Parsons, pp. 326–83.

the function of orientation to an instrumental belief is the facilitation of specific goal-attainment. Similarly, the function of orientation to an ideological belief is the facilitation of the integration of a personality or group—that is, the mitigation of conflict or stress within either of these systems.

The ideal situation of course is when cognitive convictions and moral convictions are merged, but there is usually an imperfect fit between them.

An ideological belief, it will be noted, provides a basis for making a choice in a particular value-dilemma; for example, it provides a "reason" why one should choose to be collectivity-oriented rather than self-oriented in a particular situation.

The paradigm in figure 1 might be helpful in seeing the relationship between orientation to a *value-dilemma* (for example, self-orientation versus collectivity-orientation) and orientation to a *belief system* (instrumental belief versus ideological belief).

It will be noted that participation in alternatives 1 or 2 (see figure 1, page 326), may be rejected or accepted on the basis of reality testing the belief, that is, the determination as to whether or not participation does indeed result in the attainment of a particular goal. However, such "scientific" or cognitive tests are not relevant to ideological beliefs.

Ideological beliefs, of course, should not be dismissed as simply "moralistic." Ideological beliefs perform significant functions in any society. For example, sharing such a belief is an important integrative mechanism by which conflict may be minimized in the presence of cognitive differences in a group, or which makes unity or action possible in the presence of cognitive inadequacies, that is, when it is not possible or quite difficult to determine the truth or falsity of a particular instrumental belief. A crucial characteristic of ideological beliefs is that the importance of sharing such a belief is given primacy over the question of cognitive validity. These may be some of the considerations that lead to the position that it would be much simpler if the staff would simply state to the patients, "this is the kind of place we would like this to be," rather than attempt to explain or validate the expectation to participate in the work program in terms of cognitively justifiable consequences.

In addition, an ideological belief is able to unify large numbers of people who may not be competent or interested in intellectual endeavors. Vulgarization or simplification, a glossing over complexities, is therefore usually a significant aspect of ideological beliefs. This may lead to the position that in discussing participation in the work program

Figure 1:   Value and belief alternatives in the work program

	Self-orientation	Collectivity-orientation
Instrumental belief	1. A patient will participate, or it is *useful* for a patient to participate, in the work program because such participation, it is believed, will result in the *attainment of a particular personal goal,* irrespective of whether or not the attainment of any particular goal important to the welfare of the group is involved.	2. A patient will participate, or it is *useful* for a patient to participate, in the work program because such participation, it is believed, will result in the *attainment of a particular goal important to the welfare of the group* (others), irrespective of whether or not the attainment of a particular purely personal goal is involved.
Ideological belief	3. A patient should participate, it is *right* for a patient to participate, in the work program because the patient will feel better if he does so—will feel less "guilty" and more "worthwhile."	4. A patient should participate, it is *right* for a patient to participate, in the work program because an obligation to accept this expectation, maintain it, and implement it in action is necessary to the welfare of the group (others) and this kind of commitment is a condition of membership in this group.

in a group it would be just as well for the staff to be "naive and vague," but that in individual psychotherapy a staff member has to be "sharp." Such a position of course suggests one source of strain in the hospital: obvious difficulties result from consigning cognitive standards to the realm of individual psychotherapy and moral standards to the realm of the community program. The expectation, in general, is that the individual psychotherapist operates "scientifically"; that is, specific propositions made by the patient in psychotherapy are examined skeptically in terms of cognitive standards of validity. The psychotherapist asks, "what is the evidence?" Ideological beliefs are challenged, their sources discovered; often the psychotherapist seeks to decrease the extent of the ideological realm in favor of the realm of instrumental beliefs. A great stress is imposed on the individual psychotherapist in his role as "scientist," if he is asked to orient himself toward instrumental beliefs in one setting and toward ideological beliefs in another with respect to the same problem. This says nothing of course of the strain that results in the patient's having to respond appropriately to the same psychotherapist as he takes different kinds of positions toward the same question in different settings.

On the other hand, a strain is also created whenever a psychotherapist orients himself in the direction of instrumental belief and cognitive standards in group discussion, whenever he emphasizes uncovering facts, understanding them, and skeptically challenging the validity of propositions. Such participation may sharpen differences and conflicts rather than minimize them, and—in the short run, at least—may therefore not be "integrative" as far as its effect on the group is concerned.

Appendix B
The Inauguration of the
Community Meeting

The following proposal states a rationale for the establishment of a community meeting in this hospital, written by the community program coordinator some months after his arrival. In it, he emphasizes the benefits accruing to the individual patient participating in the community program. In a "reconsideration of the community meeting," written seven or eight months after its inauguration, the emphasis is on the contribution of the community meeting to the problem-solving processes of the hospital community—namely, that the community meeting contributed primarily integrative, secondarily expressive phases, resolving strains exacerbated by earlier adaptive efforts to attain ends, and consolidating learning and commitment in preparation for new attempts at goal-achievement.

In both proposal and reconsideration the community program coordinator is beginning to view the various enterprises in the therapeutic community as interdependent, each differentiated to meet some particular imperative upon which the achievement of the aims of other enterprises depended. So, the work committee, the activities committee, the community council, the small groups, each is seen as responsible for a particular kind of action upon which the others depend for their functioning. This view is only suggested in the discussion of the relation of the community meeting to other enterprises; at times the community meeting is viewed as a supraordinate mechanism essentially including and integrating the other four, representing subsystems of the therapeutic community, and at times as simply sharing responsibility for integrative and expressive functions with the community council and small groups.

At the end of some months' experience with the community meeting, the community program coordinator became troubled by the feeling that his own contribution to the meeting—as well as that of other staff members—usually seemed to result in increasing strains in the community rather than decreasing them. One may view one source of strain in a social system as the perceived discrepancy between the *ideal* (the imagined state toward the achievement of which efforts are bent, in which shared values are actualized and shared ends realized) and the *actual* (what the current state of affairs is actually like). Staff participation tended, or so it seemed, to sharpen the perception of this discrepancy, and did little to decrease the distance between actual and ideal. The contribution of the community program coordinator as sociotherapist often involved an intellectual analysis of difficulties: differences of opinion and value, conflicts between groups or between group and individual. The more cogent the analysis, the more glum the group. Staff members felt, probably justifiably, that the staff members in a therapeutic community had to stand for and uphold certain values and norms if these were to be established and maintained, and that the community must be confronted by its halfway measures and evasions. The staff insistently held forth on values to which, it was repeatedly pointed out, commitment was inadequate, or expressed concern over the lack of adherence to norms. Staff members, however, rarely made concrete suggestions for possible action to solve various kinds of social problems, apparently often as baffled as the patients were by these or afraid, not without reason, that the staff would become—or would be seen as—too interfering, dominating, directive. The result was continual visualization of the ideal and continual "rubbing-in" the distance of the community from it

In the "reconsideration of the community meeting," therefore, its integration rather than its adaptation function is emphasized; the sharing of information and the interpretation of the causes of strain are minimized in favor of the resolution of tensions by a variety of means not necessarily verbal or intellectual. The meeting is now viewed as a place where not only patients and staff or various patient-staff committees come together, but also where the informal life of the community—especially the life of the patient-group—and the organized enterprises comprising the formal structure of the therapeutic community come together to be in some way integrated.

The emphasis on integration is useful; throwing other functions out may not be as useful. Out of discouragement and in that fatal, fortunately transient, period of exuberance when one feels one has found the answer to difficulties, oversimplification tends to occur. The community meeting may perform primarily an integration function with respect to the therapeutic community, the social system of which it is a subsystem. Nevertheless, as a system of action in itself, the community meeting in carrying out that integration function must meet the variety of imperatives—including adaptation and integration—intrinsic to any system of action: orienting to the situation, acting to achieve goals, integrating around certain norms, establishing and maintaining commitment to governing values.

Inevitably, then, a variety of kinds of participation will be required of staff and patients; frequently, and unavoidably, participation appropriate to fulfilling one need of the system will clash with requirements for fulfilling some other need. Skillful participation involves an extensive repertoire of interventions, the ability to recognize what phase a group is in, and a sense of tact and timing in contributing what is needed at the moment it is needed. In working with groups, there is no rule for the right things to do. The right intervention is always fitting in a particular context; the wrong intervention is usually one that was right the last time, but not today. "Too little, too late" and "too much, too soon" are the daily self-reproaches of any conscientious sociotherapist

Proposal. The following is the rationale for a proposed community meeting.

A daily community meeting has the following goals:

1. Each person becomes aware through community discussions of his *way of life,* as this is expressed in his way of living in the community. He becomes aware of the *consequences* of this way of life to himself and others in the community. He learns how his way of life affects his own and others' treatment, and in what way it contributes to the achievement of goals shared by members of the community.

Such awareness facilitates psychotherapy, and is necessary in order to learn how to live differently when this seems desirable. Members of the community, who live and participate in community events together, are in the best position to help each other develop such an awareness.

The development of this awareness, as well as learning new ways of perceiving and responding to oneself and others, requires an ongoing, continuous discussion, in which problems are worked on steadily and not merely intermittently reacted to.

2. In the community meeting, the community is able to learn, encourage, and maintain values that make psychotherapy possible, and to combat aspects of the setting that undermine psychotherapy and make it impossible.

For example, the community, through discussions, and the decisions and changes in attitude and ways of living that arise out of these discussions, can make an environment that helps a person to learn to face, endure, and master painful feelings. The ability to do this must be learned, and learned through experiences in the daily life of the community. Such an ability does not necessarily develop as the result of analysis of inner conflicts in psychotherapy but may actually be at times a prerequisite to effective participation in psychotherapy.

The converse is also true. An environment may encourage or make possible flight from painful feelings in a variety of ways that interfere with the further growth of the individual or that provoke and support futile, self-defeating ways of living. Such an environment cancels out the effects sought by psychotherapy. In fact, hospitalization may have as one of its goals to remove an individual from such an environment to a therapeutic environment so that psychotherapy can be productive.

Attendance at the daily community meeting should be required because:

1. The community meeting is essential to the treatment for which the individual has come to the hospital.

2. It is impossible to achieve the goals described above unless everyone in the community is prepared and does participate. As in individual psychotherapy, it is the task to be accomplished—not "authority"—that dictates the requirement.

The community meeting should follow the community work sign-up meeting (morning meeting), despite the fact that there will probably be very significant problems in effecting the transition from one to the other and maintaining a boundary between them. These problems are highlighted by the stated feelings of some members of the work committee that this plan may result in some impairment of attention to work problems, and the apparent competition among individuals, groups, and programs for the attention of members of the community. Having a different chairman for the two different meetings may help. Further, it is hoped that such problems will be outweighed by the advantages accruing to the community meeting, if it is anchored in an immediately visible part of the reality in which people live and to which they respond, and by the fact that attempting to understand and cope with these problems will be useful.[1]

The community program coordinator should be chairman of three of the community meetings because:

1. It was actually decided that the community work sign-up meeting should meet separately from the community meeting; some months after the community meeting was inaugurated, the community work sign-up meeting or morning meeting was disbanded.

1. He has a major responsibility to safeguard the treatment aspects of the community program, and to combat any anti-therapeutic processes in the community that would affect any individual deleteriously, for example, by intervening in certain ways in response to the behavior of individuals or to what is going on in the group. He is trained to see treatment issues in apparently "mere" administrative details, for example, and should clarify and respond to these issues. It seems probable that the community program coordinator can perform these functions most effectively as chairman. (The assumption here is that the hospital should not be divided into activities or areas that are the exclusive provinces of the staff or the patients; instead staff and patients share the same goals, each person contributing in his own way, out of his own resources and from his own vantage point to the accomplishment of the goals in all areas.)

2. If the goals of the community meeting are to be accomplished, strong forces and feelings are set in motion. The chairman often becomes the object of these, and the victim of various ambivalent expectations from the group. This is an unfair, if not impossible, position to put a patient in. An untrained person is more likely to take things personally, respond with discouragement, a sense of defeat, lowered self-esteem, or defensiveness, or become angry and provocative in turn. Soon it is impossible to see clearly what the issues are or to learn anything from what is going on.

Skills in responding to group processes and conducting discussions need to be learned, and some of these skills may be learned by others most effectively by observing and working with the community program coordinator.

A patient should be chairman of two of the meetings because:

1. This would implement the value that staff and patients share the goals described above and share also the responsibility for working toward them, each person by use of his own resources, skills, and understanding—as opposed to the view that responsibility in a particular meeting, effort, area, activity belongs exclusively either to the staff or to the patient group.

2. This would provide an opportunity for learning skills and practicing them.

3. This would be helpful to the community program coordinator in permitting him periodically to stand back from what is going on so that he may maintain perspective and understanding.

Possible side effects to be concerned about:

1. Feelings may be suppressed when a staff person is chairman, which would be displaced elsewhere.

2. Such a situation may make it less likely that some patients will overcome reluctance to speak up, or take initiative, as is now happening. Instead these patients may say, "Let him do it: It's easier for him; it's his meeting."

3. Magical expectations may develop that the staff chairman will solve everything, leading to disillusionment and anger.

4. Patients may feel depreciated—"he thinks I can't do it"—with consequent reinforcement of the role of being "the helpless, incompetent patient," when the community program is designed to give people the opportunity to get out of this role.[2]

Decision-making should not be a usual function of the community meeting because:

1. There is a frequently observed tendency for others to change the environment in some way when a person becomes uncomfortable as a result of interference with his illness or some vulnerability arising out of that illness. The change is usually intended to make him and others more comfortable. However, this often results in changing just those conditions that make new learning possible. If there are not safeguards preventing this, the result is cycles of arousal and reaction without the thoughtful gradual working through of an issue in discussion that makes learning possible. Discussion without eventual appropriate action and change may be sterile. Action without a prior process of sharing information, points of view, ideas, and feelings may be blind.

2. If the decision-making function is appropriated by the community meeting, there may be a gradual undermining and deterioration in the functioning of such decision-making groups as the community council, work committee, and activities committee.

3. Directing agenda items from the community council, work committee, and activities committee to the community meeting rather than the small groups will safeguard the unique asset of the small group: that it is a group in which a spontaneous discussion with maximum participation can take place among a small number of people about whatever is on their minds—the feelings, ideas, or reactions of any individual to events in the group itself or in the community.

The community meeting reconsidered. In order to avoid the danger of subcultures of sick people banding together to legitimize illness as a way of life, it is ordinarily considered crucial for the primary relation of the patient to be with nonsick rather than sick individuals. Hospital

2. It was ultimately decided that there would be four community meetings a week, all four co-chaired by the community program coordinator and a patient elected by the patient group for a two-month term. In mid-week, on the day when there was no community meeting, small groups were to meet.

treatment usually involves an effort to deprive patients of the possibility of forming a solidary collectivity that might legitimize being ill.

It is for this reason perhaps that it is not possible for a staff person to be unambivalent toward the development of a strong peer culture among patients in the hospital. This reason also provides one rationale—in addition to the interdependence of patients and staff in carrying out the tasks necessary for the achievement of the hospital's goals—for the emphasis in a therapeutic community on collaboration between patients and staff (in preference to letting the patients alone to work things out among themselves).

We may regard the patients as constituting a relatively informally structured community of interacting individuals who have a common residence (with all the ties, types of relationship, problems, and pleasures this implies), and the staff and the patients as constituting a relatively formally structured organization of interacting individuals who work together to accomplish certain goals (with the roles, job differentiations, and distributions of authority and responsibility this implies).

Then one problem is to integrate the interactions of the patient community with those of the patient-staff organization—in addition to that of integrating the various patient-staff and staff groups in the formal organization—so that there is one united effort and the treatment goals of the hospital are facilitated rather than obstructed.

The community meeting is one mechanism designed to facilitate such integrations—not, then, either a meeting of the patient community alone or of the patient-staff organization alone but a meeting in which the two come together (as well as a meeting in which the various patient-staff and staff groups in the formal organization come together).

Prototype topics, involving the integration of community and organization, are the impact of drinking, sexual behavior, noise, recreation, sharing of chores, and efforts by patients to collaborate with nurses to help each other, on members of the community, on the formal organization, and ultimately on the achievement of the hospital's treatment goals.

Prototype topics, involving the integration of formal organization groups, are concerns with the coordination of, and cooperation and collaboration (or lack of it) between, patient-staff committees responsible for government, work, and activities, and staff groups responsible for administrative and professional functions—as well as concerns with the achievements (or lack of them) of these various groups in carrying out their tasks.

The view that a sociotherapeutic function can best be performed in the community meeting follows from an analysis of the hospital as an organization, oriented to the achievement of certain goals, and in which jobs or roles are differentiated in terms of the best way to achieve these goals. Inevitably, the performance of various jobs brings individuals and groups in the organization into conflict or competition with each other from time to time, thus resulting in strains in the organization. At the community meeting, such strains should be mitigated (the sociotherapeutic function) by their becoming apparent in the process of group discussion and through the clarification of what differences, conflicts, and competitions are involved and what some resolution of them might include.

An intellectual analysis of differences as these are revealed in the community meeting—getting the group to see such differences more clearly—does not by itself help to mitigate strains in the organization; in fact, if anything, under some circumstances it appears to increase such strains. Some integrative resolution is the aim of the community meeting.

An ideal-typical problem-solving process might proceed through the following phases.[3] If we start with an adaptive phase, characterized by the attempt of group members to become oriented to the situation, then during such a phase cognitive activity, asking for and receiving orientation, asking for and receiving opinions, would be especially relevant and evident. From such a phase the group might move into a goal-attainment phase. During this phase, suggestions (instrumental moves) for the actual attainment of a goal might predominate.

A basic hypothesis is that any movement in the hospital toward the actual attainment of a goal, that is, any task-orientation, inevitably results in strains between groups, between groups and individuals, within groups, and within individuals. Such strains must be dealt with in the following phases, which are social-emotional in character rather than task-oriented. The next phases, then, are integrative-expressive, in which showing agreement or disagreement, showing tension or releasing tension, and above all showing antagonism or solidarity, predominate. The goals of such phases are to provide for tension-release and especially to increase the solidarity of the group as a prerequisite for entering a phase in which the level of satisfaction rises to a point—and in which learning becomes consolidated to an extent—that the group is again ready to enter an adaptive phase.

3. See Parsons, Shils, and Bales, *Working Papers in the Theory of Action*.

From this point of view, the function of action groups in the community (for example, patient-staff committees responsible for government, work, and activities as well as staff groups responsible for administrative and professional functions) may be viewed as primarily task-oriented and therefore as contributing to the adaptive and goal-attainment phases of problem-solving in the hospital organization.

However, the activity of such groups inevitably results in strains in the community or organization. The function of the community meeting might be especially, although perhaps not exclusively, to provide a mechanism for carrying out the integrative-expressive phases. The emphasis in this meeting is not on adaptation or goal-attainment (activities directed to these ends might on occasion be opposed to the carrying out of an integrative-expressive function) but rather on tension-release (this may be also a particular function of small groups in the hospital program) and the accomplishment of solidarity for the entire community (a unique function of the community meeting).

During an integrative-expressive phase, the community meeting would essentially attempt to reestablish the boundaries of the group in order to heal the strains or wounds resulting from moves toward task achievement in the previous phases, which have occurred typically (although not perhaps exclusively) outside the community meeting in action groups in the organization.

During such a meeting the emphasis should be on the identity of the group—what differentiates it from other groups, its characteristics and possessions, the interests and values members have in common—and on creating and maintaining a generalized, durable affective attachment among the members of the group.

The ideal output of the community meeting—in addition then to a cognitive orientation to the situation—should be above all a sense of solidarity, a decrease in intergroup strains, perhaps some reduction of individual tension, and some consolidation of learning, leading ultimately to a return to adaptive and goal-attainment phases throughout the organization.

This would seem to suggest that staff members in the community meeting should be contributing to it not merely pressures toward adaptation, goal-attainment, action, or decision, which increases strains, but also attempts to resolve the strains which have already resulted from such pressures in the organization; staff members should give special attention in the meeting to mending fences, being helpful and rewarding, increasing feelings of status and self-esteem, and showing solidarity with other staff members or groups.

An ideal community meeting might involve the gradual emergence of the wants of members of the group—initiating a process of problem-solving that may ultimately change the way of life of an entire organization—or reports orienting the group to what has happened outside the meeting and what strains have resulted from attempts to solve certain problems, achieve certain ends, accomplish certain tasks, or satisfy certain wants. The work of the community meeting then also involves resolving these strains primarily by increasing the solidarity of the group and secondarily by providing for tension-release as well as consolidating what learning has taken place from the group's experience—the latter including a process of institutionalization of norms and values (in the social system) and internalization of norms and values (in the individual personality systems of members of the social system).[4]

4. For a subsequent formulation of the functions of the community meeting and other collectivities in the therapeutic community, see *Sociotherapy and Psychotherapy*.

Index